THE CROSSWORD OBSESSION

THE CROSSWORD
OBSESSION

The History and Lore of the
World's Most Popular Pastime

CORAL AMENDE

Epigraphs by Frances Hansen

BERKLEY BOOKS, NEW YORK

B

A Berkley Book
Published by The Berkley Publishing Group
A division of Penguin Putnam Inc.
375 Hudson Street
New York, New York 10014

This book is an original publication of The Berkley Publishing Group.

Copyright © 2001 by Coral Amende.
"Groundhog Day Puzzle," "Night Lights," and "Election Day Puzzle, 1996"
have been reprinted with the permission of the *New York Times*.
Screen shots of Crossdown
software courtesy of Sam Belloto, Jr.
Screen shots of Crossword Compiler courtesy of Antony Lewis.
Text design by Tiffany Kukec.

First edition: October 2001

Visit our website at
www.penguinputnam.com

Library of Congress Cataloging-in-Publication Data
Amende, Coral.
The crossword obsession : the history and lore of the world's most popular pastime /
Coral Amende ; epigraphs by Frances Hansen.—Berkley hardcover ed.
p. cm.
ISBN 0-425-18157-X
1. Crossword puzzles—History. 2. Crossword puzzles. I. Title.

GV1507.C7—A48 2001
793.73'2'09—dc21
2001044093

PRINTED IN THE UNITED STATES OF AMERICA

10 9 8 7 6 5 4 3 2 1

CONTENTS

THE CROSSWORD OBSESSION

1.

SQUARE ONE

IN THE BEGINNING . . .

Listen, my children, and you shall hear

How a puzzle was born, and in what year,

And how it begat, and kept on breeding—

But enough of that! Continue reading . . .

A PASSION FOR PUZZLES

Human beings have a passion for puzzles: we love giving our mental musculature vigorous workouts with perplexing posers and scintillating stumpers—particularly those with a goodly dose of wicked wit. From ancient ages to modern times, the solving of cranium-straining conundrums has been one of the ways in which we have created harmony out of chaos and brought some small semblance of order, however transitory or illusional, to our lives. This edifying exercise sharpens our cerebral acuity and develops critical logical-thinking skills, as well as being enormously entertaining, and there is great satisfaction—that gratifying "Aha!" feeling—to be had in parsing a pattern or getting a grip on a puzzlemaker's sly trick. Solving (and, to an even greater degree, constructing) puzzles also allows us to use the knowledge we've collected and enhances that knowledge in a fun way (in fact, the crossword and its variants have been used to teach foreign languages to immigrants and vocabulary to schoolchildren). And all within the space of a few minutes—talk about bang for the buck!

A man is known by the company his mind keeps.
—Thomas Bailey Aldrich

The ancestors of the crossword puzzle include word squares and acrostics, both of which date from days long bygone. As far back as the sixth century B.C., puzzle-loving Greeks were inscribing word squares into statues and other artistic endeavors. These early efforts read only horizontally, although the vertical stacking of letters enhanced the visual appeal of the compositions; the later addition of lines going across and down made some look remarkably similar to the crosswords of today.

Ye olde Romans were proficient practitioners of the acrostic: Playwright Plautus used them in the introductions of his works to call out important plot points (something that wouldn't be a bad idea for some of today's theatrical offerings). Acrostics can also be spotted in the Bible, where you'll find psalms with twenty-two lines, each beginning with a different letter of the Hebrew alphabet, in order.

Will Shortz, crossword editor of the *New York Times*, is perhaps the world's foremost puzzle expert, having earned an autodidactic degree in Enigmatology (the study of puzzles) during his college days. As part of his self-designed curriculum, Shortz studied word square puzzles, which, he notes:

became popular in the 1870s. They were some of the most popular puzzles until the crossword was invented in 1913. The very first word square was in 1859. That was something that I found in my research. The first word square actually appeared in England, but it was reprinted in an American magazine within a few months. So the invention jumped the Atlantic almost immediately. As far as the first word puzzles in America are concerned, the earliest ones appeared in an almanac in 1647. This was only the twenty-first work published in the colonies. There may be only one or two copies that still exist—I've seen it only on microfilm, or microfiche. This almanac had an original versified enigma for each month of the year.

Acrostic puzzles were also originally seen in England during the nineteenth century, with one of the more interesting examples being a double acrostic (both the first and last letters of the answers spell out new words or phrases) purportedly penned by Queen Victoria for her children.

The acrostic was probably invented about the same time with the anagram, tho' it is impossible to decide whether the inventor of the one or the other were the greater blockhead.
—Joseph Addison

Among the notable puzzlers of the nineteenth century was Charles Dodgson, better known as Lewis Carroll, the author of *Alice's Adventures in Wonderland*. A superlative solver as well as inveterate inventor, Carroll created a diversion he dubbed "Doublets" (the grandaddy of modern forms such as Dell's "Laddergrams"). In an 1879 feature in *Vanity Fair* magazine, he explained the concept:

WHAT IS AN ... ACROSTIC?

A series of lines or a poem in which the first, last, or other specified letters of each line, taken in order, spell out a word, phrase, or motto.

```
O F F
F O E
F E D
```

WHAT IS A ... WORD SQUARE?

An arrangement of words of equal length stacked in a square. The words read the same vertically and horizontally (above) or, in the case of double word squares (below), differ going across and down.

```
A R M
F O E
T E N
```

*The rules of the Puzzle are simple
enough. Two words are proposed, of the
same length; and the Puzzle consists in
linking these together by interposing
other words, each of which shall differ
from the next word in one letter only. . . .
As an example, the word "head" may be
changed into "tail" by interposing the
words "heal, teal, tell, tall."*

*. . . I am told that there is an Ameri-
can game involving a similar principle. I
have never seen it, and can only say of its
inventors,* "pereant qui ante nos nostra
dixerunt!" *(I.e., "Death to those who
voiced our ideas before we did!")*

A few years after "Doublets" debuted,
an auspicious event occurred in the puzzle
world. Thirty-four men met in Manhattan
and founded the Eastern Puzzlers' League, known today as the National Puzzlers' League (NPL). The EPL went national in 1920; and in the early days of
the organization, you couldn't join up if you lived west of the Mississippi. As is
still the case, members used self-chosen pseudonyms, or *noms* (short for *noms
de plume*), to put everyone on the same social footing. *Noms*, according to the
NPL, "allow all puzzlers to meet as equals, free of the titles and social distinc-
tions that the outside world may demand." Beginning at the turn of the last
century, members composed conundrums for the organization's newsletter, *The
Eastern Enigma* (today, simply *The Enigma*): "crypt" (cryptogram), "flat" ("a
puzzle whose solution is a single, flat line of letters"), and "form" (a puzzle
whose "solution is a two-dimensional grid, like a crossword puzzle or a word
square"). Today, the NPL holds a multiple-day annual convention, "con," during
which members (known as "the krewe") get a chance to socialize and participate in no-holds-barred solving contests.

Puzzledom is a mental playground—a gymnasium for the exercise of wits.
A boy can obtain muscular development by sawing wood.
He can also get it in a gymnasium. He will naturally avoid the woodpile,
but will eagerly seek the gym on every possible occasion. Dry,
theoretical studies are mental woodpiles. What you wish is that your boy
learn to think, so give him the gym and not the woodpile.
—Sam Loyd, Jr.

Puzzle-solving had taken firm root in the nineteenth-century imagination, and Carroll's was far from the only fecund intellect feeding the frenzy: Among others, the puzzle pantheon includes American Sam Loyd and Englishman H. E. Dudeney. Loyd, a student of engineering who cast aside this promising (if rather mundane) career to take up puzzle crafting, created some of the most ingenious amusements of all time. His myriad originals included fiendish mathematical stumpers, witty word games, and marvelous mechanical puzzles (often involving the folding of paper), which were frequently commissioned for advertising purposes. (Loyd's prolific son, Walter, picked up his father's mantle—and, eventually, his first name as well—in the early twentieth century and churned out his own, less-original, series of puzzles.) Britain's Henry E. Dudeney specialized in mathematical posers but also authored entertaining word games and variety puzzles and was of the opinion that puzzle invention was the pinnacle of intellectual achievement. One innovation introduced by Dudeney was the deceptively simple crossword spin-off shown on page 8 (also a sterling example of a "pangrammatic" puzzle—one in which each letter of the alphabet is used).

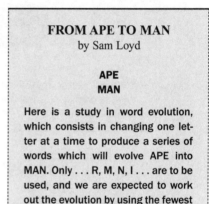

FROM APE TO MAN
by Sam Loyd

APE
MAN

Here is a study in word evolution, which consists in changing one letter at a time to produce a series of words which will evolve APE into MAN. Only . . . R, M, N, I . . . are to be used, and we are expected to work out the evolution by using the fewest possible number of words. ARE is the first; what are the others?

Sam Loyd and H. E. Dudeney (for non-crossword puzzles) paved the way for everyone. Their work is stolen all the time.
—Peter Gordon, constructor/editor

BLACK AND WHITE BALL

The popularity of particular puzzling pastimes has peaked and plummeted as public interest waxes and wanes, but no puzzle form has ever experienced the widespread and longstanding popularity of the crossword—the numero uno indoor game in America since the 1920s. Emerging from the fertile puzzlemaking epoch that was the nineteenth century, this elegant composition in black and white hit the zeitgeist of the early twentieth century with the force of a speeding train.

All I did was take an idea as old as language and modernize it by the introduction of the black squares.
—Arthur Wynne

The world's first crossword appeared on December 21, 1913, in the eight-page "Fun" section of New York's *Sunday World* newspaper. Its inventor was

"Fun" editor Arthur Wynne, a longtime puzzler originally from Liverpool, England, who brainstormed it on an occasion when he was having trouble meeting his space requirement (and his deadline!). To supplement the section's collection of head-scratchers (word squares, rebuses, anagrams, riddles, math puzzlers, and the like) and other amusements, he rearranged the traditional word square into a symmetrical, diamond-shaped composition of words reading differently across and down. Numbers identified their positions, and he supplied readers with clues to help them complete the puzzle. He baptized it the "Word Cross" (the name was changed to "Cross Word" the next month) and gave solvers simple instructions: "Fill in the small squares with words which agree with the following definitions."

These incipient crosswords differed markedly from those we see today. For one thing, two numbers were used to identify each answer word (one each in the first and final squares); for another, there weren't any rules about black-square maximums or diagonal diagram symmetry; and words were occasionally repeated within the same diagram. The use of two-letter words was also routine (a practice that was, for the most part, done away with in the 1940s).

The newly minted puzzle caught on immediately and soon became so overwhelmingly popular that the newspaper's helmsmen were deluged with wrathful missives from disappointed solvers if it was left out of "Fun" for a week. Some of the *World*'s more ambitious aficionados even tried their hands at constructing the puzzles. The first "outside" crossword was published in February 1914, a date that marked two important milestones: the premier publication of a crossword composed by someone other than its inventor, and the first constructor (Mrs. M. B. Wood) to receive a byline.

At this time, Wynne was receiving original crosswords from freelance constructors at the rate of about one a day—much appreciated, because he was having a problem finding time for construction in his busy schedule. But by the following year, the problem had reversed itself: The paper was receiving crossword submissions at the rate of *twenty-five* per day (even Will Shortz doesn't get quite that many!), and Wynne was up to his ears in new puzzles.

To ease Wynne's burden, *World* editor John O'Hara Cosgrove set out to find someone who could assist him with the puzzles in the *Sunday Magazine* ("Fun" last appeared in 1916, and the puzzles were moved). He found that helpmeet in a young woman named Margaret Petherbridge (later Farrar), who'd been his stepdaughter's roomie at Smith College. Her first instruction was to make sure the puzzle made it into print "without mistakes." Now, Margaret was no dummy, but she didn't really see what all the fuss was about: She wasn't a solver, and she wasn't overly concerned about the angry letters that came her way from irate readers (whom she dismissed as "cranks"). In fact, the crosswords that she initially chose for publication were those she felt were the most aesthetically pleasing.

Enter *World* pen-slinger Franklin Pierce Adams (a.k.a. FPA), a crossword fancier who wrote a *World* column entitled "Conning Tower." From his vantage point in the office next door to Margaret's, he razzed her about the streams of slip-ups and barrages of boneheaded blunders that regularly appeared in the crossword. When she was finally goaded into a test-solve, what she found horrified her—missing clues, misnumbering, and more. Thus convinced of the necessity for a more stringent editorial process, Petherbridge picked up her blue pencil and began taking her position very seriously. In addition to finding and fixing flubs (wrong numbers, impenetrable definitions), she consigned the dual-numbering scheme to the scrap heap and established the crossword layout rule, which still holds, of diagonally symmetrical grids with no isolated sections, or "islands," of answer words.

For about ten years after the invention of the crossword (which, rather remarkably, was never trademarked or copyrighted), the *World* was its sole publisher. But as the trickle of fans turned into a torrent, other newspapers jumped on the bandwagon and added crosswords to their lineups (in fact, the first daily crossword was published in November 1924 by the *New York Herald Tribune*), and the *World* had increased its puzzle staff to three full-time editors (Petherbridge, F. Gregory Hartswick, and Prosper Buranelli; Wynne had retired by this time). The fad didn't escape the sharp eyes of a couple of ambitious publishing tyros, Dick Simon and Max Schuster, who made the momentous decision to kick off their nascent venture with a volume of crosswords. They hired Margaret and her two editorial cohorts to put the book together for them (proving that some things in the crossword world never change, the three were given a grand advance of twenty-five bucks apiece).

Enter FPA again: Despite being a true-blue crossword nut (and friend of Simon's to boot), he was strangely sure the book would fail. His naysaying put the fear of God into the young entrepreneurs to such a degree that they decided not to use the Simon & Schuster imprint but rather Plaza Publishing (Plaza was their telephone exchange), so that if the book tanked, no one would know it was them! They determinedly gave it the old college try, though: They advertised the book in the *World* and handed out scores of free copies, hoping to entice book-sellers into placing orders. But not many took the bait, and presales grand totaled only eight hundred copies, plus—maybe—another thousand a distribu-tor was considering.

> *Hooray! Hooray! Hooray! Hooray!*
> *The Cross Word Puzzle Book's out today.*
> —*Franklin Pierce Adams, in his column on the book's day of publication*

The Cross Word Puzzle Book was published on April 10, 1924, with a seem-ingly optimistic first printing of thirty-six hundred copies—which immediately flew off the shelves! New and repeat orders poured in, and Simon & Schuster stepped up production. By the time the fledgling publishers celebrated their one-year anniversary, the book had gone to reprint several times, and two new crossword books had been hustled into the works. Combined sales of these books soon reached four hundred thousand copies, and Messrs. Simon and Schuster were launched into the publishing stratosphere.

Before long, a crossword craze was in full swing: Due to greatly increased demand, the New York Public Library was forced to limit users' dictionary time to five minutes each; a train line made dictionaries available in each of its cars for the com-muters; and a cottage industry of cross-word-themed jewelry, clothing, and trinkets sprung up (one of the more inventive items was the watch-replacement "wrist diction-ary"—yes, abridged).

A CROSSWORD-THEMED POEM OF THE 1920s

Anger, ire, temper, rage!
Era, epoch, eon, age!
Do, re, me and fa, sol, la;
Egyptian sun god, Ra, Ra, Ra!

To capitalize on their stunning, unexpected success, Simon & Schuster pre-sented ever more creative ideas to the puzzle-buying public, including a collec-tion of celebrity-penned crosswords. For this effort, Margaret wrote to renowned playwright and novelist Booth Tarkington to request a contribution—but she received a slightly different response than she'd anticipated:

My dear Miss Petherbridge:

I have had enough trouble with your two books; and if I were able to build a cross-word puzzle, I am too kind-hearted to do it.

An enemy of mine sent me the first book just as I was about to do some overdue work. Then, two weeks later, when I had just finished your first book, he sent me the second, though I had written him, begging him not to do it.

When I get finished, I hope never to hear anything more about puzzles of any kind.

Malignantly yours,
BOOTH TARKINGTON

The fans they chew their pencils;
The fans they beat their wives;
They look up words for extinct birds;
They lead such puzzling lives!
—*Gelett Burgess, of "The Purple Cow" fame*

Among Margaret Petherbridge's daily deluge of correspondence at the *World* was a letter from a rabbi, Lewis Browne, decrying "puzzle mania":

This craze has really gone too far, he complained. *I can't go down the street here without being held up by someone who ought to be at home banging on his typewriter, or by some woman who ought to be mending her husband's socks, and asked what is a seven-letter word for Eskimo gefilte fish, or the like. . . . And the worst of it is that five-quarters of the time I can give the pestiferous fans no answer. Even though I did go for years to grammar school and theological seminaries, I really don't know even the first syllable of the two-letter word for an extinct New Zealand roach or a defunct South Persian seneschal. I simply don't. The result is that I'm beginning to get an unenviable reputation among our cognoscenti for something very close to illiteracy. They call me a "Dumb Daniel" and a cretin. . . . I submit to you that it isn't right and proper. It just isn't. The first thing you know, the disappointed fans around here will be writing to the colleges from which I was not expelled to find out just how I managed to get by.*

With his letter, Browne included a puzzle, which he requested be printed with an announcement:

I don't care to be used as an information bureau by any fan, anywhere, at any time, until he, she, or it can make affidavit that he, she, or it has worked out every word in my poser. If peace does not come to me even then, I threaten to construct a puzzle containing over a hundred polysyllabic words, all taken from Bantu slang and obsolete Coptic! Maybe that will hold 'em.

MEANWHILE, ACROSS THE ATLANTIC

With their February 1922 issue, *Pearson's Magazine* became the first of the Brit pack to publish a "Cross-Word," which was described as "a new form of puzzle in the shape of a word square. . . . These new word squares are having a tremendous vogue in America just now." C. W. Shepherd, who worked as an editor for the *Sunday Express*, was persuaded in 1924 by old pal Arthur Wynne to run some crosswords (the co-author of the first puzzle printed was—yep, you guessed it—Arthur Wynne). Shepherd liked the American puzzles but found them too, well, *American*, so he changed some of the clues and answer words to suit his British audience—which, as it turns out, was the start of something big.

The fact remains that, while the mentally edentulous still have their pabulum, the cerebrally dentiferous can now command a choice of daily bread into which they can really get their teeth.
—Torquemada

Writer Edward Powys Mathers also found American puzzles too straightforward, so when he began constructing, his solution was to twist the form a bit— by using anagrams, rhymes, puns, and other types of wordplay in his clues and, eventually, dispensing with the grid conventions of the Americans. He published his pioneering cryptic creations in the *Weekly Westminster*, using the pseudonym Torquemada (a grand inquisitor of the Spanish Inquisition, notorious for his cruelty)—a tradition of *nom*foolery that continues with cryptic constructors (or "setters," in the parlance of the game) to this day. By 1926, Torquemada was the *Observer*'s full-time setter, creating "Crosswords for Supermen." And during his tenure there, he introduced several innovations: unkeyed letters (in a British puzzle, 60 to 70 percent of the letters in the grid are allowed to be "unchecked," or not part of other answer words), the "black bar" grid style (thick black lines demarcate the end of an answer in the grid, which he greatly preferred to the black-square/white-square format), and "themed" crosswords. Cryptics quickly became the puzzles of choice in England, and Torquemada created almost seven hundred for the *Observer* before his death in 1939. He was succeeded by the brilliant Ximenes (Derrick Somerset Macnutt), who concocted his own notoriously knotty creations and even wrote a book (*Ximenes on the Art of the Crossword*), now a highly sought-after collector's item.

I recall how thrilling the green poster looked: "Crosswords for Supermen." Alas, your tired commuter of today would swallow that first puzzle, verse and all, and correctly disgorge it between Charing Cross and Waterloo.

—*Torquemada, 1935*

Cryptic crosswords, well established and well known for being tough nuts to crack, came to the atten-*shun* of a few of England's intelligence men during World War II on the occasion of the publication of the *Daily Telegraph*'s five thousandth puzzle. That milestone printing, and the copious correspondence it set off, triggered an ingenious idea: Because the department was short of cryptographers, why not look for those who could solve fiendishly difficult puzzles—chess, crosswords, cryptics—with alacrity? The department reasoned that such solvers just might be prime candidates for their code-breaking efforts—a major target of which was the Germans' typewriter-size Enigma machine, used for much of their top-secret communication: warship routes and similarly sensitive information. Enigma-encoded dispatches had millions of possible solutions unless you knew the settings—which were, of course, regularly changed.

To find the key to this critical conundrum, the department had assembled a team of top minds from every field: mathematicians, linguists, Egyptologists, musicologists. (Their destination? The Government Code and Cypher School near London at Bletchley Park, an expansive estate sold to the British government by a merchant in 1938.) By 1941, they were running short on candidates—most able-bodied men were being sent to the front lines—and they desperately needed a new infusion of able brains.

So the *Daily Telegraph* was contacted by intelligence officers and asked to organize a timed contest for solvers. One entrant was Stanley Sedgewick, an accounting clerk, whose interest was piqued by a slightly misleading story in that newspaper: "A Mr. W.A.J. Gavin, Chairman of the Eccentric Club, wrote saying he would donate £100 to the Minesweepers Fund if it could be demonstrated under controlled conditions that anyone could solve the *Daily Telegraph* puzzle in less than twelve minutes."

The match was held on January 10, 1942. One speed demon finished the puzzle in six minutes, three and a half seconds, but misspelled one word and . . . outta there. Four others turned in their puzzles before the bell rang, but Sedgewick was not one of them, finding himself one word short of the finish line. "Imagine my surprise," he recalled,

> when several weeks later I received a letter marked "Confidential" inviting me, as a consequence of taking part in the Daily Telegraph Crossword Time Test, to make an appointment to see Colonel Nichols of the General Staff, who "would very much like to see you on a matter of national importance." Colonel Nichols was the head of MI8, the military intelligence department concerned with Bletchley Park, which was referred to by those in the know as BP or Station X. . . . I think I was told, though not so primitively, that chaps with twisted brains like mine might be suitable for a particular type of work as a contribution to the war effort.

The successful candidates became part of the cryptology team at Bletchley Park and were ultimately successful in their mission: The Enigma codes were unriddled, foiling Herr Hitler's battle plans and sparing scores of British vessels. While cryptic crosswords have never really grabbed Americans with the instant dog-to-a-bone fanaticism they inspired in Englishmen, they have always had a small but rabidly loyal audience who devour the works of standout Stateside setters such as Stephen Sondheim (commissioned by Gloria Steinem to create the cryptic for the new *New York* magazine in 1967) and lyricist Richard Maltby, Jr. Today's preeminent purveyors of the form are Emily Cox and Henry Rathvon, who produce the perplexing posers for the *Atlantic* and the *Boston Globe*, among others, and who wrote the book (*Random House Guide to Cryptic Crosswords*) on solving and setting—all this in addition to moderating the *New York Times* crossword forum (no, I don't think they sleep).

CONTINUING INNOVATIONS IN THE STATES

During the war years, *New York Times* publisher Arthur Hays Sulzberger became addicted to the *Herald Tribune*'s crossword and came to the creditable conclusion that his paper should have one too. Who better to oversee the paper's puzzle, he concluded, than the top name in the field: "Mrs. Crossword" (Margaret Petherbridge Farrar)? As befitted the "Gray Lady's" stature, Sulzberger decided, the *Times*'s crossword should focus on current events and the news (for the next thirty years, Margaret would be ordered to keep it "dignified"), and the daily puzzle should be solvable in around twenty minutes—the average amount of time commuters spent on the subway each morning on the way to work. The paper's first pair of Sunday puzzles appeared on February 15, 1942: "Headlines and Footnotes" was a 23 × 23 by Charles Erlenkotter, and the second was a 15 × 15 Puns & Anagrams puzzle titled "Riddle Me This" constructed by "Anna Gram" (a pseudonym used by a number of constructors, including Margaret herself on occasion—but in this case Albert Morehead and Jack Luzzatto). To introduce readers to this new form, a hybrid puzzle with an American-style grid and British-style definitions, an explanation was included: "Here are puns and persiflage, anagrams and homonyms, all fair game for the amateur sleuth." By 1950, the Sunday *Times* puzzles had become so popular that the paper instituted a daily crossword as well; the puzzle was syndicated to other newspapers beginning in the 1960s.

Farrar's innovations at the *Times* were significant and prolific. Many of the customs she pioneered have become traditions carried on by every editor since, including the practice of making the puzzles harder as the week goes by, with Monday's being the simplest to ease working stiffs into the week. (The weekend's puzzles were deliberately designed to be tougher because, she felt, it was then that people had time to look things up at home or make visits to the library.) Long multiple-word answers, previously prohibited, made their debut under Farrar's stewardship; the first was included in a puzzle by none other than future *Times* crossword editor Eugene T. Maleska. Maleska, recalled Margaret, "sent in a puzzle with the phrase SOFT-SHELLED CRAB, or maybe it was HARD-SHELLED CRAB. At any rate, it was in the dictionary and we used it. Then other constructors began coming up with phrases." She also began enforcing black-square maximums (16 percent of the total squares in the grid, which lowered the puzzle's total word count and led to more interesting answer words), publishing a "tricky" puzzle on April Fools' Day, and encouraging constructors to use wordplay in their clues.

Arguably, Farrar's most consequential contribution to crossword culture was her embrace of the topical, or themed, crossword, in which the longer grid entries revolve around a central subject or related bits of wordplay. In the 1950s, pun-friendly adman Harold T. Bers composed the first to be published in the *Times*: Its title was "Catalogue," and it contained terms like CATBIRD SEAT, KITTY HAWK, and PUSSYFOOT. (Like Bers's puzzle, early crossword themes were rather rudimentary by today's standards.)

In 1969, Farrar was ousted from her editorship, courtesy of the *Times*'s mandatory retirement policy, at age seventy-two (it was the paper's habit to foist departure on its employees when they reached the age of seventy; she'd gotten a couple of years' grace). She finished out her working days as editor of the *Los Angeles Times* Syndicate and died in June 1984.

Crossworders Remember Margaret Farrar

WILL SHORTZ: My hero, or the person I look up to the most, is Margaret Farrar. I think my puzzles are similar to hers from the 1950s. That's when she was at her peak. The puzzles then were full of lively vocabulary [and] clues that related to real life. The ways that I differ from her, I think, reflect the ways that society has changed since then. I include brand names, and there are lots more names now from popular culture. Also, there's more humor in the puzzles now, a little more trickery, certainly more themes than in the 1950s. During the 1950s, crossword themes were just coming into vogue. You could go several weeks . . . and get only one theme, and even that would be a very simplistic one. What I most admire Margaret for are the quality of her grids and the precision of her cluing.

NANCY SCHUSTER: After looking back at it after all these years, I have decided that between Margaret Farrar and [Dell editor] Kathleen Rafferty, crosswords became what they were—which was completely unlike European puzzles. They were rather prim and priggish (no barely clad girls on the covers, no off-color cartoons inside as in European mags!) and very limited—with many, many rules about what you could and couldn't say [or] put in a puzzle. A newspaper could carry any kind of suggestive headline it wanted; the puzzles couldn't. They were very, very prim.

MERL REAGLE: I just knew she was the editor—that's all I didn't know that she basically edited the first crossword puzzle book in 1924, I didn't know she was the first *New York Times* editor in 1942, and I just didn't know exactly what her place was in the crossword pantheon. I just knew that she was the editor, and so I sent her these three puzzles. One of them had ROTTEN IN DENMARK and DEAD AS A DOORNAIL in it—in the same puzzle. I didn't think another thing of it until I got the [rejection] letter back. The other one had EDEMA and RALE in it. EDEMA is not really good either. Better than ENEMA, but it's not that great.

Those two puzzles had those crappy words in them, but the third one accidentally had nothing wrong with it. The third one had triple fifteens down the center, and one fifteen across the middle. I made that puzzle when I was fifteen, and I think I sent it to her when I was sixteen. The triples down the center, one across the middle—she said, "That's pretty impressive." There are lots of guys who can't do that now. They were ALEUTIAN ISLANDS, SALES RESISTANCE, and something else . . . I can't remember. Across the middle, I remember, was INNOCENTS ABROAD. Anyway, she called it a tour-de-force, and she printed it, and she said, "If you've got anything else, send it along." I proceeded to send only the most hairy-looking stuff I had, which generally had lots of disallowable, or not the best, word choices. So she had to have a lot of patience with me, to say, "Well, yes, it's wide-open, but it's full of crap!" I would accidentally sort of get the point after a while and send her stuff that she could actually use. That was in 1966, when I was sixteen, and she was forced out in just another three or four years.

She was forced out of the *Times* daily [and] Sunday stuff, but not out of the Fireside books, or the Simon & Schuster series, and all the other things she was doing. I started sending her puzzles for her books. There were some puzzles of mine that appeared in her Simon & Schuster books, her paperback ones, which I think were from the Pocket Books series from number twenty on. I would send her puzzles, but I was still only a kid, so I didn't quite have the command that I needed to make puzzles that looked like everybody else's puzzles. But they were getting in there, and I was getting puzzles in the Fireside books of hers, the Simon & Schuster series, and stuff like that. She got to be pretty permissive with me. She'd say, "I'm going to allow this when I ordinarily wouldn't, I'm going to allow that when I normally wouldn't." When I look back on a lot of these puzzles now, I kind of cringe. Yes, the *New York Times* . . . the hard stuff, the variant spellings were all sort of okay. She frowned on most of it, but she would sort of grit her teeth and allow them more often than they do now. And you needed to with my puzzles in the early days!

BERNICE GORDON: At one time I sent Margaret a Sunday puzzle using asterisks. She questioned it, and held it for many months before publication. It was the very first time that a crossword was a bit tricky, and [puzzles] had never been done [that included] any [characters] but letters. She received many replies about it, and mailed me a huge manila envelope with letters of praise for a novel idea—and just as many downing it, saying that it was not a true puzzle.

* * *

Margaret was succeeded by Will Weng, who'd been the *Times*'s city desk man as well as a sometime crossword constructor who contributed puzzles to both the *Times* and Dell publications. Weng had a surpassing love of wordplay and the absurd, and encouraging this, to him, was much more important than enforcing the strict conventions of the puzzle world (black-square and answer-word maximums, ix-naying crosswordese, and so on). He promoted novel theme ideas (missing vowels, palindromes), and put the kibosh on a few he was seeing too often: the tired old country-plus-food equation (BERMUDA ONION, FRENCH TOAST, BELGIAN WAFFLE), colors (the tyro's most common choice), and the fifteen-letters-each trio ERNEST HEMINGWAY, THE SUN ALSO RISES, and A FAREWELL TO ARMS. To inject the necessary dose of Weng-centric humor into the puzzles he received, he blue-penciled about half the clues that came his way. As for variety puzzles, he shared Margaret Farrar's opinion of cryptics (couldn't stand 'em) and never allowed them into his pages.

Weng retired from the *Times* in 1977 at age sixty-five.

Crossworders Remember Will Weng

NANCY SCHUSTER: Will Weng made wonderful changes over Margaret, because he was much more liberal; he had a great sense of humor. He was great and the sweetest man in the world. And much better skilled with vocabulary; he had been city editor at the *Times* before becoming the puzzle guy.

MERL REAGLE: The puzzle that probably influenced me the most, coming along in my twenties, was one by Will Weng—I think it was in one of the collected books from the Sunday *New York Times*—and it was called "Thanksgiving Fare": such a bland title. But all the theme answers were things like CANNED PEAS, FREEZE-DRIED COFFEE, INSTANT POTATOES—it was like some 1950s nightmare Thanksgiving: Everything out of a can, done in thirty minutes like a TV dinner. The fact that it had this bland title and yet these surprising answers—answers with an attitude, really—struck me as very funny. It was really different and a lot of fun to solve.

And fun was what Will Weng was all about. His attitude was that the theme was the most important thing, and if the only way to get the theme answers to fit was to cross them with the crummiest words in the dictionary, then so be it. And a lot of the time they weren't even from the dictionary—they were just made up. I have four whole pages front and back of the wildest nontheme answers he ever allowed—remember, these were just incidental answers, the filler words. I remember one—it was EYE LOVE U, which was clued as "Optometrist's cherished alma mater." It had nothing to do with the theme. It was just completely fabricated. Another one I remember was SAVES LEAST, which was clued as "Emulates the grasshopper." I could understand it if it were part of a famous old Chinese saying, like "He who never thinks of rainy days, saves least." But SAVES LEAST is not even remotely conversational. This kind of wild stuff would never have been allowed by Dr. Maleska—and even the most liberal editors today would never allow it. And yet Will Weng—the *New York Times* crossword editor—was putting them in every Sunday. So I thought that was the norm. It took me a long time to realize that the theme had to be good *and* the incidental words had to be good. A very long time.

WILL SHORTZ: Will Weng I admire because of his humor. He was genuinely a funny guy, and he had genuinely witty clues in his puzzles. He encouraged more novelty and a lot more clever themes. He was the one who had the famous Tom Swifties crossword, where all the long answers finished the Tom Swifty statements. Where he wasn't so good, I think . . . he didn't care so much about the quality of his grids. The crossword grids that he published had a lot more crosswordese and obscurity in them.

JIM PAGE: Will used crosswordese. Now that I think of it, I won't say he encouraged it, but he okayed crosswordese words. In fact, he told me once that one of his references was the *Dell Crossword* [*Dictionary*], which is . . . essentially crosswordese words. He used to refer to that quite a bit. He was pretty lenient in that area. Will was a departure from Margaret Farrar in that respect. She was a lot more conservative. He liked humor—and the wackier the better.

* * *

Weng's successor was Dr. Eugene T. Maleska, who ruled the *Times* puzzle pages with an iron fist from 1977 until his death in 1993. Maleska was undeniably the most controversial editor in crossword history, for two reasons: His penchant for ripping constructors to shreds for relatively minor infractions, and for the academic bent of his puzzles, courtesy of his many years in the Brooklyn school system. Maleska's hard-core educational background produced a sea change in the *Times*'s puzzles: Humor (except of the "crossword" variety) was, for the most part, out; classic (and arcane) knowledge was way, way in. Maleska took his job seriously—very seriously—and he had a low tolerance for amateurs and those who didn't produce puzzles conforming to his strict definition of what crosswords should be. But he could be kind to constructors, as well—and no one ever forgot one of his compliments.

Crossworders Remember Eugene T. Maleska

WILL SHORTZ: Maleska had a scholarly tone. He pioneered in the quotation crossword, which became more popular once he became editor. There are many nice things that can be said about Maleska, but a sense of humor was not his strong point.

JIM PAGE: Gene started out by rejecting all my stuff that Will [Weng] had on file. It really upset me no end. I sent a letter to him, which was not very nice, about "I guess I'm now *persona non grata*." It was a hurt-feeling kind of response. That ended up in a newspaper—Gene made a comment about "one of my unhappy constructors said he was a '*persona non grata*.' " I didn't realize it would come back to me like that. That was my first experience with him, and I almost didn't bother anymore.

MERL REAGLE: I get along with almost everybody. The only person I never got along with at all was Gene Maleska.

NANCY SCHUSTER: I used to edit his puzzles for Dell. Because he was the standard in expert-category [puzzles], he was their shining star. But he spelled CHAMPS ÉLYSÉES wrong down the grid of one of his puzzles! He wrote the most god-awful clues, with the corniest sense of humor. It's okay to create "Nutcracker's suite" for NEST, but do you have to use it every three months?

He was horrible. I knew him, and what irritated me so much was . . .

when I was a real menial little freelancer, he didn't remember who I was even though it was I who made him fit for publication. When I became the editor in chief at Dell [Champion], he still couldn't manage to remember who I was, somehow. I used to see him at the bookseller's Sunday in New York, and I'd say, "Oh, hello Gene, how are you? I'm Nancy Schuster." And he'd say, "Oh, oh yeah, oh, hello. Who's next?"

JIM PAGE: He thought I was a Johnny-come-lately. I had to work like hell for years to get any kind of recognition. He asked me, "Have you been published before?" Great insult: I thought I was well known! Will Weng and I were the best of friends!

NORMAN WIZER: I made a 15 × 15 and sent it to Maleska, and he took it. Then I did two more, and he took them. As a matter of fact, in his book *A Pleasure in Words*, he mentioned me as one of the up-and-coming crossword puzzle people. That's why I told you I really liked Maleska, and I really only have good things to say about him. He might mention something once in a while, but usually he said he liked it and would accept it for the *New York Times*. When I started doing 21 × 21s, he would say he didn't need it for the *Times* but would I mind if he put it in Simon & Schuster? And I said I didn't care— as long as they published the thing. And paid me.

MERL REAGLE: Will once told me that whenever Maleska would do a little talk on crosswords, he would draw a 5 × 5 grid, and then he would put black squares in all the corners, and then he would put black squares so that it was really like a British grid. So the top word was three letters long, the middle word was five letters, and the bottom word was three. And down, it was the same thing: three, five, three. He would say, "*This* is a crossword grid." Will always thought, "Jeez, can't you even do all fives?"

WILL SHORTZ: Merl got the *idea* right, but not the precise pattern. The black squares were put in the corners, and then one more was put in the middle. The result was a 5 × 5 grid with a three-letter word, a five, two two-letter words on a line, a five, and a three. I always thought that the black square in the middle was awfully cheap, since it produced four two-letter words— what kind of crossword construction is this, anyway? And then Maleska used only words with alternating vowels and consonants for the fill—something that top constructors try to avoid, because it makes puzzles bland. The exercise really didn't explain crossword construction in any meaningful way.

MAURA JACOBSON: I was not happy with Maleska. I did not have many puzzles in the *Times* during his reign. He rejected all of what I thought were the good ones. Finally, after six or seven tries, I sent him a puzzle—it had the word ROSE repeated. He loved it.

JIM PAGE: Gene was difficult. He was a tough editor. He looked at me as kind of an interloper. I was a friend after a while, but down deep, he felt I was just a newcomer, and he was unsure about what talent, if any, I had. That changed in time, because he eventually listed me as one of his top [constructors].

NORMAN WIZER: In one of our phone conversations, Maleska said he didn't solve crossword puzzles at all—just did Double-Crostics and cryptic crosswords.

MERL REAGLE: I just assumed that Maleska was aware of what had been going on for the last eight years under Will Weng. This was in the 1970s; I was in my twenties. Those were my formative years about what could go into puzzles and what couldn't.

I got a letter from Margaret Farrar saying that she had talked to Dr. Maleska about me, recommending me as a "young promising constructor." She sent me a letter saying, "So send him some stuff. But remember, he eschews flagrant liberties." And I thought, "Hmm, what constitutes a 'flagrant liberty'? Something like EYE LOVE U?" So I sent him a couple of puzzles that had what I thought were very entertaining themes (one was about movie titles with one letter missing, like AND JUSTICE FOR AL, which was easy to clue because it actually starred Al Pacino, and the other was about puns on girls' names, like MATHEMATICAL CONSTANCE and STRUMMING AMANDA LYNN), but they also contained many iffy non-theme answers, like RAM A CAR. And I got back this now-infamous letter where he was astounded that I could send him such amateurish stuff. He didn't mention a thing about the themes. But he did single out the phrase MAKE A BUY as something he didn't like (it's a real term, but it has a drug connotation to it); and he didn't like RAM A CAR, which obviously is over the line; and, well, there was just a lot he didn't like. He did say that in the scheme of things, I needed him more than he needed me, and that what I'd sent him was pretty much the work of a hack.

ERICA ROTHSTEIN: The ego! The ego that that man had knew no bounds. For him to carry on with other constructors . . . the things we used to have to do to fix his puzzles, and we were not allowed to send them back to him—because he wouldn't fix them!

MERL REAGLE: His letter had two effects on me: One, the tone of the letter was very harsh, and that really hurt. The advice he was giving, though, was good, although it was like being sternly chewed out by your dad or something. It's just that it probably would have had the same effect if he hadn't done it in such a harsh manner. And this was the first letter I'd ever gotten from him! For the first letter to be so cutting, that's what was so hard to understand, especially since most of the other editors I'd dealt with—Margaret and Will Weng—were so incredibly polite. He was like their polar opposite. And then later I found out that virtually everybody in the biz who submitted puzzles to him got at least one letter like that—veteran constructors and newcomers alike. Almost everybody has one.

NANCY SCHUSTER: Manny Nosowsky says he got rotten, nasty letters from him. He sent somebody else a letter that said, "I can't stand your awful puzzles. Don't ever send them to me again!" Isn't that terrible? I wasn't making puzzles when he was editor—thank God!

JOHN SAMSON: I learned a lot from Eugene. Despite his gruff exterior, he was a compassionate, big-hearted soul. There were numerous occasions when he would go out of his way to help constructors who were undergoing personal crises in their lives. (When my crossword collaborator David Pohl died tragically, I wrote Eugene and told him I was giving up constructing puzzles. He wrote a long letter back to me encouraging me not to give it up.) And Eugene was sensitive to the feelings of solvers. He stopped cluing the word MORON as "Idiot" and replaced it with "City of eastern Argentina" when asked by a director of the New York State Office of Mental Health to please avoid that offensive definition. Toward constructors, however, he could be blunt and a little intimidating at times. I remember carelessly leaving out about seven clues once—I never made that mistake again! Eugene Maleska, like Vince Lombardi, had a whip a mile long and was not afraid to use it. I got used to it, though, and didn't mind it that much when I discovered all constructors were treated the same. When you did well, you were praised—when you did poorly, you felt the whip.

NANCY JOLINE: Early on, I was told by Gene Maleska that if I didn't stop making errors, he would drop me "like a hot potato." A few years later, he complimented me on the relative absence of errors in my puzzles. When I reminded him of the hot-potato message, he said, "I don't remember saying that, but I'm glad I did!" (I've since learned from a couple of other constructors that they, too, received hot-potato letters.)

My proofers have suggested that I send you to Coventry because they have a hard time keeping up with your errors. They contend that you have a tendency to "wing it" rather than checking every clue and every word. I hope that their analysis is wrong because your creations are clever. But if they continue to present me with examples of carelessness on your part, I will drop you like a hot potato lest I run into embarrassment.
—Gene Maleska to Nancy Joline, May 29, 1986

JIM PAGE: Gene had a way of getting you to be a little better. This is one of the things I really tip my hat to Gene for. He was a teacher, so he knew about trying to get you to be better in what you were doing. One of the ways he did that . . . he sent a letter to me once, and it said, "If you weren't a friend of mine, I'd drop you like a hot potato." Boy, that hurt. That really hurt. But it also got me up off my ass, to be better. I bring that up only because Nancy Joline got the same letter. I thought it was just me. Jesus. Blow my brains out. Well, it turns out that a lot of people got that letter. But it was nothing more than—it was nasty, but it was a means to make you better. In my case, it certainly had a lot to do with trying harder. Now that I think about it, a lot of things have happened to make me better, not the least of which was the rejections by Gene initially, and [then] by Will Shortz. They made me better. They made me do something different.

Sorry to be returning the enclosed puzzle, which I'd hoped to use in Series #174. It contains artificial, contrived entries that I consider unacceptable.

Please see my check marks. I hope you can fix the problems or sell the
puzzle to some editor whose standards are low and loose.
—Gene Maleska to Coral Amende, 1992

MANNY NOSOWSKY: My view of him, even after all these years, includes meanness of spirit, pettiness, and a penchant for blackmail. He hated *CROSSW RD* magazine that Richard Silvestri edited, and he tried to destroy it. It ran anti-Maleska editorials by Stan Newman. Anyhow, his chief objection seemed to be that *CROSSW RD* was selling T-shirts with the likeness of himself on it, and he wasn't being given a cut of the profits! (I have no idea why he thought I would be sympathetic to his discomfort.) Both Liz Gorski and I got letters from him that started, "I'm sick and tired of your puzzles . . ." I don't know the rest of Liz's letter, but that opening was the high point of mine.

ELIZABETH GORSKI: I am indebted to Gene for publishing the first puzzle I had ever constructed. It was called "Legalitease" and it appeared in the Simon & Schuster book series. When I submitted the puzzle to him, I included no information about myself, only that it was "my latest puzzle." (Technically, this was true. It was my first, only, and latest puzzle. I knew that he didn't like receiving puzzles from neophytes, so I just let the puzzle speak for itself.) I was absolutely thrilled when he accepted it. Gene encouraged me to send in more grids. After he had published a couple of my puzzles in the Simon & Schuster books, he asked me for some biographical info. Since I was now a "published" constructor and we had a good relationship, I thought it was high time to let him know that he had published my first puzzle. A few weeks later I received a thick envelope from Gene, in which he returned all the puzzles that I had sent to him. His cover letter opened with: "I am sick and tired of your puzzles . . ." He went on to describe my work in superlative terms—my puzzles were some of the worst he had ever seen. I guess our relationship wasn't as solid as I had imagined.

Confused and saddened, I threw in the towel on constructing puzzles. I had heard that Gene was ill and, therefore, it seemed inappropriate to pursue the matter any further. A few months later, I read of Gene's death in the *Times*. I didn't think about constructing until about a year later, when John

Samson wrote to me and asked if I'd be interested in submitting puzzles to Simon & Schuster. John encouraged me back into the fold and I've been constructing ever since.

CATHY MILLHAUSER: I remember getting a couple of acceptance letters from Eugene Maleska that were almost as bad as rejections! One scolded me, not at all gently, for violating his "one-Sunday-submission-a-year" policy, and the other I've luckily forgotten.

GAYLE DEAN: Eugene Maleska once said that there were 120 constructors who were capable of creating a *New York Times*–quality puzzle, so I suppose those top 120 constructors would probably be the best, generally speaking. I'm happy to report that Dr. Maleska included me in that list.

JIM PAGE: He was very encouraging for me, Gene Maleska. He had a gruff exterior, and he could be abrupt even to his friends, but once you got to know him—and I did get to know him, very well, because of the time we spent together—he was a very interesting guy in a lot of ways.

I know I've been piling praise on you, and I hope it doesn't go to your head. However, after having just edited your PELOTA for July 8, I must say that I've discovered a gem of purest ray serene. I'm beginning to think that you can do anything I can do better. Have you ever thought of becoming an editor?
—Gene Maleska to Nancy Joline, May 4, 1989

NANCY JOLINE: I can still remember walking up the driveway, reading this letter, and feeling as giddy as Sally Field on receiving her Oscar. "Gem of purest ray serene," indeed!

JIM PAGE: I said, "Hey, when you're in New York, give me a call—I'll take you to dinner." And he did—because he wanted a free dinner with a CBS executive who was paying the bill. That's how [the relationship] got better. From then on, he really encouraged me in lots of ways. He would send me grids, for example—unusual grids, for the Simon & Schuster books, which he was editor of as well, for me to fill out. He gave me some thematic ideas. So he encouraged me quite a bit. We became friends, and I used to visit him up in Over Jordan [Massachusetts], and when he came to New York he would have dinner with me. And he stayed here a few times, too, when he was in town. We got to be good friends. He was encouraging to me.

ELIZABETH GORSKI: I learned a lot from Gene, and I'm grateful that he didn't mince words when giving advice. When I first started constructing, I was only interested in making 21 × 21 grids. He suggested that I try some 15 × 15 grids to hone my skills—"Try some etudes before trying a symphony." That's how I want to remember him.

THE NEW WAVE OF CROSSWORD PUZZLING

A revolution is an insurrection, an act of violence by which one class overthrows another.
—MAO TSE-Tung

In the early 1980s, deep into Dr. Maleska's tenure at the *Times*, a group of constructors—spearheaded by one outspoken young upstart, Stanley Newman—decided they'd had enough of this pedant. Newman, who by this time had started his American Crossword Federation and was publishing the *Crossworder's OWN Newsletter*, made it his personal crusade to purge the puzzle world of so-called crosswordese—archaic and obscure words and phrases—and to abolish the academic tone of the crosswords of the time. Newman recalls,

I discovered all the repetition—this becomes painfully obvious when you do a large quantity of puzzles—and saw what the party line was by the people who edited the best-known puzzles; they would spout off for attribution that "Gee, crosswordese is necessary. You've got to have these words to fit the [theme entries] in." I began to discover, as my own skills improved as a puzzle-maker and editor, that it really wasn't necessary. [I] would, as an academic exercise, work on corners of the New York Times *crosswords that had two or three really crazy words. In just a few moments, this relatively new person to the business could change a few letters and make them all interesting words, or at least common words people would use in conversations that had nothing to do with crosswords.*

Newman's public critiques enraged Maleska. "I was a 'pipsqueak'—that was the word Maleska used," says Stan. "That was great—the word was a badge of honor. I had his attention, anyway."

The movement gained momentum, ultimately becoming known as the "new wave." Constructors began ignoring Maleska's strict dictums and pushing the boundaries of the crossword form: writing clues and themes that focused on trickiness and wittiness in lieu of the crossword-humor and straight-dictionary standards then prevalent. Humor, puns, and other forms of wordplay became the central features of these fresh new puzzles, and almost anything was fair game: brand names (strictly forbidden by Maleska), current slang, and phrases too new to be found in dictionaries. There are few who would argue that these changes made crosswords more accessible and "solver-friendly," and the majority of published puzzles today adhere to the new wave's conventions.

Crossworders on the New Wave

Academism results when the reasons for the rule change, but not the rule.
— IGOR Stravinsky

STAN NEWMAN: I went on the record saying that I thought Maleska was coasting, in effect, that he wasn't working nearly as hard as the editor of the most important puzzle in the country should. Maleska naturally wasn't going to admit, "You know, he's right." I learned later he wasn't the sort of gentleman who liked to be told those sorts of things. We didn't exactly get off on the right foot.

WILL SHORTZ: I don't like the term "new wave," because it suggests a radical break from the past, and that's not accurate. I call it the "new school" of puzzles, and *GAMES* magazine was definitely the pioneer of this new school, which meant that crosswords were more relevant to everyday life. More humor, more avoidance of obscurity and stupid crosswordese, and more clues pulled from everyday life and modern culture. Which is not to say that the older sorts of knowledge shouldn't appear in puzzles, just that the new school of puzzling is more balanced, appealing to solvers of all ages and interests.

TRIP PAYNE: [Stan] certainly championed it, although it was well under way by that time. Henry [Hook] and Merl [Reagle] were doing their things long before Stan came around.

STAN NEWMAN: Will [Shortz] was in the business long before I came along. Will had modern-day crosswords in *GAMES* magazine long before I ever picked up a pencil and tried to make a puzzle of my own. [But] in fact, he was part of the puzzle establishment back then, and the last thing he wanted to do was rile Maleska. Nevertheless, it was apparent to anybody who was paying attention that the puzzles in *GAMES* were hugely different from those in the *New York Times*, and it didn't take too much insight to articulate how they were different. Will's own sense of what puzzles should be: a combination of entertainment, education, a light touch, and brain-building . . . wordplay and misdirection—these were concepts that were really foreign to Maleska.

MANNY NOSOWSKY: Maleska's champions tend to be long on nostalgia, short on facts, and poor in memory. They are the ones, generally seniors (my contemporaries) bugged by Will Shortz's style. I've seen Shortz criticized for things that were invented long before even Maleska—the rebus puzzle, two-letters-in-one-square puzzles, punning, various other wordplay types—as if these were things Maleska would never have allowed. Some have even claimed that Maleska would not use a clue if it wasn't in the dictionary. One person said that Maleska was a pioneer in the fight against crosswordese. Why? Because Maleska said so in one of his books.

STAN NEWMAN: It was very easy for Maleska to say that, because he could do it without having to back anything up. I mean, nobody was going to do an investigative report of the percentage of obscure words in Maleska puzzles and how many of them could be changed and how many original clues he himself was responsible for. It was very easy for him to say, knowing that no one was going to call him on it. The truth of the matter is: Margaret Farrar had humor in her puzzles, Weng opened it up further, and Maleska pulled it back. I don't see how anyone who would look objectively at the *Times* puzzles could conclude otherwise.

MANNY NOSOWSKY: This was all too much for me; so I challenged an impartial review of three Maleska puzzles. But nobody at the time wanted to pursue that. What appears right to me to me is that Maleska avoided pop culture past, say, the 1950s. Shortz includes the current scene. I wasn't around at the time, but didn't Farrar prefer topicality in puzzles? If this line of reasoning is correct, then it was only Maleska who was pedantic, stodgy, and eschewed the present.

Nothing is more tiresome than a superannuated pedagogue.
— Henry Adams

STAN NEWMAN: One of Maleska's specialties was making his puzzles hard by using the most obscure facts he could find. I remember a clue Maleska used in the *Times* for LOA: something like "Town in Utah." I had never heard of Loa, Utah, so I went to my geographical references to find it. It turns out that Loa, Utah, had a population of around 250. To me, the use of this clue was completely indefensible. No other crossword editor would have ever considered using such a clue. That clue should never have seen the light of day. Since no one else was doing so, I took it upon myself to publicize the outrageous clues like these that Maleska was using.

MIKE SHENK: Take a beginning-of-the-week *Times* puzzle right now—[Maleska fans] probably think that it's just not enough of a challenge. They want to feel like they've gone through combat when they get done, and Maleska's puzzles were probably more like that because there were words you didn't know and meanings of words you didn't know.

If you can't annoy somebody with what you write,
I think there's little point in writing.
— Kingsley AMIS

STAN NEWMAN: I began somewhat brashly citing examples of specific puzzles and asking rhetorical questions: "Why is this stuff happening? Dr. Maleska, can you explain what this is all about?" Of course, these are things he would never answer. No doubt people who got [the *Crossworder's OWN Newsletter*] would show this stuff to him, and all I was doing was making him mad. That was okay. Again, I had his attention.

NANCY SCHUSTER: When Stan started he was rather too brash and know-it-all. I remember him then like a tornado swooping in to suck up everything in his path. He had, and still has, a very competitive nature. But look where it's got him—top dog in the puzzle book industry. Stan wanted to modernize the puzzles people face every day in their newspapers . . . and stepped on many people's toes in his attempts.

STAN NEWMAN: As I became better known in the puzzle world, occasionally people would call me for interviews. My American Crossword Federation was listed in the *Encyclopedia of Associations*, and so media looking for quotes about puzzles would occasionally find their way to me. Maleska's puzzles made him a very easy target. I would have lots of eminently quotable zingers ready, like "Maleska's knowledge of popular culture goes no further than Rosie the Riveter"—the sad thing is that statement wasn't too far wrong.

And the closer I looked, the worse it became. We must've called some sort of truce, because I actually began submitting puzzles to Maleska. And I specifically remember him rejecting two of them because of answer words I used: CAR SEATS and TAILGATE PARTIES. Not only had Maleska never heard of these words, but he either had no modern dictionary to check them out or just didn't care to. That just got me angry all over again, that the guy who's the editor of the prestige puzzle of the country was completely unfamiliar with current American English.

NANCY SCHUSTER: [Stan] really didn't have many social graces. I used to yell at him because when he started up his newsletter . . . I guess he was in a position of respecting me at the time, because I was an editor. In 1982, I must have been working for Official Publications. I used to tell him off. When he would edit his crosswords, I would send him commentary and tell him not to be fresh and not to be a smart aleck. I guess he listened. One thing about Stan, he learned fast, whether it was how to solve faster than anyone or how to get his foot in the puzzle door.

Revolutionaries are more formalistic than conservatives.
—ITALO Calvino

STAN NEWMAN: I remember doing for the puzzles [that the syndicates] were running the sorts of things that I had done for the *Times,* having now had some experience in going through a puzzle and spotting all the crazy stuff.

JIM PAGE: I think the new wave clues are less specific than the old-style puzzles. Since the difficulty of new wave puzzles is often governed by the cluing process, the clues must be made to better hide the answer from the solver. However, new wave Friday and Saturday puzzles strive for fresh vocabulary in the grid, adding to their challenge and toughness. Give me some clever clues in a puzzle and I'm happy. Old-style puzzles often had the thematic entries crossing each other in the grid. They also disallowed brand names in the grid.

NANCY SCHUSTER: I think [Stan has] succeeded very well, and he's also enormously increased the shelf space of puzzle books in the bookstore. He doesn't have to be brash anymore and behaves very kindly to people who've been good to him. He gives surprise gifts and does other little friendly things that show a lot of appreciation.

STAN NEWMAN: There are many constructors out there who are still making puzzles "the old way," what we might have called [the] mainstream of twenty or thirty years ago. They're somehow getting published, but not by me. It's 2001, and it's a whole new world. Will is at the *Times,* Mike is at the *Wall Street Journal,* Merl is at the *San Francisco Examiner,* Henry's at the *Boston Globe,* and I'm at *Newsday.* At the risk of stating the obvious, the war's over; we won.

* * *

Puzzle prodigy Will Shortz has presided over the crosswords in the *Times* since 1993 (following a brief interim period after Maleska's death, during which time the paper had a temporary editor: veteran constructor Mel Taub). Shortz recalls getting off to a somewhat rocky start:

It was interesting—I was the first person to become the Times *crossword editor whose predecessor was not still living. So it was a bumpy road for the first six months. I didn't have anyone really to advise me and no one to pro-*

vide solace when I got letters from unhappy solvers. The biggest thing, the thing that surprised me from the beginning, was how hard many of the solvers wanted the Times *crossword to be. I was used to having puzzles at mainly the medium level of difficulty—I think that's what the majority of solvers want. But the* Times *has an audience, at least in part, of really serious, expert solvers who want their puzzles to be extra-hard.*

I'll tell you what happened. First the crosswords were too easy, and I was just deluged with complaints that I was dumbing the puzzle down. That was the phrase I heard again and again: "You're dumbing the puzzle down." Then I said, "Well, I'm going to show them!" I made all the puzzles real hard—and then I got letters the other way. Eventually things settled in to how they are now, which is a range of easy to hard. There's something for everybody.

Crossworders on Will Shortz

FRED PISCOP: Will isn't afraid to use clues and themes that many other editors wouldn't touch.

JIM PAGE: One thing about [submitting puzzles to the *New York Times*] changed for the better [after Maleska], and I'm sure I'd get agreement from all the new-wavers on this: Gene's policy was to open up the puzzle area for a short time, and then he would have a moratorium. It could be a very short time that it was opened up; then the moratorium shut down and you didn't submit anything for a year or so. This did a couple of things: It made you less active in creating, and it also shut people out of it entirely. It's a lot better now, simply because Will Shortz will let you send in stuff anytime—he'll just reject a great deal of it. But the good part is, if you're somebody new, and he sees something that catches his eye, you'll get a chance. Secondarily, if you're somebody who's been around a while, like I have, and you send something in that is pretty good, he'll pick it up and publish you. And that's good.

NANCY SCHUSTER: The people who were born in the last thirty years had a whole different education than their parents. They don't know a million classic things. We "elders" also don't know the new stuff—thus the generation gap.

Will [Shortz] tries to put content in the puzzles for each group. It's such a great feeling to see a clue and say, "Hey, I know that!"

MAURA JACOBSON: I think Will, now, has really hit the right stride. He's a sweet guy.

MERL REAGLE: He's a very nice guy, and he's an excellent spokesman for the whole puzzle industry. He's got a great radio voice—in fact, Saab called him up once and asked him to audition to narrate some of their commercials. Now, it didn't pan out, but that was kind of neat. (And, funny thing, they didn't even know that Will actually drives a Saab.)

JIM PAGE: Gene [Maleska] was pretty much by the dictionary/book. I'd have to say Will Weng [was] as well. Both of those guys—what you had in the grid was important, but what was most important was that it be look-upable. Every word in the grid should be look-upable somewhere: dictionary, geography [book], movie lists, song lists, somewhere. Verifiable. Period. That had to be. Period.

Not so with Will Shortz. Lots of his words are not look-upable. You don't go to the dictionary to find AIR BUBBLE—you won't find it. You don't go to the dictionary to find SEE YA. With Maleska and Weng, you'd say, "God, what the hell is this Celebes island?" You'd go to the geography [book] and you'd find it. You can't do that with a lot of the new wave words. Not to say they're not good words—they are good words. They're words that we would probably all say, "Yeah, we know about them." But to be absolutely certain and verifiable . . . you have to say, "Yes, I know that. I guess that's right." You couldn't do that with Maleska or with Will Weng. You would have to verify everything, including initials. Everything. Anything not verifiable was no good. That's a change. Will Shortz allows, in fact encourages, brand names, which Gene would not have touched—nor would Will Weng.

The cross word, untrammeled by the strict construction rules of the Word Square, Diamond, Pyramid and other classical forms of interlocking word puzzles whence it sprang, has that very freedom of expression to thank for its universal appeal. Another reason for the infectious quality of the cross word is that in its great variety of specimens, with varying degrees of difficulty, everybody could find some to fit his taste and mentality. That's the main reason for the popularity of the cross word—everybody could solve them. Almost everybody can construct them, too.

—Sam Loyd, Jr.

PUZZLE ANSWERS

Voltaire's Enigma
TIME

Queen Victoria's Double Acrostic
NAPLES
ELBE
WASHINGTON
CINCINNATI
AMSTERDAM
STAMBOUL
TORNEA
LEPANTO
ECLIPTIC
(NEWCASTLE; COAL MINES)

From Ape to Man
APE, ARE, ARM, AIM, RIM, RAM, RAN, MAN
(8 words)

The Alphabet

2.

GAME WARDENS

---※---

CONSTRUCTION PRODUCTION

Constructors, of course, should be kept under wraps,

Either speak to them kindly or cause their collapse;

So tender their egos, from what I have heard,

They crumple completely for lack of a word!

It is not enough to have a good mind. The main thing is to use it well.
—RENÉ Descartes

Curious about the personalities behind the puzzles? The crossword clan is a diverse group, and it's ill-advised to make sweeping generalizations about its members. That said, however, you will seldom encounter a crossword constructor who is not witty and literate, with a weakness for bad puns and good wordplay. Creating salable puzzles takes a light touch; a heavy investment of time; and, I'm firmly convinced, a touch of the obsessive-compulsive in one's personality.

To gain their insights into this rather rarefied occupation, today's top puzzlemakers and editors were asked a series of questions about the biz, ranging from how they got their feet wet to the latest trends in the crossword world. Their enlightening views follow.

SQUARE ROOTS

Habitual solvers all—and from an early age? As an "only," I solved magazine after magazine of well-crafted Dell puzzles to combat boredom. Naturally, this love of solving (and intolerance of boredom) carried over into adult life, when I began to construct crosswords—and it has never left!

WILL SHORTZ: When I was a kid, I joked about majoring in puzzles when I got to college, because I really wanted to become a professional puzzlemaker. It was just a joke. In the eighth grade, in social studies class, when we were asked to write a paper on what we wanted to do with our lives, I wrote a paper on becoming a professional puzzlemaker.

PETER GORDON: I've been solving puzzles my entire life. One of my earliest memories is a math question from Martin Gardner's *Perplexing Puzzles and Tantalizing Teasers* from when I was about five. It read, "A harmonica cost a dollar more than a pencil. Together they cost $1.10. How much did each cost?" I couldn't solve it, so I asked my older brother to help. He used algebra to solve it and explained how algebra worked. I was fascinated and ended up loving math and majoring in it at M.I.T. I loved math puzzles and also liked cryptograms and "Eyeball Benders" in *GAMES* magazine.

RICH SILVESTRI: [I began solving at] about age five: the rebuses and riddles in *Humpty-Dumpty* and *Jack and Jill.*

KELLY CLARK: I once tried to solve a jigsaw puzzle with my grandmother and gave up after about five minutes.

KAREN HODGE: I probably started solving word puzzles at about age six or seven—*Jack and Jill, Humpty-Dumpty, Highlights for Children* all had kids' puzzle pages. It's hard to remember what the puzzles were like—probably crosswords and anagrams. I recall not liking word searches—and still don't!

NORMAN WIZER: I started solving puzzles as a kid. I loved jigsaw puzzles, crosswords, anagrams, and all kinds of puzzles. My aunt taught me how to do crosswords and anagrams.

WILLIAM CANINE: As a family, we played many word games.

RANDOLPH ROSS: As early as I can remember, I sat with my father and mother, trying to help them. I started on my own with the simple puzzle books.

FRANCIS HEANEY: I solved lots of puzzles as a youngster. My grandmother bought me a subscription to *GAMES* magazine when I was ten. The first thing I remember from that is my grandfather got ahold of it when I wasn't looking and started doing the Ornery crossword in pen. I was furious. He hadn't finished it—he was a pretty good solver, but he was using the hard clues. I went back and cleaned it up with the easy clues.

RAY HAMEL: My grandparents lived in the same town I did, and they solved the daily newspaper puzzle together. One solved the top half, the other solved the bottom half. I probably got interested in trying to help around age six. My grandfather also created his own crossword puzzle dictionary, which he kept in a series of small ring binders. I still have it.

RICH NORRIS: My dad started me on puzzles when I was in grade school. He used to solve the *New York Times* puzzle every day, and he'd ask me for help. My mom still tells the story of his asking, "What's a seven-letter word for 'Alcoholic beverage'?" I thought a moment (I was no more than seven, myself) and blurted out "ASPIRIN!" I always loved crosswords, though for a while in high school I had fun with Jumbles. I would try to solve all four words and the answer in my head.

ERICA ROTHSTEIN: My mother was an ardent *Times* solver. She would sit, all week if necessary, with the Sunday puzzle. She liked the Double-Crostics. Seeing her do it, as any kid [would], I used to try to get to it before she did, and I'd watch her erasing everything I ever put in. There was no such thing as a photocopy machine, so I wasn't allowed to solve her puzzle. You know, you weren't allowed to touch her puzzle on pain of death. When I finally started at least filling in a little more and having it be right, she told me to leave it alone. It was her domain, it wasn't mine. I wasn't buying it, and, therefore, I could just leave it be.

SHAWN KENNEDY: I began solving at the age of seven, and I am fifteen now. Jumbles and cryptograms were my favorite types of puzzles to solve. The first thing that I did every morning was open the newspaper and solve the word puzzles.

CATHY MILLHAUSER: The only crosswords I had seen were the crosswordese-filled ones my dad solved in the local paper. I enjoyed Scrabble and jigsaw puzzles.

NANCY JOLINE: I always loved word games. As a child, [I] did riddles, rebuses, [and] played charades. When I grew older, I took up Scrabble. Still love it.

PATRICK JORDAN: I first became interested in puzzles during elementary school, by solving the simple ones that appeared on the back page of my *Weekly*

Reader. My mother encouraged this by buying age-appropriate activity books throughout my childhood. My favorites were dot-to-dots, mazes, word searches, and picture crosswords. My first encounter with true crosswords came when I used my allowance to buy a copy of *Dell Pocket Crosswords* sometime during my preteen years. I got hooked on them and began buying Dell magazines regularly, gradually building my solving skills until I could usually finish every crossword from cover to cover.

TOM SCHIER: I started solving when I was eight years old as part of a grade-school math project. My dad mom and dad solved crosswords regularly, so I naturally tagged along.

BOB KLAHN: I've had a fascination for words and wordplay, and for structure, as long as I can remember. Crosswords involve all three, so when I first saw a crossword grid, the appeal was instant. I made my first crossword when I was eight. It was a 4 × 4, but without the four center squares, so it was just four words linked around the edges. I remember that one of the entries was BEAR, which I clued as "An animal." Obviously I didn't know too many four-letter animals, or at least I didn't think of them at the time.

I don't recall solving much of anything back then. I just remember making that one puzzle and getting a chuckle out of my parents. When I was in fifth grade I made a puzzle for the school newspaper, shaped like a Christmas tree. I made the puzzle's clues so hard, they never asked me to do another!

WILL SHORTZ: I was writing my own puzzle book when I was ten or twelve, so when did I start solving puzzles? Probably when I was eight or nine.

TRIP PAYNE: The first puzzle memory I have is [this]: When I was maybe three years old, I was sitting in the living room chair. I was looking at the *TV Guide* crossword—I guess I was just sort of attracted to the black and white pattern or something—and I would compare the old grid with the answer the next week and look back and forth between them. Eventually I got to the point where I could actually solve a good bit of the *TV Guide* crossword, even at that age. My parents saw that [it] was starting to be an interest, so they started buying me kiddie puzzle books, which I whipped through.

Eventually I got to the point where I was making small, not particularly good, crosswords for the elementary school newspaper. I remember my first one actually had a theme: The long words were PERMANENT and TEMPORARY. PERMANENT was clued as the hairstyle, and TEMPORARY was clued as "Antonym of another meaning of 9-Across." I was probably in fourth grade or so. Then in junior high, I helped edit the newspaper there, and I had my own puzzle page where I would do variety puzzles and the occasional crossword.

BARRY TUNICK: [I solved] crosswords, starting at about nine.

ELIZABETH GORSKI: My parents are Polish-born, and I learned Polish before I learned English. My father bought me Polish-language puzzle books. I especially liked the rebus-type puzzles. Perhaps that's why I was a good speller (in English). English is a breeze compared to Polish!

ARTHUR S. VERDESCA: I always enjoyed puzzles of all sorts as a child. I would guess that by age nine or ten I was doing any type of puzzle I could come across. Crossword puzzles in the newspapers, however, were not tackled until age twelve or thirteen. Perhaps my favorite puzzles to solve have been logic puzzles (and that's going back many, many years).

DAVID J. KAHN: I started as a solver at ten or eleven (I'm now fifty-eight) and spent time mostly with the daily and Sunday *New York Times* puzzles. I never paid too much attention to the authors back then, but the constructor whose work made the biggest impression on me was Edward J. O'Brien. I was dazzled by his creativity. However, I remained strictly a solver until about ten years ago.

DIANE EPPERSON: I began solving the daily newspaper crossword at about age ten. Eventually I bought a puzzle book and tried some of the other types, but always liked the crosswords best. That's also when I discovered the diagramless crossword, and when I had done them all in a book, I would do the easy puzzles as diagramless [puzzles] using graph paper.

MAURA JACOBSON: I was about eleven when I started. My father was a crossword puzzle buff, and he let me fill in what I could, and then he finished the puzzle.

DAVID MACLEOD: I began solving at the age of twelve, perhaps. My mother was an avid solver of the *New York Times* puzzles, and I would try to finish the ones she couldn't. I was rarely successful.

MARK DIEHL: I can remember doing word puzzles in the fourth or fifth grade. I enjoyed doing cryptograms, easier crosswords, and [Dell's] Laddergrams.

SYLVIA BURSZTYN: Started solving the *New York Times* daily crossword in junior high (the whole class subscribed; the paper was delivered to home room in the morning) and was usually finished before first period. If I sat anywhere near the front of the class where teachers could see the finished puzzle on my desk, they generally hated me. In high school, one teacher warned me that this would lead to the hard stuff: Double-Crostics. The warning came too late; I had discovered these too. And once I got the knack of solving them, [I] was off and running.

Throughout childhood, one of my sisters and I always played word games with our conversation. We spoonerized everything, punned everything. We still ask each other "Cow hum?" Our first language is Yiddish, so we interlanguage punned and spoonerized. At high-school graduation, everyone who signed my yearbook mentioned crosswords and wished me as much success in the future as I had with puzzles in high school. It had still not occurred to me that a person could do this for a living.

JOHN SAMSON: I began solving crosswords when I was fourteen. My uncle Tom McCarthy got me interested in solving puzzles.

TYLER HINMAN: My first puzzle book was a Penny Press variety magazine, which was about seven years ago, when I was nine years old or so. Not long after that, I subscribed to *GAMES* magazine. I still solve both of these publications today. However, I did not become focused on crosswords until I was in the ninth grade, when I was fourteen years old.

SAM BELLOTTO, JR.: I guess I started solving puzzles somewhere in high school. My favorites were always those with clever themes and lots of upbeat, trivia-based clues.

NANCY SALOMON: I think I began solving in my teens. I mainly focused on variety cryptics and acrostics.

MARTIN ASHWOOD-SMITH: I was not an avid solver. I did not really become interested in crosswords until I was seventeen, in my first year at university.

NELSON HARDY: I don't remember if I solved puzzles as a child. I'm pretty sure I didn't start solving regularly (once a week or more) until I was an adult.

WILL SHORTZ: When I got to Indiana University, I found that they had something called the "Individualized Major Program." If you were accepted, you could major in absolutely anything. So I devised a whole range of courses in puzzles and was admitted to the program, and that's how I got my degree in Enigmatology.

[The curriculum included] lots of courses on word puzzles. I'll give you examples: One was on crossword puzzles, and that was when I made my first professional-quality crossword puzzle. Every two or three weeks I would go to see the professor with a new puzzle I had made, sit and watch while he solved it and then listen to him critique it. I also took courses on subjects like the history of American word puzzles of the late nineteenth century. I took several courses on mathematical puzzles. I also took a course on logic puzzles [and] a course on the psychology of puzzles through a professor in the psychology department. I took a course on crossword magazines through a professor in journalism. I wrote my thesis on the history of American word puzzles before 1860. . . .

For my research in this course I just spent weeks and weeks and weeks in the library. What I did was look at microfilm for every magazine and newspaper that I thought had any possibility of having a puzzle column. I would dip into it every three years or so to see if there were puzzles. My main research was in the Indiana University, where I got my degree. Indiana has a terrific library. It's one of the largest libraries in the country. There are probably not a lot of universities where I could have done such thorough research. Also, I had a grant to study puzzles at the Library of Congress for a summer, and I did that in 1973. I wrote a hundred-page thesis on this, and it was printed in a magazine called *Word Ways: The Journal of Recreational Linguistics*. It appeared in four installments there in 1974 and 1975.

CROSSROADS

Becoming an established crossword constructor can take years—as well as gumption, determination, and the fortitude to press on in the face of an everheightening mountain of rejection letters.

GAYLE DEAN: After years of solving as a teen, I became tired of the same old clues and decided the puzzle world needed some fresh talent.

JIM PAGE: I was working at CBS, and I just happened to walk by the desk of somebody who was creating a puzzle. At that point in my life, I was a solver, like everybody else, and I just said, "Hey, people make those things, huh?" I never thought too much about it. She said, "Yeah." I said, "How do you do it?" She said, "Send away to the *New York Times* and they'll give you a set of rules and go from there." So I did it, and I sent a puzzle in to Will Weng many years ago. It was a piece of crap, but I didn't know that. But he was very nice about it—he was very kind about it, in retrospect. I didn't give up—I kept trying and trying and trying. Finally, he took one. I was ecstatic.

NORMAN WIZER: [I took up construction] while I was an accountant. I decided that I wanted to do it. I would come home from work and I'd be up all hours—I just couldn't go to bed until I got it. My first one took me so long that I thought, "Oh my God, how do people do these things? It takes so long! I'm not going to do another." But then I did another, and another.

MEL TAUB: I was the best solver among my friends and classmates and decided to try to make one up. I abandoned the project—too hard—but soon realized I could probably make up acrostics.

BILL ZAIS: I decided to give constructing a try; I don't remember why. Over a four-month period, I completed three excruciatingly bad puzzles. I then gave up, thinking I had no talent in this field. [Then] I decided to give it another try. All of a sudden, I found myself able to construct, even though I was using the exact same resources that I had used before. How all of this came about is a complete mystery to me.

BERNICE GORDON: When my husband was working at night, I started constructing them out of sheer boredom. I had graduated from the University of Pennsylvania [and also had] a degree from the Pennsylvania Academy of Fine Arts, so I felt I was equipped with a decent vocabulary and a fair amount of knowledge. I had no guide or mentor. I simply sent work to Margaret Farrar at the *New York Times*. I did them on loose-leaf notepaper, and the definitions in longhand.

NANCY SCHUSTER: I always was solving puzzles, ever since I was young. I used to do the Sunday puzzle all the time at the pool when my kids were growing up. The PTA president was a friend of mine, and she had to produce the school newsletter. She couldn't fill all the pages up, so she said, "Why don't you make up a puzzle?" I said, "What an incredible idea!" Of course, it was absolutely horrible, my effort, but it fascinated me because I'd never thought of puzzles from the other direction. I just couldn't get it out of my head. She really sent me into a wonderful new world. I neglected the house and the children and everything. I used to make the bed at 5:30 P.M. [just] before my husband came home.

In those days, the only reference book available was *The Dell Crossword Dictionary*, which had four-letter and three-letter words—you know, with blank spaces. The only trouble was that it included loads of crosswordese—words so obscure you'd never want to see them in a puzzle. I used to sit with a big dictionary, reading it backwards, looking for the ends of the words. When I think of how easy it is today, it's amazing. Also, I didn't know anybody else who did such a stupid thing as making up silly crosswords, which was, in a way, the attitude my husband took. Those were the days before women got libbed, and "Why wasn't dinner on the table!" I would have loved to compare notes with a fellow constructor, but there was no one to ask, and it was really a loner kind of a thing. . . .

Finally, I got published in a few of the magazines. I think most of them paid five dollars a puzzle; there was one company that paid seven-fifty. I was so excited! After that, I started to feel a little more confident, and I sent them to Margaret Farrar at the *Times*, but she didn't like any of them. Actually, she published one, finally—a daily. A little after that time, Will Weng became the editor. He published a couple of my dailies and a couple of Sundays—I guess I had gotten much better. That was in the 1960s. My husband's attitude changed when he saw my name in the *Times* magazine puzzle page. He had the puzzles laminated like a diploma!

JOE DIPIETRO: Once I was able to solve a Saturday *New York Times*, I somehow got the feeling I was the only one in the world who could do it. I thought, maybe this is my gift. So I pulled out some graph paper and kept tearing holes in it with my eraser.

ELIZABETH GORSKI: About ten years ago [1990], I was trying to solve a Sunday *New York Times* puzzle. I was having trouble solving it and decided to try to make my own. I made a copy of the blank *New York Times* grid and filled in my own words! I guess I did it the hard way!

NANCY JOLINE: I wasn't a regular solver of crosswords, but one Sunday I did a puzzle and thought, "What a dumb puzzle! I could do a better one." I studied a few Sunday puzzles, checking out themes, numbers of entries, black squares, etc., and began constructing a 23 × 23. Talk about nerve! Needless to say, it took much more time and effort than I expected, but I did finish it, and sent it off to Eugene T. Maleska at the *Times*. That first puzzle was accepted by Gene Maleska, although he grumbled that it took him four hours to edit it.

> *You are welcome to send me a 15 × 15 puzzle or two, but please do not try any large ones for me until you have developed greater skill and understanding. It took me four hours to repair your 23 × 23.*
> —*Eugene T. Maleska to Nancy Joline*

He used it in one of the Simon & Schuster puzzle books and encouraged me to do some more. I was in my fifties and had stumbled on a wonderful new life.

DIANE EPPERSON: I was a magazine editor working from my home—until the company folded. Then I was left high and dry with no chance of finding other work. My husband and I had moved to our vacation home in the desert after his stroke in 1993—we were able to do so only because of my at-home job. When the editing job went away, I was stranded in an extremely rural area near the Mexican border, thirty miles from town, where the unemployment rate is more than 30 percent and you have to be bilingual to find work. One day I was searching the Internet, looking for on-line crossword puzzles, when I happened upon the Cruciverb-L site. From that point on I was hooked.

MAURA JACOBSON: I had two copies of the *Times* in the house for some reason, and I did the puzzle; and then I started filling in words in the other blank diagram. I started with my husband's name, and it was very easy because I made up some words and wrote "variant" after [the clues]. I was very brazen—I sent it to Margaret Farrar at the *Times*. She was very gracious. Instead of sending me a rejection, she said, "I can't find these words anywhere." Then she made some suggestions as to how to correct it; and if she hadn't, I never would have done another puzzle. She was really my mentor—she and Will Weng. So I did change it, and I submitted it, and she published it. That was a daily. I was in my twenties. [Then] I wanted to get a puzzle in the Sunday *Times*, and after a few efforts, I did. I had a few puzzles in the Sunday *Times*, and then I lost interest. In 1971, I had a bad auto accident, which kept me off my feet for a year, so I had to do something with my head. I started sending puzzles to Will Weng.

KELLY CLARK: I wanted to make scripture readings interesting for the kids in my parish. My mom, who loved crossword puzzles, suggested I try to make them, using scripture readings, for the kids. Since I had no idea how to do this, I joined the Cruciverb-L forum and mailing list in 1996.

EMILY COX AND HENRY RATHVON: We came across cryptics before ever having an interest in regular American crosswords. In 1976, we were shown (by HR's father, an avid lifetime puzzle hobbyist) photocopies of a lot of cryptic crosswords written by Stephen Sondheim and Richard Maltby for *New York* magazine. We spent a month or two solving them (well, most of them) and then started writing our own, sheerly for fun at first. But we showed them to someone at the *Atlantic Monthly* (we were in the Boston area then, and the *Atlantic* had its offices on Boylston Street), and to our amazement, the editors decided to accept them. That was in 1977. It gave us the staggering notion of writing puzzles full-time to pay the rent. By 1980, we had learned to make regular American crosswords and had wormed our way into the *Boston Globe* with them.

RICH SILVESTRI: To take a break from all the mathematics in grad school, I started solving the cryptic puzzles in *New York* magazine, then tried my hand at constructing cryptics for friends. Someone suggested I try to sell the puzzles, but after discovering that there was virtually no market for cryptics in America in the late 1970s, I turned to constructing [regular] crossword puzzles.

PATRICK JORDAN: After graduating from college in 1984, I spent most of my time sending out résumés and going to job interviews. But on days when I wasn't scheduled to speak with personnel managers, I began building crosswords with graph paper and pencils. I suppose I was so intrigued by puzzles that I finally chose to try my hand at making them. In addition, I figured that if I succeeded in selling them, I could bring in some cash while waiting to accept my first full-time job.

ARTHUR S. VERDESCA: I got started with constructing in a funny way. I found myself very upset one night when one of my daughters was not yet home by her curfew hour of eleven P.M. Waiting for the phone call from the police to tell me about her rape or murder or worse, I constructed a cryptic puzzle (to keep from going crazy), which I spent much of the rest of the night defining—even though she had long since come home. It was that very puzzle which I, not knowing any better, sent on to Gene Maleska. By return mail, it had been accepted!—but he wanted me to change some definitions. Again I sent it to him, and he returned it because he didn't want it on India paper. I retyped it—and I was started! (I was fifty-six at the time.)

KAREN HODGE: Attending the tournament in Stamford back in the early 1980s was my introduction to the world of professional crosswords. I began as a (not very good) solver, and began to think that constructing might be more up my alley. I tried sending a few puzzles to *GAMES*, but the puzzles were very amateurish and weren't *GAMES* material.

TYLER HINMAN: I had only been seriously solving crosswords for a few months. I was bored one weekend, and I saw my Franklin Crosswords Solver (which I'd gotten to cheat at Penny Press puzzles) on the table. The idea of constructing a crossword, quite simply, just popped into my head. A few days later, I had a theme, a hackneyed one: foods with nationalities in their names. And so I began. The construction matched the weakness of the theme—far too many black squares, as well as very obscure abbreviations and names. It was absolutely terrible. My skills improved rapidly, though.

FRANCIS HEANEY: I started as a constructor when I first moved to New York, which would have been around 1992. I had some time on my hands. I was taking a sort of semivacation from working because I was too stressed out from moving. I was sitting around the apartment thinking about what I could do with my time, and I thought, "I'm a smart guy. I could probably write some puzzles if I wanted to."

CHRIS JOHNSON: The challenge: "I have heard they are harder to compose than to solve."

NORMAN WIZER: In 1979, someone gave me a crossword contest puzzle book. It contained puzzles of well-known constructors. You couldn't get into this book until you'd been published three times. I thought, "This book is awfully easy. I think I'll get published."

TO MARKET, TO MARKET

No crossworder ever forgets his or her first sale—or the first check that arrives in the mailbox. These events, of course, are usually separated by many months!

STAN NEWMAN: Eventually I had a couple of puzzles published in *GAMES*. That was real swell, of course. My first published anything!

CATHY MILLHAUSER: After trying to solve—and enjoying—a Sunday *New York Times* puzzle for the first time (in my early thirties), I began making up little puzzles for my dad and for the house organ at my hospital job. But the real breakthrough came when my local high school offered an adult education class in crossword construction led by a guy named Sidney Frank, who gave me the basics and a list of crossword editors.

ELIZABETH GORSKI: I made my first sale to Eugene Maleska when I was about thirty years old. He published it in the Simon & Schuster series, under the title of "Legalitease." It was a 21 × 21 featuring puns on legal phrases. I was lucky—Gene purchased my first puzzle. I was elated. Later on, after accumulating some rejections, I came down to earth and realized that acceptances weren't all that easy to come by.

JOHN SAMSON: I had enjoyed solving the *New York Times* crosswords edited by Will Weng; and when Eugene T. Maleska succeeded Mr. Weng, I decided to take a shot at constructing my own crosswords. I guess I felt less intimidated approaching a new editor.

GAYLE DEAN: I sold my first creation to Will Weng in 1984 . . . a 21 × 21 puzzle, featuring entries like GRANDMOTHER CLOCK and FATHER-OF-PEARL.

SYLVIA BURSZTYN: Got started in the puzzle business when early in 1980 I got a postcard in the mail from one Barry Tunick, a fellow member of the National Puzzlers' League, who needed a grid-filling partner for a crossword gig: a puzzle for the Sunday *Los Angeles Times* exclusively. A few years earlier, I had considered writing and submitting crosswords. My inquiries snuffed that notion: the *New York Times* was paying fifteen dollars for a 15 × 15. I knew I could write puzzles, having written some just to prove it to myself, but a fee like that wasn't worth the effort.

BT and I wrote one 21 × 21 on speculation for Art Seidenbaum, [*Los Angeles Times*] *Book Review* editor, and sweated out a few months of waiting for him to say we were in. The decision to get into puzzle-writing seemed to make itself. I was between ambitions at the time and was stuck doing temp office work to pay the bills. It was a few years before I could afford to quit my day job and let puzzle-writing support me. Our first puzzle appeared in April 1980, and our thousandth—we called it "A Grand Occasion"—appeared in May 1999. Our first submission was our first sale.

MARK DIEHL: I received [Jordan] Lasher's *Crossword Puzzle Compendium* as a gift in the early 1980s, and thoroughly enjoyed it. The chapter titled "How to

Construct Crossword Puzzles" piqued my interest, and I decided to give it a go. Following the hints, suggestions, and guidelines laid out in the book, I tinkered with several puzzles before finally submitting one a few years later. Through sheer luck and naïveté, my first submission and sale was to the *New York Times* under the editorship of Eugene Maleska. It was a 21 × 21 puzzle titled "Off the Rack," with entries like FAMILY TIES and BRAKE SHOES.

SAM BELLOTTO, JR.: After many years, solving was no longer much of a challenge. One fine day I got the bright idea to raise the bar, so to speak, by constructing my own. I still have a copy of it. After a couple of shaky starts, I sold my first puzzle to the *New York Times Sunday Magazine*, edited by Eugene T. Maleska. That was February 18, 1979; I would have been about thirty-two.

KAREN HODGE: I sold my first puzzle to Eugene Maleska at the *New York Times*. I was thirty-six or thirty-seven years old. It was a crossword puzzle with a bird theme—entries like PIGEONHOLE, ROUND ROBIN, TURKEY TROT, and JAYWALKING.

Do you think my mind is maturing late, or simply rotted early?
—Ogden NASH

NELSON HARDY: I've always loved wordplay and puns. In the late 1980s, I discovered cryptic crosswords and became a huge fan. On a whim, I decided to try creating some cryptics myself. It hadn't occurred to me to attempt making American-style crosswords because the grids seemed much too difficult to construct. But filling a cryptic grid looked like something I could handle, and writing cryptic clues looked like it might be a lot of fun. I was right on both counts. My first sale was a batch of five cryptics to Dell magazines in 1990. I was thirty-six years old.

FRED PISCOP: I started constructing cryptic crosswords before I started constructing conventionals, and I got into that after I joined the National Puzzlers' League in 1989 or so. I think cryptics are more interesting puzzles than conventional crosswords.

WILL SHORTZ: I sold my first puzzle when I was fourteen, to my national Sunday school magazine, a magazine called *Venture*. I became a regular contributor for the Dell puzzle magazines when I was sixteen, [with] original types of puzzles. I had a feature called "Time Test," which consisted of five little word teasers. The idea was that if you had long enough to spend on this test, you should be able to solve everything in it, or virtually everything. Once there was a time limit, though, that made solving a little harder. After you finished the puzzle, you got a rating, depending on how high your score was. After I went to college, I went on to get a law degree from the University of Virginia, and while I was there I got a monthly puzzle column in *Science Digest* magazine—and again, this was [with] original puzzles: numerical, logical, and other varieties as well as word puzzles.

RAY HAMEL: I started writing crossword puzzles in high school as a way to kill time in study hall. Eventually, I tried sending a few out for publication just to see if I was doing anything right. I made my first sale to Penny Press just out of high school. I sent three crosswords, and two were accepted.

FRANCIS HEANEY: I wrote some up and I sent them to *GAMES*, and they got rejected because they were very bad. They were just sloppy. They were decent enough that they saw fit to give me some pointers on how to do better next time. I took their advice, and I sent in some new things, and those were bought.

TRIP PAYNE: I decided to start at the top, and I sent my first submission to *GAMES* magazine. Will [Shortz] was the editor, and back then Mike Shenk was there, and Wayne Schmittberger, and Curtis Slepian, and all those guys. Mike didn't take my first puzzle, but he did take the second one. It was published in 1983, when I was fifteen years old. It was called "Shining Examples," and it was a repeated-word theme—phrases that had LIGHT in them. It was three fifteens and two elevens that each crossed two of the fifteens. Mike wrote back and said, "Normally we wouldn't take this because it's a repeated-word theme, but because you interlocked them so well, we're going to take it." He had to clean up a third of the grid or so, though. After that, I got really encouraged, and I started sending him these overstuffed envelopes that would have eight or ten puzzles of various kinds in them. Normally, I would get back a reply detailing exactly why he was rejecting each of them. But it was very, very nice of him, I thought—he wasn't just sending a form letter or something. I guess he thought that I had some talent that could be encouraged. He was very good to me. Once in a while there would be one thing in one of those packages that he would take. *GAMES* was my first market, and then I moved on and started submitting to the Simon & Schuster book series and a couple of others.

BOB KLAHN: While I had made unclued grids off and on for years, I didn't decide until 1991 to get serious about making complete puzzles. I thought it would be great if my first placement was in the *Wilmington News Journal.* [Klahn lives in Wilmington.] So I approached the paper and said I was a crossword constructor, that I had made a number of puzzles over the years, and that I was now ready to hit the marketplace. I said I'd love to have my first published puzzle in the local paper; could I interest them in that? They filed the information.

A couple of months later, on April Fools' Day, the paper called back. The features editor was looking for a new slant on something they do annually—they've called it various things, but more often than not it's been the "Delaware Almanac." It's published in the Sunday edition and usually comes out sometime in July. It's a series of sections on various aspects of Delaware life and is aimed as a sort of orientation booklet at people relatively new to the state. So the features editor thought, "Why not have, on the front page of one of these sections, a Delaware-themed crossword?" I thought that was a great idea. I immediately started working on it, gathering information about Delaware and coordinating with the paper. We settled on a twenty-three-row, thirty-one-column size; this was going to be a puzzle that would take up the full page. I had the idea to call it "Delawareness," and that became the final title. The features editor held a couple of sessions with his staff to brainstorm theme material, and I met with him at the paper a couple of times.

Once I had the grid together, the paper's graphics folks got involved. Delaware's colors are blue and gold, so the grid's themed "white squares" would be yellow squares, and the rest of the page beyond the grid would be a graduated range of blues. The wife of the overall editor of the paper had made a puzzle or two herself, so she became my clue editor.

The big day arrived. Sharon and I got up when we heard the paper hit our doorstep. At six A.M. we flipped to "the" section. The puzzle page was beautiful.

Then I looked at the clues. Over a dozen of them were missing! Others were misnumbered, many had typos, and some had been "corrected" by a layout person during page setup. For example, for DAH, "Doo follower" became "Duo follower." All of the fill-in-the-blanks underlines had been set as ellipses. It was a disaster!

After I died a thousand deaths, I called the paper's public editor, and we ended up getting the overall editor of the paper out of bed. "What's wrong?" I detailed the disaster. As a result, the following day, Monday, a detailed correction notice and apology appeared on the front page of the features section. But even the "corrections" had errors.

I had volunteered to come down to the paper to proof the final copy, but the features editor had said, "No need, we'll handle that." I learned later that that final proofing never occurred.

Now, eight-plus years later, we still keep a framed camera-ready copy of the puzzle page hanging downstairs. It's a terrible puzzle by my standards today. Perhaps it was one disaster deserving another. But it's a reminder of my beginnings, and I think of it as a valuable experience.

TOM SCHIER: When I was fifteen years old, I was solving the *New York Times* crossword daily and thought that there would be a greater challenge by constructing crosswords. I was published on November 5, 1966, in the daily *New York Times*. Perhaps I was fortunate, or the guidelines were not as stringent.

TYLER HINMAN: My first sale was a normal 15×15 crossword to the *New York Times*, at fifteen years of age. I received the acceptance letter in May, and the puzzle was printed on the Fourth of July!

MARTIN ASHWOOD-SMITH: I started by drawing cartoons for the university student newspaper. I suppose I was just curious when I wanted to try my hand at constructing a crossword for the college paper. The first crosswords I ever got paid for were self-edited and appeared on and off in a small local weekly newspaper in the early 1980s. These were standard American-style 13×13 crosswords. My first "official" sale of a crossword to a crossword editor was in 1990 (I was thirty-three years old). It was a seventy-eight-word 15×15

that featured a quip. I sent this crossword to Eugene T. Maleska at the *New York Times*. He accepted the puzzle, and it was published in the *New York Times* about a year later. This was the first crossword I ever sent anywhere, and I was lucky enough to have it accepted on first submission. I submitted at least a dozen other crosswords to Maleska, all of which were accepted.

MIKE SHENK: I probably started [solving puzzles] in high school. After a while I just decided to see what it would be like to try to make [puzzles]. What I was making then probably wouldn't have been anywhere close to a real crossword. [I] probably wasn't following all the rules. I really started seriously when I went to college. I started making one for the college newspaper, and that's really both where I learned and where I got started. Then [after college] I finally got up the courage to try to send off some puzzles. I think I sent a couple to the *Times*, to Maleska, and some to *GAMES*, to Will Shortz.

STAN NEWMAN: I thought it would be swell to learn how to make puzzles and send them off to *GAMES*, since Will knew who I was. [*Newman had recently taken top prize in Shortz's annual crossword tournament.*] I made all the mistakes every beginner makes.

SHAWN KENNEDY: I made my first sale when I was thirteen years old. I sold my very first puzzle to *GAMES* magazine. It was a small word game where the solver had to figure out the common trait that eight words shared.

MIKE SHENK: I think I sent two daily ones to the *Times*, and [they] took one of them. *GAMES*—I don't remember how many I sent the first time, but I remember Will [Shortz's] letter back to me started with "Whew!" because he was surprised the puzzle was better than a lot of the stuff he was getting. It may be partly because I had been making puzzles for five years or so before I got up the courage to actually send them anywhere.

RICH SILVESTRI: My first published work was a daily *New York Times* puzzle: January 12, 1978. I was a mere lad of thirty at the time.

RICH NORRIS: Somewhere back in the 1970s or 1980s, I tried to make a crossword and failed miserably. I always dreamed of seeing one of my own puzzles in the *New York Times*—but not having my name on it was a big turn-off. When Will Shortz took over as editor and began running bylines, my interest was piqued again. This time I had a computer dictionary program with a wild-card feature, which made it much easier to find words to fill the puzzle with. I made a couple of puzzles and sent them to him. Luckily, Will liked one of the two puzzles I sent. I had sent them separately, and ironically, he saw the second one first. He bought it. So my first-ever submission resulted in a sale. It was the *New York Times*, it was a 15 × 15 puzzle, and I believe the acceptance letter came in March 1994. I was forty-seven years old.

KELLY CLARK: I completed my first puzzle (an American-style 15 × 15 crossword) in March 1997. I sent it to Will Shortz at the *New York Times*, and he bought it. I was amazed and delighted! It's funny, but the second puzzle I ever made was also accepted by Will Shortz. While I remain very pleased about this, I also believe it gave me a rather false impression that selling puzzles to such an august publication was easy! That impression was very quickly dispelled!

MARTIN ASHWOOD-SMITH: The first puzzle I ever sold to the *New York Times* had actually been turned down by a local magazine—the editors felt that a crossword feature was too lowbrow. Oddly enough, they had no problem with an astrology column.

PATRICK JORDAN: When I sold my first puzzle to the *New York Times*, a story about me appeared in the local newspaper, where I work in the advertising department. Not long afterward, a couple of women came into the department to place an ad for a church event. Although they dealt with one of my colleagues, I noticed that they kept looking at the nameplate on my desk and whispering to each other. When they had finished their advertising business, they approached me and asked if I was "the crossword guy." When I told them that I was, one of them actually gave out a squeal of delight, told me that she was a big crossword fan, and generally behaved as though she had just met a movie star! I happened to have a magazine at my desk that day which contained one of my puzzles, and I asked her if she'd like to have a copy of it. She let out a startled gasp, then asked, "Would you autograph it for me?" I've never seen her since then, but it's nice to know that I actually have a groupie out there somewhere!

JIM PAGE: I think [my] thematic ideas were not creative enough [at first]. Will [Weng] had a good sense of humor. He was a nice man—a very nice man, great sense of humor. And his puzzles, I think, reflected that. I got rejected because I was just immature. I knew nothing about creating puzzles. It was a real lark that I even tried it. I almost didn't pursue. But because I got one published, then I did pursue [it] and got to know a little more about what they wanted.

PETER GORDON: Shortly after starting at *GAMES*, I decided that I had to get better at crosswords. I never really liked crosswords because of all the three- and four-letter words that come up over and over that are never used in actual conversation, plus all the names of the old actors and actresses always annoyed me, since they died before I was born. But I decided that I'd better get good at crosswords, so I did the *New York Times* puzzle every day for a year, keeping index cards of words that I didn't know. I got better fast.

PATRICK JORDAN: Penny Press bought the very first crossword I ever made, sometime during the summer of 1984, when I was twenty-two years old. It was a 19 × 19 standard crossword with no theme. Actually, I was quite fortunate [in that] my initial effort was accepted by the very first company to whom I offered it. I sold Penny Press about a dozen more crosswords after that, all with themes, and I don't recall that they ever sent me a single rejection notice. However, when I decided to start offering my works to other publishers, I began to learn that some of them had higher expectations of their contributors, and I started getting some of my puzzles sent back for revisions. The hardest market to break into was the *New York Times*, which rejected at least four of my puzzles before—much to my surprise and delight—accepting two of them at once!

RICH SILVESTRI: My first puzzle, submitted to the *Times*, was rejected by Gene Maleska because of too many (fifty) black squares. The second was accepted.

GREG STAPLES: I made my first sale in about April of 1999 to Stan Newman for *Uptown Puzzle Club*. A week later, I got an acceptance for a Sunday *New York Times*. These were the first Sunday-size puzzles I made, so I consider myself pretty fortunate to have hit the big time so early.

RANDOLPH ROSS: I started in 1988. I saw Stan Newman's invitation to [send crosswords] for the *Newsday* puzzle and decided to send him my own creation. He liked it, helped me to present it properly, and I was published—and hooked. My first accepted puzzle was called "Circular Reasoning," printed in Sunday *Newsday*. My first published puzzle was actually in *GAMES*, a 17 × 17 called "The I's Have It."

MANNY NOSOWSKY: It took me three months of repeated effort to even find a theme acceptable to Stan Newman.

NANCY SALOMON: I sold my first puzzle. I didn't have many rejections, but I did learn that editors shy away from anything the least bit grisly or off-color, especially with theme entries. I also learned that a lively, colorful fill was very important in making sales of 15 × 15 puzzles to the top editors. I work with a lot of rookies, and I've probably seen ARSE in half of their grids. I laugh because I had it in one of my early puzzles before an editor expunged it. It's such a useful combination of letters—too bad.

THE WRONG STUFF

Novice constructors tend to make the same kinds of mistakes: trite themes, overuse of obscurities, carelessness in cluing, and so on. Editors who receive such submissions have different ways of handling them, but however diplomatic they are, beginners must inure themselves to the slings and arrows that are routinely shot their way. Often, rejection has little to do with the quality of the work; rather, it's editorial overload or other vagaries of business at a particular establishment. Still, tyros are well advised to grow tough hides.

BILL ZAIS: Contrivances were my biggest problem. I felt that if I could define it, I could use it. I put esses on anything that would stand still long enough.

MEL TAUB: My first crossword submission was to the *New York Times*, in 1954. Editor Margaret Farrar returned it with a note saying she could see I would someday land in the puzzle corner, but . . . The puzzle was replete with obscure crosswordese culled from *The Dell Crossword Dictionary* which defined just about every arcane entry in Merriam-Webster's second unabridged dictionary. Among others, I had DJO (Japanese measure) crossing OONT (Anglo-Indian camel). Crossing two obscurities made it virtually impossible for even the most astute solver to finish the puzzle. My second submission was declined because of contrived abbreviations. The third attempt succeeded, and I've been at it since.

GAYLE DEAN: I sold [Will] Weng my first puzzle attempt. With that encouragement, combined with my ignorance of the publishing world in general—I didn't realize one was supposed to start at the bottom and work one's way up—I immediately sent my second puzzle creation to the top: Eugene T. Maleska, then editor of the *New York Times* [crossword puzzle]. It was 1984. Eugene was a bit crankier than Will, but he was also very helpful—he sent me a style sheet and a few suggestions, along with the return of my rejected puzzle. He said that the puzzle diagram *must* be symmetrical, "p-nut" is not a word, a puzzle can't have 40 percent black squares, etc. Using Eugene's suggestions, I reworked the puzzle three or four times, and it was finally accepted and published in the Tuesday, February 12, 1985, *New York Times*. Eugene sent me a note after the puzzle was published and asked me how I had gotten "so good so fast?" I was thrilled and immediately launched into my new career.

> *After being turned down by numerous publishers,*
> *he had decided to write for posterity.*
> *—George ADE*

JOHN SAMSON: The first crossword I sent Eugene [Maleska] was so bad he wrote back: "This is really amateurish. Do us a both a favor and never send me another one again. One of your entries OX MORGUE, clued as 'Where dead oxen are carted off to,' is ridiculous; also, your diagram is not symmetric, and on top of that it contains unkeyed letters." Needless to say, I noticed he had taken the time to reply to me (written in longhand), which prompted another effort on my part. I contacted a friend, David Pohl (an excellent solver), and together we submitted a puzzle titled "Menagerie" (a theme based on people with "animal" names). Eugene was a little surprised by this more professional submission and accepted it for publication in the Simon & Schuster crossword series. Our next two puzzles were accepted for the Sunday *New York Times*.

JIM PAGE: I have very often found that the thematic entries of mine that I like best are the ones that I get rejected for. It's probably because I'm stretching things or pushing things too far or something—but I happen to like it. This happened to me with Maleska a lot. It was like the one thing he kind of frowned on was the thing I liked the best.

TRIP PAYNE [On receiving letters from Eugene Maleska]: They were brusque. They weren't overtly rude, but they were brusque. Most of the puzzles I sent to him were wide-open 21×21s, but they really weren't that good. Looking back, I call that my "honing-my-skills" years, because I was just learning how to make grids. There really was a lot of garbage in those puzzles. Foreign words you've never heard of and incredibly long partials and just a lot of obscurity.

JOE DIPIETRO: I was rejected six times before my first acceptance. These early offerings had quite a lot of obscurities. I learned to try to see puzzles more through the solver's eye.

NANCY JOLINE: Gene Maleska never rejected a puzzle of mine. He did take me to task early on for careless errors—leaving out an entry or a number. I learned that you can't be too careful in creating a puzzle and developed a couple of methods for catching mistakes.

WILLIAM CANINE: My mother, a *New York Times* aficionado, suggested I try [construction], and so I did. My first attempt was a 23×23! I confidently sent it off to Maleska. Maleska returned the puzzle with a long letter of advice, pointing out where I'd gone wrong. Maleska took exception chiefly to my theme. I have forgotten just what that was, but I do recall it was gloomy. Mr. Maleska pointed out to me how many crossword fans are ill people, stay-at-homes, etc. who do not need to be reminded of their woes.

KAREN HODGE: Too many short words, too many words overall, themes that weren't particularly original. I think the *New York Times* rejected four or five puzzles before finally accepting one. To keep trying was the most important thing I learned. Dr. Maleska was quite encouraging, and once the *New York Times* had taken a puzzle, it seemed to help with other publications.

RANDOLPH ROSS: I was lucky that my first puzzle was accepted; subsequent ones were rejected, usually due to inconsistency in themes. Editors were helpful—including Gene Maleska, who had a reputation for being ornery.

NELSON HARDY: The mistake I made in my early cryptics was mixing too many types of wordplay in the clues and making them too convoluted. The mistake I made in my early 21 × 21 themed crosswords was placing the theme entries in a way that rendered construction very difficult.

SAM BELLOTTO, JR.: The first few puzzles that Maleska rejected contained some pretty bizarre words. My beginner's error was finding letter combinations that worked and then scouring the main New York Public Library for definitions that fit. Things like "Maori moon god." Maleska's encouraging rejection slips taught me much about entry choices and constructing for the solvers rather than myself.

Why should you mind being wrong if someone can show you that you are?
—A. J. AYER

NANCY SCHUSTER: When I would send the puzzles in, these little 15 × 15s or even 13 × 13s, to the magazines that I saw on the newsstand, they would get rejected because they were so bad. I would use the most obscure words—I figured, "If it's listed in *The Dell Crossword Dictionary*, I can use it." Or I might even put in a word spelled wrong because I was in such a rush I didn't notice it. I would make all sorts of mistakes.

CATHY MILLHAUSER: [My first sale] was a 21 × 21 titled "Fame and Misfortune," [which] appeared in the Sunday magazine section of my local Gannett paper. The theme entries weren't bad—things like BLACKEYED SUSAN, TUMBLEDOWN DICK, etc. But the grid now makes me cringe—ninety-one black squares! Only one [puzzle] was rejected before my first sale, because it had even more black squares. But I then got a rejection from *GAMES* magazine because the theme was too contrived. It had various (not necessarily common) animals linked with nonanimal terms. The worst one I can remember was MASCARABAO [*a CARABAO is a Philippine water buffalo.*] *GAMES* accepted my next submission, though. Will Weng also accepted a number of my early puzzles for his book series and *Crosswords Club.*

MARTIN ASHWOOD-SMITH: My first *New York Times* rejection didn't come until Will Shortz took over. Will accepted my first submission (a themeless) but rejected my second because I had used a six-letter partial (ONE AT A). Will also rejected another themeless because he thought that several of the longer entries lacked interest. What I learned from this was (a) not to use six-letter partials! and (b) to make *all* of my longer entries sparkle. For example, in a themeless with several stacked fifteen-letter entries, I make sure that all the fifteen-letter entries are phrases, rather than dull dictionary words (like STEREOTELEMETER and REMORSELESSNESS).

KELLY CLARK: Whenever I received a rejection from Will, I always learned something: primarily, to keep my themes clever and tight. This one from Will cracked me up because, after enumerating all the things wrong with the puzzle, he (as he unfailingly does in his correspondence) ended it on a charmingly polite note:

> *Hi Kelly,*
> *Thanks but regrets on your latest 15×, "Signs of Love," whose theme, I'm afraid, doesn't appeal to me. For one thing, I've never heard of HUGS FOR TEACHERS, and I can't believe I'm alone on this, so this is a peculiar entry to start a puzzle around. Also, I'm just barely familiar with the phrase BUTTERFLY KISSES. And I would think that there are usually an equal number of X's and O's in XOXOXO. . . .*
> *So for me this theme is a complete washout! Sorry!*
> *I do appreciate the look, though.*
> *—Will*

The price one pays for pursuing any profession, or calling, is an intimate knowledge of its ugly side.
—James Baldwin

RICH NORRIS: I sold my first submitted puzzle. The next half dozen were rejected for a variety of reasons. Themes either were flawed—Will [Shortz] always explained why—or had been done before. I decided I might have better luck with a themeless puzzle, so I made a couple of those and sent them in. Will accepted them both. I guess you'd have to say that was a turning point for me, since over the past three years I've been the most published *New York Times* constructor, and the huge majority of my puzzles are themeless ones that appear on Saturdays.

TYLER HINMAN: I had difficulty coming up with an original theme. My skill in grid designing was poor, and I tended to accept any fill, no matter how obscure the words were. In my first submission to the *Times*, editor Will Shortz didn't like the theme and felt that some entries were obscure or uninteresting. On the second one, he liked the theme but felt that it was inconsistently applied. The third one, he said, just didn't excite him enough. I hit pay dirt with the fourth submission. From my rejections, I learned to try to put more interesting and less obscure words into my puzzles, and to make my theme clever and tighter.

MIKE SHENK: Most of the really basic rules, like the symmetry, I just kind of figured out on my own by looking at other puzzles. I guess probably before I sent puzzles to Will, the book by Stan Kurzban and Mel Rosen [*The Compleat Cruciverbalist*] had come out, and that probably gave me some ideas about the right way to format things and the finer points that I might not have known about. I don't think I ever felt [using crosswordese] was desirable, but at the beginning I'm sure I didn't hesitate to use it to solve a problem. I remember doing them for the college paper—I had to blacken in each square and type the numbers into the squares. I usually blacked in the squares fine, it was just numbering—I used to always leave out one number and that would screw up everything!

DIANE EPPERSON: My worst mistake was including too many abbreviations. I just wasn't paying any attention until an editor asked me to revise a puzzle for that reason. Then I was appalled when I counted them up. I found that with a little extra effort, it wasn't that hard to eliminate most of them, and the puzzle was improved because of it. Another mistake was not checking the spelling or meaning of a word before filling the grid. One landmark puzzle I had to revise twice after finishing it. The first time I was at the cluing stage when I came to the entry GRESHAM (*"The Firm* author"), whose name is spelled *Grisham.* I redid that corner, went back to cluing, and came across EARING ("Lobe adornment"), which is spelled *earring.* A little extra effort early on, and I would have saved myself a lot of time. Fortunately, I caught these *before* sending [the puzzle] out.

DAVID MACLEOD: In my early ignorance, I had too many words or too many blocks or a weak, shallow theme. I probably had five puzzles rejected before my first acceptance. On the whole, what I learned from the rejections were the editors' preferences, a valuable factor in deciding where to submit.

MARK DIEHL: With *Crossword Puzzle Compendium* [by Jordan Lasher] as a guide, I was able to avoid most technical pitfalls like asymmetry and unchecked squares. Rampant crosswordese filled many of my earlier creations; yet few were rejected for this shortcoming, and those that were could usually be reworked to pass muster. Some rejections have come because the theme was too esoteric, gimmicky, or pop culture. On occasion, a rejection comes with the deflating "didn't interest me."

WILLIAM R. MACKAYE: One of the worst [mistakes beginners make]—and this is one that really bites on me—is too many entries. The size of the page in the *Post* and the design of the puzzle page means that even 142 entries is crowding it; 144—practically impossible to get on the page without having the whole puzzle consist of two-word clues. My 140 limit is really pretty inflexible. I've seen puzzles with 150, 156 entries. Just hopeless. I couldn't use it even if it was [a] worthwhile construction.

The other thing is a lot of puzzles I get fail because they're full of crosswordese that I just can't stand: ORTS and ENES and TERNS and ERNS. No. No, no, and no! If it's a wonderful theme idea, I'll write back and say, "It's a wonderful theme idea, but you've got to do a better job of constructing it, and you've got to get rid of these words."

I had one puzzle from a constructor who will remain nameless. I bought the puzzle sort of against my better judgment, and the more I looked at it . . . the gimmick was fine, but there were too many really awful entries. I went back to the constructor and said, "You know, I really think you need to do some more work on this puzzle, even if I've bought the puzzle." The constructor said no. I said, "Okay." I got in touch with another constructor, and I said, "I've got this troubled puzzle here. I'd like you to reconstruct it for me." I spent half the fee again on getting the puzzle fixed, and I haven't bought any more puzzles from constructor number one.

SAM BELLOTTO, JR.: After three or four helpful rejections, Maleska purchased my first puzzle—and I don't recall a single rejection thereafter.

JIM PAGE: Gene Maleska came onboard and rejected all of the puzzles of mine that Will Weng had accepted. I wasn't aware that that kind of thing could be done. I found out the hard way that not only can it be done, it *is* done. I'm not talking a lot of puzzles, but I didn't realize that kind of thing happened. That was a shocker.

BILL ZAIS: I once had an editor accept one of my puzzles, sit on it for a year, and then return it without comment.

SYLVIA BURSZTYN: Over time, hustling for gigs outside our flagship *Los Angeles Times*, we've had enough rejection and have eaten enough invoices to balance out [the immediate sale of the first puzzle Barry Tunick and I created] but good. Our rejections have had less to do with the puzzles than with business. The lessons we learned were to be more cautious and better at the business side of construction. Our rejections usually went like this: A magazine would order a dozen custom-written 13 × 13s. Some weeks after delivery, we would inquire about payment on our invoice. "Oh," they would say, "we've decided we don't need puzzles after all. We'll send them back, okay?"

SHAWN KENNEDY: Surprisingly, the first puzzle I ever submitted to a company ended up being purchased. Some of the puzzles I made later on were rejected, but I wasn't upset by the rejection slips—I used them as a learning experience. Most constructors are discouraged by rejections. I knew that they were not rejections of me as a person, but of my work. Puzzles that are rejected may be very high-quality work; sometimes the publisher already has a similar puzzle in existence or the work may not be suitable for the company's current needs.

FRED PISCOP: I guess everybody makes the same mistakes. Inconsistent themes— that still bugs me. I should be better at pulling themes together than I am. Sometimes I hit a dry spot. But I think that was my biggest mistake. I had an early knack for cluing and grid fill, and I had an early cognizance of cross- wordese and stuff that should be left out. I got a rejection letter from . . . I don't want to name the editor. I had submitted some cryptics to a publica- tion, and he wrote me a very nasty letter. He included with it—I'm para- phrasing this—"There is no polite way to say this, so I'll just be myself: Your stuff stinks!"

RAY HAMEL: I'm sometimes baffled by the reasons puzzles get rejected: "I don't like French"; "How dare you use the word TOILET in a puzzle!"

MARTIN ASHWOOD-SMITH: I did get a really scathing [rejection] by a magazine assistant editor (who shall remain nameless). She had accepted quite a few of my crosswords and had often been complimentary. Unfortunately (for me), I chose to use a Byron quote in a puzzle, and she absolutely hated Byron . . . called him a "male chauvinist pig" and ranted on from there!

NANCY SCHUSTER: [Margaret Farrar] told me that she didn't like my entry KISS- ING DUG that appeared in one submission. I clued it something like "A germ on campus." It was too bad-news for her. I think the puzzle was even- tually accepted elsewhere. I used to go down the line, starting at the top with the *Times*, who paid the best.

MARK DIEHL: A puzzle with a dental theme (FILLING STATION, PAPER PLATES, CROWN PRINCE, etc.) was [once] summarily dismissed as unusable, since dentistry is a completely unpleasant field—so much for my attempt at putting a positive spin on my oft-maligned profession. Fortu- nately, I did find another editor who had better memories of dental treatment and [who] even admitted to having friends who were dentists.

CHRIS JOHNSON: When I came across *GAMES* magazine, I sent off an inquiry. Will Shortz said he was interested and told me the criteria he used. I set a puzzle and sent it off. I gave a copy to my editor [*Johnson works a day job at a newspaper*], and he came back five minutes later with it solved. "Oh, well," I thought, "I'd better make a harder one to send to *GAMES*." I got to work and produced a much harder one. Before I could send it off, I received a reply from Will Shortz saying that the original one was too hard for his readership!

BILL ZAIS: Mel Rosen at *Crosswords Club* rejected my first submission, saying in part that THES was a plural he had *never* seen before.

NANCY SALOMON: If you like gallows humor, Will Shortz once wrote me about one of my early submissions to him that the fill looked like it had been generated by a computer! It hadn't, but I learned a lot from that rejection. I've concentrated on getting lively fills for my grids ever since.

LEONARD WILLIAMS: After having two puzzles rejected, I learned rather quickly that it was important to have a theme—and one that could stand the test of time (not too oriented toward current events). The initial rejections stimulated me to be more attentive to the structure of published puzzles, from which I learned how to make a puzzle with a tight, coherent theme.

ARTHUR S. VERDESCA: I didn't have any rejections before my first sale. In retrospect, I see that I was incredibly lucky. Even when I began to do [construction regularly], I didn't have any rejections until I had shifted to a significant increase in my output of puzzles. However, I have had my share of rejections subsequently. I've learned a few things from my rejections: Make sure that the thematic entries have strong internal consistency; avoid obscure words and crosswordese like the plague; if an editor suggests fixing a puzzle, it is easier (except in rare cases) to redo the whole thing rather than to spend hours on repairs. Perhaps because of my initial luck regarding rejections, I tend to become very down with any letter of rejection.

JIM PAGE: If you're any good and you find out because somebody gave you a chance, that's what's important. Because I would never have known. If you said to me twenty-five years ago that I would be where I am in that area, I would've said, "You've been drinking heavily." It's like everything else in life—unless you try something, you don't know whether you're any good at it. You have to enjoy words. You have to be very, very compulsive, nutsy, crazy—and you have to stick to it, too.

RICH SILVESTRI: In general, rejections from various editors taught me that editors are idiosyncratic.

WITH A LITTLE HELP FROM MY FRIENDS

Many crossword neophytes have been pushed along in their careers by the helping hands of other, more experienced constructors. A majority of top editors (the *Crosswords Club*'s Mel Rosen, the *Washington Post*'s Bill MacKaye, Random House's Stan Newman, the *New York Times*'s Will Shortz) give generously of their time and wisdom to new entrants into the puzzle fray. Their good advice is invaluable to novices.

MERL REAGLE: In the early days, I was pretty much untutored in everything. Even when I doing stuff for Margaret Farrar—no matter how much she said, "Kind of just toe the line, kind of keep it in," I would never really do it.

SHAWN KENNEDY: I got started in the puzzle business by talking with some people who constructed puzzles in their free time. From what they told me, I knew that making puzzles was what I wanted to do.

TYLER HINMAN: The person who got me interested in crossword puzzles was my history teacher from ninth grade. She, as well as many of my friends, solved my puzzles and gave me their opinions. They helped me improve my skills. Also, the people on the Cruciverb-L forum are a huge help when I need them.

MARK DIEHL: Constructing tends to be a solitary pursuit and any input and suggestions from fellow enthusiasts is often welcome as well as useful for honing one's craft.

MEL TAUB: Margaret Farrar, the *New York Times* editor, liked my chances, albeit on her terms. She pointed out what was good and what wasn't, and I was guided accordingly.

MARTIN ASHWOOD-SMITH: I suppose Maleska was kind of a mentor, but I found him a bit odd to deal with. Sometimes he'd say very little, and other times he'd talk about things in detail. I remember once, in a note, he wrote about his one and only appearance on [Late Night with] David Letterman. He ended by telling me, "I don't think I'll be asked back."

GAYLE DEAN: Dr. Maleska was very helpful and encouraging.

RICH SILVESTRI: Gene Maleska—he was very generous with praise and included constructive criticism in his letters of acceptance. He referred my work to other editors (at the time I was largely unaware of other outlets for my puzzles.) He listed me as one of the top constructors in his book *Across and Down.*

ARTHUR S. VERDESCA: Eugene T. Maleska was my mentor. After I had gotten into the swing of cryptics, he suggested I do a regular crossword. When I told him I couldn't, he said, "Yes, you can. Send me a 15 × 15." I did—and he published it on a Saturday! Similarly with 21 × 21s and 23 × 23s: When I said I couldn't do them, he repeated the same advice and orders. Finally, he encouraged me to do diagramlesses in the same way. He believed in me and wouldn't listen to my words of insecurity.

> *The man who gives [the student] the benefit of the revealed canon . . .*
> *should be known as his guru.*
> *—Laws of MANU*

SAM BELLOTTO, JR.: Gene Maleska took the time and effort to guide me to my first sale. Afterward he was always quick to point out anything I did that was innovative or especially clever. Even today, I still learn much from John Samson, who fights a never-ending battle for inventiveness, fresh content, and skill in the American crossword format!

WILLIAM CANINE: If Gene Maleska had rejected my first effort out of hand or had he in any way ridiculed it or even ignored it, I certainly would never have tried again. Both he and Mrs. Farrar would be my mentors. In addition, they made points of putting me in contact with other editors.

NANCY JOLINE: Gene Maleska was certainly a mentor. He'd pass along suggestions for puzzles and began encouraging me to try daily-size puzzles with fewer and fewer entries. He thought I could equal the existing record of fifty-eight entries, and, with his encouragement, I did. Then, when someone did a fifty-sixer, he challenged me to equal that. That I did, too. Never would have tried these without his belief in me.

ELIZABETH GORSKI: In his own way, Eugene Maleska mentored me for a year or so. He told me what not to put into puzzles. Later, when Will Shortz assumed the editorship of the *New York Times* puzzle, I received invaluable guidance from him. Even when a puzzle was rejected, I kept track of my mistakes and tried not to repeat them.

STAN NEWMAN: Will [Shortz] is responsible for me being in the business. He brought alternatives and pathways to my life that I would never have had. I owe Will more than I could ever repay, but it's been great to have been in a position to help Will with various things over the years.

DAVID J. KAHN: One day in December 1989, I just felt like writing a puzzle. It was a 21 × 21 and wound up being published by Will Weng of the *Crosswords Club* because I was having no luck impressing the *New York Times* crossword editor at the time. Until Will Shortz became the *New York Times* crossword editor in 1993, I had only had two puzzles published, both by the *Crosswords Club.* My first *New York Times* puzzle, a daily, appeared in March 1994, after two rejections. For the rest of 1994 I had a dry spell, since it had yet to sink in that my submissions had too much crosswordese and sometimes inconsistent themes. Will Shortz, however, was very supportive and gave me very constructive criticism (pun unavoidable), which encouraged me to keep writing puzzles. Will, I'm sure, enjoys his role of recognizing new talent, and became a mentor to me, as he has to others.

MERL REAGLE: It was Will Shortz at *GAMES* magazine who finally turned me around. I met Will and Mike Shenk—both *GAMES* magazine guys—in 1979 at the Stamford tournament. I think I made my first puzzle for Will in 1980. And that's when I realized that the way puzzles should be made was a whole other thing—that I'd gone through my twenties with the wrong idea. What Will said was, "Now, if you just put a couple of extra black squares here and there, the word choice improves 9,000 percent." The idea at *GAMES* was to make all the answers interesting and colorful and, above all, *common,* so that solvers would always have heard of the answers no matter how they were clued.

The other thing I learned at *GAMES* was how Mike Shenk made puzzles. His crosswords were incredibly wide open, and yet even his three-letter words were real words, not strange abbreviations. He was really something else. Whenever I went to New York, I'd hang around the *GAMES* office for three or four days. I would do the same at Dell, with Erica Rothstein—I would hang around Erica's office. I would split my time between those offices. That was from the early 1980s through the early 1990s, and that really influenced me a lot.

So the inspiration to do funny themes came from Will Weng; the inspiration to have solid words in the grid came from Will Shortz; the inspiration to do wide-open grids came from Mike Shenk; and the inspiration to make just solid, good-quality puzzles on a regular basis came from Erica [Rothstein].

FRED PISCOP: Will [Shortz] I have to put on top of the list. He has been such a great friend to me. Over and above that, he's recommended me to countless people to do custom work. I'm one of his right-hand men at the annual tournament—I'm the chief scorer. There's just been such a great friendship there, and he's been great. He's the one. Another person I have to mention is George Bredehorn. He's not a crossword person at all. He was my teacher for two years in elementary school, and he recognized my talent for wordplay and got me interested in anagrams and all sorts of other fun with words. Forty years later, we're still best of friends. If not for George, I probably would never have found my way into the crossword business.

Others I should mention are John Samson, who uses a ton of my stuff at Simon & Schuster, and Mel Rosen from the *Crosswords Club,* who's been a good friend since my early [National Puzzlers' League] days and who uses my puzzles regularly. And there's Nancy Schuster, the former editor in chief of Dell Champion crosswords—she's been test-solving my weekly puzzles on my Web site, macnamarasband.com, for a couple of years now.

RICH NORRIS: My mentor was, and still is, Will Shortz. I always sent him a cover letter with my submissions. After a few acceptances, I felt comfortable enough to begin to ask him all kinds of questions: about constructing, editing, and the industry in general. He never once left a question unanswered. I can't begin to tell you how much I learned from those exchanges with him. One time I proposed a theme to him, and he surprised me by telephoning me at home to discuss it. After that, when I had questions, I called him or e-mailed him. To this day I still e-mail him with questions about constructing and editing, he still answers every one, and I still learn.

WILL SHORTZ: I think I publish more different constructors than any other editor. There were about 120 different constructors in the *Times* last year. I work very hard to find good new constructors and work with them, tell them what I like and what I don't like.

JON DELFIN: Stan Newman, Mike Shenk, and Nancy Schuster have all been very patient with me.

TRIP PAYNE: Around 1985 or 1986, Stan Newman called me out of the blue. What happened was he called home—he got the number from *GAMES* or something—and my mom got the phone, and Stan asked to speak to me. My mom said, "He's at school." Stan took this to mean that I was a teacher, and was very, very surprised to learn my age. After that, he wrote to me and said, "I've seen your puzzles in *GAMES*, and I've seen your stuff in Simon & Schuster, and I like how you're trying to do all these great things, but you've really got to work on your fill—you have to cut out all the obscurities. If you can do that, then I want you to start working for me too." Back then, he had *Crossworder's OWN Newsletter* and various book series and so forth. That really opened up a lot of markets to me. Mike [Shenk] was really my first mentor and the one that in a sense I owe everything to, but I also owe a whole lot to Stan, because had he not written me and forced me to get better with my entries, it would have taken me a lot longer to get better as a puzzlemaker. It would have taken me a lot longer to find markets. So I owe Stan a good deal. I have a good relationship with him to this day.

RANDOLPH ROSS: Stan Newman [was] certainly [my mentor] at the start. I really have learned a lot from Will Shortz and Mike Shenk (my favorite constructor, along with Manny [Nosowsky] on a Saturday), Rich Silvestri, and the work of Merl Reagle (best sense of humor in the business).

MANNY NOSOWSKY: Stan Newman walked me through my first puzzle, and I used to ask thirty questions at a time through regular mail.

NANCY SALOMON: Stan Newman offered in one of his puzzle publications a minicourse to anyone who agreed to do the homework. The result of the course was a 15 × 15 puzzle which Stan bought from me. I was off to the races after that.

PATRICK JORDAN: When I began submitting daily-size puzzles to Stanley Newman for his *Newsday* crossword feature, he often complimented me on what I had done right and made suggestions for fixing poor fills. In addition, in his capacity as the editor of *Times* Books's puzzles and games division, he often tells me when his employer has published a particularly handy reference work which should be added to my library.

My other mentor was John Samson of Simon & Schuster. I sent him examples of my daily-size puzzles, and he encouraged me to try constructing larger crosswords for his book series. He has always made himself available via e-mail to comment on theme ideas and to answer questions about the acceptability of certain fill words.

> **AN EARLY CONVERSATION BETWEEN MANNY NOSOWSKY AND STAN NEWMAN**
>
> Nosowsky: "Can I use clues that other constructors have used?"
>
> Newman: "You mean you're asking if you can steal someone else's brilliant, clever, and creative clues, essentially claiming them as your own? Well the answer is, 'Only in moderation.' "

STAN NEWMAN: Will [Shortz] is a great diplomat, and I believe he's nurtured a few—maybe more than a few—of Maleska's contributors and got[ten] them [to be] more modern. But there are, in fact, constructors that you might call low maintenance, and [then there are those that are] high maintenance, who send a puzzle and then you have to go back and forth with them three or four times before it's publishable. And Will, God bless him, is very patient and diplomatic, but I'm juggling too many chain saws to engage in that. I think there would be a few constructors who would tell you, if you get around to them, that I had something to do with getting them started. I'm very pleased that I had something to do with a few people whose names are near the top.

CATHY MILLHAUSER: Stan Newman, Mel Rosen, and Will Weng were all very supportive when I was getting started. I also relied heavily on Rosen and Kurzban's book *The Compleat Cruciverbalist*.

WILLIAM R. MACKAYE: I get submissions from people who don't know what they're doing, who I try to deal with kindly, telling them what they need to do before they submit again.

RICH NORRIS: I try to encourage talented new constructors whenever I can. When possible, I work with constructors at all levels to improve their puzzles. As with so many things in life, the more I put into it, the more I seem to get back.

PETER GORDON: I was extremely lucky to have Mike [Shenk] teach me. Many people, myself included, feel he's the best puzzlemaker there is, and he helped me every step of the way. If I was working on a puzzle, he'd stop by my office and check out how it was going, giving me tips and suggestions all the time. I remember one time in particular: I was making [a puzzle called] "International Breakfast," and I was having trouble in the area with 53-Across. He happened to walk by and took a look and suggested that I try STOOD FOR at 53-Across. I had been working on that area [and] getting nowhere, but as soon as I tried STOOD FOR, I was able to finish. He just has a sixth sense as to what will work and what won't. Amazing.

MEL TAUB: Kathleen Rafferty, the Dell editor, was nice and patient with me. My first puzzle submission ever was an acrostic to Dell magazines in 1951. It was rejected with an encouraging letter from Kathleen Rafferty, who gave a detailed critique. She offered to reconsider if I would rework the puzzle. I did. Before long I was turning out acrostics en masse for Dell and other publications.

RAY HAMEL: I didn't ask for spec sheets (I didn't even know I was supposed to), so I sent a crossword submission that looked like a crossword with the answers in the grid, and the clues written beneath. Fortunately, I had a patient editor in Janis Weiner, who quickly straightened me out. . . . Janis Weiner was instrumental in setting my feet on the right path when it comes to puzzle construction. Manny Nosowsky was tremendously helpful in introducing me to new editors.

RICH NORRIS: A constructor once sent me a puzzle that I rejected for two reasons: It was flawed, and I'd recently done a puzzle on the same subject. In my letter, I made one or two suggestions as to how (s)he might improve it. (S)he subsequently sold it to another newspaper. A week or two later I got a note from the constructor with a $5 check enclosed, my "commission" for my contribution to the puzzle's success. (I put the $5 in the collection plate at church the next week.) The constructor's total pay for the puzzle: $35.

LEONARD WILLIAMS: Rich Norris—I sent my first attempts at puzzle construction to him, totally out of the blue. He was kind enough to offer an encouraging word, even while turning down puzzles. Without that, I may not have been willing to keep trying. Nor can I fail to mention the reference to John Samson that he gave me.

KAREN HODGE: I found my first real niche with Emily Cox and Henry Rathvon at the *Four-Star Puzzler*. They really liked my puzzles and were willing to work with me on both American crosswords and cryptics. They were willing to respond quickly and personally to just about any questions I had. On my early cryptics, Henry would offer a clue-by-clue rundown, complimenting good clues and explaining the problems with bad ones.

NELSON HARDY: When I made my first *New York Times* puzzle, I sought advice from *New York Times* regular Manny Nosowsky, and he was very kind. Veterans such as Nancy Salomon, Rich Norris, and Merl Reagle have also been extremely generous with their help and advice.

KELLY CLARK: Manny Nosowsky has coached and encouraged me in theme, grid design, construction, and cluing since I started making puzzles and continues to do so. What I treasure most about Manny is that he doesn't really care why I'm making a particular puzzle—he just wants me to strive for excellence. Whether I'm working on something for potential sale to a major market or just making a puzzle as a gift for a friend, he's always there to offer advice, encouragement, and a desire [that I] do the best I can do.

BOB KLAHN: Manny Nosowsky—I forget how we first hooked up. In late 1994 we produced a 23 × 23 Sunday puzzle for the *New York Times*, titled "Working Together," entirely through e-mail. We had never met, and we had never talked, and we didn't either talk or meet until months later. We thought our 140-character quote was quite possibly the longest ever done; perhaps it was. And perhaps we were the first team ever to construct a puzzle in this long-distance manner; Manny thought some good publicity could come out of that. We don't know if we were the first such team or not. Manny's a real nice guy, very encouraging. He thought I had talent. Well, *I* thought I had talent. I'll always appreciate the encouragement he provided.

BILL ZAIS: Franny Hansen and Nancy Salomon—Franny kept me going during that first difficult year. Nancy has also helped me get through the interminable delays, and she has also helped me improve every aspect of constructing.

SHAWN KENNEDY: Nancy Salomon and Kelly Clark have been outstanding mentors. They helped me improve my cluing skills [and] grid-building skills, and they taught me how to make a puzzle more entertaining for the solver.

DAVID MACLEOD: I got invaluable suggestions from Nancy Salomon and Manny Nosowsky. Were it not for them, I would still be struggling.

GREG STAPLES: Nancy Salomon was a tremendous help. She took an early puzzle and gave me very beneficial feedback. I still value Nancy's advice tremendously. She is "the" mentor among new constructors.

MANNY NOSOWSKY: You know, I never even heard the word *mentor* as applied to puzzling until recent years. Ever since the Internet started, people have sent me puzzles to critique, and being retired, I have done so, and I've enjoyed it. But I've kept my involvement just to the level where I'm asked. One time I commented on more than I was asked, and that pissed off the constructor no end, so I learned my lesson. Mostly, I'll comment on theme proposals or word quality in the fill or optimizing black-square placement. Sometimes I'll make suggestions for improvements, but not usually; in fact I rarely offer any comment on anything I was not specifically asked, and I avoid the whole cluing part of crosswords since that's so subjective. Once in a while I'll check for clue accuracy, agreement in number and tense, etc.

At this level, I think I've mentored tens of constructors at one time or another, maybe even a hundred. I don't think of it as anything unusual, since when I started, while there was no Internet, there were several busy editors and other constructors who would do similar things for me by phone or regular mail. There was one editor who helped me even when he knew the puzzle was to be sent elsewhere. I have helped Kelly Clark more than others, since I see all of her puzzles. She test-solves everything for me and has been very helpful, so it comes out even.

DOLLARS AND SENSE

Economics and art are strangers.
—WILLA Cather

One hard fact of life as a crossword constructor is that one's remuneration typically has little correlation to the time and effort expended. In fact, there are some puzzles that end up taking so long to complete that crossworders are lucky if they make minimum wage!

JOE DIPIETRO: No attempt to make a living. I'm just trying to show off as much as possible.

BARRY TUNICK: There are more and more good young constructors, but on the downside, there are fewer and fewer traditional markets as syndicates and mergers take their tolls. Even though payment rates are edging up, publications' and editors' insistence on buying all rights to puzzles has limited constructors' income.

WILLIAM CANINE: Puzzling was never more than an avocation for me.

RANDOLPH ROSS: I do this as an avocation, not for a living.

ELIZABETH GORSKI: I'm a professional musician, so whatever income I earn from puzzlemaking is supplemental.

BARRY TUNICK: [In] 1979 . . . the *Los Angeles Times* . . . paid $250 for a cryptic crossword about the *Times*, plus a crypto-quote. The *Times* bought about twenty-five [crypto-quotes] over the next two years. Sylvia Bursztyn's and my first crossword sale was to the *Los Angeles Times* in May 1980. For four to five years in the early 1990s, the *Los Angeles Times* ran our crosswords along with either our [crypto-quote], word search, or Double-Crostic. When they shrunk the page size to save paper, the second puzzle had to go—along with a big chunk of our income.

NELSON HARDY: I used to create many different kinds of puzzles for Dell, but when they slashed their prices in 1997, variety puzzles were hit hardest, and I stopped making them. I also stopped making cryptics, because I was never able to increase my clue-writing speed to the point where I was making a decent hourly wage. I make only American-style crossword puzzles now. I don't know if you could call my annual income a "living." It's slightly more than what I was making as a stock clerk in the 1970s.

NORMAN WIZER: You have to love it and [know that] you would do it regardless of pay. There was a man who tried to start a Crossword Hall of Fame. He thought that all constructors should be paid better, as part of his agenda. Someone stood up and said, "It doesn't matter what they pay us. If they paid us nothing, we would still do puzzles"—which is the truth.

NANCY JOLINE: I certainly couldn't make a living at it, nor could anyone who isn't a puzzle editor. We constructors are in the game for love.

BOB KLAHN: This isn't about money. I'm too slow, and I'm too fussy. I spend too much time per puzzle. I'd have to change how I do things to turn this into more than a secondary source of income.

TYLER HINMAN: I am unable to make a living off of crosswords, nor do I need to. (I'm only fifteen as I write this.)

BILL ZAIS: I'm not even close to making a living at it, but that isn't my motivation anyway.

MARK DIEHL: [I] could never make a living at it (at least compared to my "real" job).

DAVID MACLEOD: A living? Not at this pay rate.

CATHY MILLHAUSER: A living? You jest.

MEL TAUB: I was never able to make a living at it. No—strictly a sideline/hobby.

KELLY CLARK: No, I couldn't live on my earnings, alas—fortunately, I've got a business that takes care of food, shelter, and things like that.

PATRICK JORDAN: I certainly do not make enough from freelance crosswords to earn a living. However, I do pride myself on the fact that, when I purchased my first house, I was able to furnish it solely from puzzle revenue!

RICH NORRIS: I haven't been able to make a living from selling puzzles alone, but I've made a nice side income in each of the last three years—in excess of $10,000 per year.

MARTIN ASHWOOD-SMITH: I do not make a living from crosswords, but I do find the extra income very handy.

PETER GORDON: [There are] maybe two hundred constructors, and two dozen make their living doing it.

STAN NEWMAN: The crossword editor of the *New York Times* has always been paid reasonably well, so of course Will is earning a fine living in his career. Merl [Reagle], I know for a fact, has built up his own businesses that have been very successful for him.

JON DELFIN: Does anybody make a living exclusively from constructing besides Merl? And maybe Henry Hook?

GAYLE DEAN: I do make a living at it—but "a living" is a relative term . . . I'm a very frugal person.

FRED PISCOP: I'm starting to do okay now. I had a couple of lean years, but I think they're behind me.

TRIP PAYNE: Except for a six-month period, I have been solely freelance. There was a six-month period where I lost my two biggest clients, which meant two-thirds of my income out the window. In that time, I worked at a bookstore while I built my client base back up. I figured if I had to work someplace awful, at least I should make it a bookstore. I was very glad to get out of there.

EMILY COX AND HENRY RATHVON: In 1982, we were invited by Will Shortz, then an editor with *GAMES* magazine, to come to New York and work at that publication. We did, but in 1985 we went to full-time freelancing, and we still get by on it. Our jobs these days (besides the *Atlantic*) include Sunday puzzles for the *Boston Globe*; acrostics every other Sunday for the *New York Times*; monthly crosswords for the US Airways in-flight magazine, *Attache*; and a weekly cryptic puzzle for a Canadian newspaper, the *National Post*.

GAYLE DEAN: Invest weeks of time and energy to the neglect of all else—forget children, pets, and dirty dishes—and create a "perfect" puzzle, and someone will pay you a paltry sum for it. Keep doing this for fifteen or twenty years, and then you can be sure that every perfect puzzle you create will also be purchased for a paltry sum. In other words, constructors are artists—satisfaction comes from the creation of the work.

DON'T GIVE UP YOUR DAY JOB

WILLIAM R. MACKAYE: It used to be said in Washington that most of the constructors around Washington worked for the National Security Agency. [William] Lutwiniak did. I used to try to get him to talk a little bit about the agency, but not a word, not a peep did I get out of him about what happened there, what he did there, or anything else.

MARTIN ASHWOOD-SMITH: I am a taxi driver (night shift).

RICH NORRIS: I'm treasurer of a small corporation that owns photography-related businesses, including a processing lab, and I'm associate editor for Farrar Nichols Associates, which supplies the crossword puzzles for the *Los Angeles Times* Syndicate.

KELLY CLARK: With my business partner, Alden Thatcher, I own and run an ad agency/design studio in Boston, along with a company that represents freelance graphic artists.

JON DELFIN: Pianist/accompanist/vocal coach (etc., etc.).

ELIZABETH GORSKI: Professional violist.

RICH SILVESTRI: Math professor at Nassau Community College, Garden City, New York.

RAY HAMEL: My regular job is as a librarian at the Wisconsin Regional Primate Research Center. I'm responsible for answering reference questions, managing an audiovisual collection, and maintaining an informational Web site.

CHRIS JOHNSON: I used to be a graphic designer, but gave that up about twelve years ago. I sometimes teach chess in schools and privately. I do some contract computer programming.

JOE DIPIETRO: I own a bar in Manhattan.

PATRICK JORDAN: I sell advertising and perform computerized layout work at my hometown newspaper. It's the only full-time job I've ever held, and I recently completed my sixteenth year with the company.

DAVID J. KAHN: Actuary and employee benefits consultant.

DAVID MACLEOD: No day job now; working on developing a forestry invention. Have spent most of the last two decades as a silviculturist.

CATHY MILLHAUSER: I previously worked many years as an occupational therapist.

TOM SCHIER: Retired from Exxon Corporation after thirty-four years of service.

MEL TAUB: Now retired. Former job was as insurance company executive.

ARTHUR S. VERDESCA: I'm in the active practice of internal medicine.

LEONARD WILLIAMS: Professor of political science.

SAM BELLOTTO, JR.: [I have] no day job, thankfully. Between my constructing and my software business, I'm quite comfortable. I'm so lucky to be able to do this.

JIM PAGE: I left CBS about fifteen years ago to write a book and to stop working for a while. I'd worked all my life and just wanted to stop for a while—just plain stop, with the intent to go back. I realized when that time came I was not able to do nine-to-five anymore. Of course, when you're a kid and you're doing nine-to-five, you figure that's the way life is. Everybody does nine-to-five. You get up, you go to work, go home, go to bed—that's the way life is—then you die. But if you ever get away from nine-to-five, it's a whole different world. I've turned down some jobs for that reason. It's just simply the time—I don't want to devote that much time to working. I fully intended to go back. I got lucky—the puzzle thing turned into something more than I had anticipated in terms of editing. Plus I did some editing for Simon & Schuster, some of their fiction and nonfiction. That also helped. All of that kind of worked out, so I didn't ever go back to nine-to-five.

EXTENDED PLAY

All work and no play . . . as they say.

MANNY NOSOWSKY: I am a pool hustler in my spare time.

MARTIN ASHWOOD-SMITH: Music, both classical and electronic.

GAYLE DEAN: I love Scrabble and Boggle, of course. And math problems.

SAM BELLOTTO, JR.: I like acrostics. But I spend too much time on the computer, between making puzzles and working on my software. When I can, I like to get out with my dog and run around.

SYLVIA BURSZTYN: My pursuits are solitary ones. Reading, TV, movies, puzzle solving, keeping two cats from felicide (why can't they see in each other what I see in them?). I got a little bit involved in cat rescue a few years ago, but found I just don't have the constitution for it—so heartbreaking. For a while after my first cat died, I fostered cats, but now have two more of my own. I'd keep fostering if space permitted. And I take long drives, just to explore and think.

KELLY CLARK: My favorite game is charades, but nobody will ever play it with me.

WILLIAM CANINE: Music, especially opera; reading, particularly nowadays the genre headed by such as Elmore Leonard; gardening; sports on TV, first and foremost college basketball; birds and butterflies and my despair at their gradual disappearance; politics; golf; etc.

RICH NORRIS: Golf, softball. Writing of all kinds. I've written fiction, and I write a monthly inspirational article for my church newsletter. All sports, actually—I love to watch sports. I played them all when I was younger. Now it's mostly golf. Music. I studied piano starting at age seven, and now I'm the regular pianist at church as well. I've played in small ensembles—trios, quartets—all classical music: Beethoven, Mozart, Brahms, Schumann, to name a few. I've also accompanied vocalists in concerts. I sing, too. My wife and I and two friends have formed an a cappella quartet. We do a lot of rock 'n' roll and some light swing and jazz.

JOHN SAMSON: I love playing hearts on the computer. (When I win with a perfect zero score, my day is complete.)

JON DELFIN: Entertainment, reading, current events. Is pinball a game?

DIANE EPPERSON: Reading (mystery, thriller, horror); solving, of course; solitaire and mah-jongg; Scrabble.

PETER GORDON: I love all kinds of games. Other interests include baseball, bowling, postcard collecting, and movies.

RAY HAMEL: I am a huge trivia fanatic, and have a collection of about 150 trivia games and hundreds of trivia books. I also enjoy bowling and playing guitar.

MAURA JACOBSON: Until recently, I was a tennis player. We [my family] play Trivial Pursuit, we play bridge; Scrabble when we go on vacation, but not otherwise.

CHRIS JOHNSON: Chess, classical music, computer programming, reading (mostly mysteries and science fiction at present), drinking beer, pipe smoking, making furniture (bookcases more than anything else, from necessity), playing trivia games, designing Web pages.

NANCY JOLINE: Family get-togethers, travel, my book group, tennis, ballet, gardening. I enjoy Scrabble, charades, and hearts with my grandkids.

PATRICK JORDAN: I have collections of comic books, animation cels, and vintage radio programs on audiotape, and I perform community service through my membership with the local Lions Club. The only game in which I engage regularly is my computer version of *Jeopardy!*.

DAVID J. KAHN: Sports, Scrabble, and playing with my fifteen-month-old grandson.

DAVID MACLEOD: Golf.

CATHY MILLHAUSER: I sing in a local choral group. I enjoy playing anagrams. I try to hike or ride my bike whenever I can.

FRED PISCOP: Several friends of mine and I had a Tuesday-night regular word-game group, and Stan [Newman], in 1989, maybe, started the crossword in *Newsday*, which is our local paper. The week he started, there was a little bio about him in the paper, and we figured we'd give him a call and invite him down. He came down and never left—he's been a part of the group ever since.

RICH SILVESTRI: Visiting brewpubs. Listening to '50s rock 'n' roll. Every Tuesday night I get together with fellow word-gamers at the home of George Bredehorn to play games that George has created.

NANCY SALOMON: Word games of all kinds; spectator sports; gambling; TV.

TOM SCHIER: Play golf four times each week. Enjoy traveling with wife and family. Collect stamps. Enjoy Scrabble.

MEL TAUB: Not avid at game-playing. I spend my time writing (or trying to write) humor, exploring New York City, and doing some volunteer work. I'll be teaching a course in puzzlemaking for senior citizens this summer.

BARRY TUNICK: I'm president of the Culver City Friends of the Library and Culver-Palms Meals on Wheels. I enjoy traveling with my wife and family. I regularly play Scrabble and WordBluf, the invention of John Suarez (Bluff in the [National Puzzlers' League]), and by far the best word game I've ever played.

ARTHUR S. VERDESCA: Detective fiction (I have a library of over six thousand titles); classical music (for eleven years back there, I had a weekly one-hour radio program on which I discussed classical music, etc.); horticulture (at one time I had a houseful of cacti—over three hundred miniatures—growing under banks and banks of lights); translating from the Italian or German; writing short stories. For over twenty years, I have been a judge (now senior judge) of the American Publishers Association in their field of scholarly publications.

LEONARD WILLIAMS: Writing, film, poetry, and tennis. I play Scrabble and some election-related games.

BILL ZAIS: Billiards and card games.

CODE NAMES

You might not be solving who you think . . .

MIKE SHENK: I'm the puzzle editor for the *Wall Street Journal*. . . . Once in a while [I also construct them], but so far that's only been under various pseudonyms. It's just because I think it looks better than having "Edited by Mike Shenk, puzzle written by Mike Shenk." Sort of like, "Well, why did he bother editing it if he wrote it himself!"

GAYLE DEAN: At times, an editor may wish to use more than a few of a constructor's creations in the same book and will use a pseudonym.

RAY HAMEL: I used pseudonyms while writing for Dell Crosswords, at their request.

MARTIN ASHWOOD-SMITH: A few of my Dell Champion puzzles were published under the name "Andrew Rowan." Dell Champion asked many of its regular contributors for pseudonyms so they could run our puzzles closer together (i.e., same page).

CATHY MILLHAUSER: I think the now-defunct Dell Champion used a pseudonym when I was having a lot of puzzles published there. I created the anagrammatic name "Hillary Mustache" for such purposes, but it never got used except on the cover of *CROSSW RD* magazine.

RICH NORRIS: The first time was when John Samson, the Simon & Schuster editor, told me he wanted to run a couple of my puzzles on facing pages, so he wanted a pseudonym for one of them. I used my son's first and middle name: Geoffrey Louis. Now, as an editor of *Los Angeles Times* puzzles, if I need a special-occasion puzzle on short notice, I make it myself and publish it under a pseudonym. My current pseudonyms are anagrams, a page I stole out of Mike Shenk's book. He's published a couple of puzzles in the *Wall Street Journal*, for which he's the puzzle editor, under the name "Marie Kelly," which is an anagram for "Really Mike." My pseudonyms: "S. I. Murphy II" (if you spell out *second*, it anagrams into "Rich's pseudonym") and "Alastair Dusay," which I use only for an occasional *Los Angeles Times* Saturday puzzle, and which anagrams into "Saturday Alias."

TRIP PAYNE: [At *GAMES*], I had been doing nine to eleven puzzles per issue, some under pseudonyms. My rule of thumb there was that anything I made that was a crossword or a crossword variation would never get a pseudonym. For the variety stuff I sometimes used pseudonyms, because it didn't matter so much—I'm not going to get corporate assignments because people know me for making a crisscross puzzle. I used "Georgia Mann"—very clever, I know [*Payne lives in Atlanta*]—and "Penny A. Roman," which is an anagram of my real name, Norman Payne.

PETER GORDON: In my left-handed puzzle, I got the *Times* to print the grid on the other side so that righties could understand the problems lefties face (and I had the byline read "Peter [Lefty] Gordon" even though I'm a righty). Another byline change was my [*New York Times*] St. Patrick's Day puzzle: "By Peter O'Gordon; Edited by Will McShortz."

NORMAN WIZER: Bernice Gordon and I have such a good time doing [puzzles] together and laughing about it. [Our pseudonym] "Monica Brenner" is an anagram of Bernice and Norman. Monica was born in Stamford. We were sitting around the bar talking crossword puzzle nonsense and a theme popped up. We did the layout and definitions together. By the way, [when] a friend of mine saw an obituary for Monica Brenner, she said to herself, "That name sounds awfully familiar," until she realized that was our pen name!

JOHN SAMSON: In the *Globe* and *National Examiner* I drop my last name and go by John McCarthy (McCarthy is my middle name.) This keeps the Irish side of my family happy.

PETER GORDON: I sometimes used "Ogden Porter" in *GAMES* when there was another puzzle by me or when I was the editor and I didn't want my name appearing too often. "Ogden Porter" is an anagram of "Peter Gordon."

FRANCIS HEANEY: I was all over *GAMES*—and probably more so than it seemed at first, because I was under numerous pseudonyms. Back when Trip Payne was still writing for them, we didn't want it to be completely obvious that he and I were writing like a third of the magazine, so we had numerous pseudonyms. I wrote the cryptograms under the name "Bob Lynch" because it was sort of a letter change on my [National Puzzlers' League] pseudonym Lunch Boy: Lynch-comma-Bob, Lunch Boy. I did the 500 Rummy under a pseudonym, because there's been a longstanding tradition of people using pseudonyms there, like Mike Shenk wrote it as "Jack Schneider." I wrote it as "Trey Yarborough," taking his cue as card for the first name-[and-]card-game term for the second name. I think a Yarborough is from whist—I had to work really hard to find a card-game term that sounded like a last name.

PATRICK JORDAN: Simon & Schuster has a rule stating that a constructor may have no more than three puzzles published under a single name in any volume of their crossword book series. Recently, one volume was scheduled to include seven of my works, so I was asked to create two pseudonyms. I chose "Bud Gillis" (combining my father's nickname for me with my mother's maiden name) and "Jay Hackney" (my middle name, followed by the tiny Kansas township where I spent most of my formative years).

NANCY SALOMON: I did a partner puzzle with Bob Frank. Stan Newman didn't have room for both of our full names on the byline. He decided to use "Frank Salomon." That generated some interesting mail. One hapless Cruciverb-L member asked me if Frank was a relation of mine. If so, he suggested I give him a cluing lesson!

MEL TAUB: Margaret Farrar would use a generic pseudonym on Sundays, "Charles Cross," when she felt a constructor was appearing often enough to make other constructors envious. I was "Charles Cross" now and then.

ARTHUR S. VERDESCA: Because my early output was so great, Gene Maleska suggested I use pseudonyms. So I was also "Mike Salvatore," "Dave S. Carter," and "M. D. Randolph."

TREND SPOTTING

Since the genesis of new wave crosswords, there haven't been any radical changes in the puzzle world. But crosswords do continue to evolve, as do construction techniques.

SAM BELLOTTO, JR.: I am totally mystified over the upsurge in old-style, straightforward, themeless puzzles. Sure, they may have a very low word count, but solvers don't give a darn about that. I have a feeling that constructors of these boring efforts make them largely for self-gratification. We have a word for that.

MANNY NOSOWSKY: I happen to believe that we're living in a golden age of puzzling.

NANCY SALOMON: I don't think there have been any decided trends since new wave puzzles became popular.

RANDOLPH ROSS: The best trend has been the emphasis by Will [Shortz], Mike [Shenk], and others on wordplay in the clues, as opposed to esoterica.

MARTIN ASHWOOD-SMITH: Many of the trends are good, especially with the *New York Times*. Crosswordese is at an all-time low. Crossword fills on average are better than ever.

KELLY CLARK: I enjoy seeing the use of everyday words and phrases, cleverly clued, over lengthy, little-used words, which I understand was once the vogue in construction.

MERL REAGLE: It's hard to see trends in general. I don't remember too many of these change-a-letter, switch-a-letter, add-a-letter, drop-a-letter themes before I started doing them in the 1980s. I don't remember them appearing much at all under Maleska. I don't remember seeing them ever under Will Weng, or under Margaret—they might have been around, but I don't remember seeing them. For me, the changing of a letter for humorous effect, or dropping a letter, or adding a letter, or switching two letters around, seemed to have tons of possibilities for crossword humor.

PATRICK JORDAN: I think puzzles are generally getting better. There seems to be a real effort to reduce crosswordese to a minimum and greater use of bylines so that solvers can recognize their favorite constructors. And today's younger puzzlers (especially people like Frank Longo, Matt Gaffney, and Patrick Berry) are raising the art of the wide-open grid to new heights.

DAVID J. KAHN: I see a trend toward more pop culture and less crosswordese in puzzles, and that's good. It gives the puzzles a more immediate look.

NANCY JOLINE: The recent trend away from crosswordese and obscure words is a good one, I think. Will Shortz deserves a lot of credit for that.

TYLER HINMAN: I'm glad we're moving away from crosswordese and moving toward livelier entries, like singers, actors, names in the news, etc. Crosswords have to stay modern; otherwise the flow of new, younger puzzlers will decrease. I hope that more youths like myself get into puzzle construction. Right now, I only know of four teenagers, including myself, who are serious about puzzlemaking. (There may well be others, but if so, I don't know them.)

NELSON HARDY: I've noticed only good trends: more humor and fewer obscurities. Crosswords in the past seemed to be aimed at people with insanely large vocabularies and no sense of humor. I'm glad we're moving away from that.

SHAWN KENNEDY: Today's puzzles are becoming more lively and entertaining. Crosswords used to be more strict and proper. Nowadays, editors allow wordplay and more creativity.

GAYLE DEAN: The clues that were becoming so boring and that spurred me to creating puzzles in the early 1980s have changed. This has contributed to more interesting and more challenging puzzles. The human creative potential is boundless, and I'm sure the trend toward more interesting puzzles will continue. Clues like "Was outstanding?" for OWED and "Backward butter?" for MAR are priceless.

CATHY MILLHAUSER: I'm happy that there's been a loosening of restrictions [in terms of] multiword entries, brand names, and terms that are risqué only in the eyes of the beholder.

RICH NORRIS: Two good trends: (1) The advancing state of puzzlemaking software. Notably, Antony Lewis of England continues to improve his Crossword Compiler for Windows [CCW] program, which I think is state-of-the-art. No software is a substitute for imagination and hard work, but CCW certainly eases a lot of the drudgery of puzzlemaking. (2) [The] influx of new puzzlemakers. I may be wrong about this, but it does seem that more and more new names pop up under puzzles in places like the *New York Times* and [*Los Angeles Times*] than when I first joined the ranks. New constructors are putting out quality work, and many editors are open to looking at it.

Bad trend, if it is a trend: money. Pay rates are too low to begin with, and are standing still at an alarming rate. Admittedly, there are economic laws at work here: 99 percent of puzzle constructors have no pretensions about making a living at it; it's a hobby, and they enjoy it, so money is not a priority. But that doesn't make it fair.

SYLVIA BURSZTYN: The bad trends I see are not so much in construction as in business. Publications reuse old puzzles to avoid spending money on new ones. Some years ago, constructors were paid on acceptance; today, the trend is payment on publication. I don't see high standards for originality or creativity in the general puzzle market. The good trends? No matter how high tech the world becomes, there are still kids coming along who love to solve puzzles on paper, and kids who want to create them, too.

PETER GORDON: I'm not a big fan of themeless crosswords. A quality theme is what makes a puzzle great. It should be totally consistent and very tight. The reason I don't write more puzzles is because themes are hard to think of. They should be themes that haven't been done already, and the filler words should be good—no crappy words at all. . . .

I like to make my puzzles easy. Unless we keep attracting new solvers, puzzles will die out in a generation. And new solvers need easy puzzles. Look at the puzzles I [do]—they all have tight themes, and most are easy. And there are probably only a few lousy grid entries in the entire stack. One thing I don't agree with most constructors on is the goal of a low word count. Ask an average solver, and they'll have no concept of what a low word count is. I'd much rather have seventy-eight words in a puzzle, that are all familiar, than seventy-four words, where one is obscure and one is a partial.

RICH SILVESTRI: Good: There's a lot less crosswordese and fewer obscure entries in puzzles nowadays. There's more of an emphasis on clever cluing. Bad: There are too many unthemed puzzles, which I find boring. It seems like anyone with a decent software package can churn out a puzzle loaded with Qs and Zs, and that's supposed to be creative.

WILLIAM CANINE: The editors of old (Maleska, Farrar, Weng, Rosen, Osborn, Samson, Lutwiniak) rarely tampered with your work, beyond correcting an obvious error or occasionally improving a clue. Today's editors seem to impose themselves rather heavily on the final product. This is okay, I guess, but since the puzzle is published under the constructor's name, it can be annoying when you preferred your own work!

BILL ZAIS: The worst trend I see is the continuing dearth of snappy themes. For my money, much of the humor found in puzzles of the 1970s and 1980s is now gone. There are too many compilation and cookie-cutter puzzles being published.

ARTHUR S. VERDESCA: [I see] an unfortunate trend to emphasize popular culture at the expense of culture in general.

A WORLD OF GOOD

Our intrepid band of constructors provides opinions on that most subjective of subjects: What makes a good crossword puzzle?

WILLIAM R. MACKAYE: It has to be amusing. It has to be clued in a way that's tricky, but that when you discover what the trick is, you slap your head and say, "Why didn't I think of that!"

GAYLE DEAN: I like themed puzzles using wordplay: puns, anagrams, clever gim-micks. And, of course, most solvers disdain crosswordese: ANOA, ESNE, etc.; obscure rivers, communes, combining forms, abbreviations. I try to limit abbreviations to one well-known abbreviation per puzzle, and I think the rule (that some editors enforce) prohibiting abbreviations and obscurities in corners is a good one. There is nothing more frustrating for solvers than to be stuck in a corner.

RANDOLPH ROSS: A good crossword is one that is solvable with a little work and some divergent thinking. Good clues, interesting words, and a sense of humor all make a good puzzle. My underlying feeling, though, is always "it's only a game—don't take it too seriously, but learn from it."

TRIP PAYNE: A good crossword should be first and foremost entertaining. The solver should have fun with it. It needs to be filled with lively, interesting words—not crosswordese, and a minimum of boring words like ASSESS. There should be stuff where the solver thinks, "Oh, cool" when he writes it into the puzzle. It doesn't necessarily have to have a theme, although it's always nice to have something that's going to make the solver laugh, whether it's in the theme or in the clues. If somebody laughs, you know it's a good puzzle. And a lack of things that most people won't know; It's fine to put in information about a common word that they might not know, but if so, it should be something that they will find interesting and not just trivial. If a puzzle can have a punch line, that's wonderful. Merl [Reagle] is great at those. But you can't always have that. Barring that, a fun theme, or just fill it with great words and good clues.

MARTIN ASHWOOD-SMITH: Fresh, interesting themes; good, lively fill; and creative cluing.

ELIZABETH GORSKI: My favorite puzzles use up-to-date language. I make sure that my fills contain new words that are accessible to most people. Themed puzzles are really two puzzles: (1) The theme itself, which should be interesting and fresh. (2) A colorful fill, which I consider the subtheme. Even after a solver catches on to the theme, a puzzle should continue to entertain by providing a snappy fill.

RICH NORRIS: My general philosophy is to make my themes interesting and consistent, to put quality words and phrases into my puzzles, to write clues that are fresh and entertaining, and to avoid obscure words and names to whatever extent possible, if not entirely. I try to vary the references in my clues as much as possible: a little movies, a little TV, literature, sports, science, drama, etc. "Fairness" is my prime directive.

I think puzzles should primarily entertain. I also think that to a limited degree, a puzzle can teach. A good puzzle can be structured so that the solver, whether a beginner or a pro, can learn something from it. For instance, it was in a crossword that I learned that "jai alai" means "merry game" in Basque. Sure, you can look that up in a good dictionary, but who ever would?

SAM BELLOTTO, JR.: To me, a clever theme is first and foremost. Next I strive for an "open" grid design. Finally, the rest of the clues should be a mix of trivia, straight definitions, and puns. The idea is to make a good American crossword. If the British format is your thing, move to England.

RICH SILVESTRI: A clever theme and an absence of French words.

WILLIAM CANINE: Be as original as possible. Find themes and words that are intrinsically interesting. And, of course, that which is for me most difficult: clues that "excite."

SYLVIA BURSZTYN: I like silly wordplay in a crossword; inventive themes; lively cluing. I like to see that the constructor put some thought into unifying the puzzle, so that some filler is clued to relate to the theme. I like evocative clues, ones that set your mind off on its own nostalgic trail. For example, rather than "Appendage" for HAND, why not "Spicoli's history teacher" or "Penn: Spicoli; Walston: _____" [from *Fast Times at Ridgemont High*]? I think a puzzle is successful if the solvers feel as if they themselves have come up with this wordplay, these puns, as they discover the theme answers from a few entered letters.

JON DELFIN: Theme first, then fill and clues free of trash.

NORMAN WIZER: I really like words that are in common use. I like definitions that are clever—not necessarily stumping. To me, the whole thing is fun. You have to get a kick out of some of the definitions. I love to do humorous puzzles.

MARK DIEHL: First, entertainment value. Second, lively entries and cluing. Third, minimum of crosswordese. Fourth, my preference is for more white squares.

DIANE EPPERSON: The usual mantra from the editors: tight, focused theme; lively fill; fresh clues in a variety of styles (definition, puns, fill-ins); minimum of crosswordese, obscurities, abbreviations; open grid with a minimum of "one-way-in-only" corners.

GREG STAPLES: A good theme is the most important. "Aha" themes or original themes are the best. Original and humorous clues are important. Crosswordese and trivia should be kept to a minimum.

NANCY JOLINE: I try to make my puzzles challenging but doable. If no one can solve it, what good is a puzzle? I try to avoid stodgy words and to include fun entries like SLURPEE or COOLIO when possible. I enjoy solving puzzles that have some humor in them.

PATRICK JORDAN: The buzzword for me is *fairness*. A good puzzle must have no blind crossings (in which two uncommon words intersect) and adhere as closely as possible to everyday vocabulary. Aside from this, a good puzzle will have an interesting theme, a lively fill with a few contemporary references thrown in, and just enough partials or "gimme" clues to allow solvers of all levels to find a foothold (unless it's meant to be especially challenging, of course).

SHAWN KENNEDY: A good puzzle should not be so difficult that it's no longer fun to solve. However, it shouldn't be so easy that the solver can fill in the grid without even thinking about what he or she is doing. A good crossword is like a good workout: variety and exercise are important.

DAVID MACLEOD: I look for witty word combinations, solid themes, lowish word counts, and that extra *je ne sais quoi* that contributes to construction elegance. Clever cluing is icing on the cake and is the most fun for me in constructing.

CATHY MILLHAUSER: The best puzzles are those that make you laugh out loud, scratch your head until you figure out the theme, or have such clever clues that the theme almost doesn't matter. And if a gimmick, such as dropping a letter, is used, the result should be funny or meaningful in some other way, not just a gimmick for gimmick's sake.

MANNY NOSOWSKY: If it's fun, entertaining, and solvable, it's good.

NANCY SALOMON: Good theme (for themed puzzles) and a colorful, lively fill (for all puzzles).

TOM SCHIER: I love to integrate as many theme-related words and clues in a daily or Sunday grid as is physically possible. Entering three or four related theme words or phrases just doesn't cut it, in my opinion.

MIKE SHENK: I try to keep all the words in the puzzle . . . familiar words. I'd much rather have the clues be the tricky part, not have obscure words. That's largely based on just laziness on my part, because it makes it so much easier to clue it if I know what the word means already. It really started out of laziness on my part. So that, I think, is important, and I think that puzzles should be entertaining fun—much more important that they be fun than that you learn anything from them. The main thing is you should have fun solving it. You shouldn't finish it and think, "Well, that wasn't very interesting," [and] you shouldn't not be able to finish it and think, "Well, this isn't fair." Ultimately, the solver comes first.

MEL TAUB: Avoiding arcane crosswordese and defining words imaginatively. Fresh clues and themes keep solvers interested.

BARRY TUNICK: Puzzling should be fun first—by a long ways—then informative. (While puzzling does increase one's knowledge and vocabulary in the long run, it's a very inefficient and scattershot way of doing so.)

LEONARD WILLIAMS: One that has a tight theme (hopefully not a groaner) and that makes little use of abbreviations and rarely used words.

JOHN SAMSON: A good crossword is both entertaining and challenging. The bonus of a good crossword is a newfound fact or word. A solver in her early nineties once approached me and told me how much she enjoyed solving the Simon & Schuster crosswords. I asked her what she liked most about the puzzles. She told me it was because she learned one new thing in every puzzle. I had always played down the educational value of crosswords, but since that conversation I've modified my views. It's nice when you're learning something while being entertained at the same time.

MERL REAGLE: [There were] people that I really liked seeing because I really liked their stuff a lot: Jordan Lasher was one, A. J. Santora—these were guys that could really open up a diagram, and seemed to do it effortlessly. A lot of the stuff that Jordan Lasher was doing—he was pretty wild also. But A. J. Santora wasn't. His stuff was just clean as a whistle and wide open as hell—I was just amazed at his stuff. Those are the guys that I sort of idolized.

TRIP PAYNE: Merl [Reagle] is the person with the best themes, just continually. Just solving for fun, I will solve Merl's before anyone else's. He's the person who will make me laugh the most. Mike [Shenk] is the person I've tried to model myself after. He is simply the best grid-maker out there, I think. He doesn't use a computer to help him fill—he's just better than the programs are. I still love the fact that Eric Albert made an Ornery for *GAMES* with a really, really wide-open corner, and there was one thing in it that Mike had a tiny problem with, so he just threw out that corner and made a better one. That's just the way he is. He'll make these wonderful grids filled with amazing words, and you just think, "It doesn't get better than this."

Henry [Hook] over the years has done a lot of good stuff. Frank Longo I think is very, very good. I like Patrick Berry, who does great variety puzzles. His Rows Garden that runs in *GAMES* is my favorite thing in that magazine. He's just really good at variety stuff. David Kahn is very good. There are people that I wish constructed more. I wish Donna Stone would come back. I really enjoyed her puzzles. Early on in my career, one of the people I really admired was Jordan Lasher. And a lot of A. J. Santora's early stuff. They were both inspirations to me.

MARTIN ASHWOOD-SMITH: Mike Shenk, Merl Reagle, and Henry Hook: These were (and still are) the big three for me. All are masters of wide-open interlock, highly original themes, and creative cluing.

NELSON HARDY: My favorites are the ones who put a lot of humor into their puzzles: Merl Reagle and Cathy Millhauser immediately come to mind. I appreciate the clever themes and lively fills of Manny Nosowsky, Nancy Salomon,

Rich Norris; the wide-open grids of Bob Klahn, Martin Ashwood-Smith, Frank Longo . . . there are more, too many to name here.

ERICA ROTHSTEIN: I love Merl. I absolutely love him. I think he is the single best constructor in the country. Without hesitation—there is absolutely no one who can touch him. Merl understands the solver like nobody else out there does. Merl understands that a puzzle isn't any good if nobody can solve it.

RANDOLPH ROSS: I like Mike Shenk because he is so creative and such a good cluer. Rich Silvestri is a great cluer and always has tight, inner consistency in his themes. Merl is funny and versatile. Manny Nosowsky has great fill. Cathy Millhauser has a great sense of humor. Cox & Rathvon are great pros and do everything well. David Kahn always does something interesting.

SAM BELLOTTO, JR.: Aside from myself, Gayle Dean, and John M. Samson, I also like Ray Hamel. There are others, but these few come to mind immediately. The reasons are clever themes, fresh clues, and lots of trivia.

JON DELFIN: Reagle, Hook, Shenk, Millhauser, Longo, Cox & Rathvon, Ashwood-Smith, Nosowsky, Kahn, Klahn, and I'm sure I'm leaving out many.

PETER GORDON: Merl Reagle has great themes. Mike Shenk is the master of grid-making. Henry Hook is a super clue-writer. Cathy Millhauser never disappoints me—she always has great themes, grids, and clues.

RICH NORRIS: There are so many different kinds of puzzles, and within each kind there are different levels. Merl Reagle makes terrific puzzles for the average to intermediate solver. Henry Hook makes terrific brain-busting puzzles—many of which are beyond me. Cox & Rathvon make great cryptics, and recently they've gotten into acrostics, which they seem to have an affinity for as well. There are dozens of different kinds of novelty puzzles, too, and all I know about them is that Will Shortz seems to be able to make them all.

As far as American-style crossword puzzles are concerned, I can say who some of my favorite constructors are. I apologize in advance to the dozens of fine constructors I just can't think of at the moment. Some names that really stand out: David Kahn, Cathy Millhauser, Manny Nosowsky,

Mike Shenk, Cox & Rathvon (again), Frank Longo, Matt Gaffney, Peter Gordon, Joe DiPietro. I could mention a dozen more, but I'd rather leave out more names than less. It's important to note that there are three basic skills that go into making a crossword: theme development, grid-building, and clue-writing. In the above list, I think Mike and David stand out as constructors who can do it all. Cathy and Cox & Rathvon are great at themes and clues. Manny, Matt, and Frank are among the best grid-builders around. David, Frank, and Peter are especially skilled at squeezing lots of theme into small spaces (as is Merl Reagle, mentioned above).

MAURA JACOBSON: I'd say Merl Reagle. Frances Hansen—she's a doll. Henry Hook is another one I think is a great constructor. A new one coming up who's great is Cathy Millhauser.

RICH SILVESTRI: Cathy Millhauser, because of the wordplay in her puzzles. Maura Jacobson, because of her wonderful puns. Randy Ross, because every so often he'll come up with a theme I wish I'd done. Merl Reagle, because of the sheer zaniness of some of his puzzles.

PATRICK JORDAN: In my opinion, the best constructors combine technical skill, clever clues, and humorous wordplay. My favorite puzzlemakers who are capable of this remarkable triple feat include Henry Hook, Cathy Millhauser, Merl Reagle, Harvey Estes, Maura Jacobson, Patrick Berry, and Emily Cox and Henry Rathvon. If we count just the first two criteria, the list would grow to include Frank Longo, Trip Payne, Mike Shenk, Manny Nosowsky, Matt Gaffney, and many others.

JOE DIPIETRO: Manny Nosowsky, Rich Norris, Frank Longo, Cox & Rathvon. They make the difficult look easy.

DAVID J. KAHN: My favorite puzzle writers, in no particular order, are Merl Reagle, Manny Nosowsky, Bob Klahn, Joe DiPietro, Frank Longo, Cathy Millhauser, Randolph Ross, Matt Gaffney, Peter Gordon, Patrick Berry, Mike Shenk, and Nancy Joline. All are creative and can really put together a fabulous grid.

DAVID MACLEOD: Merl Reagle, because he's very entertaining and sometimes actually makes me laugh. Manny Nosowsky, because he never ceases to satisfy, and some of his grids are works of art. Bob Klahn, because he's sneaky tough. Brendan Quigley, because he's always tough. Cathy Millhauser, because she's so creative. Rich Norris for his prolific output. Nancy Salomon for the assurance that there's no funny business or contrivances. There are many others.

CATHY MILLHAUSER: I enjoy Merl Reagle's puzzles—he has the wacky sense of humor that I love and is especially good at coming up with creatively specialized themes. One such puzzle, which had NAPA in the title, had entries relating to both truckers and wine. But I also admire those who can come up with wide-open grids and outstanding fill, things that are still difficult for me.

STAN NEWMAN: Henry [Hook], Mike [Shenk], and Merl [Reagle are] the three I think of together as the top tier, although many new ones are pretty close these days.

KELLY CLARK: Manny Nosowsky, without question, because he makes it look so easy. Merl Reagle cracks me up (his clues alone are worth the price of his books!). I enjoy the quip-style puzzles Martin Ashwood-Smith makes, along with his incredible themeless works. Rich Norris deserves his *New York Times* title: "Mister Saturday." For early-in-the-week puzzles I love Elizabeth Gorski, Nancy Salomon, and Mary Brindamour. Frances Hansen makes beautifully witty limerick puzzles that I admire very much.

MANNY NOSOWSKY: Merl Reagle. His puzzles are the most entertaining and the most fun, at least for me. (Gee, that sounds flat.) Merl Reagle is a *bloody genius*!

NANCY SALOMON: Henry Hook, Merl Reagle, Cathy Millhauser, Manny Nosowsky. There are lots of honorable mentions.

TOM SCHIER: Henry Hook and Merl Reagle. Their creativeness and imagination have set the next plateau for crossword constructors.

NANCY SCHUSTER: I used to play Scrabble at lunch every day with Henry Hook at work. He was at *GAMES* at the time. I first met him at a small New Jersey tournament, though I knew his name from editing his Dell puzzles. I thought he was a fantastic constructor. Across the room we each noticed the other twiddling thumbs while every other contestant was still working away, so we sent messages back and forth in the form of an acrostic puzzle made up on the spot from a sentence or two.

Henry's biggest dream—and Merl's, too, in those days—was to have a whole book of puzzles of their own published. It's amazing to see how they've achieved that goal. And I wanted to be their exclusive editor. We all were scrambling together. It's so interesting to see how they reached the top of the profession.

I used to write Merl's clues for him. He couldn't stand to write his clues. He's marvelous, but he liked best to run off the grids, you know, and then have somebody else deal with the clues—not for all of his puzzles, but I guess for the ones he had submitted to Dell. He figured that since I was going to edit them, why not just have me write them from scratch?

Fred Piscop (for his Web site) and Manny [Nosowsky] send me their puzzles before they submit them to see if there are any changes or suggestions I have for them. Fred's a quiet kind of guy. He used to do freelance editing for me at Dell, and he did it terribly! I said to him, "How is it when you suddenly set up your own Web site, you have great discrimination and wonderful clues, but when you were working for me you were so bad?" He says, "Well, I guess I had to learn sometime!" He's become really good. That's what's funny—because I've watched these people really grow up in their career.

Manny's a really great constructor, and he's become a dear friend.

MIKE SHENK: I certainly would be happy to name both Henry [Hook] and Merl [Reagle] in that list [of top constructors]. There are a lot of good people out there—it's hard for me to pick just a couple when I'm also editing, and I don't want to hurt the feelings of people who might be sending me puzzles if I don't name them.

TYLER HINMAN: I thoroughly admire the work of expert open-gridded constructors, particularly Frank Longo, Manny Nosowsky, and Martin Ashwood-Smith. Few things are more impressive than an eye-popping, low-word-count puzzle. I also admire Merl Reagle, as well as anybody else who can produce a top-quality 21×21 puzzle *every week*.

MEL TAUB: Over the years, my own personal favorites have been Maura Jacobson and A. J. Santora.

WILL SHORTZ: Boy, where do you start? Some of my favorites are, besides [Mike Shenk and Merl Reagle], Rich Norris, Joe DiPietro, David Kahn, Frank Longo, Rich Silvestri, Peter Gordon, Elizabeth Gorski, Cathy Millhauser. Cathy just continues to amaze me at her humor and her new ideas, and then the quality of her constructing and clues . . . really, she does everything well. She's a constructor that I really don't feel I have to edit much. So she's terrific.

Martin Ashwood-Smith: He does marvelous constructions with fifteen-letter answers running parallel to each other. I admire that a lot. Here's someone I should've mentioned earlier: Manny Nosowsky. He has lots of crosswords in the *Times*. His constructions are just beautiful, and he's a pleasure to work with, a pleasure to get puzzles from.

Alan Arbesfeld has done a lot of remarkable things, like the D-Day puzzle in which every clue started with the letter D, and all the theme answers were familiar two-word phrases starting with Ds as well. Wow!

Nancy Salomon is very good. I accept most of the puzzles she sends me. She's a wonderful person, too. She mentors other crossword constructors. She seems happy to look at puzzles that new constructors have made and comment on them and tell them what she likes and what she thinks will sell with crossword editors. Randy Ross—he's one of the top-notch people. Fred Piscop—should've mentioned him before. He's one of the best cluers. I hardly edit his clues at all. He's fast, he's good, he's easy to work with. Here's another newcomer—he just started contributing to me last year, and I think other markets within the previous six months or so: His name is Greg Staples. He's done some very innovative puzzles. Bob Klahn: He's another top-notch puzzlemaker, who was responsible for some of the most celebrated puzzles I've edited. Those are a few people who jump to mind—not an exhaustive list.

BARRY TUNICK: No constructor is far and away the best, but I enjoy the work of a large tier of top puzzlemakers. In no particular order: Mike Shenk, Matt Gaffney, Rich Norris, Nancy Salomon, Harvey Estes, Bob Klahn, Merl Reagle, Sylvia and me, Richard Silvestri, Stan Newman, Mel Rosen, Trip Payne, Rathvon & Cox, Francis Heaney, Frank Longo, Manny Nosowsky, Henry Hook, Fred Piscop . . . and five people whose names will no doubt come to me as soon as I [finish this].

FRANCIS HEANEY: Mike Shenk and Henry Hook are personal favorites of mine. In terms of non-"straight" crosswords, Patrick Berry is probably the best. He certainly has the broadest variety of puzzles. Mike Selinker is very good, although having edited him, I know he's not perfect. Patrick is close; Mike is very close. I did some of his early puzzles which had some dubious entries, and I think they fit perfectly well with the standards of the time, but I think the standards have upgraded as the years go on. Mike Selinker is such an envelope-pusher—sometimes he just goes crazy. But that's a good thing. That should happen more. Merl's another one who's great. I'm also fond of Cathy Millhauser.

BOB KLAHN: Mike Shenk, Henry Hook, Cathy Millhauser, Merl Reagle. I love Emily and Henry, too.

ARTHUR S. VERDESCA: Frank Longo, Joe DiPietro, Martin Ashwood-Smith. The latter for his incredible grids. Longo for his overflowing talent in words, themes, inventiveness. DiPietro for his great word skill. Merl Reagle is very, very fine but a little self-indulgent.

LEONARD WILLIAMS: The names that come to mind are Fred Piscop, Manny Nosowsky, and Rich Norris.

WILLIAM R. MACKAYE: New folks have been coming along. I am particularly interested in getting in as much as I can with the younger crowd, so I'm always looking for young constructors. Matt Gaffney is one of my protégés. He now is all over the place, but he started with me. He lives here in Washington, and he's one of the few constructors that I actually know personally. Carole Anne Nelson, who also I think constructs only for us, works here in Washington, and I know her as well. Other than those two, it's pretty much the standard crowd—the people that you see in the *Times*; many of them submit here as well. It's Lou Sabin, or Lou and Francine Sabin, Alfio Micci.

BILL ZAIS: Manny Nosowsky, Nancy Salomon, Franny Hansen, and Mike Shenk are my current favorites. My all-time favorite constructor was Ernst Theimer, followed by William Lutwiniak and Eugene Maleska.

SUNDAY BEST

These are a few of their favorite themes.

MERL REAGLE: I did one called "Hit Song": It was Sean Penn's version of "My Way." It took a long time to get the phrasing right, because I wanted MY WAY to be the very last five-letter entry in the lower right corner of the puzzle. So it had to start with a five-letter entry at 1-Across to make the symmetry work. And it helps if you sing it: I'M IN A / RUSH, NO PICTURES / PLEASE, OR / ELSE YOU'LL LEARN THE / BLACKENED EYE WAY / THE RECORD SHOWS I'LL / BUST YOUR / NOSE IF YOU GET IN . . . / MY WAY. Of course, this was way back then in the 1980s when I was actually creative.

NANCY JOLINE: The one I'm most proud of is the one Will Shortz asked me to do for one of the millennium issues of the *New York Times* magazine last year. There were six of these issues during 1999. I was the only woman to do a puzzle for one; and it was, of course, the issue about women. (The puzzle theme was famous females in film.) These puzzles had to be 25 × 25, and required two sets of clues: hard and easy. I was given six weeks in which to complete the job. Constructing a 25 × 25, I found, is not just a little harder than a 21 × 21 or 23 × 23, it's ten times harder. There are so many more areas feeding into each other! I'd wake up at night thinking, "I can't do this!" But eventually I did, and it turned out quite well, although I'm not in a hurry to do another any time soon. (When I read one day that these millennium issues were going into the *Times* time capsule, I said to my husband: "I'm going to be in the *Times* capsule!" "Do you think you'll fit?" he replied.)

BOB KLAHN: Certainly my greatest thrill as a constructor came in helping New York City lawyer Bill Gottlieb propose to his fiancée, Emily Mindel. Because Emily solves the *Times* crossword religiously, day in and day out, Bill thought it would be a great medium for his early 1998 proposal. Bill contacted the *Times* and Will contacted me. The resultant 15 × 15 featured the Jonathan Swift tract (A) MODEST PROPOSAL, Gary Lewis and the Playboys' 1965 THIS DIAMOND RING, and the Paula Abdul 1992 hit

WILL YOU MARRY ME, plus BILL G (clued in terms of Bill Gates), EMILY (in terms of Ms. Dickinson), MINDEL (split horizontally into MIND and ELope), and various entries dealing with bachelorhood, high hopes, love, sharing, and nervousness—all designed to resonate with Emily as she solved. The puzzle ran, it resonated, sleepless Bill popped the question, and Emily responded with 57-Down, "Hoped-for response to 56-Across," YES.

[Another] of the puzzles I most enjoyed constructing was the one Will asked me to do for Bill Clinton's second inauguration. Titled "Presidential Punditry," it featured entries such as THE BIG TIPPER, DIRECTLY TO YALE, and CHELSEA GRAMMAR. Clinton was given an advance copy of that weekend's *New York Times Magazine*; and, according to press secretary Mike McCurry, he was far more interested in solving my puzzle that Saturday than working on his inaugural address. Later he spoke about my puzzle in an address to the Democratic National Committee. He mentioned HOPE DREAMS, but said his favorite entry (mine also) carried the clue "Mathematical rules governing the Vice President's macarena?" The answer: AL GORE RHYTHMS.

The grid came out quite well. The theme entries were spaced at equal intervals, from the fourth to the twentieth row. My goal for the background fill was to have three triple stacks of lively sevens across the top and the same across the bottom; I was able to achieve that, and I think the result is quite beautiful.

Another favorite, which Will also commissioned that year, was "World War True," published on the fiftieth anniversary of VE-Day, again a 23 × 23 with five twenty-three-letter theme entries, each being a little-known fact about the war. There you learned that (1) "The German troops' marching song was derived from _____" (HARVARD'S "FIGHT! FIGHT! FIGHT!"), (2) "Hitler's blitzkrieg theory was based on the _____" (WORK OF A BRITISH HISTORIAN), (3) "The first non-Britisher to receive Britain's Dickin Medal for Gallantry was a _____" (CARRIER PIGEON NAMED G.I. JOE), (4) "Negotiations leading to the surrender of German troops in Italy _____" (HAD THE CODE NAME "CROSSWORD"), and (5) "The BBC promoted V-for-Victory in musical Morse code by frequently broadcasting _____" (BEETHOVEN'S FIFTH SYMPHONY).

SAM BELLOTTO, JR.: The puzzle which, to date, I've received the most fan mail about has been "Rosetta Stone," published by Simon & Schuster. "Rosetta Stone" was a quotation-themed puzzle. Interestingly, the quotation was by Ralph Waldo Emerson on acrostics. What made it original was that the thematic entries were encrypted. The solver, therefore, not only had to solve the crossword, but solve the cryptogram as well. This in itself would be way too difficult. That's where the title "Rosetta Stone" comes in. To make it a bit easier, the cryptogram used a simple alphabet-offset key. The clue to 1-Across was "Genie offering/Key to puzzle's theme." The answer was WISH. But if you look at it another way, the answer was W is H: the key to the alphabet offset.

W X Y Z A B C D E F G . . .
H I J K L M N O P Q R . . .

I got quite a bit of mail, all of it very positive if frustrated. And I'm still getting comments from solvers!

JOHN SAMSON: In 1999, I was asked to construct a special puzzle to publicize the launch of Stephen King's *Bag of Bones*. It was a 15 × 15 puzzle that appeared in an ad in the *New York Times*. The theme of the puzzle was a blurb to buy the book. I was sent an advance copy of the book, which I later asked Stephen King to sign. Not only did he sign it, he drew a little crossword diagram on the title page with the following clues: 1-Across "Not just good" (4 letters); 2-Down "If they were horses, beggars would ride" (6 letters). When solved, it read BEST WISHES; and on the next page was, "Thanks for Everything!—Stephen King." (I was later told Mr. King solved Simon & Schuster puzzles as preparation for the crossword references in this book.) I wrote him back saying the crossword showed promise, and any time he wanted to submit a crossword to me feel free to do so—"I like helping talented new constructors get published!"

FRED PISCOP: There was one I did for the *Times* that was a lot of fun. It involved puns on Indian tribes. Things like APACHE FOG, SO SIOUX ME, THE SAD SAC, and so on.

TRIP PAYNE: This is one of my favorites: it was called "Career Woman," and there were seven theme entries, most of them intersecting. This was a 21 × 21. All of the clues were things like, "Résumé item: 1993," "Résumé item: 1985," and so forth. They all led to very different things. There was BASEBALL PLAYER, PRESIDENTIAL CANDIDATE, TEACHING ASSISTANT, and so on [*see below*]. And you're thinking, "Who on earth has this résumé?" The last entry across is "Owner of the résumé," and it's BARBIE. That was one of my favorites—I was very happy with the way it turned out. That's an example of a good punch line, because it's the last entry across.

"Résumé item: 1965" = STUDENT TEACHER; "Résumé item: 1985" = BUSINESS EXECUTIVE; "Résumé item: 1985" = TV NEWS REPORTER; "Résumé item: 1990" = ICE CAPADES STAR; "Résumé item: 1991" = NAVAL PETTY OFFICER; "Résumé item: 1992" = PRESIDENTIAL CANDIDATE; "Résumé item: 1993" = BASEBALL PLAYER; "Owner of the résumé" = BARBIE.

[Another favorite was titled] "AAAA into Solving" (17 × 17, *GAMES World of Puzzles*, 1995). [It included] "Long-simmered veggies" = STEWED TOMOOOOOOOO; "Immediate celebrities" = OVERNIGHT SSSSSS; "Gibson Girl's time" = THE GAY TTTTTTTTT; "Traveling worldwide, perhaps" = SAILING THE CCCCCCC.

NORMAN WIZER: One of my favorite puzzles I did a long time ago was on *Casablanca*. I had all the stars in it, clued as "Actor from London," "Actor from Sweden," "Actor from Hungary," "Actor from New York," etc. In the middle, I had going around in a square: HERE'S LOOKING AT YOU, KID.

My favorite puzzle is one that I sent to [Simon & Schuster]. It was a flapper puzzle and was a story. The definitions are, "She thought he was _____ (THE CAT'S PAJAMAS) in his raccoon coat!" "He thought she was _____ (THE BEE'S KNEES) in her _____ (FLAPPER DRESS)!" "He took her to a speakeasy where they had _____ (BATHTUB GIN)... and danced the _____ (CHARLESTON)." "She shimmied like _____ (MY SISTER KATE)!" "He asked, 'How about _____ (MAKIN' WHOOPEE)?" "She pondered, _____ (WHAT'S A GIRL TO DO)?"

MERL REAGLE: I did one called "Spot the Fake," and this was a puzzle where there were names of famous paintings where you had to pick out the ones that were the real ones. Let's see.... AMERICAN GOTHIC? That's real. WASHINGTON CROSSING THE DELAWARE TURNPIKE? That's a fake. BIRTH OF VENUS? That's real. MADONNA AND JULIA CHILD? That's a fake.

JIM PAGE: [*On his* New York Times–*published puzzle "Unglue the Clues," in which you "unglued" the clues to come up with the answers. For example: STONEWALLED = BOULDERSTREET MCMAHON (Stone; Wall; Ed)*]: Gene [Maleska] sent me a note apropos of that puzzle—I happened to be going to Russia at the time—and he said, "Well, it's a good thing you're going to be in Moscow when 'Unglue the Clues' hits the fan." He liked that puzzle, but that was kind of early on in his career at the *Times*, and he was a little concerned about the viewer reaction to it. There was quite a bit of it, to say the least. But Gene was adventuresome.

I did one I rather liked called "Buried Cities," which had cities buried in the thematic entries. For example, QUINTESSENCES has the city ESSEN buried in it, and [the clue] was "German city comes across with top grades." "Pennsylvania city is involved in unforgettable event": EXPERIENCE; ERIE.

[Others were] "Do the Math" (for Will Shortz): Clue numbers plus added numbers = the grid answer (22 + 43 = RETIREMENT AGE; 32. − 32 = FREEZING POINT). "Playing with Matches" (for Eugene Maleska): Tuskincisor = CLENCHED TEETH; Saxantler = LOCKED HORNS. "Clueless" (for Shortz): Used clue numbers only; for example 21. GAMBLERS CARD GAME; 13. ROMAN XIII.

> ## THE SHORTZ REPORTZ
>
> Who's had the most Sunday puzzles in the *New York Times*? (Date range: November 21, 1993, the beginning of Shortz's editorship, through October 22, 2000.)
>
> 1. Tie: Cathy Millhauser and Nancy Joline (24 puzzles each)
> 2. Randolph Ross (21)
> 3. David Kahn (17)
> 4. Tie: Matt Gaffney and Richard Silvestri (14)
> 5. Tie: Rich Norris and Manny Nosowsky (13)
> 6. Tie: Frances Hansen and Nancy Salomon (12)
> 7. Charles Deber (11)
>
> This list includes everyone who's in double digits. Following them are Harvey Estes and Frank Longo (9); Dean Niles, Fred Piscop, and Robert Wolfe (8); Elizabeth Gorski, Bob Klahn, and Fran and Lou Sabin (7); and Joe DiPietro, Peter Gordon, Martin Schneider, and Bryant White (5).

DAVID J. KAHN: One puzzle I'm particularly fond of appeared in a Sunday *New York Times* in December 1996, titled "To Make a Long Story Short." The horizontal theme entries were:

EDWARD TUDOR A ROYAL HEIR
MEETS TOM CANTY A POOR LAD
BY CHANCE THEY SWAP ROLES
EDWARD WITH TOM'S SUPPORT
REGAINS RULE BY LOCATING
THE GREAT SEAL OF ENGLAND

Interlocking with all of the above was THE PRINCE AND THE PAUPER reading vertically through the middle of the grid.

Another favorite was one I co-authored with my daughter Hillary, titled "Green Eggs and Hamlet." It appeared in the *New York Times Sunday Magazine* on May 17, 1998. The eight theme entries, all reading horizontally, were:

I DO NOT LIKE MY DAD'S BROTHER
POISONED KING, WED MY MOTHER
I LET THEM THINK THAT I AM MAD
OOPS! I STABBED OPHELIA'S DAD
NOBODY HELPS ME IN MY PLIGHT
NOW LAERTES AND I WILL FIGHT
SWORDS ARE SWITCHED IN A JAM
A THEATRICAL ENDING; HAM I AM

Genius . . . is the capacity to see ten things where the ordinary man sees one, and where the man of talent sees two or three, plus the ability to register that multiple perception in the material of his art.
—EZRA Pound

JON DELFIN: I once made a deliberately unfair puzzle full of wretched puns and jokes and invalid grid entries. [It] was distributed with annotated answers. [The] only bit I can remember without digging it out: For clue "Stout relative," the answer was JANE, and the annotation said "Have you ever *seen* my aunt Jane?"

MAURA JACOBSON: One of my favorite themes was . . . it was like a story. I started out by saying, "A monastery was in financial trouble, so they went _____" The answer was INTO THE FISH AND CHIPS BUSINESS. I forget what the words were in the puzzle, but . . . "A customer knocked on the door and a robed figure answered. The customer asked 'Are you the fish friar?' " And the answer was NO, I AM THE CHIP MONK.

MERL REAGLE: I like cooking a theme—that is, I like doing a theme that, once it's done, no one else can do the same theme without repeating all the same answers. I did a puzzle called "Inside Woody Allen" in which all the theme answers contained the word ANGST. Now, there are not too many phrases that actually contain ANGST. So you get ANGSTROM UNITS and GANG-STER and HANGS TEN, and I think I even had CHANG'S TWIN, clued as "Eng." The last one down at the bottom was TOO DANG STUPID, and the clue was something like, "Vern, how come I can't solve these here cross-word thangs?" "Well, Ernest, because you're _____."

CORAL AMENDE: One of my favorites from the old days (pre–*Los Angeles* maga-zine) was the blandly titled "A Number of Things." In the grid were ONE FINE DAY (clued as "Time to pay parking tickets?"), TWO-TIMERS ("Hour-glass, stopwatch"), THREE CHEERS ("Yippee, huzzah, ole"), FOUR TOPS ("Basque, halter, shirt, pullover"), FIVE STARS ("Regulus, Sol, Arcturus, Bellatrix, Pollux"), SIX-SHOOTERS (".22, .30–30, .32, .38, .44, .45"), SEVEN SEAS ("Black, Red, Dead, North, Arabian, Coral, Beaufort"), EIGHT BALLS ("Foot, snow, soft, eye, cue, basket, hand, base"), NINEPINS ("Safety, bobby, hair, straight, clothes, bowling, king, stick, hat"), and TEN-SPEEDS ("R, N, 1, 2, 3, 4, D, fast, slow, rapid").

For the sophisticated, sarcasm-loving *Los Angeles* magazine audience, I liked what I call "snotty" themes. These include things like "How to Be an Actor" (SLEEP WITH MADONNA; RUN FOR SENATOR; DENY THAT YOU'RE GAY) and "How to Be an Actress" (SLEEP WITH WARREN BEATTY; DO A WORKOUT VIDEO; DENY YOU HAVE IMPLANTS).

NANCY SALOMON: It's hard to pick a favorite, but I think my two top picks in the 15 × 15 category are both *New York Times* puzzles. The first ran on Septem-ber 23, 1997. The theme entries, all clued with "Dieter's Credo," were

LIGHTEN UP, TAKE A LOAD OFF, BE A GOOD LOSER, and THINK FAST. My other choice is a 15 × 15 I co-authored with Harvey Estes. It ran in the *New York Times* on December 16, 1999. The three theme entries, all running vertically, were TARZAN THE APEMAN, SOMEBODY GREASED, [and] THE VIIIIIIIINE. The latter two entries are clued as last words of the first entry.

Bill Zais and I partnered on a 15 × 15 puzzle that ran in the *New York Times* on December 9, 1999. In addition to the three "normal" theme entries related to buried treasure (SPANISH MAIN, [X marks] THE SPOT, and TREASURE MAP), there were two diagonal entries forming an X (DIAMONDS AND GOLD, EMERALDS AND JADE).

WILL SHORTZ: Cathy Millhauser did a puzzle called "Eland." This was a Sunday *Times* puzzle in which the only vowel was E. That was a tour-de-force construction. Then there was a very nice puzzle recently by a new constructor named Bill Zais, along with Nancy Salomon, that had a treasure hunt–related theme. The theme answers included SPANISH MAIN, TREASURE MAP, and things like that. When the puzzle was finished, the main diagonal from the upper left to the lower right spelled DIAMONDS AND GOLD, and the other diagonal, running from the lower left to the upper right, formed EMERALDS AND JADE. That was quite a feat of construction. It's hard enough just to have words interlock in two ways. To have a triple interlock like that is amazing.

LIKE MINDED

Crossword constructors tell us what they like about their avocation.

SYLVIA BURSZTYN: When I was a kid I wanted to know everything. Now that I write crosswords, people think I know everything.

RICH SILVESTRI: All the groupies. No, wait—that's the best thing about being a mathematician.

MARTIN ASHWOOD-SMITH: Getting paid for a hobby!

PETER GORDON: Getting to solve puzzles all day.

SAM BELLOTTO, JR.: Sleeping late. Not having to wear ties. Being able to watch afternoon cartoon shows on TV. I love cartoons. Going to Mendon Ponds with the dog at a moment's notice. My dog likes the latter very much, as well.

MAURA JACOBSON: Since I had to stop tennis because I have a knee problem, I find that if I didn't have [construction] to do, I think I'd go bananas. I enjoy doing it. I'm a puzzle person. And I get to work at home, which is great.

GAYLE DEAN: The creativity that it requires always challenges me, and I love being able to live in any part of the country and work at home. It's also very nice to be able to work while traveling.

NELSON HARDY: Coming up with horrible puns. Walking into a grocery store two thousand miles from my home and seeing my name in a magazine. And being able to wear my pajamas all day if I want to.

ELIZABETH GORSKI: I like to entertain through my puzzles.

WILLIAM CANINE: It is just so much fun—and so satisfying.

NANCY JOLINE: (a) I love the rush I get every time I take up my pencil to begin a new puzzle, with the grid and theme entries in place. Each puzzle is a new challenge. I guess I love the mental exercise. I described it to someone once as feeling as if my brain cells were tiny gymnasts doing their thing for me in my head. If that sounds nuts, so be it. (b) I love the constant learning of new things that puzzle making brings. (c) I love the friends I've made through constructing, getting together with them for lunches in New York, or for the tournament in Stamford, or by e-mail. (d) I love hearing from friends and acquaintances, and the occasional strangers, who have seen my puzzles in different parts of the world.

PATRICK JORDAN: I think it's the knowledge that, whenever one of my puzzles is published, I am entertaining thousands of people across the country and yet remaining anonymous enough to go to the grocery store without having to wear dark glasses!

DAVID MACLEOD: The knowledge that on publication day there are millions of solvers around the world doing my puzzle. I can't sing, dance, or act, so this is how I entertain people.

CATHY MILLHAUSER: I love making the grids—the challenge of solving difficult areas of the grid without resorting to a computer program. And I like hearing from people that I've brightened their day—that my puzzle has made them laugh or think about something in a new way.

MANNY NOSOWSKY: It's fun!

ARTHUR S. VERDESCA: It is a creative outlet. It isn't the Sistine ceiling; it isn't the late Beethoven quartets; but it is creative nonetheless.

LEONARD WILLIAMS: It's a fabulous way to pursue my longstanding fascination with words and to have an outlet for creative expression.

DAVID J. KAHN: The creativity involved.

BILL ZAIS: Tapping into any form of creativity is always a rush.

TOM SCHIER: The freedom to create when I want, where I want, and on any subject I want to integrate into a grid.

MEL TAUB: It's a stimulating, creative pastime that has provided great pleasure over the years, not to mention a little extra spending money and a touch of celebrity (only a touch).

PETER GORDON: Watching strangers on the train or in the park solve my puzzle, then introducing myself and seeing their strange reactions.

RICH NORRIS: I was in my local auto dealer's waiting room while my car was being serviced. The guy across from me was solving the day's *New York Times* puzzle, which just happened to be one I'd constructed. I waited for him to finish, then asked him how he liked it. He said it was fine, "not too hard," and said to me, "Did you solve it yet?" I said, "I wrote it." He looked a bit surprised, and said, "Really? Are you"—and here he glanced down at the puzzle in his lap—"Will Shortz?" (The constructor's name is there, of course, under the puzzle. It's just that it's about one-fifth the size of Will's name, which appears at the top.)

CHRIS JOHNSON: Sadistic pleasure in watching people try to solve my puzzles. Being able to work from home doing something I enjoy.

SHAWN KENNEDY: I find satisfaction in knowing that my puzzles provide entertainment for other people. I also enjoy the fan mail that I receive. It encourages me to keep on going.

TRIP PAYNE: It is nice, occasionally, when I mention what I do, and they say, "Oh, I think I've seen your puzzles." Whether they have or not, that's nice to hear. I actually have had a few people where I haven't said what I did, I've just said my name, and they knew immediately who I was. Not often.

NANCY SALOMON: I enjoy making puzzles, and I am delighted with all the friends I've made in the crossword construction/solver community. There's quite a bit of ego gratification in seeing one's puzzles in print.

RICH NORRIS: The people I've met and gotten friendly with. The camaraderie and supportiveness within the industry. People help each other at all levels. Yes, there's competition, but there's very little backstabbing. The other guy actually wants to see you succeed. And of course, I like the challenge of working on each new project, and the infinite varieties that our language offers.

BARRY TUNICK: Working and playing with words, and meeting people who like working and playing with words. Also the looks I get when I tell people what I do.

CROSSFIRE

Woe betide the puzzle editor who fathers deformed brain children, or is a victim of the typesetter or proofreader. Puzzle solvers take their pastime mighty seriously and will not overlook even the occasional faux pas permitted other departments of a publication. The puzzle man is expected by his editor in chief and his public to sail along pretty close to 100 percent with respect to accuracy, if he hopes to preserve his job and his good name.
—Sam Loyd, Jr.

WILLIAM R. MACKAYE: A recent puzzle that I thought was an absolute tour-de-force: [the *Washington Post*'s] Fourth of July puzzle [of 2000]. What the constructor [Richard Thomas] had done was take the postal abbreviations of the names of the thirteen original states, and put those two letters in a single square. That was how the puzzle was laid out: Each one showed up just once, and nowhere else in the puzzle did those particular combinations of letters appear. That was a brilliant construction job.

I got letters from people who just could not understand what was going on. "Why in the world were the two letters in the same square? There's something wrong here! There's some sort of horrendous mistake!" They just didn't understand, and they didn't pick up on what the letters were that were doubled up—they didn't see that even though they crossed. It was strange—it was like solver blindness. The idea of putting more than one letter in a square is not all that unusual; what was unusual about this puzzle was that it wasn't always the same pair of letters. But if you studied what the letters were, it soon became evident that this was the thirteen original states. I was so pleased with it. I'm sure there were people who loved it, but there certainly were those that hated it as well.

MERL REAGLE: I *hate* making mistakes. I think within one month I made two pretty big ones. That bothers the hell out of me. I had Troy Aikman going to the wrong school, going to USC instead of UCLA, and that was a huge mistake. There are some things you just won't know. I had SKEIN in a puzzle, clued as "Ball of yarn." Of course, it's not a ball of yarn; it's a thing that you roll into a ball of yarn. I heard from a professional yarn person. And when I looked it up, I said, "You're right." All these years, I thought it was a ball of yarn.

Some things you don't even realize could possibly be wrong are wrong. I had OTTO in a puzzle—and I should have a whole list of Ottos, and I do: Kevin Kline played Otto in *A Fish Called Wanda* . . . other than the usual "Otto von Bismarck" things. But I thought I remembered that Harvey Lembeck had played Otto Von Zipper in all those Frankie and Annette beach movies. But it's *Eric* Von Zipper. Otto Zipper is a big car dealership in Beverly Hills. I used to live in L.A.—that's how I got them mixed up. I hate making a movie mistake in the *Los Angeles Times*. Hate it. I know those movies—I've seen them a million times. So I have an editor now who checks all those things for me—probably long overdue. It's one of those things where you think, "Oh . . . yeah . . . right . . . crap!" You looked at it a couple of times, and it just looked as right as it could be. We do like to rely on our knowledge—that is one thing about crossword puzzle people. If you aren't kind of sure of what you know, you probably aren't going to be in the business anyway. But sometimes it'll bite you.

WILL SHORTZ: Stephen Sondheim wrote me pointing out an error in a crossword that related to one of his own lyrics. He's a solver and a puzzlemaker himself. The clue was " 'Aren't we _____' " (Sondheim lyric)" for the answer A PAIR. He wrote me that he was pleased to see his name in the puzzle, but that the lyric was actually "*Are* we a pair." He was very nice about the mistake.

SYLVIA BURSZTYN: Early on, we used to get letters from solvers who assumed we also wrote the weekday puzzles. One peevish solver complained that the weekday puzzles were awful, amateurish, and simplistic; that they couldn't hold a candle to the work of his idol, Margaret Farrar. I tried to be as flat in tone as possible in my reply, which was that the weekday puzzles were supplied to the *Times* by Margaret Farrar.

BARRY TUNICK: One big mistake was the *Los Angeles Times*'s replacing its regular Sunday crossword with my cryptic—with no instructions on how to do

ORGANIZATION MAN

How Eugene T. Maleska classified his "civilian" correspondents:

Sleepers: Satisfied solvers who think highly of editors and constructors and usually write in with pats on the back; when they think they've found an error, they're incredulous.

Squawkers: Bitter pills who write to the paper's editors complaining about things over which the crosswords editor has no control or who are really mad they couldn't finish a puzzle.

Leapers: Those who rush to dash off a nasty letter correcting something that doesn't need correcting.

Quibblers: "Somewhere between squawkers and leapers"

Gotchas: Letter writers who make valid corrections to clues and other factual errors; Maleska called them "a mixture of cool customers who know their onions, their literature, movies, geography, foreign languages, sports, music, and other fields in which I occasionally reveal my humanity by making an error."

cryptics! They got four thousand letters and phone calls about it, of which ninety-nine-point-something were against the switch. (Subscription cancellations were the least of it: There were suicide and death threats. A typesetter told me his neighbor threatened to burn his house down if the standard crossword wasn't reinstated.) After four weeks, Sylvia Bursztyn's and my regular 21 × 21 appeared. Looking back, our first puzzles were awful—lots of "var." and "obs." entries, and unimaginative cluing. When we readied them for our Random House anthologies, we rewrote entire sections—as much as half of a puzzle. Some of our biggest mistakes weren't that early. My cluing BOULDER, COLORADO, as "Air Force Academy site"—it slipped past Sylvia and our two proofers. I spent a week apologetically answering solvers' "Gotcha!" letters.

JOHN SAMSON: Simon & Schuster [*for whom Samson edits crossword collections*] has two sets of copyeditors and proofreaders, who carefully scrutinize every crossword book. (Don't ask me how mistakes manage to find their way in there!)

MERL REAGLE: Here's one funny thing that happened. I had a puzzle called "United Nations." The idea was that all the theme clues were only half there—you had to add "nation" to all of them to get the real clue, which in turn led to the real answer. For example, if the clue were "Stag?" you first had to add "nation" to it to get "stagnation" and that was the real clue, so the answer would turn out to be POOL PROBLEM, or some such. Well, one of the clues was "Tar?", which led to "tarnation," which led to the answer, FARMER'S EXCLAMATION. Now, the M of FARMER happened to cross the M of NIHILISM. And I got a letter from a lady saying she accidentally wrote in NIHILIST instead of NIHILISM and got quite a surprise.

ERICA ROTHSTEIN: I'll never forget: Somebody wrote to us about a Maleska puzzle called "Euphemisms." He had things in it like DARN YANKEES and LILLIAN HECKMAN. Somebody actually wrote to us to say, "Don't you know the name of that play is *Damn Yankees*?" None of the other things in the puzzle—she didn't complain about any of them. It was only DARN YANKEES! Nothing else was wrong. It was like, "Well, I guess this one didn't work for you, honey!"

WILLIAM CANINE: I remember once when I'd defined OMNI as "Home of the Hawks," this solver informed me that nowhere in his ornithological experience had he heard of a hawk's nest so described.

MEL TAUB: In my working days, I commuted from Brooklyn home to Manhattan office by subway. One day, a woman seated next to me marveled at the speed with which I completed the daily puzzle. Her husband was good, said she, but I left him in the dust. The lady got on the train the stop after I did, and we'd meet fairly often. One Monday, she got on carrying Sunday's magazine section. She showed me the puzzle page. Her husband had completed the main puzzle, but my Puns & Anagrams at the bottom was in mint condition. Her spouse, said she, didn't know how to do them. I offered to explain the tricks which she, in turn, could explain to her husband. After analyzing several clues with her, I went on to complete the puzzle in a couple of minutes. She was aghast. After a bit of banter I pointed to the byline and said, "That's me." She wouldn't believe it until I showed some ID.

BARRY TUNICK: Once, as a crossword contest judge in Los Angeles, I was confronted by an audience of ace solvers who asked why I didn't make the *Los Angeles Times* puzzles harder. Alluding to *The Rocky Horror Show*'s Dr. Frank N. Furter's response to Janet (who didn't like Rocky), I said, "Well, I don't make them for you!"

LOADED QUESTIONS

Funny how most civilian solvers seem to be curious about the exact same things.

WILLIAM CANINE: Behind all the questions lies amazement that a human being actually constructs these crosswords. I wonder where they think they come from.

BARRY TUNICK: I'm sure I'm not the only constructor to have been asked, "Which do you do first, fill in the grid or write the clues?"

RAY HAMEL: "Do you write the puzzle or the clues first?"

PETER GORDON: "Do you write the grid first or the clues first?"

JON DELFIN: "What comes first, the answers or the clues?"

MIKE SHENK: Everybody in the business, the one question they probably think of first is the silly one where people ask if you do the clues first or the grids first.

NORMAN WIZER: They all say, "How do you do it?" But I think the funniest question I was ever asked was, "Do you do the definitions first or do you do the answers first?" It's also funny that some people do not realize that the grids are symmetrical.

FRANCIS HEANEY: Mostly they just want to know how the heck I got into this business. They have no idea. They're sort of curious about how many people have that job. I know Trip Payne's favorite complaint is people who ask him whether he writes the grid or the clues first. I was relating that story to someone else, assuming them to be a clever person, that they would immediately grasp what I was saying, and they were like, "But which one *would* you do first?"

ELIZABETH GORSKI: The most common question is "Why do you make puzzles?" My answer is, I don't know why, I just like to do it. I consider it an art form.

TRIP PAYNE: There are the unanswerable questions and comments, like, "Boy, you must be really smart." "You must know a lot of words." "What did you study at Emory to get here?" Their thought is, "What did you take in school that led to puzzles?" Then there's the inevitable, "Well, I don't really solve crosswords much myself. I'm not very good at that. But my uncle Harold— he does them all the time, and he does them in ink, and he can do the *New York Times* crossword puzzle in an hour usually." I'm supposed to care. It's like, "Oh, you know somebody who does crossword puzzles! What a coincidence!" It's not like there aren't fifty million active solvers around.

KELLY CLARK: Most people presume that, because I make puzzles, I must be an expert solver. So the most common question I get is "How can you do that? I can't even solve puzzles, never mind make them!"

JOE DIPIETRO: "How much does a puzzle pay?" "Where do you get ideas from?"

RICH NORRIS: "Where do you get your ideas from?" "How much do they pay for a puzzle?" "How long does it take to make a puzzle?" "How many puzzles do you make in a week/month/year?" And my favorite of all: "When you make a puzzle, do you write the clues first, or put the words in the little boxes?"

RICH SILVESTRI: "How long does it take you to make a puzzle?" "How much do you get paid?" "Can I have your autograph?" (Two out of three are true.)

DAVID J. KAHN: "Civilians" sometimes ask me whether the clues are written at the beginning or the end of the process.

MERL REAGLE: The most common question I get is just, "How the hell do you do it?" I think, for a lot of people, it's beyond understanding. If they really thought about it, though, they would see it's really a straightforward, A-B-C process, no pun intended. Even if the puzzle has no theme, there's a way to go about doing it. I think it's because they've never really thought about it seriously, and don't know what the rules are. You can't be clever on every clue, nor should you be.

NELSON HARDY: "But aren't they all made by computers?"

SYLVIA BURSZTYN: A well-meaning friend of mine once asked why is it that I always have to get my part of the job done first. "Why can't Barry do his part first?" [*Bursztyn composes the puzzle grids; Tunick writes the clues.*] "How long does it take to write one?" "How did you get into it?" "How much do you get paid?" "Where do you get those words?"

MARTIN ASHWOOD-SMITH: Have I ever constructed a standard crossword without any black squares? (Answer: NO!)

DIANE EPPERSON: "How do you do that?" "You must have a big vocabulary."

GAYLE DEAN: How I got started constructing puzzles. How to break into the business.

PETER GORDON: "What does Will Shortz do as an editor?" "How much does the *Times* pay for a crossword?" (They're always shocked at how little it pays.)

TOM SCHIER: "How do you start to design a crossword?" "How long does it take?" "Is it profitable?"

SAM BELLOTTO, JR.: "Can you make a living just constructing crosswords?" (No.)

CATHY MILLHAUSER: Most people want to know how long each puzzle takes to create and how much it pays. Unfortunately, there is no correlation.

MAURA JACOBSON: "Where do you start?"

PATRICK JORDAN: They usually want to know (1) how I build puzzles, and (2) where I get my theme ideas.

ARTHUR S. VERDESCA: "How do you do them? And where do you find the time?"

SHAWN KENNEDY: "Where do you get your ideas?"

MANNY NOSOWSKY: "Gee, you must know a lot of words."

NANCY JOLINE: Without exception, everyone wants to know, "How long does it take you?"

LEONARD WILLIAMS: "How long does it take to make a puzzle?"

BARRY TUNICK: By far, "How long does it take to make a puzzle?" Second: "How did you get started in the business?" Followed by "Why don't you make the puzzles harder?" and "Why don't you make the puzzles easier?"

MEL TAUB: "How long does it take to make one up?" "How do you go about constructing one?" "Where do you get your ideas?"

BILL ZAIS: "Where do you get your ideas?" "Where in the grid do you start?"

CHRIS JOHNSON: "How long does it take to compose a cryptic?" "How do you go about creating a puzzle?" "Are you that bastard . . . ?"

* * *

Note: For the answers to these and other burning questions about crossword construction, see chapter 4.

EDITORIAL DEPARTMENT

And what about the hands that hold the reins? A puzzle editor's job is rewarding, if difficult—often it means you're doing more construction, in the form of rewriting clues and redoing grids, than editing!

ERICA ROTHSTEIN: Everybody at Dell, at least in the old days, had to be a solver first. If you weren't a solver, you couldn't get a job there, because you wouldn't be able to relate to the people buying the magazine. You didn't have to like everything, but you had to have a basic love of puzzles in some sense.

WILL SHORTZ: I knew exactly what I wanted to do. I'll tell you—during my senior year at Indiana University, I decided I wanted to work for a crossword magazine company for the summer before I went to law school. First I wrote to Dell, because that's where I'd been selling puzzles. They had never had an intern, and they weren't interested in one. So then I wrote all the other companies, and the one that gave me a job was Penny Press. I went to Stamford, Connecticut, and worked there for the summer. Then I worked there for each of the following summers during law school, and then the first seven months as a full-time job after I graduated from law school.

GAMES started in 1977, which was the year I graduated from the University of Virginia Law School. I was twenty-five then. When GAMES came out, I was just enthralled by it: This was the sort of publication that I wanted to work for. Some of the [puzzles] were harder, but more important, they were more sophisticated. There was more care put into their construction. Plus, it wasn't just crosswords—it was all varieties of puzzles. I was just excited by the whole format. I worked for Penny Press from summer 1977 until January 1978 while GAMES was starting up.

Around January or February of 1978, I saw an advertisement in the *Times* for a puzzle editor. It mentioned "quality puzzles." The advertisement was phrased in such a way that I was virtually certain it was for GAMES, even though there was no name attached to the ad. You were supposed to apply to a box number. So I had the brilliant idea that I would beat all the competition by walking into their offices and announcing that I was there for the job. So I put on a coat and tie, I went into *GAMES* and announced I was there for their position. It turned out it was not their ad; they did not have a job open. But the editor saw me anyway, and we hit it off, and later in the year I did get a job with them. Well, for years and years I was the editor of "Pencilwise," which was a sixteen-page section in the middle of the magazine of pencil puzzles: crosswords, Double-Crostics—anything that you can do with a pencil.

The exciting thing about *GAMES* was that it had a younger audience than almost any other puzzle publication. The Dell puzzle magazines—and most newsstand crossword magazines—have quite an older audience: people in their fifties, sixties, and up, and also overwhelmingly female—at least two-thirds, and probably 75 to 80 percent female, whereas *GAMES* had an audience with an average age of thirty-five to forty and was about evenly split between male and female. So it had an audience that was more diverse, more interested in innovation.

TRIP PAYNE: I graduated high school in 1986. My graduation present from my mother was a trip to New York so that I could attend the 1986 U.S. Open tournament, which turned out to be the last one. I went as a judge. I had talked to Will on the phone and asked him if he would mind if I judged, and he said, "Great." I went up there, and at the opening reception party, that was where I met everybody for the first time—I met Mike and Will and Henry and Frances Hansen, and all these people. I was sort of starry-eyed at all of them. I'd never been around a group of people like that before. These were all these names that I knew so well. That was a lot of fun. Toward the end of that tournament—I guess I had a lot of gall—I went up to Will and I said, "Will, I would like to spend my summers working for *GAMES*, as an assistant or whatever you need." And he agreed.

I went to Emory University and helped put myself through college with puzzlemaking. I did make several thousand [dollars] a year, even at that point, with my stuff, to the various books series and so on. During my summer breaks, I went up to New York and worked at *GAMES*. I would stay at Columbia University in one of the dorms, because that was very cheap, and take the subway down to *GAMES*. I started off just sort of being a low-level play-tester, a sub-proofreader, and so on. When there was a simple puzzle that needed to be made, [Will] would sometimes give that to me. Gradually, I started getting more and more responsibility there, and by the end, I certainly wouldn't say I was an equal of Mike [Shenk], but I was getting higher up the editing chain there. I was remaking submitted puzzles, making harder puzzles for them, writing introductions to sections, and all sorts of things he would never have let me do at the beginning. By the end, it was clear that this was going to be my career. That was the plan. I was going to go work at *GAMES* and be an assistant editor. But two days before I graduated from Emory, *GAMES* folded. Two days before!

STAN NEWMAN: Talking to some business colleagues of mine, they thought that I should attempt to do something a bit more to leverage my new [American Crossword Puzzle Tournament winner] titles, [so I] started something called the American Crossword Federation in 1983. Analyzing it with my limited insight at that time, I thought that if I wanted to be in the puzzle business, I needed to be a puzzle editor rather than a constructor. Unwilling to wait for someone to die, which is basically the way puzzle editors get their jobs, I decided to take an unconventional route. Looking back at the earliest newsletters that I published . . . well, I had a lot to learn, but I owned the publication. So I learned how to become a puzzle editor by editing puzzles, developing my own sensibilities and so forth, and developing my own point of view, which eventually I began expounding upon at length in the pages of [*Crossworder's OWN Newsletter*]. There was a domino effect of things after that as a result of the newsletter. As a result of the newsletter, I got my first book contract.

NANCY SCHUSTER: With Will Weng, once he became the editor [of the *New York Times*], I asked him if he needed an assistant. I just wanted to worship at his feet. He didn't, but he said that he knew that Dell used freelancers for crossword editing and recommended me to Kathleen Rafferty.

ERICA ROTHSTEIN: When I got out of college and wanted to move out of the house and move into New York, I went to an employment agency that had found my cousin a job. Oddly enough, it was an employment agency that Mickey Mantle and Joe Namath had put their names to. It was called the Mantle-

Namath Agency. I don't even know why they did such a thing—they weren't there. I was the typical liberal arts college grad who had an interest in a lot of things but no particular burning desire to do much of anything—because I didn't know what was possible.

I was interviewed by someone who said, "I have this job [for a] gofer at Dell, and I think you would be very good for it." I went there and took their tests: There was an editing test and a proofreading test, and I had to write a letter—the same tests we used for the next twenty-five years. I was called back to meet with the editor in chief, who told me that no one had ever done worse on the proofreading test! Fine, okay—I never pretended that I was a good proofreader. I didn't know anything about proofreading. But they ended up calling me and offering me the job. I mean, I never did figure out quite why.

WILLIAM R. MACKAYE: I started working for the *Washington Post* in 1966 and became associate editor of the Sunday magazine about ten years later. They had at that time a so-called puzzle page in the Sunday magazine, in which they were using syndicated puzzles. It was dreadful. It was put together by people who didn't know anything about puzzles, including the crossword that they were using—they didn't understand that you had to run the title. They just tossed away the title and ran it without. I pointed this out to the then-editor, that this wasn't being handled right, and that part of the secret of Sunday crossword puzzles was that solvers needed the title because it told them what the gimmick was in some sort of indirect fashion. He said, "You understand puzzles," and I said, "Yes, I do. I solve them." He said, "Why don't you take over the puzzle page?"

I started shepherding the page, and toward the end of my time there—this would be the early 1980s—I said, "Look, the *Washington Post* is a grown-up newspaper, and it really is pretty stupid that we don't have our own Sunday crossword puzzle, that we're just using a syndicated puzzle which sometimes is okay and sometimes is not okay." They said, "Well, put together a proposal," so I put together a sort of halfhearted proposal of what we might do, and it was floating around in 1986 when I got from the *Post* an offer of a buyout. They were once again going to redesign the magazine, and we had a new editor coming in.

He called me into his office shortly after he arrived, and he said, "Look—I'm going to deal with you straightforwardly on this. I have run up against one of the problems that people have at the *Washington Post*. Namely, I've been handed this assignment of reconfiguring the Sunday magazine, but I was hired into an operation in which there are no empty slots. I have talked with upstairs, and I am prepared to offer you a year's salary to take early retirement so that I can hire my own person." I thought about this, and I'd already been through three redesigns of the magazine. I said [to myself], "I can't stand another redesign of the magazine. Working for the *Post* isn't any fun anymore. Why don't I just get out of here?" So I said, "You've got to give me time enough to refinance my house, and then I'm gone." So I did. I think partly because I was so agreeable about the whole thing, the editor said, "Well, I would like you to take a little part with you— there's this proposal floating around of creating the *Washington Post Magazine* puzzle. Why don't you do it, and we'll take you on as a contractor to do so?" I said, "Fine."

PETER GORDON: When I was thirteen, I bought a subscription to *GAMES*, starting with the March/April 1980 issue (issue #16). I immediately knew that I wanted to work there. I sent them a letter asking if I could work there during the summers. I said that I didn't need to be paid. They said I could work there once I turned eighteen. So two summers during college I worked there, and when I graduated, I knew everybody who worked there. I called the editor, Wayne Schmittberger, and asked if he had any jobs. He said no, but if anything opened up he'd let me know. Two weeks later, someone quit and I got the job. I worked there for five years; then they went bankrupt. When they revived the magazine, I came back and worked there two more years.

FRANCIS HEANEY: I did little bits and pieces here and there. I did a few crosswords for the *New York Times* and some proofreading for Dell. About the time that I got fed up with being a temp and was taking an extended vacation from that, which was about three years later, that was when *GAMES* got bought by the many-tentacled octopus that is Kappa. They had just moved to Philadelphia, and the staff didn't want to move there. They spent a while looking for people to hire in Philadelphia. After a while, they were like, "Huh. Don't have anybody." They started considering other options. Mark

Gottlieb, a friend of mine, was interning with them at the time, and he jokingly said to me, "So, you want an editing job?" I was like, "Well, actually I do need a job." So I called up and said I'd be happy to work as a freelance editor, but I wasn't about to move to Philadelphia. They took me up on it. For a while, I would go out once or twice a month, and they'd stick me in a hotel for a couple of days. I'd do some stuff there and take some stuff home with me—mostly worked by e-mail and fax. The more we did that, the more they realized there wasn't really any point in me actually coming out there.

ERICA ROTHSTEIN: My job was "the desk." I was called "the desk." I barely had a name. I answered the phone and I typed up all the requisitions. I used to type up the requisitions that Will Shortz used to get, because he was a contributor to us when he was sixteen. I'd do Kathleen Rafferty's mail, or whatever else anybody wanted me to do; fill her water bottle. I used to say I was so low on the totem pole that I was the part underground. There just wasn't anything lower on the totem pole than I was. I actually even used to go sit in Dag Hammarskjold Park at lunchtimes and cry because nobody would talk to me. I mean, it was terrible—it was my first job [and I was] away from home. I was lonely.

WILLIAM R. MACKAYE: I didn't know squat about running a puzzle at that point. I knew how to solve puzzles, but I didn't know anything about the crossword puzzle business, which meant that, among other things, I had to find a colleague who knew a lot about it. I came up with William Lutwiniak, now dead, who I signed on as my partner in crime in this operation, as much as anything because he knew who the personnel were in the constructing world. I didn't, and I didn't know how to reach them. So Bill and I formed a partnership, and for the rest of his life we operated as a team. Then, after he died, I took over solo, and I've been doing it since 1986. He could create a very acceptable 15×15 in about thirty minutes. It was just amazing watching him. What I would run into with him—I hate to say I did most of the work. It was his reputation but my back that did a lot of the stuff. When we would get a puzzle that both of us really quite liked, but there would be a section that didn't work too well, I'd say, "Bill, this isn't working, and I really think we need to get rid of this offensive word here." He'd say, "Well, let me scratch my head over it." He'd call me back in about twenty minutes, and he would have redone the corner, and it would be lovely. This happened again and again. Or he would look at it—he had some sort of inner sense on this, and he'd say, "It can't be done. You'd have to redo the whole puzzle. It's not worth the energy."

STAN NEWMAN: I began in 1993 a nine-month consultancy for Random House and submitted what can loosely be called a business plan—I didn't go to business school; I had no idea what a business plan was supposed to look like. I discussed their various books and what I thought was the state of the competition and places where I thought they could do things better and differently, and [how they could] expand. I presented that business plan to the top three or four people in the corporation, from the CEO on down. Before I left the building, they had created this job for me and were offering it to me: to run their puzzle-publishing program. I accepted.

MERL REAGLE: [Stan Newman is] perfect for that job. He's half entrepreneur, half puzzle guy. To be in that position is just great.

PETER GORDON: At Sterling, before I got there, they had no puzzle editor. Most of their books were garbage. They had no idea what they were doing. Now we publish only quality stuff.

NANCY SCHUSTER: Will [Weng] recommended me to [Dell's Kathleen Rafferty], and she interviewed me, and they hired me as a freelancer. In fact, they gave what to me was a great job, because I had to edit the expert-level puzzles—about four per issue. They wanted the challenger puzzle—one per issue—in the style of the *Times*, to make a little departure from their typical style. In those days, what Dell did mattered a great deal in the industry. Puzzle magazines were second in importance only to the *Times* puzzle and were very big sellers on newsstands and by subscription. . . . They were hot stuff then, and maybe the stuff that people used to write about magazine people is true. But it certainly was a different world then. They were high-flying people—they had big expense accounts, and they were glamorous, I suppose you could say.

I worked freelance for Dell from the 1970s until I think about 1980, at home. Then my kids were grown, and I wanted to go out to an office a couple of days a week. I got a job at a publication that lived for a year, and I learned a little bit about the production of puzzles. When that collapsed, the boss suggested we go over to Official Publications—he said, "They hire everybody!" Must've been true, because they did hire us—the artist and me. I was with Official Publications from 1982 until 1988.

ERICA ROTHSTEIN: It was a very small office; only women. Kathleen Rafferty wouldn't have hired a man to save her life. We used to call it Kathleen Rafferty's Catholic Kindergarten for Girls (when they started talking to me, at any rate). It was a very unusual place to work. She was, however, absolutely brilliant as an editor. She never, ever, ever got the credit in the puzzle world that she deserved. She *made* Dell. I mean, without her, Dell puzzle magazines would not have existed. She was an absolute genius.

The other thing was she knew how to hire very good people. She hired Rosalind Moore, who was a crackerjack editor. She taught me about writing and about editing. The two of them were just beyond compare in terms of knowing their business, knowing their solvers, and knowing how to put magazines together that people wanted to buy. And they have never, ever, ever gotten the credit they deserve.

NANCY SCHUSTER: When I was at Dell Champion and I had about five editors, my job was to check what they did or teach them or make final changes. I'd sort of be the last word about what would go. There were many other aspects of the job, but too numerous to mention. It was hard work.

FRANCIS HEANEY: [At *GAMES*] I would get a heap of "Pencilwise" puzzles and was sort of an official "nudge." If I got a crossword and I thought one corner could be improved, I would either do it myself, or if I thought it would be too hard for me to do or I was too busy, I would just point it out to [the constructor] and say, "Why don't you fix it?" I would do that with any puzzle I got—see something I didn't like and either fiddle with it or just complain about it. I did that mostly with clues, because writing clues is far and away my least-favorite part of puzzle constructing. So if I saw a clue I didn't like, I would just basically give [*GAMES*] a list of the clues I wasn't fond of. Grid fixes I would be more likely to do.

ERICA ROTHSTEIN: We were allowed to do freelance work, and we made a lot of puzzles. When we didn't get enough puzzles from constructors to supply our needs, we could make them on our own at home. Other people in the office would test-solve them.

TRIP PAYNE: Nancy Schuster gave me a job at Dell Champion as a proofreader and editor. I did that for about three months (it was a temporary thing that Nancy had given me while I was getting on my feet, which I certainly appreciated), and then got a job editing *Herald-Tribune* crossword puzzles. I was the overall editor there. I edited three titles: *Crossword Puzzles Only, Large Print Crosswords*, and *Crosswords and Other Word Games*. They were all just dreary magazines. How it worked was we would take puzzles that had originally been printed in the 1940s or so, and somebody would reclue them and somebody else would proofread them, and then they'd go into the new issues. There were no computers, nothing. It was just photocopy the puzzles, then cut and paste with glue stick—I'm not kidding. Being editor didn't carry a whole lot of cachet. I also had to answer phones and bag back issues and so on. I kind of appreciate having had that experience, because it really showed me a lot of what goes on behind the scenes that I hadn't really seen before.

I really couldn't stand those puzzles, but Cathy Greenwald, the publisher that I worked with there, was insistent that that's what the people wanted. It was an older audience and people who were very set in their ways, and they liked these old-style puzzles. So I said, "Fine, let's compromise. We'll keep two of the books this way, but in one of the books you have to at least give me a section that I can make interesting." And she agreed to that. With *Crosswords and Other Word Games*, I got Mike Shenk and Mel Rosen and Donna Stone and a bunch of other people to send me two puzzles per issue. It wasn't a lot of money—just forty bucks a puzzle; I think many of them agreed to it just because they could appreciate what I was trying to do. Every issue, I would have twelve or fourteen of these puzzles with themes, with interesting words, with captions. There wasn't much room on these pages, so the clues couldn't get too lengthy or clever, but certainly the grids were a whole lot stronger. So I got to have at least a little fun there, at least. For the other titles, I tried to get my freelance editors to at least take the worst crosswordese out of the grid.

NANCY SCHUSTER: I used to make variety puzzles for Dell—I accepted them myself! Wasn't that nice! I used to only make them when we needed something of the sort I wanted and we didn't have any.

ERICA ROTHSTEIN: [Dell's puzzles] were all right to be solved by kids. Parents didn't have to worry about, when their kid picked up a copy, that the kid would find things that were inappropriate. If a child was intelligent enough and had language skills high enough to be able to solve the puzzles, there wasn't anything in any of our magazines that would have made a parent uncomfortable. Until the famous pill ad.

Once we had to start taking ads, we got this new advertising director who got this ad—it was on the back page of most of our magazines—and it was for these pills. They were supposed to increase your energy and all this other stuff, but there were things on there that were sex-related; the pills were in shapes, and it made it look like they were candy. I went ballistic when I saw the ad. It was a terrible ad. I got into a lot of trouble, because I sent a very, very strong memo about my feelings to my boss, and to my boss's boss. My boss was furious with me. But we also got zillions of letters from people who said they would look for that ad and would never buy that ad, because it wasn't appropriate to leave on the table. And they were absolutely right! We got some of the same letters when they started taking cigarette ads, and they finally stopped. It was meant to be a family entertainment, and it was a disgrace to have something like that on the magazine.

NANCY SCHUSTER: Let me say a good word about Dell: That's the place I was taught to have very high standards of accuracy and not to tolerate any errors at all. They created many kinds of popular puzzles, sought the best constructors, and fully deserved their great success for entertaining and quality puzzles.

ERICA ROTHSTEIN: There was a woman who once asked what the carrot was that Kathleen Rafferty held out in front of us to get us all to work so hard. She had incredibly high standards, and nothing less than perfect was good enough for her. Of course, we couldn't get to perfect, but we damn sure tried. I would hold my hand up at a certain level and I'd say, "If our standards are up to here, people are going to come up to here," and I'd put my hand a good three inches below that. I'd say, "If we lower our standards to here"—which was below the second hand—"people aren't going to work up to that level, they're going to come down." I just saw an article about establishing standards, and how you can't expect people to work up to nothing—that if you don't have standards and you don't have a level of expectation for performance, people will never work up to their full capacity. I mean, they won't even try.

I once had a boss who was not a puzzle person at all—he was a direct-mail expert—and he wanted me to quantify how many mistakes in a magazine were okay. I said, "You can't quantify something like that." He said, "Aw, you can quantify everything." I kept arguing with him, and he insisted, and I said, "Well, fine. If you want a number of how many mistakes is okay in a magazine, the only possible number is zero." He said, "But that's not possible." I said, "Well, of course it's not possible. But that's the only number that's acceptable." That was the philosophy at Dell, from before I started to when I left. That was the philosophy: There was no mistake that was acceptable.

NANCY SCHUSTER: In 1988, a funny thing happened. We played what we called musical chairs. I had become the editor in chief at Official by this time, and I was approached by Dell to become the editor in chief of Dell Champion. At the same time, Penny Press wanted to hire Wayne Williams, who was the editor in chief at Dell Champion. The editor in chief at Penny Press was Doug Heller, and they wanted him at Official. So we all switched jobs in 1988. I always thought I got the best of the deal, because I was very happy to be at Dell, since I had worked for them for years before that and learned editing there, and now I could do anything I wanted because they had the new division, which was Champion.

ERICA ROTHSTEIN: [Dell Champion] was the result of a threat to Roz Moore. They decided on high—this was the Doubleday people—that we should increase our output of magazines by 30 percent in one year—without giving us any more people, without hiring, without doing anything. Roz put her foot down and said, "That's impossible." It was impossible—it was ridiculous. I don't even know how many more magazines that turned out to be, but it was 30 percent—it was a lot. It would have been physically impossible for us to do.

We had this woman who had come in who was supposed to be this general administrator. She'd come from *Parents* magazine, and she knew nothing about the puzzle business. She knew how to be an editor of a consumer magazine, which was different than what we were doing. She said, "Well, if you won't do it, I'll start another puzzle department." It was like, "Oh, if you think that's so easy to do, you go right ahead and do it."

They got a headhunter, and they ended up with Wayne Williams—but they thought they were getting Will Shortz! They knew that there was a "Will" around, but Roz said, "That's Will Weng, and he's retired from the *New York Times*, you idiots!" We always felt that they thought they were hiring this young whiz kid, and they thought they were getting Will Shortz, and they got Wayne.

We wouldn't help him. It was really too bad for him. Because after all, we'd been told that anybody could do what we did—anybody. So it was like, "Well, f—— you—if you think it's so easy to do, and that what we do is so easily replicable, you go ahead and do it!" So when they came to us and said, "Help him," it's like, "Why? You said it was so easy to do! He's supposed to be this wonder boy; let him do it." We wouldn't have anything to do with him.

NANCY SCHUSTER: I had free rein—it was great. I was able to compete with *GAMES*. You know, I wanted the more modern kinds of puzzles, and I didn't have to join the basic Dell group, which was where I had been working in the 1970s. But they had changed in the interim. After Rosalind Moore died and Erica Rothstein took over, they became ever so much more rigorous in their rules—and restrictive. For instance, PETE ROSE wasn't allowed reference in a puzzle, because he was such a bad egg. And NIXON was a no-no too.

In a word search, you weren't allowed to use the word DOG. Do you know why? It spells GOD backwards. I'm not kidding. A bluenose attitude prevailed lest a reader took offense. If they got one letter from a Kansas farm wife who took issue with a minor point, a whole new group of rules went into effect. So they kept the puzzles old-fashioned. And they wouldn't permit two-word fill-in-the-blank phrases. For example, to clue TOA, they would use "Warrior of Samoa" instead of "One_____customer." I guess they thought Mrs. Kansas wouldn't catch on, even if they said "2 wds." The other reason, and I was actually told this, was so the solver would feel the need to shell out some cash for *The Dell Crossword Dictionary*.

ERICA ROTHSTEIN: We wouldn't give [Champion] constructors—why would we? We needed them for our own magazines. If we'd had extra, we would have been able to increase our output. It was like, "If [Wayne Williams is] going to come in and tell you he can do this with one arm tied behind his back, let him go ahead and do it." All he could do was copy *GAMES*. And that's exactly what he did. Now, Dell never copied anybody. We went out there and we did an original. If somebody sent us an idea that was currently being used in another magazine, we didn't take it. We wanted new stuff that people weren't using elsewhere. Other people copied us; we did not copy anybody.

NANCY SCHUSTER: During their heyday in the 1950s, [Dell was] on top, and they wanted to stay there and thought nobody could ever come close to them—to the point that they never even opened a competitor's magazine. Then, when they did open a competitor's magazine, all they said was, "They've copied us." They were very, very much on their high horse with their head in the sand (picture that!). So they didn't see the puzzle world and people's tastes changing about them. I think this is what eventually led to their demise.

ERICA ROTHSTEIN: We had, quite frankly, no respect for [Wayne Williams], because after all, we knew where he started. We knew that he didn't have any taste and he didn't know what he was doing, but he fancied himself a puzzle editor. (Some things never change.) So he struggled, and we wouldn't help him in any way, shape, or form. I'm sure he hated us. Tough.

That's how Champion started, and we literally had no respect for it, because it was just a copy—a copy of something successful. A copy of something that was an original piece—no question about it. *GAMES* wasn't like Dell. Will [Shortz] and the people who started *GAMES* magazine did something original. We respected [them] for that.

NANCY SCHUSTER: [Dell] Champion and Dell "basic" were two separate entities, each with their own editor in chief, each having free rein over his product. While there's always a strong need for easy puzzles, there was a dearth of modern, more amusing puzzles out there on the newsstand. At Champion, I tried to fill that vacuum.

My goal was to present a broad spread of puzzles, from easy to tough, all top quality. In the easy market of word searches, when they were turned over to Champion editors, we way, way outsold what had been published before by Dell basic, making them the top Dell titles. But I couldn't achieve that goal with the harder crosswords and variety puzzles without the support of our marketing or subscriptions directors, whom Erica had convinced that *New York Times*–style puzzles wouldn't sell. With the exception of *Champion Logic Puzzles*, which took off splendidly in sales, subscriptions weren't offered on magazines with the same issues per year as other Dell publications, because the subscriptions guy was too uncertain it would pay, in spite of many, many requests from solvers. Little effort was made to place Champion titles in the proper newsstand locations. Of course, they wouldn't sell in downscale areas, but they would've done well with careful placement. It's true Champion had a niche market; we just had to cater to it, but that wasn't done. Solvers who were able to find Champion titles kept writing asking for better availability, without success. C'est la vie.

ERICA ROTHSTEIN: It was East Germany and West Germany. I'm serious. [Dell Champion and Dell basic] didn't talk to each other. Not only was it not one happy family, it was the McCoys and the Hatfields. They couldn't compete with us. They just couldn't compete. The solvers that were out there wanted what we offered. The solvers that they were trying to get didn't believe that Dell would do that kind of stuff.

NANCY SCHUSTER: If you have to sit in a conference with all the department heads and keep listening to Erica tell how bad your own magazines and editors are, when the world is telling you otherwise, it's unpleasant, to say the least. Erica kept treating Champion like a foreign invader to the other executives, passing along to me the resentment she felt toward my predecessor. The other department heads weren't specifically puzzle people; puzzles were just their selling tool, of course, so they bought whatever was told to them loudly and emphatically. I tried to promote my magazines and their potential worth without the histrionics, but I was the newcomer in this group and wasn't credited with much know-how.

By the time I left [in 1997], [Penny Press] had bought [Dell]. The bottom line was virtually their only interest. But, of course, they had big competition from Official Publications, who had swallowed up all the small puzzle publishers, and who had begun to flood the market with computer-generated puzzles. The quality [of Dell's puzzles] didn't change at that time [of the sale]. I had turned around *Dell Word Searches* to lead the market, and I also had faithful readers for Champion's logic puzzles, variety puzzles, and crosswords, so [Penny Press] didn't make any changes right away. Penny had fired Dell's executive staff within months of taking over; I was the only one they left alone, probably because I hadn't been throwing money down the drain. But since the Champion market was really a niche market, faithful though the buyers were, they dropped most of the magazines and dumped me too.

ERICA ROTHSTEIN: The way I like to look at it is at least I had it once. There are zillions of people in this world who never know what it is to be so proud of what you do. How blessed we were, to have worked with [people] as demanding as Kathleen Rafferty and Rosalind Moore, who believed so devoutly in what they were doing that they could infuse all these other people with that same need to strive, month after month after month, to put out the very best puzzle magazine we could possibly put out. And clearly, there were literally millions of people every year who agreed with us. There was nobody else who ever did what we did there. I would only wish for everybody to have at some point in his life, for however brief a period of time, to have something that was that fulfilling and that rewarding—and I certainly don't mean in the monetary sense! But in terms of feeling good about what you do and what you could do, and the end product—that you were capable through this product of touching the lives of hundreds of thousands of people and making them better.

MERL REAGLE: They stopped Dell Champion a few years ago. I don't think it was ever very profitable, or [know] if it made any money at all. It started out at 80,000 or 90,000 circulation in 1982—which isn't even that much, by Dell standards; but it eventually was down below 30,000. When I started making puzzles for regular Dell, in the early 1980s, it was around 220,000 circulation. And now, regular Dell, original Dell, sells maybe 50,000 copies. [Since Penny Press's acquisition of Dell], I don't think the quality in Dell "official" has gone down too much. The pay for constructors there, though, is a lot less now. In the late 1980s, I was making in the high [one] hundreds, and in the 1990s, I was making $250 per puzzle. But that's because I was one of Erica [Rothstein's] favorites. She said that generally she got such dreck, even from the people who had been submitting puzzles for years.

NANCY SCHUSTER: Every editor has his own writing style, his own preferences and dislikes. As with authors, some people love 'em and some hate 'em. You either prefer Henry James or Elmore Leonard. And when people complain about a puzzle's quality, they invariably blame the editor. What they don't realize is that the puzzles published by an editor have everything to do with what his boss lets him pay for the puzzle and nothing to do with the editor's own taste, to a large degree. We never recognize the valiant efforts that must have gone in to making a puzzle at all publishable—you can't believe how much bad stuff is submitted every day, to every editor. Everyone submitting a puzzle probably starts with the highest-paying place, then goes down by degrees of either price or reputation of the publication until they find acceptance somewhere. The top editor can pick and choose; the littler guys have to make a bad puzzle at least publishable; they've got fewer puzzles to choose among.

WILLIAM R. MACKAYE: It was quite a struggle I had with the [*Washington*] *Post*. I noticed when we were paying $250 [and then] the *Times* [rates] went up, there was a falloff in really top-notch puzzles. I was getting a lot of puzzles that looked to me as if they had visited the *Times* first. I started complaining to the *Post*. It took me a year, but I finally got them to raise the rates. I must say in some ways it was a bitter pill—in order to get the rates up there, I wasn't able to pry out any more money for myself. They promised me the next time around I would get some more too, but this time they said they were going to do this increase, but I had made a good case that it had to go all to the constructors.

WILL SHORTZ: Sixty to seventy-five puzzles [are] submitted to me each week.

STAN NEWMAN: For *Newsday*, I get many fewer puzzles than Will for the *Times*, who I believe gets about seventy-five submissions a week for seven spots. So he has to reject 90 percent of what he gets! I get maybe about 120 percent of what I can use in the course of a month. Of course, I have the advantage of working a little differently than most editors [in] that I prefer working with a smaller group of people. By and large, I get a regular set of puzzles from a small group of people every month.

RICH NORRIS: Right now I'm averaging anywhere from twenty to thirty submissions per week. Six are published.

WILLIAM R. MACKAYE: I don't get as many submissions as I would like to get. I get probably five a week, maybe, and I would really be happier if I was getting twenty a week. I just don't have that much to choose among. On the other hand, if you do submit to me, your chances of selling me something are better. Most of my new people are coming to me off Cruciverb-L now. I do a fair amount of chatting on that [forum], and people know who I am. I've never constructed a puzzle. I don't think I could.

ERICA ROTHSTEIN: I've never been a constructor, but I've always been a solver. I think that you can be an editor without being a constructor, but you can't be a constructor without being a solver.

STAN NEWMAN: Puzzle editors—and Will [Shortz], I know, would agree with me on this—are entertainers. You don't think of Charles Schulz as an entertainer, but in fact he was listed in *Forbes* magazine's richest entertainers, or highest-income entertainers. That really is our business. The few square inches we have in a newspaper every day, or the little space we take up at a bookstore—people are buying our books or trying our crosswords each day, more, in general, for entertainment than for intellectual development.

ERICA ROTHSTEIN: We did send our hearts and souls out every month. We really gave it our all, and it showed.

I grow old ever learning many things.
—SOLON

3.
WINNING HANDS

SUPER SOLVER

His skill is enormous, his talent immense,

He wins all the prizes at puzzle events;

Such a wonder he is, such a whiz, such a champ,

You'll be seeing him soon on a postage stamp!

Crossword-puzzling is America's number-one indoor sport and has been for the better part of a century. Why? Well, many good reasons: It's portable and inexpensive; puzzles are widely available, even abroad; and it doesn't require a huge time commitment—plus, there's something about filling in that last white square that makes you feel you've really accomplished something (solving, as constructor Barry Tunick notes, provides "a series of success experiences quite unlike that provided by real life").

Crossword people tend to be those who are the most busy, whose minds are very active, always racing.
—Will Shortz

Most expert-level solvers, like most constructors, had an early fascination with puzzles and tend to have pretty large vocabularies and strong logical-thinking skills (as well as a skull stuffed with useless knowledge!). Education can be a factor, too, although it's less important than a naturally curious mind. David Wagner, a college sociology professor, says he makes "frequent reference in some of my classes to puzzle solving as a process parallel to scientific investigation." Many other teachers use crosswords in the classroom to enhance the vocabulary and comprehension skills of students of all ages.

Becoming a competent crossword solver requires time, patience, and practice, just like any other discipline, and each individual tends to have a slightly different way of tackling the grid, struggling through a difficult corner, or parsing a series of tricky clues. With that in mind, however, generally speaking, most solvers go for the "gimmes" first—those definitions that have only one possible answer (like the majority of fill-in-the-blank-type clues). Then they try to get the diagram entries that cross them (it is, of course, easier to guess an answer if you have a hint or two in the form of filled-in letters, especially if the constructor is being devious!).

Don't get scared if you can't guess the first horizontal word. Go through the list till you find a definition that you're sure of. Don't spend too much time with the long words unless you are sure of them.
—The Cross Word Puzzle Book, 1924

Here are a few general solving tips:

- Until you are sure of an answer or have become particularly proficient, it's best to work in pencil so your grid doesn't end up looking like a piece of abstract art.

- Think like a constructor. Sometimes you can ferret out indications that he or she is trying to pull the wool over your eyes: A question mark is a good tip-off, as are words like *perhaps* and *maybe.* But, of course, deliberate misdirection is always possible!

- Do some educated guessing (best accomplished with a pencil!). Write in what you think are strong possibilities for particular clues: S for plurals, -ED for past-tense verbs, and so on. If you think you've got it, check out the crossing words to make sure you're on the right track.

- Don't assume that all plurals end in S (examples that don't: *cacti* and *men*).

- Shorter, more common words are typically found in the corners of puzzles. You might start there to see if you can find an easy in.

- Talk to other solvers (in person or on-line) and work on your skills together. To get started, read on!

SOLVERS' SAY

The top solvers whose quotes are featured in this chapter come from all walks of life and from diverse backgrounds—but they all have one thing in common: their devotion to solving crosswords. The group includes six-time American Crossword Puzzle Tournament champ Doug Hoylman ("I've been entering crossword tournaments regularly since 1986. I've won the American Crossword Puzzle Tournament six times, the North Jersey Crossword Open twice, and the Long Island Crossword Open three times."), plus Ellen Ripstein, known as "the Susan Lucci of crosswords" because she has competed in all but one (1979) of Will Shortz's annual American Crossword Puzzle Tournaments, and although she has placed toward the top of the heap in most of them, she never won one until 2001! Ellen has parlayed her skill as

a solver into a lucrative career as a test-solver, copyeditor, proofreader, and researcher for various puzzle publications and a major game show. She spent years in the insurance business before beginning a second career as a word maven and puzzle expert, and she is a sterling example of how hard work and dedication—even to a "mere hobby"—can pay off . . . in spades. She says:

ELLEN RIPSTEIN
Photo by Nancy Shack

I'm thrilled that I've been able to make puzzles and games a career as well as a hobby. I'm doing exactly what I want to do professionally. [For the game show,] I research and fact check questions, as well as do some copyediting and proofreading of the material.

I'm one of the test-solvers for the Los Angeles Times *Sunday puzzle. I also work for the* New York Times: *I'm the final pair of eyes checking the print puzzles before they are released. I then cut-and-paste from the print files on Will Shortz's machine at the* Times *to create files in Across Lite format for on-line [use]. I administer and grade the at-home version of the Stamford tournament.* Crosswords Club: *I proofread Mel Rosen–edited puzzles.* Dell: *Right now, I'm just test-solving all their Cross Sums, though I also have proofread* Champion Variety [Puzzles], Crosswords Crosswords, *and other books.* Random House: *I'm test-solving a series of old* Times *puzzle reprints to make sure they are still current.* Sterling: *occasional editing or proofreading. Last project was the* Beat the Champs *book where Jon Delfin, Doug Hoylman, and I were the "champs." We solved and timed all the puzzles. I've also done work proofreading puzzles for Uproar, Official, Running Press, and Book of the Month Club. I was also solutions editor of the* Enigma *for the National Puzzlers' League for three years, but this was for no pay and was the first to go when the TV work came up.*

I'm way too busy and usually exhausted, but also thrilled to be able to make a living doing my favorite things. It definitely beats MetLife (where I worked for seventeen years)!

THE WRITE STUFF

Never a pen, never.
—Will Weng

One of the never-ending controversies of Solverland is "Pen or pencil?"

MARY BUERGE: I always work in pen.

ANDY CLAYTON: Saturday *New York Times* in pencil and Sunday *New York Times* usually in pen.

NOAH DEPHOURE: I currently work in pencil when I bother to print the thing or find myself forced to get the puzzle from the newspaper, but I solved in ink for years for showmanship and because a sharp pencil on the older, rougher newsprint tended to tear the paper, and erasing tended to take the paper off with the lead. I prefer pencil. Though I don't erase even with a pencil (I just write corrections over the incorrect answer—and write in lightly when I suspect I could be wrong), it makes less of a mess on those occasions when I have to repeatedly correct my answers.

RICHARD GUHL: I work in pencil, because I get answers wrong.

ELLEN HARLAND: I solve on-line or with erasable pen.

DOUG HOYLMAN: I use pencil (or erasable pen for slick paper).

LLOYD MAZER: Always use ink.

RICHARD MERRIFIELD: Pencil.

JANICE NICHOLS: I always work in pen.

DENISE (DEE) O'NEILL: Pen.

MARY LOU PERRY: Pen.

ELLEN RIPSTEIN: I work mostly in pen.

AL SANDERS: I only use pencil. I think the concept of working in pen being an indicator of solving prowess is a fallacy. I'm much more interested in speed solving, and thus want to be sure I can erase as fast as possible.

BARRY SPIEGEL: I work in pencil. One of my brothers laughs at this, saying that a real man would take the risk and use a pen, but I know better.

DAVID WAGNER: I always solve with a pen.

FRAME OF REFERENCE

Everybody is ignorant, only on different subjects.
— Will Rogers

"Mrs. Crossword," Margaret Farrar, felt that the use of reference materials was "all a matter of one's own conscience." However, she added, "Puzzles should be fun, not work. Besides, the solvers may learn something in the process of looking words up."

MARY BUERGE: I sometimes use my *Webster's New World Crossword Puzzle Dictionary*.

ANDY CLAYTON: Mainly Web searches to find movie personality names, authors of books, etc.

NOAH DEPHOURE: Only when I really can't get the answer, or if after having got the answer, I still don't know what the hell it is. Random House's unabridged dictionary when the easier-toting *Merriam Webster Collegiate*

[*Dictionary,* Tenth Edition] fails me; Random House's single-volume encyclopedia, and Web searches.

JOHN GOSNELL: There is a difference of opinion whether it's okay to use reference works. The people I know who think it's not okay explain their position with these three points: (1) If you can get all the answers without having to look them up, you'll feel more satisfaction for your accomplishment. (2) If you can't do the puzzles without help, then you shouldn't take full credit. (3) It's cheating. I say: (1) I certainly agree with the first point, although to me it's not that big a deal. It just means the puzzle was too easy for you and that you didn't learn anything. (2) I disagree with the second point. If you can't finish without the help of references it means the puzzle was too hard for you and that you did learn something. (3) The third point is tautological and, therefore, specious. I would not finish maybe a fourth of the puzzles if I eschewed my references. As I see it, you will surely learn a lot more if you do use references, and I truly do consider learning to be a really good reason to play crosswords.

RICHARD GUHL: When someone throws an impossible puzzle at me, I use whatever I can find. Fair is fair when the clue is "North African wash."

ELLEN HARLAND: Almost never.

DOUG HOYLMAN: I rarely use references for standard crosswords. For cryptics, the most useful book I've found is *Longman Crossword Solver's Dictionary*, from Britain.

LLOYD MAZER: Only as a last resort—and that is very rare. When I resort to references, it is a hard-copy dictionary, or the Internet.

RICHARD MERRIFIELD: Only if I'm hopelessly stuck—I regard their use as a defeat.

JANICE NICHOLS: I never use reference materials—it spoils the fun of working it out!

DENISE (DEE) O'NEILL: Yes: dictionary, atlas, thesaurus, sports almanac, and [the] *A–Z Crossword Dictionary*.

MARY LOU PERRY: *Funk and Wagnall's Collegiate* [*Dictionary*] 1973, road atlas, *Information Please Almanac*, and the Internet when I'm really stuck.

ELLEN RIPSTEIN: No. Of course, when I proofread, I use tons of references to fact-check: CD-ROMs of the *Random House Unabridged Dictionary*, MS Bookshelf, Cinemania, and the Internet (judiciously).

AL SANDERS: Absolutely not. That's cheating!

ZULEMA SELIGSOHN: I use reference material sometimes. I consider the solving a learning experience, and I like to do research, so often I look up first clues that I know I cannot know—sports people, actors, etc.—in my books (almanac in particular; atlas; my Larousse). There seem to be fewer and fewer things to look up as the puzzles rely more on what the constructors think are cute answers and way too many interjections to answer with other interjections—infinite variations of AHH, UH-OH, OH-OH, AHA, UMM, etc. I sometimes look things up afterward—names I have never heard of, movies and actors—in the IMDb on-line, though for movies I have always enjoyed Halliwell in a real book. Right now, that book of mine is in Europe and I miss it.

DAVID WAGNER: For the first five or ten years of my solving career, I used anything I could get my hands on that would help—most notably, crossword puzzle dictionaries. However, once I developed my skills, I stopped using them. I almost never consult references anymore. I usually don't even feel the need to check my answers against the solution. The only time I look anything up anymore is if I am curious to learn more about the subject of the answer word.

PRACTICE MAKES PERFECT

You can't get better without a little sweat o' the brow—and if you want to be a competition solver, it takes a lot more than a little! All kinds of puzzles, not just crosswords, should be grist for the mill. . . . I asked our group of solvers to tell us what they liked, the publications they prefer (both in print and on-line), and the frequency of their solving sessions. (Thanks to the Internet, there are more solving opportunities than ever before. The best part? Many on-line puzzles are free.)

MARY BUERGE: I love cryptic crosswords, anacrostics, and difficult themed regular crosswords.

ANDY CLAYTON: All kinds of puzzles, mainly [the] types found in *GAMES* magazine.

NOAH DEPHOURE: *New York Times*–style crosswords.

RICHARD GUHL: Plain-vanilla crosswords, diagramlesses, Puns & Anagrams, cryptics (American and British), Cross Sums, crostics, Petal Puzzles, crosswords with more than one letter to a box, etc.

ELLEN HARLAND: *New York Times* crosswords, acrostics, diagramlesses, cryptics occasionally, many varieties in *GAMES* magazine.

DOUG HOYLMAN: I do most kinds of puzzles, both word and number. *GAMES*; *GAMES World of Puzzles*; *The Enigma* [National Puzzlers' League]; *Tough Puzzles* (British); *Dell Math Puzzles & Logic Problems*.

JOEL LIPMAN: Crosswords mostly; only the Friday, Saturday, or Sunday *Times*, and the national competition [puzzles].

LLOYD MAZER: Mostly traditional U.S.-style crosswords. . . . [I] also like diagramlesses very much. I solve all six daily *New York Times* puzzles; also the following weekend and Sunday puzzles: the *Wall Street Journal, Philadelphia Inquirer*, the *Washington Post,* and Creators Syndicate.

RICHARD MERRIFIELD: Regular crosswords (mostly *New York Times*), acrostics, diagramlesses, Puns & Anagrams, cryptograms.

JANICE NICHOLS: I solve the *New York Times* daily; also the *Wall Street Journal* puzzles and all of Merl Reagle's puzzles.

MARY LOU PERRY: *New York Times* Thursday through Sunday; also the *Wall Street Journal, Philadelphia Inquirer*, and *Washington Post* weekend puzzles.

ELLEN RIPSTEIN: Crosswords, math puzzles, and variety word puzzles. I'm not very interested in cryptic crosswords.

AL SANDERS: Primarily newspapers, especially *New York Times* puzzles. Besides traditional crosswords, I also enjoy acrostics, cryptics, and diagramlesses.

ZULEMA SELIGSOHN: Only crosswords and only *New York Times*, although now that they are available from the *New York Times* [on-line] forum, I do solve the other puzzles they post, such as the weekend *Wall Street Journal*, *Philadelphia Inquirer*, *Boston Globe*, etc.

DAVID WAGNER: I'll try any puzzle, although when time is restricted I focus my effort on the most difficult puzzles—I find them the most entertaining. On vacation (or when I'm just feeling perversely "word-happy"), I go on a cryptic, or even a variety cryptic, binge.

MARY BUERGE: *GAMES* magazine, *GAMES World of Puzzles*, *GAMES World of Crosswords*, *Dell Variety Puzzle Spectacular*. I solve on-line at *Washington Post* and *Philadelphia Inquirer* Web sites. I also do some cryptics at the *London Times* Web site.

ANDY CLAYTON: *GAMES* magazine, *GAMES World of Puzzles*, *Puzzler* (Japanese magazine, when I can find it).

NOAH DEPHOURE: I occasionally buy a *GAMES World of Crosswords*, but only rarely. I solve the *New York Times* religiously every day, and do the "Saturday Stumper" and "Sunday Challenger" from CrosSynergy and Creators Syndicate (I don't know which goes with which). I have in the past bought *New York Times* puzzle books. If I have idle time, I'll do the other daily puzzles from the last two sources.

RICHARD GUHL: Dell crosswords of various types, Penny Press (ditto), *GAMES* (and *GAMES World of Puzzles* and *GAMES World of Crosswords*), Random House *Hard Crosswords*, *New York Times Toughest Crossword Puzzles*, Double-Crostics, *Fun with Crostics*, *Times Crostics*, and various logic-puzzle books. The Across Lite site has a lovely area called Frank's Parlor. I also try to solve at the *Times* and Sunday *Times* puzzle site, and at the *Philadelphia Inquirer*, *Boston Globe*, and *Los Angeles Times* sites. I also sign on to CrosSynergy every once in a while.

ELLEN HARLAND: *GAMES World of Puzzles*; spiral-bound acrostics and Sunday puzzles (for travel).

LLOYD MAZER: I do not buy any puzzle publications. I get all my puzzles directly off the Internet. I usually print out [on-line puzzles in] Litsoft format.

JANICE NICHOLS: I solve the *New York Times* [on-line puzzles] with the Across Lite program. I don't actually solve while on-line, but download to the computer to solve off-line. I rarely use printed puzzles anymore. I download the *Philadelphia Inquirer* puzzle from the *New York Times* forum, and also the *Wall Street Journal* puzzle.

DENISE (DEE) O'NEILL: I print them off from the *New York Times* [Web site] and its puzzle forum.

ELLEN RIPSTEIN: Lately, I have not done many puzzles I haven't been paid to solve (too much work). I buy Random House and Simon & Schuster books, *GAMES* and Dell magazines; also *Uptown Puzzle Club* and the National Puzzlers' League's *Enigma*. [On the Internet,] CrosSynergy, *Newsday*, puzzability.com. And I proofread the *New York Times* [puzzles] and create its on-line files.

AL SANDERS: *New York Times* collections, Merl Reagle collections, Stan Newman's *Masterpiece Crosswords*, Henry Hook collections, and *GAMES* magazine. I subscribe to the *New York Times* "Diversions" service to get access to *New York Times* dailies on the Internet. I print the puzzles from the Internet, and then solve on paper (since I always time my puzzles, pencil and paper is much faster than Across Lite software). The *New York Times* site is my primary source. I also print off the *Wall Street Journal*'s, Merl Reagle's, and the more difficult CrosSynergy and Creators Syndicate puzzles. I get to these either through links in the *New York Times* crossword forum or through Will Johnston's link page [on the cruciverb.com Web site].

DAVID WAGNER: *GAMES* magazine (charter subscriber!), *New York Times* books (puzzles edited by Shortz, Maleska, or Weng), anything composed by Cox & Rathvon, Merl Reagle, Henry Hook, and a few others. At various times, I have subscribed to a number of different (generally now defunct) crossword or cryptic monthlies. The most notable (and far and away the best) of these was the *Four-Star Puzzler*. I do the *New York Times* puzzle almost every day, though I download it and solve it on paper as often as I solve it on-line.

MARY BUERGE: I solve about five to ten puzzles daily.

ANDY CLAYTON: Probably twenty-five to thirty crosswords per week, plus most of the puzzles in the *GAMES* magazines I get monthly.

NOAH DEPHOURE: At least nine a week: one a day, two on Saturdays and Sundays. If I've got the time and the will, I might do as many as three or four a day: *New York Times*, CrosSynergy, Creators Syndicate, and on Fridays, the *Wall Street Journal*.

RICHARD GUHL: Two or three a day, on the average.

ELLEN HARLAND: Six to seven hundred annually.

DOUG HOYLMAN: Each day I try to do at least one regular crossword, one cryptic, and one number puzzle; I usually do more than that.

JOEL LIPMAN: Three a week.

LLOYD MAZER: A minimum of seven 15×15s and five 21×21s per week.

RICHARD MERRIFIELD: One a day.

JANICE NICHOLS: About fifteen per week.

DENISE (DEE) O'NEILL: At least one per day.

MARY LOU PERRY: Seven to ten weekly.

ELLEN RIPSTEIN: I can't begin to count. I proofread *New York Times*, *Crosswords Club*, Sunday *Los Angeles Times*, and all Dell Cross Sums. I usually also do CrosSynergy and *Newsday*, and various puzzles from books.

AL SANDERS: Five to ten a day.

BARRY SPIEGEL: Probably five per week of the newspaper variety is most accurate, so 250 or so of those per year. Of course, this doesn't count the thirty or so in *GAMES* that I'll get to each year.

DAVID WAGNER: My best guess is about five hundred a year.

BEAT THE CLOCK

Think you're pretty fast? Time yourself against the experts.

PETER GORDON (editor/constructor and one of Will Shortz's test-solvers): Since I time myself on the *New York Times* puzzles to report to Will Shortz, I know what my averages are: Monday, five minutes; Tuesday, seven; Wednesday, ten; Thursday, fifteen; Friday, twenty; Saturday, twenty-five to thirty; Sunday, twenty-five. *Wall Street Journal* is around twenty.

MARY BUERGE: I can usually do a difficult puzzle in fifteen to twenty minutes.

ANDY CLAYTON: Five to fifteen minutes for the daily medium-difficulty *New York Times* and similar crosswords.

NOAH DEPHOURE: *New York Times* goes something like five or six minutes for Monday; eight minutes for Tuesday, ten minutes for Wednesday; a bit more for Thursday; and Friday, Saturday, and Sunday are too variable to say. When the Sunday is easy, I can do it in about forty-five minutes, or maybe a bit less at times. I really don't know very much, so I'm easily thrown by two crossing factually clued answers

JOHN GOSNELL: My best time so far, which was on a Monday, of course, is four minutes, forty-eight seconds. I'm sure the people who win crossword puzzle contests would laugh at such a time, but I so rarely finish in under six minutes that I despair of breaking the five-minute barrier ever again. (But keep in mind that while I'm crosswording I'm also listening to NPR radio and occasionally petting either of the two overly friendly cats I have and drinking from a can of diet Coke–brand cola, all of which have the effect of hurting my times.)

RICHARD GUHL: Depends on the type of puzzle. Between five minutes for an easy puzzle in a newspaper and never for that puzzle by Jordan Lasher that was used as a bookshop promotion.

ELLEN HARLAND: *New York Times* Monday through Thursday, five to eight minutes; Friday through Sunday, fifteen to twenty-five minutes.

DOUG HOYLMAN: Five to ten minutes for standard crosswords; fifteen to thirty minutes for variety cryptics.

JOEL LIPMAN: Friday and Saturday [*New York Times*], fifteen minutes; Sunday, thirty minutes.

LLOYD MAZER: From Monday through Saturday for the *New York Times*, it starts at five minutes for Monday and increases to one hour (or more) for Saturday. Sunday about thirty minutes.

RICHARD MERRIFIELD: *New York Times*, Monday, five minutes; Saturday, thirty minutes.

JANICE NICHOLS: Monday *Times* in about five minutes; Friday, Saturday, and Sunday in about twenty.

DENISE (DEE) O'NEILL: Fifteen minutes to up to an hour for Sunday puzzles.

MARY LOU PERRY: Weekday [*New York Times*], thirty to forty minutes; weekend, one and a half to three hours.

ELLEN RIPSTEIN: I'm one of the fastest solvers in the country. Three to eight minutes on the daily *New York Times* (Monday through Saturday); ten to fifteen minutes on Sunday.

AL SANDERS: Easier daily-size puzzles (like Monday or Tuesday *New York Times*) I can solve in under four minutes. My record for a Monday *New York Times* is two minutes, twenty-four seconds. Tougher daily-size, like Saturday *New York Times*, is more like eight to fifteen minutes. Sunday puzzles are also eight to fifteen minutes depending on difficulty.

BARRY SPIEGEL: I can usually handle the *Times* puzzles in under forty minutes for most of the weekdays. The Saturday puzzle usually vexes me, though. I can polish off most of the Sunday puzzles in the *Times* in under two hours of work, but that is often spent in pieces.

DAVID WAGNER: Most 15 × 15s I solve in ten to fifteen minutes; larger puzzles take half an hour or so. Cryptics take maybe twenty minutes most of the time. (Of course, all of this is affected by the relative difficulty of the puzzle.

Some of the most fiendish puzzles take me up to an hour, though I usually do get all, or almost all, of the words eventually.)

FAVORITES

NOAH DEPHOURE: The open-format *Times* Friday and Saturday puzzles are the best. Themed crosswords don't usually excite me. It's rare that the theme is all that interesting, and they usually have lots of three-, four-, and five-letter words, which are always the usual suspects clued the usual way.

RICHARD GUHL: It depends on my mood. I like British puzzles when I feel like getting a headache, and I like pretty diagrams when I feel like being aesthetically pleased. There is an epidemic of abutting long [answer words] lately. I think they are fun. They are good to look at but not necessarily difficult to solve.

DOUG HOYLMAN: Cryptic crosswords: They're challenging and entertaining at the same time.

JANICE NICHOLS: I prefer puzzles that challenge the intellect and not one's knowledge of pop culture. I especially enjoy solving the old Maleska puzzles.

DENISE (DEE) O'NEILL: Themed crosswords: I like figuring out the mystery.

MARY LOU PERRY: I like old-fashioned, Maleska-edited, arcane-knowledge-based puzzles.

ELLEN RIPSTEIN: Cross Sums: totally addictive. I test-solve all the Cross Sums for Dell, but I'd probably do it for free. I could do the same book over again and never notice.

AL SANDERS: My favorite is a really tough *New York Times* Saturday that I can sink my teeth into for ten to fifteen minutes. This is the most challenging puzzle—the closest I can get to a puzzle of the caliber of the final puzzle at Will Shortz's Stamford tournament, which is definitely the ultimate puzzle of the year.

ZULEMA SELIGSOHN: I like puzzles that ask me to remember certain facts, cultural data, things that I may have almost forgotten, and those that have what at the *New York Times* are called HOF (hall-of-fame) clues, though those are very subjective. Good clues are those that make you think of many contexts. I don't like Puns & Anagrams or cryptics.

BARRY SPIEGEL: Any clue that makes me rediscover something I already knew is good.

DAVID WAGNER: The more difficult puzzle the better; I need the challenge. I also have a real weakness for a very exotic kind of puzzle that Trip Payne used to put together. It didn't really have a name, as I recall, but he would string together words into long answers that generated an extremely wide-open grid. Trip's clues for these "compound" words were always hilarious and the puzzles were challenging.

THE GOOD STUFF

... Wherein we get the solver's take on the same question asked of constructors in the previous chapter: What makes a good puzzle?

MARY BUERGE: A great puzzle has clues that are unusual or cryptic.

ANDY CLAYTON: Inventiveness, creative cluing, and attractive visual presentation, requiring a new way of reasoning to solve.

NOAH DEPHOURE: Good words, clued well. Anything I think is particularly clever or amusing.

RICHARD GUHL: Ingenuity. I like to have a bit of a struggle to solve the puzzle, so it doesn't seem like a chore; but at the same time, I like to be able to finish the puzzle, so it doesn't seem purely frustrating. A tough combination to achieve, and I am surprised at how often it happens.

DOUG HOYLMAN: Clues that require a wide range of knowledge, together with clues that are tricky yet fair.

JOEL LIPMAN: Unusual and new words; humor; difficulty.

LLOYD MAZER: Challenging clues and a great theme. I especially like themes where more than one letter, word, or number are used in a single square.

RICHARD MERRIFIELD: Ambiguous clues, but not impossibly so. Clever and original themes (the "Aha!" factor). Doable without arcane knowledge or crosswordese.

JANICE NICHOLS: A great puzzle is one that really makes me use my brain—[one that's] not just an exercise in filling in squares. The harder the better!

DENISE (DEE) O'NEILL: Tongue-in-cheek clues; for example, "Dey job" = L.A. LAW and "Fretter's name" = STU.

MARY LOU PERRY: A good mix of creative entries, the need for searching out answers, tough decisions about clue meanings, and a bit of wordplay to boot.

ELLEN RIPSTEIN: For a regular crossword, interesting clues and interesting word patterns.

AL SANDERS: Wide-open grids; fiendishly misleading clues; interesting and original word and theme selection.

ZULEMA SELIGSOHN: A great puzzle makes me feel that I have connected with the mind of the constructor and, of course, that I like that mind as it comes through in the puzzle. Also, [I like puzzles that are] difficult, but [ones where] solving them will be satisfying and will be worthwhile, not because the constructor has decided to trick us or has been self-indulgent.

DAVID WAGNER: I guess the best puzzles are ones that force you to stretch your mind a bit, to think outside the box. I am happy if I'm forced to rethink a noun as a verb or vice versa. In other words, the clues make the puzzle.

BAD EXAMPLES

Is there anything constructors do that's just plain unfair? Most solvers have very definite affirmative opinions, with only one of our respondents—Mary

Buerge—having a more liberal attitude: "Anything is 'fair play' in puzzles," says she.

ANDY CLAYTON: Awful crosswordese and obscure trivia; puzzles that require guessing instead of only logic.

RICHARD GUHL: Blind corners (esoteric acrosses teamed with recondite downs), and misdefinition.

DOUG HOYLMAN: Useless, obscure facts like Siberian rivers and Hawaiian trees, especially when they cross one another.

ELLEN HARLAND: Incorrect clues.

LLOYD MAZER: Lots of obsure and arcane words.

RICHARD MERRIFIELD: Specialized words; for example, sports and entertainment figures that can't be worked out from the crosses. Two such words should never cross.

JANICE NICHOLS: Bad grammar [and] slang.

DENISE (DEE) O'NEILL: Questionable word usage; for example, in a recent puzzle, "Dresses for dinner" = LARDS.

MARY LOU PERRY: Duplicative words in both clues and entries, or in two entries.

ELLEN RIPSTEIN: Not really, other than complete obscurity. I don't do puzzles that have entries no one has ever heard of.

AL SANDERS: Too many obscure words—crosswordese—especially when they have equally obscure crossings. I hate solving older *New York Times* Sunday puzzles (that is, from the 1940s and 1950s), which are primarily exercises in research.

ZULEMA SELIGSOHN: Most of my American friends who live in Europe have a very hard time with the *New York Times*'s puzzles because they have become so culture and popular-culture bound rather than being, as at one time, word-play [based]. Manny Nosowsky's April Fools' puzzle April 1 [2000] in the *New York Times* was totally unfair, but it was an April Fools' puzzle. Still, I told him I felt I should have gotten the $75 for solving it rather than he for constructing it.

BARRY SPIEGEL: I realize that in many cases it becomes necessary to the constructor, but I think an overuse of opera-, Bible-, or Shakespeare-related clues (which I see as obscure, and doesn't that say so much—or so little?—about me) and answers turns me off.

DAVID WAGNER: We all have our pet-peeve obscurities, but those don't really bother me as long as there aren't too many of them. The only thing that really bothers me is a poorly constructed clue—one that doesn't really mean what the constructor/definer thought it did.

CONSTRUCTION CREW

And speaking of construction, who do our solvers think are the best of the best?

MARY BUERGE: I enjoy puzzles by Henry Hook, Merl Reagle, Eric Albert, and Emily Cox and Henry Rathvon.

ANDY CLAYTON: Will Shortz is my favorite editor, by far. I love the variety cryptic crosswords by Cox & Rathvon, and also their and Merl Reagle's standard crosswords.

NOAH DEPHOURE: Manny Nosowsky is my favorite constructor. He's by far the most consistently clever cluer, and has come up with what I think are some of the better themes recently (he's only been making themed puzzles for a year or two, I think; before that, it was all Friday and Saturday open-grid stuff).

RICHARD GUHL: [My favorite] used to be Thomas H. Middleton; now it's whoever does the *GAMES* contests, which I believe varies. I didn't like Eric Albert when he did them because he often resorted to definitions best characterized as unknowably highbrow.

ELLEN HARLAND: Cathy Millhauser, Manny Nosowsky, Nancy Salomon; anyone that Will Shortz chooses.

DOUG HOYLMAN: Constructors: Henry Hook, Merl Reagle. Editor: Will Shortz.

JOEL LIPMAN: Bob Klahn.

LLOYD MAZER: Manny Nosowsky and Will Shortz.

RICHARD MERRIFIELD: Shortz.

JANICE NICHOLS: Maleska, Merl Reagle.

DENISE (DEE) O'NEILL: I like the *New York Times* gang.

MARY LOU PERRY: Eugene Maleska, editor; Martin Ashwood-Smith, constructor.

ELLEN RIPSTEIN: Most of the new wave: Mike Shenk, Henry Hook, Merl Reagle, Stan Newman, Will Shortz, Barry Tunick, Frank Longo, Trip Payne.

AL SANDERS: Will Shortz is far and away the premier editor. Favorite constructors would include Merl Reagle, Rich Norris, Joe DiPietro, Manny Nosowsky, and David Kahn, among others.

ZULEMA SELIGSOHN: I loved Will Weng, and then I got used to Eugene Maleska. I hated, as many did, Will Shortz, but he has learned. Two constructors that are great favorites of mine are Cathy Millhauser and Glenton Petgrave, two very different constructors. I used to never pay attention to who the constructor was, but I know how difficult it is to do.

BARRY SPIEGEL: The gold standard, I think, has to be Will Shortz. His work in *GAMES* was influential to so many others. I like Henry Hook's work, and that of Rathvon & Cox (or do they normally list their names the other way?). Still, the one whose name alone makes me shiver is Merl Reagle.

For some, construction seems a natural outgrowth of the solving hobby— and in fact most constructors started as habitual solvers. But, as most find out, the two are quite different endeavors. . . . One of very few solvers who has succeeded in beating the odds, Noah Dephoure, hopes this book won't "inspire too many more people to take up writing crosswords. It's difficult enough as it is to get one by Will Shortz!"

MARY BUERGE: I have constructed word searches with English-Spanish vocabulary and some crosswords with the help of crossword software. The kids like them. [*Buerge is a teacher.*]

ANDY CLAYTON: No, I'm a very happy solver.

NOAH DEPHOURE: Yes, a daily *New York Times* style crossword. I'm a hobby constructor. I've had two *New York Times* puzzles published (a third is forthcoming) and many of my *New York Times* rejects have appeared in *GAMES World of Crosswords* and a few other random places.

ELLEN HARLAND: Yes—a 15 × 15, using existing patterns, and [with] personal (for birthday presents) or professional themes. The results were good, but my cluing is somewhat pedestrian.

DOUG HOYLMAN: Years ago I tried constructing crosswords, but found I didn't have the patience.

LLOYD MAZER: Yes, but with no success. I truly admire the skill of a constructor.

ELLEN RIPSTEIN: I have no interest in constructing, but I do like to fix other people's puzzles.

ZULEMA SELIGSOHN: Not long ago, I tried to construct, since there is so much talk among the constructors on [the *New York Times* on-line] forum, but found it very difficult. Also, from their talk, one gathers that there are many different kinds of puzzles, and that these are subjective kinds. The people in this forum seem to all know each other, and I gave up even trying when I saw how cliquish this community is.

BARRY SPIEGEL: I've just started constructing 15 × 15 daily puzzles. So far, the results are an increased appreciation for what it takes to put one together.

DAVID WAGNER: Yes—I once constructed an acrostic that is unfortunately about twice as long as is commercially viable. Most recently, I constructed a 15 × 15 themeless crossword that Will Shortz will publish in the *New York Times* later this year.

MY FORAY INTO CROSSWORD CONSTRUCTION
by John Gosnell

Here's how I write a crossword from scratch:

* To get started, create a grid. This alone is damnably difficult . . . in fact, I've found it so time-consuming that of the half-dozen or so puzzles I've written I've used the same basic grid for every one, because I really don't want to have to go through all that work again. And then, of course, at some point you have to make sure you've got the clue-numbering exactly right, which is tedious but at the same time wholly unsatisfying.

* Anyway, once you've decided on your grid, generate a list of theme answers you want to consider adding. The longer this list is, the easier your subsequent work will be. Then just bear down and start filling in answers that intersect those theme answers. Do not worry about the clues till you've filled in the grid completely, because filling in the grid is by far the tougher task. By far.

* If you've beavered away for too long on a particular area of the grid, you might have to face the fact that a theme answer will have to be replaced, which of course messes up any other work you've done in areas that intersect whatever you're replacing. It's hateful, but sometimes you have to do it.

* As you're choosing your answers, keep in mind the level of experience of your intended readership. The puzzles I've written were for people whose crosswording experience is no different from that of the general public, so I made each puzzle as easy as I possibly could, and at that I'm sure most of my special group of readers did not even attempt them.

* Once you've finally gotten the answer grid filled in, the easy work starts: defining the clues. If you're an experienced *New York Times* crossworder, you'll have little trouble inventing clues that conform to the proper style and character. If you really want to get everything right, you have to pay attention to the fiddly stuff, such as whether it's "Eskimo's home, Var." or "Eskimo's home: var." or "Eskimo's home: Var." (It's the last one.) Generally speaking, you want each clue to be as short as possible and consistent with how difficult or clever you want it to be.

* There are two ways to make a puzzle more difficult: The obvious one is to use lots of obscure answers (and get them to intersect a lot). The less obvious and much easier way is to use obscure clues for nonobscure answers. For example, for the answer MUSIC, don't use the clue "The Sound of _____," use the clue "St. Cecilia's sphere." For the answer COLUMBUS, don't use the clue "Italian who discovered America in 1492," use the clue "Caesar's male pigeon."

* Writing even a small, crappy crossword is hard, as you'll find out if you dare to try. Writing big, good ones is an art that few people appreciate.

You can read more of John's crosswording philosophy at his well-done Web site (http://members.aol.com/barelybad).

GOOD ADVICE

Who better to get solving advice from than regular—some would say compulsive—solvers?

ANDY CLAYTON: For crosswords: practice practice practice, do them every day, and you'll get much better.

NOAH DEPHOURE: Crosswords method: Try to solve it as fast as I can. For every answer of which I'm not certain, I instantly look at the crosses and try to answer them with the letters of the original answer. Key in on uncommon letters. If you fill in DOZE in one direction, see what goes with the Z in the other direction. Look at endings: Is the answer plural? Do you expect it to be a present participle? If one is a *New York Times* solver, one should get accustomed to answering with short phrases. Especially common are those that include UP, ON, IN, FOR—all those short prepositions. These can really be a pain in the ass if you're looking for a one-word answer.

RICHARD GUHL: I start by filling in what I can and hope that eventually it all links up. I am not hung up on solving the upper left corner first or whatever. Once I solve a clue, I try to link as much as I can on that basis.

ELLEN HARLAND: If 1-Across isn't a gimme, I fill in all the answers that I know for certain, then work the crosses to those.

DOUG HOYLMAN: I just read through the clues until I find a word I can enter, then work from there using crossing words. My only tip is to try different interpretations of a clue.

LLOYD MAZER: I go through all the clues quickly and write the answers to the obvious clues first, then try the crossing clues to fill in.

RICHARD MERRIFIELD: Look through the clues for a gimme and proceed Scrabble-style from there. It is a minor defeat if I have to look for a second starting place. If I seem to be stuck, it usually helps to leave it and come back later.

JANICE NICHOLS: I do the across clues first and then the down, repeating this until the puzzle is completed. If I am ever stumped, it definitely pays to walk away from it for a minute or two and come back with fresh eyes. Miracles can happen if you take a break.

> *If you are hopelessly stuck, try another puzzle.*
> *Inspiration sometimes waits for a return engagement.*
> —The Cross Word Puzzle Book, 1924

DENISE (DEE) O'NEILL: Just attack, fill in what you're pretty sure of and hope it all comes together.

MARY LOU PERRY: I go through the across clues until I find one that I know, then start to build the pattern by using the crossing clues from that first word. Once I have entered all the across and down clues that I can easily figure out, I move, again, through the across clues and find another spot to fill. Once I have gone through the across clues, I start with the down clues. By going once or twice over all the clues and using the crossings for hints, I am usually pretty well finished with the puzzle. If not, I will start to use the grammatical tense and formation of the clues to help me fill in some letters, such as past tense (filling in -ED), and plural (filling in -S). This will sometimes help jog my brain so that I fill in more areas of a hard puzzle. Then I look up words in the dictionary to see if the definition yields any easy synonyms or helpful information. Then I will put the puzzle down for a while—perhaps even overnight. If things aren't filled by then, I go to the on-line forum for *New York Times* daily puzzles and look for or ask for hints for the daily puzzle. This usually gets it solved. (However, I have been working one really hard puzzle since January 1999—I get a word or two in it every now and again.)

ELLEN RIPSTEIN: I just sit down and solve. No real tips, other than "read a lot"— know current events and be familiar with usual types of clues.

AL SANDERS: For superspeed (that is, under three-minute) puzzles, I'm always looking at the next clue while writing an answer. I always double-check every entry against the clue, which is different from other speed solvers, but accuracy is key. For really hard puzzles, I try not to jump around too much; I look for a foothold and try to work outward from there.

ZULEMA SELIGSOHN: I seem to start at the bottom, and I skim the puzzle for some clues that I can answer with certainty. Generally, I go about it as if it were Scrabble. I solve with a ballpoint (easier on the eyes), and unless I am certain of the answer because it cannot be otherwise, I always check the across clues for the same kind of certainty—or even likelihood. Then I know I can put it in. I never guess and very seldom have to write over—but then, I don't solve for speed; quite the opposite. My best help, I think, for people, has been the advice not to guess answers. One wrong word can throw a puzzle off for hours—days sometimes.

BARRY SPIEGEL: My approach is to first start at the top left and try to fill in the corner. If that looks unlikely to happen anytime soon, I scan the clues for what I perceive as easy—movie, sports, or political references, or fill-in-the-blanks. If this works, great; if not, I just try to dig in harder.

DAVID WAGNER: I have no fancy solution techniques, but I do follow different strategies for different kinds of puzzles. (1) Easy-normal crosswords: Start in the northwest corner with the first across word, then try to get all the down words that start with 1-Across, then all of the across words that stem from those down words. The fill spreads across the puzzle like an infection. Sometimes, to create more of a challenge, I will try to perform this without skipping a clue throughout the puzzle. Or I may try to fill the grid using only the across clues or only the down clues. (2) More challenging normal crosswords: Gain a toehold anywhere and work from that point out. Sometimes, I've even successfully solved puzzles when I started by filling in a few obvious -S or -ED endings, although that is rare (and, of course, subject to—eminently fair—clue trickery on the part of the constructor). (3) Cryptics and variety cryptics: I almost always look for some apparent anagram clues as a way of getting started.

PUZZLING IT OUT

A return to our crossword constructors to ask, Does being a crossword puzzle constructor mean you're a top-flight solver?

FRED PISCOP: You name it, I'll do it. I'm a nondiscriminatory puzzler.

NELSON HARDY: I used to enjoy acrostics, logic problems, and other variety puzzles, but in recent years I've stuck to crossword puzzles exclusively.

MARTIN ASHWOOD-SMITH: I wouldn't call myself an expert solver, but I am probably faster than the average solver. My time on an average 15 × 15 is about five to seven minutes.

SAM BELLOTTO, JR.: I still like to solve them. I prefer themed puzzles with well-designed open grids. These themeless puzzles I see cropping up all over the place that hark back to the more traditional crosswords of thirty years ago are a crushing bore!

PETER GORDON: I'm an expert math- and logic-puzzle solver. I was a member of the U.S. team at the World Puzzle Championship in Budapest, Hungary, in 1999. The team came in first place.

RAY HAMEL: I'm a pretty good speed solver when it comes to crosswords. I've finished in the top ten at the American Crossword Puzzle Tournament in my last two tries.

MAURA JACOBSON: I guess I'm an expert solver, for crosswords, of course—it's my work. I love cryptics. I can usually get most of the cryptic puzzle. In *New York* magazine, they have two puzzles: One is mine and one is a cryptic. I would say I get most of the cryptic, but I often have to use help, like the [electronic] Franklin crossword [completer].

NANCY JOLINE: I can always solve all the *Times* puzzles, as can everyone I know who's a constructor.

NELSON HARDY: I don't know if I'm an expert solver or not. I rarely encounter a puzzle I can't finish, if that means anything.

PATRICK JORDAN: I seem to be quite good at word puzzles in general. I solve them in ink, with few mistakes. (This habit began in my early teens, while I was living at home with my sister. She would sometimes find my puzzle magazines with the answers written in pencil, which she would then erase and fill in herself. So I began solving in ink to thwart her!) In addition to standard American crosswords, I enjoy cryptics, diagramlesses, and just about any kind of word puzzle that doesn't involve abstract concepts (I stink at logic problems!), and that doesn't simply give you a list of words for placement in a diagram (I don't care for fill-ins or crisscross puzzles).

DAVID J. KAHN: I'm a very good solver, but not one of the elite. I did finish in the top 25 percent at the 1996 American Crossword Puzzle Tournament, the only one I've entered.

SHAWN KENNEDY. I am an expert when it comes to the Jumble. I can solve the whole puzzle in well under a minute. People stand over my shoulder and ask how I do it. I just tell them that my solving ability comes from experience. If I do get stuck, I have a few solving methods, such as writing the letters out in a circle or getting out Scrabble tiles so that I can actually move the letters around. Crosswords are a different story. Out of all the crosswords I've started, I've only fully completed about 1 percent of them. I am much better at constructing than solving.

DAVID MACLEOD: I'm not sure what defines an expert solver, but I am rarely stumped and I do not use reference materials when I solve. My solving times are about fifteen minutes for a Monday *New York Times* to about an hour for a Friday-level.

RANDOLPH ROSS: I guess I'm pretty good. I love wide-open themeless puzzles. I'm not too good with cryptics.

NANCY SALOMON: I never solved American crosswords regularly until after I began constructing. Even then it took me a while. I don't consider myself an expert solver, but I've gotten to be fairly adept. I solve the *New York Times* and [*Los Angeles Times*] puzzles daily. I also solve lots of CrosSynergy puzzles in our peer-review process. I sometimes solve the *Wall Street Journal* puzzle. I still solve acrostics and variety cryptics, but not nearly as often as I used to. Once I started constructing lots of puzzles, I found that the lure to solve them was not as great. I guess it's kind of a busman's holiday now.

TOM SCHIER: I have not had time to devote to solving. I do not have a photographic memory.

MIKE SHENK: I'd say I'm a pretty good solver. I generally try to do the *Times* daily puzzles with just the down clues and try to figure out what the across words are by the letters I get from the down clues. I can usually do, I'd say, through Thursday, and sometimes can do Friday and Saturday, which is much more satisfying, I find, than just doing it the regular way. If you can do a Saturday puzzle with just the downs, that's really satisfying. It's interesting, because I can tell certain constructors have a style that's more similar to my own, and I have a much easier time on their puzzles because I can say, "Well, I would've filled in . . ." It helps to solve. The one person who I feel right now is fairly similar to me, and it's just purely coincidence, I guess, is Joe DiPietro. There's something about his choice of using a multiple-word phrase over just a single word—a lot of what he does is what I like to try to do.

GREG STAPLES: I had never successfully solved a *New York Times* puzzle when my first Sunday was published on July 4, 1999. I've gotten better, but I'm no expert. I do crosswords exclusively now—to see what is being done in the market and for enjoyment.

ELIZABETH GORSKI: I'm not an expert solver. It's much easier for me to make puzzles than it is to solve them.

SYLVIA BURSZTYN: Over the years my own favorites to solve have varied. There was a time when I would stay up for days until I had finished a logic puzzle.

There were times I would solve twenty or more Double-Crostics. Nowadays, it's a variety of variety puzzles that keeps me from getting ordinary household chores done. I'm expert at solving variety puzzles—not all, just the ones I like. I miss the defunct publications that offered hypermodern and supertough crosswords, with a handful of black squares in a 27×27, or the hardest possible clues for simple entries.

RICH SILVESTRI: I consider myself a very good solver of crosswords and cryptics.

JOHN SAMSON: I don't have the time anymore to solve puzzles—many hours are spent editing/constructing crosswords and attending soccer, basketball, and Little League games (I have two children: Elsie and Robbie). Also, I'm busy with my own publishing company, Nene Books, which I cofounded in 1998 with Norman Wizer, a veteran crossword constructor.

RICH NORRIS: I solve traditional crosswords and an occasional acrostic. I can solve a *New York Times* Monday in about five minutes. The "real" experts do them in less than three minutes.

ARTHUR S. VERDESCA: I consider myself an expert solver. (In the old days, I used to enter tournaments and do rather well.) I'm very good on crosswords and diagramlesses, but I also am rather fast on cryptics. I think I'm very fast on Double-Crostics. (I'm old enough that I used to correspond with Elizabeth Kingsley about her Double-Crostics!)

BILL ZAIS: I don't know if I'd call myself an "expert" solver. I do not use reference books for solving, and my only problem is an occasional Friday or Saturday *New York Times* that I can't finish. I would put my solving ability in the top 10 percent, but not in the top 5 percent.

BARRY TUNICK: I can solve a puzzle in mid-Stamford time, but that's in an ideal, no-stress situation. If I were in a contest, I'd probably panic and/or freeze.

KELLY CLARK: Some people find it rather comical that I'm generally unable to solve my own puzzles.

SAM BELLOTTO, JR.: Crosswords are a leisurely, solitary activity to be enjoyed with your morning coffee, for example. They ain't an Olympic sport.

STIFF COMPETITION

I've never entered any contests—crossword or otherwise. (I take that back. I did enter a freckle contest when I was eight years old. I won first prize and was awarded a small plastic airplane. That was the last contest I ever entered.)
—John Samson

Beyond the regular solver is the competition solver. These people, who train for puzzle events just like athletes, put themselves through a rigorous routine that includes daily solving of multiple puzzles (the harder the better), learning all they can about the words that frequently pop up in puzzles (including obscurities, foreignisms, and, of course, the ubiquitous remnants of crosswordese), and time-testing themselves on every puzzle. Yes, almost anyone can do it—but it takes persistence and single-minded dedication, and it can mean putting your life on hold until you reach your "fighting weight."

The first crossword competitions coincided with the craze in the mid-1920s. One of the more notable contests was held in May 1924 at New York's Ambassador Hotel, where entrants struggled to solve a tough little puzzle by one of the *New York World*'s editors, F. Gregory Hartswick. The winner, William A. Stern II, was crowned the "Cross Word Puzzle Champion of the World" after cracking the creation in a little over ten minutes. In January of the following year, the country's top universities staged a public competition at the Roosevelt Hotel in New York City. Vying for top prize were Harvard (the solving team included eminent alumni Heywood Broun and dramatist Robert Sherwood), Yale (team included Stephen Vincent Benet), Princeton, Wellesley, and the City College of New York. And the winner was . . . Yale (appropriate, considering how often "Old ELI" pops up in puzzles!).

Today, the number-one game in town—any town—is Will Shortz's American Crossword Puzzle Tournament (surf to www.crosswordtournament.com for the complete scoop), held annually in Stamford, Connecticut. The event is a three-day puzzlefest that includes much revelry and rivalry, culminating in the Sunday solve-off, when the three top contestants from the previous day's solving do battle for the championship in a nerve-racking challenge: solving a superdifficult puzzle in full view of the entire audience, via overhead transparencies or on whiteboards. Yikes! Speed, of course, is important (contestants are given bonus points for turning in a completed grid before the deadline bell), but submitting a completely accurate answer is paramount.

Past winners have included some of crossword construction's leading lights, notably Nancy Schuster, Stan Newman, David Rosen, Jon Delfin, and Trip Payne (a complete list of winners appears on p. 183).

WILL SHORTZ: This is something I had been dreaming about for years, but it came about fortuitously. I was living in Stamford, Connecticut, working for Penny Press. The Stamford Marriott Hotel had just opened, and the director of marketing was looking for ways to bring in weekend business. He remembered when he had commuted into Manhattan every day that many people solve crosswords on the train, so he had the idea of holding a crossword contest, which would attract people to the hotel. He made various inquiries: first he called Maleska at the *Times*, who gave him the name of someone else, who recommended me—I just happened to live in Stamford. We publicized this first event, advertised it in the *New York Times*, and we had a huge success—and we've had it every year since. The first one had 149 contestants. Nancy Schuster [won the first tournament]. She had made some crosswords before, but she really went into puzzles as a career after that.

NANCY SCHUSTER: In 1978, Will decided to revive the national crossword puzzle tournament that existed in the twenties. I won the first prize in Stamford. Then I won second prize the second year, and sixth prize the third year. I proceeded down to number nine, the reason for that being that the real smarties like Stan Newman, who was so fast, didn't even know about the contest in the first few years. It was an open field. I never studied for the darn thing. I just took what I had learned from editing and constructing—you have to have your nose in dictionaries all the time. But I was always terrified—just scared stiff every time I'd sit down to a contest puzzle. I also felt that it wasn't such a good idea for an editor to be a contestant. I didn't want people to know.

WILL SHORTZ: Another person who used his win at Stamford—parlayed that into a career—was Stanley Newman. He won in 1982, I believe. He went on to . . . well, you know what he went on to.

STAN NEWMAN: I wanted to see how good I was, I think, and what I got out of it was far more than I had anticipated. Setting aside for the moment how I did personally: The level of insight, how articulate the other competitors were—about how these puzzles were constructed, and these clues and this diagram—these were all completely foreign notions to me. I was fascinated by the depth of understanding these people had about the whole crossword business. I found it fascinating. I finished, I think, in thirteenth place out of around 130 people. But I had found something here in puzzle-solving that I thought I could get better at in a measurable way. Over the next year, I did, by my estimation, well over fifteen hundred crosswords from all kinds of sources: *GAMES* magazine, the *New York Times*, books, etc., learning all the words that I could, learning how fast I could do a puzzle without making care-less mistakes. [I] would [later] look up all words I was unfamiliar with, all references and factual-type things that weren't in dictionaries. [I] actually kept a file box with alphabetized cards that I would review every few weeks just to see if I still knew these words.

By the time I showed up at the Marriott the next year, I found, to my astonishment, that my skills had improved by a quantum amount compared to everyone else in the room. I remember noticing a few people who had completed the puzzles faster than me the previous year and had gotten them right while I made a few mistakes. One of the goals I had was to someday become as good as they were, actually one person in particular (no names, please). So this year, I positioned myself close enough to this person that I could see how well I was doing, and I was surprised to see myself getting the

---

AMERICAN CROSSWORD PUZZLE TOURNAMENT: SCORING

Scoring is based on accuracy and speed. Score as follows:

1. 10 points for every correct word you entered across and down
2. A bonus of 25 points for each full minute you finished ahead of the suggested solution time—*but* reduced by 25 points for each missing or incorrect letter (but not beyond the point the bonus returns to zero)
3. A bonus of 150 points for each completely correct solution

For the purpose of scoring, a "word" consists of any series of letters written between black squares in the grid, or between a black square and the border of the grid, whether it is a single word, a phrase, or other combination.

puzzles done first. As it turned out, I did well enough to make the final three. The final tournament puzzle was done on an overhead transparency, with three of us sitting in front of overhead projectors. You didn't know how the other two people were doing, and in fact I thought I wasn't moving all that quickly. I was nearly done, maybe had a few squares left, and the person to the right of me said, "Done." Of course, I wasn't happy about that, but continued to complete the puzzle. I said "Done" a few moments later. (I don't think the third person finished.) Then Will announced that the person who had finished before me had a couple of mistakes and I didn't have any, which made me the winner. It was pretty heady stuff!

My wife and infant daughter came up on the train from Brooklyn to Stamford. *People* magazine just happened to be there, and since I was the one who won the tournament, I was the one they did the article on. It was a remarkable day. I discovered later that no one had really done what I had now done—devote a huge part of their spare time to doing puzzles every day and tracking progress. I know a number of people have [since] followed in one way or another the things that I have done, and many have gotten better as a result over the years. But I guess getting there first made all the difference. As well as a healthy dose of dumb luck.

Where luck played the greatest part in the start of my puzzle career was the year that I won the Marriott tournament just happened to be the same year that Will was running his first U.S. Open Crossword Championship. I went through the various qualifying rounds and found myself there in August 1982 at NYU [with] the 250 best puzzle-doers in the country. Of course [I] continued to train very seriously. As you may recall, I won that event too. But the competition at the Open was much more intense than at the Marriott. Nevertheless, I distinctly remember that on at least two of the puzzles I finished one full minute faster than anyone else in the room. Through dumb luck, I just happened to improve my solving skills enough just in time to win that first U.S. Open. And my entire puzzle career can be traced back to that day in August 1982.

NANCY SCHUSTER: When Will had the *GAMES* tournament—that was in 1982— when they had it down in Washington Square in New York, *GAMES* sponsored a tournament for about three years, which is [another] that Stan won.

He was wearing black kneesocks, blue basketball sneakers, a Hawaiian shirt, and plaid shorts. I'm not kidding! That time I won fourth prize, and I was glad because the top three had to go up on the stage and do the playoff. I didn't have to do that, which was very nice. After that, Will made me a judge, thank God. I was able to sleep at night and really enjoy the tournament. I've never missed a single one since.

PETER GORDON: I wrote a puzzle for the Stamford tournament, and before the tournament, I got together with Will Shortz . . . to test all the tournament puzzles with David Rosen, a four-time tournament champ. I had written the puzzle a while earlier, so I had forgotten much of it. Sure enough, during the testing, he beat me at my own puzzle! The next year, I had a puzzle again, so this time I reviewed it the night before. But since it was a big puzzle, David was able to beat me again! So the following year, when I had another puzzle, this time a 15 × 15, I memorized the puzzle grid the night before. That morning I reviewed it. On the subway on the way over, I looked it over again. Right before the testing, I ducked into the bathroom and studied it one more time. Sure enough, I was finally able to beat David—but only by fifty seconds! He had never seen the puzzle before, and took only fifty seconds more than it took me to write in the memorized letters! Incredible.

MARTIN ASHWOOD-SMITH: I attended Stamford in 1998. I think I came in around 124th out of over 250 entrants.

MANNY NOSOWSKY: I've competed at Stamford, and I've done poorly there.

NANCY SALOMON: I entered one Stamford tournament. I don't like speed-solving, though, and didn't even try to be a contender.

NANCY JOLINE: For the past two years I've competed in Stamford at the annual crossword puzzle tournament. I will never be anywhere near as fast as the top people. I was happy to finish in the middle both times.

PATRICK JORDAN: I have attended the American Crossword Puzzle Tournament four times, and garnered a total of eight trophies, ranging from fourth to tenth place. In my first appearance at the tournament, I became the first person in its history to win four trophies in a single year (sixth place overall,

AMERICAN CROSSWORD PUZZLE TOURNAMENT: WHO COMPETES?

Contestants simultaneously compete in all events for which they are eligible:

Division A: Everyone

Division B: Contestants who have not won a Division A or Division B prize during their last three tournaments

Division C: Contestants who have not finished in the top 20 percent during their last three tournaments

Division D: Contestants who have not finished in the top 40 percent during their last three tournaments

Division E: Contestants who have not finished in the top 65 percent during their last three tournaments

Age Divisions: Solvers 25 years and under (Juniors), 50–59 years (Fifties), 60–69 years (Sixties), and 70+ (Seniors)

Regional Divisions: Solvers in each of eleven geographical regions (Connecticut, Other New England, New York City, Long Island, Westchester/Upstate New York, New Jersey, Other Mid-Atlantic, South, Midwest, West, Foreign)

Rookies: Contestants competing for their first time. Rookies are not eligible for Division D or E prizes.

third place in the B Division, first place in the West Regional Division, and Rookie of the Year).

RICH NORRIS: I did win the D Division championship in 1998. That means I was the best of about the middle third of the entire competing group.

RANDOLPH ROSS: I enter the tournament at Stamford. I've won the B Division but can't match the top A solvers.

CATHY MILLHAUSER: I only competed once at Stamford, and I was in the bottom third.

KELLY CLARK: Sure, I've enjoyed the Stamford tournaments for the past four years. Last year I came in second to last!

KAREN HODGE: One year, I made it onto the first page of solvers at Stamford—I think I ranked somewhere in the top forty.

FRANCIS HEANEY: My highest finish was ninth. It's pretty good. I'm a very competitive person, so I need to do that at least once a year. Traditionally on Saturday night at the [National Puzzlers' League] conventions, there is a big multipuzzle extravaganza. I've been on teams with people who are a little stressed out by the speed at which I want to do things. This year, I made a distinct effort to go slowly, [to] try to include the new person. Even after that, the new person was like, "I felt very left out and I'm kind of angry." I'm like, "Oh God. I tried!" Welcome to the NPL.

PETER GORDON: My first crossword tournament was the North Jersey Open in 1988 (or maybe 1989 or 1990). There were 105 contestants. I came in 104th place, beating out only a Frenchman who didn't speak much English. I've steadily gotten better, every year improving. In 1998, I won the D Division at Stamford. In 1999 I won the C Division and finished in 37th place (or somewhere around there). I was also a member of the U.S. team at a competition in Bjelovar, Yugoslavia, in which I had to construct a crossword for twenty-four hours straight. Team USA won, making a puzzle over fifty meters long (and twenty-five squares wide).

NANCY SCHUSTER: I'm also involved now with the World Puzzle Championship, an international puzzle group whose U.S. organization is headed by Will Shortz. They took me free to the tournament last year in Budapest, which was very nice, and so I said, "Well, how can I pay you back?" And Will said, "Well, you'll work for us. You're going to recruit more countries." So I've been spending the winter e-mailing people all around the world. Quite interesting.

It's a five-day event, with ice-breaking parties, some sightseeing, and much puzzle-solving. The puzzles—I can't solve a single one of them! They're language-neutral puzzles. There's no English involved in anything. They're so intelligent, these people—I can't believe it!

TRIP PAYNE: I won [the American Crossword Puzzle Tournament] the third time I entered, which was 1993. I was the youngest person ever to win—I was twenty-four. I'm still the only person to have won while still in the Junior Division. Five years later, in 1998, I won again. I had a bunch of seconds and thirds in the meantime—of my nine tournaments, I've been to the finals six times. I've never finished lower than eighth. I'm pretty consistent there. Unfortunately, the year that *Nightline* did their piece was the year I made one error that kept me from going to the finals, where I would have won the final without question—because none of them finished it, and I finished it in six minutes. C'est la vie. It's always nice to get into the finals and play up on the big board. I'm sort of a ham—when I'm frustrated, I play to the audience with my body language. Everybody always says it's fun to see me when I'm up on stage next to Hoylman, because he's "The Iceman." He barely moves—you can practically see the letters just magically filling in the squares. He's very methodical, whereas I'm hyper and jumping around and flailing my arms.

The merest attempt to examine my own confusion would consume volumes.
—James AGEE

STAR-CROSSED

With the millions of people who routinely solve crosswords, you'd guess there'd be a famous name or two in the bunch, wouldn't you? You'd be right.

My name appeared as an answer in the New York Times crossword puzzle.
—SELA Ward on how she knew she'd made it

Franklin P. Adams

Bernard Baruch (statesman and presidential adviser)

Robert Benchley (author, *From Bed to Worse*)

Ben Bradlee (newsman/writer)

SYLVIA BURSZTYN: Lots of constructors use names like Ruta Lee, Shelley Berman, and Orson Bean in their puzzles. As the *Los Angeles Times* constructors, we get letters from these people saying what a Sunday-morning thrill they got out of seeing their names in our puzzle. Kenneth Anger sent me an autographed copy of his *Hollywood Babylon II*, which I treasure. Marsha Hunt sent a copy of her spectacular coffee-table book, *The Way We Wore*.

Heywood Broun (journalist)

Gelett Burgess (poet, "The Purple Cow")

Ellen Burstyn

Roz Chast (cartoonist)

Winston Churchill

Bill Clinton (an expert "ink" solver)

In July 1997, President Clinton, who's an accomplished solver, discussed one of my recently published Sunday New York Times puzzles, called "Technophobe's Delight," at a White House conference on technology and the Internet. He needed some laughs, which the puzzle apparently provided.
—David J. Kahn

MIKE SHENK: [Will Shortz] and I, when we were at *GAMES*, did a puzzle for then-candidate Clinton, which he solved in his hotel room when he was in New York. The puzzle had a quote in it from . . . Senator Pell? I forget. When he was running for president, we made a special puzzle for *GAMES* that we took up to his hotel room in New York, and he solved it while timing himself. He did it in something like seven minutes. Half of that time he was on the phone with somebody else!

Joseph Cotten (loved Eugene Maleska's Stepquote crosswords and became Maleska's friend)

Noel Coward

Judith Crist (film critic)

Marlene Dietrich

Queen Elizabeth II (cryptics)

Ron Ely (TV's Tarzan and, of course, a frequent crossword answer himself)

Nora Ephron (screenwriter, *Heartburn*/director of *Sleepless in Seattle*)

Henry Fonda

Judy Garland

Greer Garson (actress, *Mrs. Miniver*)

Sir John Gielgud (cryptics)

Julie Harris (actress, *The Member of the Wedding*)

Ben Hecht (screenwriter, *The Front Page*)

Leona Helmsley (hotelier and tax evader)

> *I get a lot of letters from mid-level celebrities whose names appear in the crossword, and they get such a kick out of that. One that jumps to mind was from the CBS newswoman Rita Braver, who wrote me a real amusing note about how surprised she was at how many of her friends do the puzzle at seven A.M., which is when her phone started ringing the morning her name appeared in the puzzle.*
> *—Will Shortz*

Keith Hernandez (baseball player)

John Hersey (writer, *A Bell for Adano*)

Celeste Holm (actress, *All About Eve*)

Brit Hume (TV newsman)

Lee Iacocca (auto executive)

George S. Kaufman (playwright, *You Can't Take It with You*)

Helen Keller (solved puzzles in Braille)

Burt Lancaster

SYLVIA BURSZTYN: Many years ago, I worked temp in Beverly Hills for an entertainment law firm. I never met him, but I was told about their client Burt Lancaster. They said he never showed up at their offices without a book of crosswords. He sat in the reception area working crosswords. He filled any pause in a lawyer-client meeting with crosswords. And all the hours an actor spends on a movie set just waiting, Burt Lancaster spent working on crossword puzzles.

American Crossword Puzzle Tournament: List of Winners

Year	Number of Contestants	First Place	Second Place	Third Place
1978	149	Nancy Schuster (Rego Park, NY)	Eleanor Cassidy (Fairfield, CT)	Murray Leavitt (Pound Ridge, NY)
1979	154	Miriam Raphael (Port Chester, NY)	Nancy Schuster (Rego Park, NY)	Merl Reagle (Santa Monica, CA)
1980	128	Daniel Pratt (Laurel, MD)	Miriam Raphael (Port Chester, NY)	Joel Darrow (Greenburgh, NY)
1981	125	Philip Cohen (Aliquippa, PA)	Joel Darrow (White Plains, NY)	John Chervokas (Briarcliff Manor, NY)
1982	132	Stanley Newman (Brooklyn, NY)	Philip Cohen (Aliquippa, PA)	Joseph Clonick (New York, NY)
1983	146	David Rosen (Buffalo, NY)	Stanley Newman (Brooklyn, NY)	Ellen Ripstein (New York, NY)
1984	115	John McNeill (Austin, TX)	David Rosen (Buffalo, NY)	Stanley Newman (Brooklyn, NY)
1985	110	David Rosen (Buffalo, NY)	Rebecca Kornbluh (Mundelein, IL)	Eric Schwartz (Newton, MA)
1986	130	David Rosen (Buffalo, NY)	Rebecca Kornbluh (Mundelein, IL)	Ellen Ripstein (New York, NY)
1987	118	David Rosen (Buffalo, NY)	Ellen Ripstein (New York, NY)	Ed Bethea (New York, NY)
1988	137	Doug Hoylman (Chevy Chase, MD)	Jon Delfin (New York, NY)	Ellen Ripstein (New York, NY)
1989	134	Jon Delfin (New York, NY)	Doug Hoylman (Chevy Chase, MD)	Ellen Ripstein (New York, NY)
1990	143	Jon Delfin (New York, NY)	Ellen Ripstein (New York, NY)	Doug Hoylman (Chevy Chase, MD)
1991	149	Jon Delfin (New York, NY)	George Henschel (Springfield, VA)	Doug Hoylman (Chevy Chase, MD)
1992	172	Doug Hoylman (Chevy Chase, MD)	Ellen Ripstein (New York, NY)	Trip Payne (Atlanta, GA)
1993	192	Trip Payne* (Atlanta, GA)	Ellen Ripstein (New York, NY)	Doug Hoylman (Chevy Chase, MD)
1994	216	Doug Hoylman (Chevy Chase, MD)	Al Sanders (Nashua, NH)	George Henschel (Springfield, VA)

Year	Number of Contestants	First Place	Second Place	Third Place
1995	232	Jon Delfin *(New York, NY)*	Doug Hoylman *(Chevy Chase, MD)*	Ellen Ripstein *(New York, NY)*
1996	239	Doug Hoylman *(Chevy Chase, MD)*	Trip Payne *(Atlanta, GA)*	Jon Delfin *(New York, NY)*
1997	255	Doug Hoylman *(Chevy Chase, MD)*	Ellen Ripstein *(New York, NY)*	Trip Payne *(Atlanta, GA)*
1998	251	Trip Payne *(Atlanta, GA)*	Jon Delfin *(New York, NY)*	Ellen Ripstein *(New York, NY)*
1999	254	Jon Delfin *(New York, NY)*	Doug Hoylman *(Chevy Chase, MD)*	Al Sanders *(Fort Collins, CO)*
2000	286	Doug Hoylman† *(Chevy Chase, MD)*	Ellen Ripstein *(New York, NY)*	Trip Payne *(Atlanta, GA)*
2001	322	Ellen Ripstein *(New York, NY)*	Patrick Jordan *(Ponca City, OK)*	Al Sanders *(Fort Collins, CO)*

*At age twenty-four, the tournament's youngest champion.

†First six-time champion and, at age fifty-six, the tournament's oldest champion.

Michael Learned (actress, *The Waltons*)

Ernest Lehman (screenwriter, *The Sound of Music* and *North by Northwest*)

Phyllis McGinley (poet)

Princess Margaret (won a puzzle-solving competition held by *Country Life* magazine in 1954)

Walter Matthau

MAURA JACOBSON: Stephen Sondheim once recommended me to Alexander Cohen, the producer, who wanted to have some puzzles as publicity for one of his plays. There was a benefit that we attended, and Stephen Sondheim was there, and as we all left the premises, I saw Stephen Sondheim. I went over to him and I said, "I have to thank you, because you once recommended me for a very nice job." And he said, "Yes, okay, thank you," and walked away. I never identified myself! I think he would've been a little more cordial if I'd told him who I was!

Liza Minnelli

Kathleen Norris (author, *Through a Glass Darkly*)

Nancy Olson (actress, *Sunset Boulevard*)

JON DELFIN: Dick O'Neill (character actor—Cagney's father on *Cagney & Lacey* and in *Wolfen* and *The Jerk*, among many) was addicted. For many years, I'd send him the Stamford puzzles, and he always complained that they were too easy.

Emily Post (etiquette expert)

Mary Roberts Rinehart (playwright and novelist, *The Circular Staircase*)

Andy Rooney

Tom Seaver (baseball player and sportscaster)

Beverly Sills

I sent Beverly Sills a puzzle I wrote with her name in it, and she solved it, signed it ("Love! Beverly Sills"), and mailed it back to me.
—*Peter Gordon*

Frank Sinatra (an "ink" solver and friend of Eugene T. Maleska)

JIM PAGE: Gene [Maleska] got me into a dinner with Frank Sinatra. Sinatra was a big crossword solver, and there was a group on the West Coast and the East Coast that got together every Sunday over the phone about the puzzle: Sinatra on the West Coast; Arlene Francis and some other people on the East Coast here. They did the puzzle over the phone every Sunday. They got together in New York for dinner, and Gene happened to be in New York at the time and was staying with me, and invited me along. It was a great experience to be with Sinatra and all these notables. They were all solvers. Sinatra was cute—we talked about [*Page's puzzle*] "Unglue the Clues," and he said he thought the puzzle was a gas. He told a bunch of stories, one of which I thought was sort of interesting, about how he got started in puzzles. He used to work on Wall Street as a runner as a kid. One day he was taking the ferry or the train from New Jersey to Wall Street, and he saw this guy doing the *Daily News* puzzle in ink, and he thought, "Boy, that's cool." That's how he got started—he thought that was a very cool image, so he started doing puzzles in ink. Kept at it and became a good solver. He was just exactly what you'd think he'd be like. He was what he was. All his parts were walk-on parts, really, and that's exactly what he was. Told great stories about Las Vegas—about being behind two hundred grand. A long, interesting night.

Jean Stafford (novelist and short story writer)

Rex Stout (detective who created Nero Wolfe)

Richard Wilbur (poet)

P. G. Wodehouse (humorist, *Anything Goes*)

MAURA JACOBSON: Anne Meara—some years ago I included her name in a puzzle on comediennes, and she wrote back that she was very flattered to be included with some great names. Then we went to a benefit, and we saw her there, and I asked my husband, "Do you think I ought to go over and tell her who I am?" And he said, "Oh yes, by all means." So I did, and she was very . . . almost excited about it. Her son Ben was there, and she introduced me, and he was very unimpressed. But then we went after the show—the play was somewhere up in the nineties in Manhattan—to Elaine's. We were having a sandwich, and Anne Meara walks in, and loud and clear, she says, "Oh, the Jacobsons are here!" Everyone turned around to look. That was my fifteen seconds of glory.

I think puzzles are wonderful ways to keep your mind working and to help continuously learn new things.
—Andy Clayton, solver

4.

CONSTRUCTION PAPER

---- ✴ ----

WORDS TO A WOULD-BE CONSTRUCTOR

ESNE, OLIO, ANOA,

RAREE, MOA, EMU, GOA;

These are in your puzzle? Maybe

You should stop constructing, baby!

Constructing is a lot like solving, just with different rules.
—Jon Delfin

Constructing crosswords, as any crossword constructor will tell you, can be a frustrating, low- and slow-paying, time-intensive endeavor. It is also, however, an eminently satisfying one that supplies education, entertainment, and a gratifying sense of achievement. If you've ever thought you might like to try it, or if you're just curious about how it's done, read on.

How does one get started? Well, that's a question with no easy answer. The first thing a prospective crossword constructor should do is to evaluate his or her skill set. It's helpful to have a background in puzzle-solving, English proficiency (in spelling, grammar, word usage), a good memory, a sense of humor (especially an affinity for puns), and well-rounded general knowledge, including at least a passing acquaintance with today's music, TV shows, and films, plus the notables in each of these fields. Free time is a factor as well (you'll need it!)—although less so now than in the days before we had computer programs to help with the more mundane construction chores. Software such as Antony Lewis's Crossword Compiler and Sam Bellotto, Jr.'s Crossdown can greatly reduce the amount of time it takes to whip a puzzle into salable shape.

The process of creating crossword puzzles from scratch (that is, without using software) could consume an entire volume—and has. If you're serious about getting into the crossword game and mastering the tricks of the trade, it behooves you to locate a copy of the unfortunately out-of-print *Random House Puzzlemaker's Handbook* (formerly titled *The Compleat Cruciverbalist*) by noted puzzle editor Mel Rosen and his cohort-in-crime, Stanley Kurzban. The principles, methods, and techniques outlined in that volume are invaluable in learning how to create and market your efforts from square one.

But back to computers: One of the first decisions the nascent puzzler has to make is whether or not to use crossword-construction programs such as the aforementioned industry-standard "big two": Crossdown and Crossword Compiler (also known as Crossword Compiler for Windows, or CCW), both for the Windows platform (Mac users, your options are sadly limited). There are pros and cons to using such programs, but my strong feeling is that they take so much of the drudgery out of the construction process (I can remember hours spent with graph paper, a fat black felt pen, and a ruler, coloring in the solid squares in my diagrams) that constructors can't afford *not* to have at least one. They completely eliminate former banes of the constructor's existence (such as misnumbering), enforce diagram symmetry, and keep track of clues that have been used. CCW also features an "AutoFill" function that links to dictionaries (in list form) or user-defined word lists, and generates the grid's nontheme answer words (known as "fill").

The downside of having software generate your fill is that unless you spend time developing word lists—deleting the lousy, obscure, and just plain boring words and adding snappy slang and zippy phrases—your puzzles will be rife with dull and unacceptable entries. Maintenance of word lists and dictionaries is a critical and very time-consuming task, if you're going to use the software effectively. Even then, in many cases you'll be forced to redo portions of the puzzle because the same darn words, particularly of the three- (ELI) and four-letter (ARIA) variety, reappear in puzzle after puzzle. We'll take a closer look at constructing puzzles with software after running through a few basic exercises for new constructors.

BASIC TRAINING

If you're completely new to the game, it's best to start small: try some elementary crossings. Dig out some graph paper and draw a 3 × 3 grid. Can you fill it in using no duplicated words? Try using words with alternating vowels and consonants, as shown on the next page.

```
T I P
A R E
```

```
F O R
A R E
```

Once you've mastered the 3 × 3, try a 4 × 4, then a 5 × 5. Proper names are fine, but try not to use any crosswordese (ANOA, ERNE). Next, try reducing the number of plurals you use, then try cluing your entries.

```
F A D S
. . . .
. . . .
E A T S
```

```
Y E A R N
O L L I E
K A P P A
. . . . .
. . . . .
```

Once you've mastered smaller grids (a skill that will come in handy when it comes time to fill in sections of larger grids), go bigger: to a 13 × 13 or 15 × 15 grid. Ah, things are exponentially more complicated now, aren't they? Where do the black squares go? How will the longer words fit? Let's see how computers can help.

It doesn't matter if a cat is black or white, as long as it catches mice.
—*DENG Xiaoping*

Crossword Compiler has a set of stock grids to help get you started, so let's give them a whirl. First, we should come up with a set of "theme" (long) entries to insert into our grid. Three should do the trick for a simple 15 × 15, and we'll make them each fifteen letters long. How about three traits every crossworder should have: ADVENTUROUSNESS, MISCHIEVOUSNESS, and PERSPIC-UOUSNESS. Browsing through CCW's grid store, you'll find that there are quite a number that fill the bill. (Some need slight modification to remove "cheaters.") Here's what the process looks like:

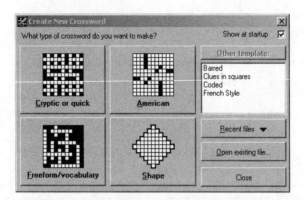

Choose "American."

Choose "15 × 15."

Browse through the selection of stock grids (each pattern will appear in the grid on the right as it is selected on the left) and choose one that will accommodate three fifteen-letter entries.

Because the theme entries haven't been entered in the puzzle diagram, choose "Put the words in myself." (CCW can create an entire puzzle from scratch—but it can't come up with themes!)

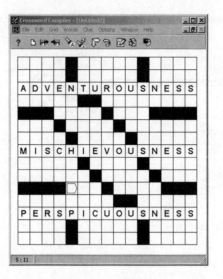

Here's one of CCW's stock grids, slightly modified (we removed cheater squares and moved one black square to increase the "stair-step" layout, a procedure that also breaks up long white-square chains into more manageable areas), with theme entries in place. (Note that they're placed so that they're pretty well separated from each other, which makes filling in the grid quite a bit easier.) Keep an eye out for oddball letters (I, V, U, J, Q, Z) that appear at the ends of words. Another thing to look at is the common crossings: answer words that contain letters from two or more theme entries. In this case, we have links between ADVENTUROUSNESS and MISCHIEVOUSNESS (S to S, on the right-hand side of the grid in the upper half) and MISCHIEVOUSNESS and PERSPICUOUSNESS (H to P, lower left). The second of these crossings is a possible problem (there probably aren't many words that fit the pattern H ? ? ? ? P), so we'll check in our CCW dictionaries (each gets its own tab) for possible matches.

Hmm . . . let's try switching ADVENTUROUSNESS and PERSPICUOUS-NESS and see what crossings that gives us.

Seems a little more reasonable: S to S and H to N. Using CCW's "Find Word" feature again, we see there are quite a few more words that fit H to N than H to P, so we'll leave the entries as-is.

Where can you find dictionaries or word lists to use with CCW or Cross-down?

* You can make your own—a laborious process, to say the least.

* You can use and modify CCW's related Word Web program (additional fee; does not come with the base package).

* You can search on-line for freely available dictionaries. A good place to start is at the cruciverb.com Web site.

Next, we'll use CCW's AutoFill feature to complete the rest of the diagram. Let's take a look at the result:

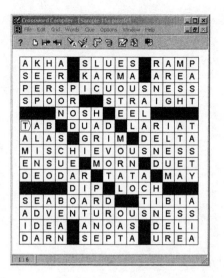

Ugh! Look at all that crosswordese: AKHA, LAC, ANOAS, UREA, and so on. You'll also note the presence of two forms of the same word (a big no-no): SEABOARD and AT SEA. This is one of the crossword constructor's complaints about such "autofill" functions: The result often takes so much work to fix that it's easier and quicker to generate the fill yourself. CCW does, however, let you use AutoFill with many different options (including assigning a numeric value to each word and choosing to fill your grid with words of a minimum numeric value)—and you can always modify the word lists and dictionaries to delete the objectionable entries. If you plan on constructing crosswords regularly and using this feature, the effort is well worth it.

Crossword Compiler's cluing function allows you to see numbers on the left, clues on the right, and to type in your definitions in between.

Double-clicking on any clue brings up the clue database, allowing you to look at, edit, add, or delete existing clues. You can also use existing clues in your current puzzle.

When the diagram is finished and the clues written, you can export your puzzle in a variety of formats for use in Microsoft Word or desktop publishing programs.

Now let's look at the same process using Crossdown.

First, choose "Construct" → "New" → "15×." All the standard commercial sizes are here, but CCW gives you a bit more flexibility in being able to create diagrams of nonstandard sizes (such as 11×15 and 27×27).

The next step is naming your puzzle and saving it to a location on your hard drive (the default save folder is PUZZLES in your Crossdown installation directory).

Up pops a blank grid in the size you selected. No stock grids here, so we'll place our own black squares. When the black squares have been entered, theme entries are typed in.

Under "Options" → "Preferences," you'll find the "Tools" tab, which allows you to link to any dictionary and/or thesaurus software installed on your computer. Crossdown does not have an autofill function, so you'll need to fill in the grid yourself (with the aid of your dictionary and thesaurus software or hardcopy references). An optional add-on to Crossdown, the Cluebank program, keeps track of the answer words and definitions you've used in the past.

When you're ready to send your puzzle to market, you can choose from a variety of file formats for export.

* * *

As you see, software—while not perfect—can greatly ease the construction process, leaving you more time for the fun stuff, like theme creation. On to the crossword constructor's rules of thumb.

If you don't do it excellently, don't do it at all. Because if it's not excellent, it won't be profitable or fun, and if you're not in business for fun or profit, what the hell are you doing there?
—*Robert Townsend, from* Farther Up the Organization

GROUND RULES

Here are some general tips for new constructors.

MARTIN ASHWOOD-SMITH: Aim to construct the kinds of puzzles that you really like to solve. I've always liked to solve themeless 15 × 15s with unusual and interesting grids.

BILL ZAIS: I enjoy solving complex, devious puzzles, so those are the kind I enjoy constructing.

NANCY SALOMON: I can't recommend regular solving of quality crosswords enough to new constructors.

RICH NORRIS: Solve lots of quality puzzles, and pay attention to how themes are constructed.

NELSON HARDY: Solve a lot of puzzles, and take notes. What's the average word count? What's the average number of theme entries? What percentage of words in a puzzle are unfamiliar to you?

- Do your homework: solve, solve, solve. You won't know what's been done or what contemporary styles are unless you do some research into the crossword marketplace. Stick with established puzzle sources such as the *New York Times*, Random House and Simon & Schuster crossword publications, and so on. This has an additional benefit: You won't waste your time on themes that have already been done, and you just may find inspiration in someone else's clever creation.

Read, read, read.
—*Sylvia Bursztyn*

■ By reading books, newspapers, and publications such as *People Weekly, Entertainment Weekly, Time, Newsweek*, and the like, you can pick up ideas or gain knowledge you'll use in constructing puzzles. You'll also familiarize yourself with current goings-on in music, film, and television—subjects that appeal to a broad audience, and subjects with which that audience is familiar.

MARTIN ASHWOOD-SMITH: Join the crossword community on the Internet. Cruciverb-L is a great place to meet constructors and solvers, beginners and experts.

■ Don't be afraid to ask for help. If you don't have any contacts of your own, participate in the Cruciverb-L forum, on the Internet at www.cruciverb.com. According to Rich Norris, "You can get quite a lot of helpful feedback there. Some skillful constructors, such as Nancy Salomon and Manny Nosowsky, make a habit of mentoring new constructors. I've been doing some of that lately, as well, in my role as associate editor of the *Los Angeles Times* Syndicate crossword puzzles."

STANDARDS AND PRACTICES

■ Diagrams are typically perfectly square, with an equal, odd number of squares across and down (resulting in a central column and a central row); the standard sizes are 15×15, 21×21, 23×23 (for commercial markets, there is rarely any deviation from these sizes). The *New York Times* features 15 × 15 puzzles Monday through Saturday, and 21 × 21 or 23 × 23 puzzles on Sundays.

- No word is an island: Each entry in the grid must be part of both an across and a down word.

- Your answer words must be at least three letters long (some publications allow two-letter words for supereasy puzzles, but this is the exception rather than the rule).

- Your black squares must be diagonally symmetrical in your grid. If you have a black square in the uppermost left square, you must also have one at the lowermost right.

GRIDLOCK

- Beginning constructors may find it easier to use others' diagrams (say, from a *New York Times* puzzle, from Crossword Compiler's set of stock grids, or Crossdown's library of sample puzzles) rather than having to create them from scratch.

ERICA ROTHSTEIN: Merl [Reagle] used to say he used to try to make every single puzzle have a different design of black squares. I said to him, "Why? You don't actually think solvers are going to put them up on the wall to compare them and say, 'Oh no, he used this one already!' do you? That's a thing for you—it has absolutely nothing to do with constructing or solving a puzzle. And that's a ludicrous waste of time. What do I care if you use the same diagram over again? Turn it on its side. It doesn't matter."

- If you're doing your own grid construction, make things easier on yourself by beginning at the center of the puzzle when placing your black squares. Start with a stair-step arrangement that gives you a series of four- or five-letter words that run through the center of the grid from the upper left to the lower right or vice-versa. If you're doing a themed puzzle, place your black squares in a logical, stair-step arrangement first, then remove or rearrange them as needed to create space for the longer entries.

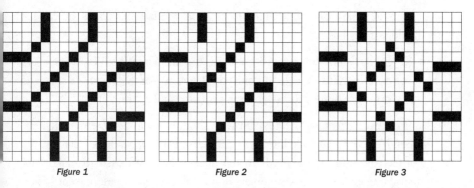

Figure 1   Figure 2   Figure 3

Figure 1 contains four "islands" (isolated areas with no common letters) of grid blocks. Switching just a couple of black squares yields a much more user-friendly diagram (Figure 2), albeit one with a few only-one-way-in sections. Rearranging again yields a strong diagram ready for the filling (Figure 3). This grid also illustrates a constructor's trick: If you have a semi-isolated area of words in the grid, instead of placing black squares in a stair-step design, as in Figures 1 and 2, flip two of them so that they still split the longer entries but allow for a more open grid design. Figures 4 and 5 illustrate this principle.

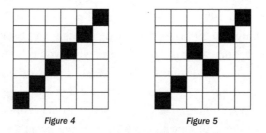

Figure 4   Figure 5

Bob Klahn has an interesting take on grid construction: "Grid-building is still the part of crossword constructing I love the most, the part I find by far the most exciting. Fundamental to my jungle theory of grid construction, and to my thinking, is that grids already exist; I just discover them. Filled grids live in multidimensional grid space. Where in multidimensional grid space are the cities? Where do the grids cluster? Where is "New Jersey," and where is "Wyoming"? Some grid sections are very easy to change; they live in the cities. Others cannot be changed but must be ripped out and replaced; they live in the boonies. Others are somewhere in between; they live in the 'burbs. Which black-square structures promote cities, and which tend to promote the boonies? Yes, that's what it's like inside my brain."

- Keep your three-letter-word count as low as possible. Why? There are comparatively few of them, and you'll notice—as will your editors and solvers—the same culprits cropping up time and again.

- What are "cheater" squares and why shouldn't you use them? Cheaters, per *New York Times* editor Will Shortz, are black squares "that do not affect the number of words in the puzzle, but are added to make constructing easier." Frankly, solvers don't care if cheaters are present or not, so why are they frowned upon? You'll have a hard time sneaking too many of them past quality editors, who feel that they detract from the elegance of the grid design. (Don't worry if you need a couple in a particularly knotty puzzle, though—*occasional* use is almost unavoidable.)

BOB KLAHN: I'm Will Shortz's grid doctor—which is not to say that any grids that get changed from what the constructor submits are my work. Will makes all the simpler edits and most of the not-so-simple edits, but he also sends quite a number of grids my way. I've studied his work, and I know what he likes. One day, back in 1994, I noticed a *New York Times* grid that I thought could've been quite a bit better. So I made it better, and I sent him a copy. I said, "It's my bet that there are many times when you need to edit grids. I'd like you to consider me as a resource." He liked the work sample I'd given him, and pretty quickly after that he sent me a couple of grids just to see what I could do with them. He was pleased with the results, so he sent me more. I've been doing this backroom work ever since, and it's very gratifying.

SQUARE DEAL

Due to limited printing space, most editors have established maximum black-square and word counts. The general guidelines are given here.

ERICA ROTHSTEIN: Solvers don't even know there's such a thing as a limit to the [number of] black squares. What does it do? A lower word count—it makes for longer words, true. So what? It can also make for puzzles that are hard to solve and hard to start. We always had one absolute rule [at Dell]: You don't cross an unknowable with an ungettable.

- As a general rule (see Will Shortz's thoughts, below), no more than one-sixth of the grid should be black squares (because of space constraints, maximum word counts may also apply—check with your editor). Here's how this translates:

13 × 13: 28 or 30 black squares

15 × 15: 38 (*New York Times* maximum word count: 78 for a themed puzzle, 72 for an unthemed)

17 × 17: 48 or 50

19 × 19: 60 or 62

21 × 21: 74 (*New York Times* maximum word count: 140)

23 × 23: 88 or 90 (*New York Times* maximum word count: 168)

WILL SHORTZ: The old one-sixth rule really applies only to themeless puzzles. In themed fifteens, it's not unusual to see forty, forty-one, or sometimes even more black squares—and this is true for most of the top markets (including the *New York Times*).

Actually, the old one-sixth rule doesn't even apply to themeless puzzles, which tend to have many *fewer* than one-sixth black squares. The important thing for constructors is to avoid large clumps of black squares, which are cheap and visually off-putting. If a puzzle has a low word count and avoids black clumps, by definition it'll be well under one-sixth.

- Most editors allow marginally higher word counts in themed puzzles than in themeless puzzles. And speaking of themes . . .

THEME PARK

Rem tene; verba sequentur (Grasp the subject; the words will follow).
—CATO

No one can tell a new constructor how to think up themes. It's a skill developed over the course of years—years spent solving puzzles, punning, and playing with words. That's not to say that there are no sources of inspiration, however: other constructors' themes can lead to interesting new ideas (don't plagiarize another's work, though!); thesauruses can help with building lists of related elements; and books, TV shows, and movies can trigger one's imagination.

The most common mistake [beginners make] is using an overworked theme such as colors or parts of the body.
—John Samson

- Don't use a theme that's been done before unless you have an unusual or interesting twist. Editors have seen variations on flowers, animal names, clothing, cities, and so on ad nauseam. Repeat-a-word themes are trite too, and you'll find few outlets for such efforts. Strive for originality—one good reason to solve others' puzzles: You can't know what's been done unless you've seen what's out there.

Never express yourself more clearly than you think.
—NIELS Bohr

- For quotation themes, look for a lesser-known, humorous citation and make sure you get it all—in order—into the grid. A nifty plus: Include the name of the quote's author in the grid.

- As with your fill (see below), don't use themes focusing on "downer" topics (guns, diseases, other unpleasantries) or rarefied terms specific to a particular art or occupation.

BOB KLAHN: The more potential theme entries you generate before thinking about grid layout, the better the eventual puzzle is likely to be, because you've given yourself more options.

- When possible, don't begin construction of a themed puzzle until you have a good surplus (at least twice what you'll need) of potential theme entries.

- Don't hesitate to trash a theme entry if it doesn't fit naturally into the grid—even if it's your best one. If you can't bear to toss it, redesign the puzzle or come up with more candidates.

- Don't try to stuff too many theme entries into a grid. The general minimums for common puzzle sizes are three theme entries for a 15 × 15 (four, better) and six for a 21 × 21 (eight, better; ten or twelve, fabulous; although, as always, length plays a part—if your theme entries are fairly long, you'll get by with less).

- If you're basing your theme on a recognizable, fairly small set of items (for example, the Seven Wonders of the World), include all members of the group. You must also treat each entry in the same manner—that is, don't drop letters from one entry and add letters to another.

- Nancy Salomon makes a couple of very good points on the Cruciverb-L Web site (both Nancy and Cruciverb-L are great sources of useful information for new constructors): First, your theme must be consistent (verbs should be of the same tense; nouns should be singular or plural, not both). Second, if you're using puns based on clichés or other common phrases, make sure they're just that: common, and immediately recognizable to the average solver.

- Organize your theme entries. Group prospective theme answers by letter count (put all of your ten-letter entries together; then your eleven-letter entries, and so on). All theme entries—except those running down the center of the puzzle vertically or horizontally—must be diagonally symmetrical within the grid (that is, if you have a fifteen-letter entry starting three squares down the left edge of the grid, you must also have a fifteen-letter entry starting three squares up from the right edge of the grid). If you'd like to interlock theme entries (a nice touch that also allows you to fit more into a diagram), you will need to identify common letters in key positions. For my own constructing efforts, I have a table (created in Microsoft Word) into which I enter prospective entries sorted by letter count. Then, I go through the list and write in each entry's third and third-to-last, fourth and fourth-to-last, and fifth and fifth-to-last letters, along with the central letter for odd-letter-count entries (the fifth letter is the center of a nine-letter entry; the sixth for elevens; seventh for thirteens; and so on). Here's what the layout looks like with sample theme entries (from a 21 × 21 crossword titled "The Ten Commandments of Modeling," originally published in *Los Angeles Magazine*):

Size	Entry	3-1	3-L	4-1	4-L	5-1	5-L	Ctr.
15	ESCORT ROCK STARS	C	A	O	T	R	S	O
	DENY BEING A BIMBO	N	M	Y	I	B	B	N
13	BECOME BULIMIC	C	M	O	I	M	L	B
	HAVE HISSY FITS	V	O	E	F	H	Y	S
11	KEEP THE RING	E	I	P	R	T	E	H
	GET A BOOB JOB	T	J	A	B	B	O	O
10	CHAIN-SMOKE	A	O	I	M	N	S	
	DEMAND VSOP	M	S	A	V	N	D	
9	PACK EVIAN	C	I	K	V	E	E	E
	TAKE LIMOS	K	M	E	I	L	L	L

Here's how they were matched up:

1. I looked first for "3-1" entries with matching "3-1" or "3-L" entries. Here, we have a perfect fit: the "C" in the 3-1 position of ESCORT ROCK STARS matches with the "C" in the 3-1 position of PACK EVIAN, and the "M" in DENY BEING A BIMBO (3-L) matches with the "M" in TAKE LIMOS (3-L). *Note:* Because of the diagonal-symmetry grid rule, if we come up with a match for the upper left, we must also have a match for the lower right, with identical letter counts.

2. There are also center-letter matches: on the "O" in ESCORT ROCK STARS and the "O" in GET A BOOB JOB; however, since the former was used in the upper left corner of the grid, center-grid entries weren't possible. (Why only odd-numbered entries for central grid placement? Because even letter counts result in a different number of squares before and after the central entry, violating the symmetry rule.)

3. Next, the first set of interlocking entries was placed into a 21 × 21 grid:

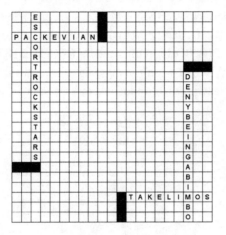

4. Black-square placement was dictated by the position of the theme entries (a black square ends each, and two additional squares were added to make a block of three—a necessity due to the location of the theme entry, since putting black squares to the left or right of the one at the end of the entry would result in two-letter entries: not allowed).

5. The nine-letter entries dovetail perfectly with the eleven-letter entries, creating a row twenty-one squares across, so those were placed next:

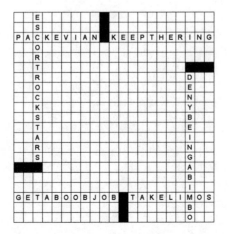

6. Next, I did some nosing around to see if I could cross any more theme entries. In this very atypical case, everything fell into place and all entries fit—with interlocks! CHAIN-SMOKE's second letter fit vertically with KEEP THE RING, and DEMAND VSOP's second-to-last letter fit vertically with GET A BOOB JOB; same for BECOME BULIMIC and HAVE HISSY FITS. (No, it wasn't really quite this easy—it took hours of hard labor, with many prospective theme entries attempted and discarded.)

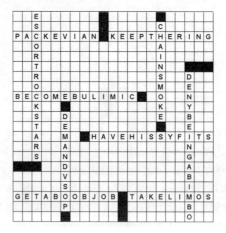

7. I placed the remaining black squares in such a way as to minimize contact between theme entries, some of which are very close together; then I filled the rest of the grid (ooh, look at them cheaters!).

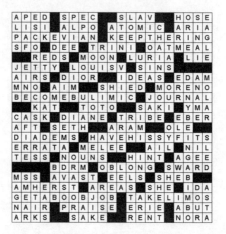

- There is no minimum-letter-count rule or requirement for theme entries, but a good rule of thumb for 21 × 21 puzzles is nine letters (10 + 10 or 9 + 11 combinations create a perfect 21-square row with one black square separating them, and tens can be split into 4 + 5; nines into 4 + 4; and elevens into 5 + 5).

- Theme entries should be symmetrical within the grid, and fill words should generally be of lesser length than the shortest theme entry.

Erudition, n.: Dust shaken out of a book into an empty skull.
—Ambrose Bierce

- Don't show off your outstanding grasp of the Ugric tongues in the seventeenth century; make your theme accessible to a wide audience.

- Give your puzzle a title that will clue the solver in to the nature of your theme.

INSPIRATION POINT

MERL REAGLE: David Letterman's top-ten lists are the most real-world manifestations of what a crossword theme is like: One thing at the top, then ten things under it. Of course, he doesn't have to make them fit [in a grid]. And very often, his are whole sentences. Like, he'll do "Nicknames for Robert Bork's beard": THE AMISH OUTLAW, things like that. When they're things like that and they're short, that's the exact kind of thing a crossword puzzler uses. . . . Do lines heard in every kind of genre film. So if you're going to see a sci-fi movie, someone's going to say, "That's funny, my watch stopped too." It's the kind of thing that makes you crack up because of the recognizability. In a Disney film: "But I don't *want* a lot of dogs. I want Sparky."

NANCY SCHUSTER: I've been inspirationally challenged. I don't know where they keep coming up with new themes. It astonishes me. My last good puzzle was *Men in Black*—the year that movie came out, I guess that was two or three years ago, I did a puzzle about that. After that, I went dry. I don't even enjoy it anymore. When you know there's a program out there that's going to throw the words into a grid by itself, you sort of don't even want to bother. I used to pore over every little corner—two weeks on one corner just to see what I liked best. It's too much like work.

RICH NORRIS: In the beginning I did a lot of brainstorming. Nowadays I'll plan sessions for myself in which I sit down with a favorite reference book and look for words, phrases, titles, names that have some relationship to one another. I keep a theme notebook, which has completed theme ideas as well as snippets— dozens of them—that are just waiting for that one last phrase to complete them. For instance, there are reasonably well-known people whose first names are Adam, Eve, Abel, and Seth, but no one famous whose first name is Cain. Someday that person will arrive, and I'll finally get to do my Genesis theme.

RANDOLPH ROSS: The muse has to visit to come up with a theme. I'm inspired by what makes me chuckle or groan. I think I have a sense of what's clever and [am able to] extrapolate cleverness into themes. I'm always writing theme ideas on scraps of paper. Other constructors inspire me as well.

RICH SILVESTRI: I wait for the muse to visit and suggest a theme. Then I try (sometimes fruitlessly) to come up with matching theme entries. Once they fall into place, the rest is grunt work until it comes time to write the clues.

KELLY CLARK: What usually happens with me is a theme idea will hit me while I'm doing something else: working, reading, taking a shower. Sometimes I'll jot it down (except when I'm in the shower). I have fun making up quips, funny observations, riddles, and such, and then rewording them so that they work symmetrically.

MERL REAGLE: The trouble with themes is [that] you can't tell people, because you're ruining it for them. It's like telling them how a mystery ends, like, "Read my book, and by the way, here's how it ends."

SYLVIA BURSZTYN: All our crosswords have themes. Perhaps five of our fifty-two or fifty-three *Los Angeles Times* puzzles per year are from themes Barry suggests. The rest are my themes. I don't know how to explain where the themes come from. "Salinas" is my stock answer. When I sit down to write a puzzle, I pick up my gray legal pad and stare at a page blank except for the puzzle's date and number. I look at my [chronological file] to see what my last four or five themes have been so as not to repeat a theme style too soon. Somehow, something clicks in, and I have a theme to start developing. Often, the theme I end up with is only marginally related to the one I started with. The first theme entries I think of, the ones that suggest the theme, often don't make it into the final grid because of letter-count requirements (the "ones that got away"). I keep a stock of half-developed themes and occasionally check to see if I can develop any of them further. New movie titles, new songs, fresh famous names, etc., that have come on the scene over time can save one of those dormant themes. Usually I write a puzzle from a theme just thought up.

MERL REAGLE: I do a lot of just straight pun puzzles. Like Ralph Lauren's CLONE FOR MEN, clued as "Type of perfume that makes you smell like the next guy." That one also had LIFE WITHOUT THE POSSIBILITY OF PEROT. It's very similar to Johnny Carson's Carnak character, where he holds an envelope to his head, says an answer, then opens the envelope to reveal the question. The answer is ALL SYSTEMS GO. The clue is "What happens when you eat peanut butter and chili peppers and Coke?" NO FLY ZONE: "The worst place to be for a frog." THE BARN SWALLOW: "What's the hardest act to follow at a county fair?" They work in puzzles because they're "joke jokes," they're funny in a real-world sort of way. You could pull them out of the puzzle and just tell them as jokes. That was the main thing I was trying to do in puzzles that I felt wasn't being done. I just thought that if a puzzle is supposed to be funny, you're supposed to laugh. It's the setup and the gag, so that a complete non-crossword fan might laugh.

NELSON HARDY: I keep a list of theme ideas, which come to me while reading or watching TV or driving around or eating breakfast; in other words, any time in the course of a day. When I sit down to make a puzzle, I'll start with one of these basic theme ideas and see how many theme entries I can come up with. If I can come up with enough good entries, I make it a 21×21 puzzle; otherwise, it's a 15×15. I place the theme entries in the grid, place black squares where they seem to be conducive to construction, and start filling in whatever appears to be the most problematic spot. If necessary, I rearrange the black squares as I go.

ELIZABETH GORSKI: Themes come to me at all times of the day, whenever I hear an interesting word or phrase. I keep a notebook of potential thematic ideas.

JOHN SAMSON: Themes come right out of the blue. They appear when I least expect them. I was watching a documentary on Coney Island a few days ago when the roller coaster theme popped into my head. (I may also do another puzzle just on Coney Island after watching that show.) Crosswords are constructed similar to houses: first comes the frame (long thematic entries) and then the rest of the house (other words.) I'm big on themes—I only accept themed puzzles for Simon & Schuster. A crossword without a theme is like a movie without a plot.

BOB KLAHN: One thing I haven't done—and I'm not planning to do—is to catalog themes. I want my theme ideas to be my own—I don't want to poison my mind any more than it's already been poisoned!

SAM BELLOTTO, JR.: The best puzzle ideas are not forced—even [for] those markets for which I do a regular puzzle and know beforehand what the general theme must be. I like to go jogging with my dog, and this has a tendency to bounce some really good concepts out of my brain.

WILLIAM CANINE: Ideas for themes come from anywhere and everywhere, sometimes just the sudden intrusion on your consciousness of a peculiar word. Every puzzle must begin with the thematic entries, as they determine the grid. I have a file full of ideas. Some may take years until fruition.

JON DELFIN: Themes occur and get scribbled down. Sometimes they're run past Will Shortz and Stan Newman. Eventually, I will pick up the folder and start making a puzzle, often during blizzards. Global warming may end my constructing career.

GAYLE DEAN: Coming up with fresh themes is a difficult task. Word lists and word groupings often provide ideas for themes. I keep a notepad by my bed and often wake up at three A.M. with a flood of ideas to jot down. Friends and family also provide grist for the mill.

PETER GORDON: I have a notebook full of theme ideas. Often they're too complex to execute. Sometimes I have an idea and I need another example of a certain length before I can make it. Sometimes that comes much later.

MAURA JACOBSON: I do kooky puzzles. I'm working on one about mergers. The merger of Polydent, Warner, and Keebler would be POLYWARNER CRACKER. They're usually groaners, but people seem to like them. Another one I have, and I like this one, is "What is the result of a merger of Xerox and Wurlitzer?" And the answer is REPRODUCTIVE ORGAN. I prefer humor. But you can't do this every week.

MERL REAGLE: Very often, a single word leads to an entire theme. I once looked at the phrase EYE-CATCHING and thought, "Gee, that sounds like an event at a county fair that I *really* would not want to take part in"—which led to a puzzle called "The Stephen King County Fair." Now, this particular theme took more than just a day or two of thinking, because what it specifically involved was common expressions that have nothing overtly to do with Stephen King, but which can nevertheless be clued in a Stephen King way. This took about a month, just saving them up until I finally had enough. Plus, they had to be paired together by letter length because of the symmetry rule. In fact I had to think of about twenty or twenty-five of them in order to winnow it down to just a dynamite ten. It had things like TALKING HEADS and MONSTER TRUCKS. That puzzle turned out pretty well. Another one was "Top ten things your butcher gets tired of hearing," like WHERE'S THE BEEF? and IS THIS LIVER YOUR WURST? and THIS LAMB IS YOUR LAMB, THIS LAMB IS MY LAMB, etc.

NANCY SALOMON: How one comes up with themes is an often-asked and, in my opinion, unanswerable question. Sometimes I can re-create my thought processes, but more often, I have no idea where my theme ideas spring from. I can tell you that working on one set of theme entries often leads to other ideas. I keep a book with half-baked theme ideas in it.

NANCY JOLINE: Coming up with new themes is the hardest part of puzzlemaking for me. Everything has been done before, and many times. I do keep a file of ideas; if I'm not happy with a selection of theme entries I'm working on, I'll stick it in the file for a while. When I retrieve it later, I may come up with a new slant on it.

PATRICK JORDAN: First, I come up with the theme. Like most other constructors with whom I've spoken, I keep a notebook in which I scribble potential theme ideas whenever I happen to think of them. Most often, themes occur to me when I hear or read a common phrase containing a key word that belongs to a certain category (car parts, species of rodents, etc.). Then, I try to think of other phrases sharing this trait, often using library resources to help me. If I'm lucky, I eventually build a list of four to ten themed phrases that have lengths that can be placed symmetrically in a grid.

However, themes can also come from surprising sources. Once, I was watching a *Roadrunner* cartoon and, as usually happens at the start of those films, the Roadrunner halted in midstride while a fictional Latin name (something like Fastus Furious) appeared beneath him. This inspired me to come up with a list of phony taxonomical terms, using real words ending in the "-ous" sound, which could describe other fictional characters. They included BOGUS ADONIS for Austin Powers, RAUCOUS IGNORAMUS for any of the Three Stooges, and COVETOUS COLOSSUS for the giant from "Jack and the Beanstalk." Stanley Newman used this crossword in his *Uptown Puzzle Club.*

In addition, I frequently discover theme ideas while solving other constructors' crosswords. No, I don't mean outright plagiarism! But sometimes, a theme answer can belong to two different categories. For example, I was once solving a puzzle by Trip Payne, whose theme involved phrases containing things you can find in a dining room. One of his theme answers was TABLE-HOPPER. When I wrote it into the diagram, it occurred to me that many TABLE-HOPPERs are also NAME-DROPPERs. A bit of research turned up two more eleven-letter rhyming terms for general types of people, TEENYBOPPER and SHOW-STOPPER. I placed the four entries into a 15 × 15 grid, and it became the second puzzle I sold to the *New York Times.*

Anyhow, once the theme entries are determined, I seek out a suitable grid and begin filling the diagram. First, I come up with possibilities for the longest nontheme entries, using interesting words, names, and phrases in lieu of single dictionary words whenever possible. (Some of my recent efforts have included such nontheme entries as GENE AUTRY, BE MY GUEST, and NOVA SCOTIA.) I plug these potential entries into their places and see if I can finish the sections in which they appear without resorting to crosswordese or creating spots that are impossible to fill. Once the grid is completed, I write the clues. This often takes nearly as long as the construction process, because I strive to avoid overused clues when I can. It involves a lot of thought and research, especially for such frequently occurring words as ERIE and ARIA.

BOB KLAHN: My wife, Sharon, helps me with theme and clue ideas. I definitely think that most of "my" best themes "have Sharon in them."

DAVID J. KAHN: I never sit down to actually start writing a puzzle until I've thought about whether the theme really excites me and whether I could do it in a way that's fresh. If I'm not sure, I don't do it. Since the ideas I think are good don't pop up that often, I don't really have an inventory of ideas for later use.

MANNY NOSOWSKY: Don't keep a list. Themes just come.

DIANE EPPERSON: I solve several crosswords a day and occasionally will get an idea for a theme from one of those. For instance, say a puzzle uses various synonyms for "strike": HIT the bricks, POUND the pavement, etc. I write down the salient terms/clues, author's name, and date so I won't inadvertently duplicate his or her work. This gives me the idea to find various terms for, say, "leap": JUMP the gun, etc. I might see a headline in a magazine or newspaper, hear a clever phrase from an announcer, whatever. I write it down and put it into my theme folder. I was reading a mystery novel in which the hero decides to confront his nemesis at the local eatery, called the Whine Cellar. That got me started making a list of homonyms for use in future puzzles.

DAVID MACLEOD: I have lists of [theme] possibilities. Some of them are years old. For themes, some phrase or term may just pop into my mind and I'll build on it. Sometimes I ask my siblings for input. TV and printed news are also good sources for themes.

CATHY MILLHAUSER: Anything is grist for the mill: current trends, kids' language stumblings, a comic strip. I do keep a notebook of possible ideas.

FRED PISCOP: If I have an idea and I can't get the lengths correct or I can't get enough [entries], I'll jot it down and put it in a folder and [later] I'll pull it back out again.

TOM SCHIER: I start with a theme, develop theme-related words, and go for it. I try to use eight to ten theme words in a daily grid. Lists! I have lots of lists with lots of ideas and themes. I'm always on the prowl for quotes, fifteen-letter words, puns, names, etc., etc.

GREG STAPLES: I have a pile of potential ideas that I go through, especially when I don't have anything hot. The hot ideas get worked on immediately. Theme ideas can come at any time—hearing conversation, seeing a film, reading the paper. My constructor subconscious is always lurking, looking for ideas.

MEL TAUB: [I] start thinking about a theme and keep jotting down words and phrases that fit. In any given case, one or another reference book could help the process.

ARTHUR S. VERDESCA: First I get a theme idea, then I make long lists of all possible thematic entries (usually three to five times more words than I eventually end up using). Then you work and work at it. I certainly do keep all my thematic lists for possible use in future puzzles. I get theme ideas from my reading, from reference works, from my wife, friends, anywhere.

LEONARD WILLIAMS: I've arrived at themes from various sources. I started out with material from my work. I've since been inspired by items in the newspapers or on the radio, by comments made by friends, and other such sources.

BILL ZAIS: I construct themed puzzles only, since my grid-filling abilities aren't very good yet. The process is a bit eclectic and about 80 percent inspirational. I do keep a list of ideas, and some of those ideas can lie fallow for a long time. I just finished a puzzle that had been on my idea list for a year and a half.

FILLING STATION

Fill is the term used for all of the nontheme answer words in a crossword diagram. You will hear editor after editor say that one of the most important construction tasks is the creation of "lively" fill. Now, that adjective is subjective, obviously, but the essence is that you should try to populate your puzzles with colorful, interesting, or uplifting words and phrases rather than dull, oft-seen entries or crosswordese, particularly in your longer (six-plus-letter) non-theme entries.

MERL REAGLE: Then there are taste considerations. One word with excellent letters that would have bailed me out of many a tough corner is ENEMA, but, as we say, it comes up a little short in the entertainment department.

WILL SHORTZ: I love phrases in crosswords, because they tend to be fresh and colorful, they mix up the letter patterns, and generally they add difficulty without obscurity.

- Contemporary slang and phrases (BOOM BOX, WEB SITE) are always appreciated.

> *Slang is a language that rolls up its sleeves, spits on its hands,*
> *and goes to work.*
> *—CARL Sandburg*

- Do not make up phrases (STOLE IT, GOT A BILL) for the sake of filling a tough section of your puzzle.

> *The Greeks had a word for it.*
> *—ZOË AKINS*

- Keep foreign words and abbreviations to a minimum. When you do use them, make sure they are well-known by most solvers (OLE, IRA).

PETER GORDON: Partial phrases, foreign words, actors that were famous fifty years ago, etc., should be avoided as much as possible. Why do we need to know names of people who have been dead for fifty years and weren't that famous even then? It really annoyed me when I first started, but after a few years, you learn the few you need to know (INA Balin, UNA Merkel, etc.). Foreign-language phrases that aren't part of English annoy me, too. And partials (OFLA: *Man____Mancha*) aren't fun.

- Technical jargon is understood by only a select few. For example, as a Web developer I'm familiar with the acronym ASP (which can mean either Active Server Pages or Application Service Provider), but the average solver is going to scratch his head if he sees a clue like this.

JIM PAGE: A lot of people create puzzles—they get a clever idea and they use a theme, then they fill the grid with whatever fits into the grid that will be sensible. I think that's a bad direction to be going in. So I have this list of my own which I add to every day. . . . I happen to think it's critical that the [fill] words in the grid are fresh words, and there are not enough of those. What I've done for the last ten years, or at least since Will Shortz came on board [the *New York Times*], is I have underlined any words I come across in my reading of papers, magazines, books, whatever—any word that I think is a good, fresh word, I underline it, and I put all of those in my computer. So I've got this word list of about twenty thousand words—which are really pretty damn good words, pretty fresh words. I put as many of those in the grid as I'm able.

- Avoid words related to negative topics such as war, disease, drugs, death, and the like. Also, make sure you don't inadvertently include phrases or words that might offend certain ethnic groups (GYP). And, as Erica Rothstein notes (below), each editor has his or her own likes and dislikes (this is why you send away for style sheets!).

ERICA ROTHSTEIN: I never allowed DONUT in a puzzle. Never. There were certain things that some people would've thought were silly, and this is completely personal, but once I got to be editor, I said, "I can do it." I didn't want NIXON in a puzzle. Purely an expression of my own political beliefs, but I didn't care. I just didn't want him in puzzles. There were certain things we didn't mention. . . . If we had a puzzle that was astrological signs, I didn't care if CANCER was one of them. When you see the word isolated on a page, it's not the astrological sign you think of. . . it's a terrible disease.

- Begin filling your puzzle in the most difficult areas. This has two benefits: You'll suss out design problems before you're too far into it, and your construction chores will get easier as you complete the puzzle.

WILL SHORTZ: Partial phrases seem like flawed entries, because inherently they're incomplete. Actually, I don't mind them much when they're short (like OF A and IT IN). Sometimes they're necessary for a constructor to finish a tough corner or a tricky crossing. And I'd much rather have I'M A, which is familiar, than IMU, which is not. (That's an Hawaiian baking pit.) There were lots of words like IMU in old-style crosswords. Ugh! I almost never allow partial phrases that are longer than five letters. The short ones are excusable if they set up interesting [and] lively long answers. But the long answers themselves should not be partial phrases.

■ What are *partials*? Portions of *well-known* (only) phrases that are occasionally allowable as nontheme entries. Editors' policies on partials differ; if you must use them, keep in mind that most editors prefer the colorful (RED ROSE) to the mundane (IS THE).

MERL REAGLE: The word I get tired of cluing the most is ELI. There are only four or five ELIs that people actually know, but in my puzzles it just comes up constantly. Out of complete frustration, I think I once clued it as "Man's name that becomes a girl's name when 'nor' is added." Like, "I'm just tired of looking at it."

NANCY SCHUSTER: I almost said hello to Eli Wallach in the street. He was in tennis clothes, and I was playing tennis at the time. I said, "Oh, hi!" Then I realized, "I don't know you!"

■ Proper names are okay, but don't include the plural form of a name if there's only one famous example (the *Washington Post*'s William R. MacKaye mentions a particular favorite: EARTHAS). Don't include names from any source, including the Bible, that most people aren't likely to have heard of. Ditto for mythological characters and geographical references.

BOB KLAHN: What really turns me on is being able to insert a high percentage of lively material into a grid without also inserting any below-average entries. I avoid inflections as a rule, and entries crossing on inflections (for example, two plurals crossing on the terminal S) in particular. If you were to go through all of my published puzzles, you'd only find a few such crossings. I dislike most partials. Ideally, I want to use colorful vocabulary with lesser-used letters. I tend to use too many names sometimes, but it's all with the goal of making the grid vocabulary itself as colorful and varied as possible. That's always my thrust.

- For beginners, fill words with alternating vowels and consonants are easier to place than words like STYX.

KELLY CLARK: I use what I call the "mom test." Now, my mom, who was a very smart lady, had only an eighth-grade education. So my personal test on every entry is this: "Would my mom know what this word or phrase means?"

- It's tempting to lengthen a puzzle's fill words by making them plural or changing tense with -ED or -ING (these suffixes are sometimes called "stretchers" because they "stretch out" an entry); instead, try finding more interesting words or rearranging the diagram. Never add the RE- prefix when it would result in an uncommon or contrived word (RESTEAL).

NANCY SALOMON: One of the most frequent mistakes I see from rookies is settling for inferior grids. There's a temptation to feel that as long is one is able to find any fill, the puzzle is a good one—not so.

> **MANNY NOSOWSKY:** "Dear Mel, I notice that you changed my clue for CHURRO to an extinct African beast. A CHURRO is a Mexican cruller. Enclosed is a photograph of a churro stand. They're all over California!"
>
> **MEL ROSEN:** "Hmm, I just noticed that they're all over Florida too. Shows what a little sensitizing will do."

- Minimize or omit prefixes, suffixes, and combining forms in your puzzles.

- If you've got a lot of time on your hands, attempt a pangrammatic puzzle—one where every letter of the alphabet is used. Although most solvers don't notice or care if a crossword is pangrammatic, you will almost certainly end up with some interesting words in your grid—not to mention the undivided attention of your editor.

FRED PISCOP: I've never used ESNE in a puzzle. A funny story about ESNE: the very first puzzle I submitted to Will Shortz—which incidentally was the first daily that he ran under his editorship, and also the first daily *New York Times* puzzle in history to run with a byline—one of the entry words was SERF. I clued it ESNE and dared him to leave it in, and he did! That started a kind of tradition: the "I dare you" (or "IDY") clue.

- Crosswordese (ANOA, PROA, STOA, and the like): Although its usage is becoming rarer, there is occasionally no other choice than to use an obscurity to complete a tough grid. When the inclusion of crosswordese is unavoidable, make sure all entries crossing it are common, everyday words. *Never* allow two obscurities to cross in your grid unless you don't want to sell your puzzle.

NELSON HARDY: Remember that not all solvers are crossword maniacs. If you make a list of words commonly seen in crossword puzzles—such as ALEE, ETUI, OLIO, etc.—and run it by someone you know who isn't an avid solver, you may be surprised to learn how much your vocabulary has been skewed by frequent solving.

- Most crossword editors now allow familiar brand names, if only sparingly. (Eugene T. Maleska never did, feeling that he didn't want to provide free advertising in the pages of the *New York Times*.)

Words, like men, grow individuality; their character changes
with years and with use.
—Frederick E. Crane

- Do not overuse exclamations (AHA, OHO, HEHE).

ERICA ROTHSTEIN: We didn't want to include anything that someone could construe as a downer. We didn't talk about scandals. Puzzles are supposed to be fun, and supposed to take people away from whatever it is that's bothering them. They can get all the bad news they want by turning on the television or opening the newspaper. It wasn't necessary to include in a puzzle—any kind of a puzzle—anything that could be construed as sad or depressing. We kept in mind always that the solver was our friend, and like a part of our family—that no matter how big a company Dell was, that we were a very small operation, and that we cared very much about the solver. I think that came through on every page.

- Never use more than one form of the same word in a puzzle (FEEL; FEELER), even if the words, like these two, can be clued as completely different animals.

Simply stated, it is sagacious to eschew obfuscation.
—*Norman Augustine*

BAD FILL
(by Merl Reagle)

EERY and IRANI: I would not use them except as a last, embarrassing resort. My reason is that the mainstream press doesn't recognize them as acceptable, and thus readers don't either. I'm not quite ready to give up on the traditional notion that, in addition to being all those good things we talk about—clever, entertaining, sometimes mind-blowing—crosswords should also be helpful in spelling and vocabulary. If we at least cover this base, we go a long way toward ensuring that crosswords will remain a fixture on the American literary landscape.

I'm all for blazing a trail when it comes to words everyone says but that are rarely seen in print (like UEY or WELL, EXCUUUSE ME), but if the *New York Times* and the *Los Angeles Times* and the *Philadelphia Inquirer* and the *Chicago Tribune* and *Time* and *Newsweek*, etc., etc., etc., *never* use these variant spellings, then to me, they are *verba non grata* in crosswords.

I read a lot. I follow domestic and world news. I keep notebooks on words and usages. I have never seen IRANI outside of a crossword. Period. This doesn't mean I myself have never used it in a puzzle. I've been making *New York Times*–style crosswords for thirty-one years. I've used practically every crappy word on anyone's crappy word list. Volume 3 of my Sunday crosswords has EMEER in it twice, both times clued as a variant. But I think it's healthy—and vital—for crosswords to avoid these words. I think it's important for crosswords to seem connected to the real world. The more they do, the more we all stay employed, and employable, and the more our horizons broaden rather than contract.

If you're a fledgling constructor and your grid has answers in it that you can't find anywhere, alarms should go off in your head. Even if you do find a legitimate clue for it, you've still got a puzzle that can be sold *almost nowhere*. Your job as a beginning constructor is to maximize your chances for success. This is done by using all easy-to-medium words and cluing them interestingly. This was the rule at *GAMES* even for the Ornery crossword—the Ornery was supposed to be a one-star puzzle that could be clued easy or hard. Striving for wide-open patterns is fine—heck, that's just about all I did in my first ten years of constructing, and my stuff pales in comparison with what some of the young guns [of today] can do—and striving for the *New York Times* is fine, too. But let's not lose sight of the fact that what we are trying to foster are solid, well-made, well-clued, *real-world* crosswords. If we do that, editors will line up to pay us.

GET A CLUE

RANDOLPH ROSS: Keep your entries accessible to the solver. They should have some feeling of satisfaction when they do a puzzle, even if it takes a little work. One other thing: The cluing is harder than the filling in. Finding and cluing a good theme is hardest of all.

■ Strive for humor and wordplay in your clues, but don't go for cleverness at the expense of intelligibility. That pun may make perfect sense to you but leave others scratching their heads. If you're unsure, run your pun past the folks on the Cruciverb-L forum.

Variety is the soul of pleasure.
—APHRA BEHN

■ One of the things that makes a puzzle hard is unfamiliar clues for familiar words. If you're writing an easy-level crossword, include a majority of gimme clues. Even if the puzzle is intended to be expert-level, solvers need a way in, so take care not to make things so difficult that it frustrates anyone who attempts it.

JOE DIPIETRO: The entries must be lively. The livelier the word, the more likely you can clue it in a fun or interesting way.

NELSON HARDY: Keep it user-friendly. If the solver can't finish the puzzle without a stack of reference books at his elbow, you've done something wrong. And inject humor wherever you can.

- Never clue a word with a different form of the same word.

> *"Whom are you?" he asked, for he had attended business college.*
> *—George ADE*

- Make sure you're using words correctly (that is, don't use *conscience* when you mean *consciousness*).

- Never rely on your memory: Look it up!

> *In art, economy is always beauty.*
> *—Henry James*

- Don't be too verbose (editorial space is limited), but don't be too terse, either—a puzzle with nothing but one- and two-word clues is a yawn.

> *True art selects and paraphrases, but seldom gives a verbatim translation.*
> *—Thomas Bailey Aldrich*

- When cluing an abbreviation or acronym, try to use another abbreviation or acronym in the definition rather than including the parenthetical "abbr." hint. Conversely, don't include an abbreviation in a clue unless the answer is also an abbreviation. Clues and answers should match.

- Similarly, clue slang answers with slang clues ("Noodle" = BEAN).

PATRICK JORDAN: For cluing, I use Infopedia, Grolier's CD-ROM encyclopedia, and a program called A Million Kazillion *Clichés* when I want a fill-in-the-blank clue using a common phrase. It's also provided theme ideas on occasion.

- Clue for your market, always keeping in mind the target audience's solving expertise. If you're writing for an industry- or region-specific market, lard your puzzles with answers and clues that are specific to that market (for example, if you were writing for a Los Angeles–area paper, you'd include more entertainment-biz references than you would for *Newsday*).

TYLER HINMAN: Rare letters in the fill can add to a puzzle's quality, if the words that use them aren't obscure. Phrases are also excellent. And, of course, interesting and witty clues help. Dictionary definitions are boring.

- Match tenses in clue and answer.

- Don't give overly vague definitions for your answer words ("Tree," "Man's moniker," "Item of apparel").

- Wordplay in the constructor's cluing arsenal includes alliteration ("Film-dom's Finch" = PETER), puns ("Porky pig" = HOG), rhymes ("Vacation destination" = ISLE), and homonyms ("Deer girl" = ROE). There are, of course, many more options—limited only by your imagination.

BOB KLAHN: I'm writing clues all the time. I find that super-fascinating. I was quite bad at this when I started, as I expected I would be. I think I'm quite good at it now. I learned to write good clues mainly by solving a huge number of top-of-the-line puzzles and by studying what techniques are and are not used by the best constructors. Because I do all my solving on my computer, as a by-product of my work I've built up a huge storehouse of published clues. After writing clues without reference to this "cluebase," I often look to see what's been previously published. I may then use something there instead of what I've written, or I may be inspired by one or more ideas I see there to come up with something even better. I avoid clues that my cluebase shows to be clearly associated with a specific individual, although I don't mind it when others use one of mine. And when they actually ask first, I'm gratified.

THE BEST FROM THE REST

Deliberate misdirection is fine, within limits, and clues like those are to be valued because they're very hard to concoct properly.
—Stan Newman

What you'll find in puzzles created by the experts:

- Fewer fill-in-the-blank clues ("Happy___lark")
- Lesser-used letters (Q, Z, X, J, W, V, F)
- Fewer plurals
- Few or no partials
- More theme answers (eight, ten, or twelve in a 21 ¥ 21 puzzle)
- Clever cluing with lots of wordplay
- Elegant grid design with a minimum of cheaters
- Fewer vowel-consonant-vowel-consonant fill words
- More lively fill words (SNAPPY)
- Six-, seven-, or eight-letter words stacked atop each other
- Theme entries that interlock

I SUBMIT TO YOU

JOHN SAMSON: Eugene T. Maleska was my mentor. He instilled in me a professionalism that remains with me today. His golden rule: "Polish, polish, polish!" Do I have any words of advice for aspiring constructors? Yes. "Polish, polish, polish!"

- Check your work carefully. Make sure your grammar, spelling, and punctuation are correct.

Look everything up, even if you think you're sure. Spelling in particular.
—Jon Delfin

- Don't be satisfied with version one of any puzzle. Set it aside for a day or two, check it again—thoroughly—and and if it still looks good, send it out!

> *The first precept was never to accept a thing as true until*
> *I knew it as such without a single doubt.*
> —RENÉ *Descartes*

- Cite any words or phrases that aren't likely to be found in common dictionaries. (The exception is brand-new phrases that haven't yet made it into reference works—but be sure those phrases are very familiar.)

- Send for the style sheets of the publications to which you intend to sell, and research their requirements thoroughly before mailing.

STAN NEWMAN: Anyone sending me a puzzle ought to take the time to see what it is I want and to see the sorts of puzzles I publish—they're available on the Web. Anyone with e-mail who sends me a puzzle of seventy-six words that doesn't have a theme—I mean, they're not paying close attention.

- Pick your prospective sales carefully—first submit to publications that pay relatively well and publish constructor bylines. Submit to only one publication at a time. If a puzzle doesn't sell after repeated submissions, you probably need to rework it.

ERICA ROTHSTEIN: In the old days, there weren't names on the puzzles. One reason was because Kathleen Rafferty didn't want solvers to know how few constructors we were dependent upon. And she believed that the only name that mattered was the name Dell.

- In general, you will need to send a solving grid (blank, with numbers and black squares but no answer words), an answer grid (complete grid, with answer words), and double-spaced clues and answers, as well as a self-addressed stamped envelope or e-mail address so editors can return your puzzle(s) if need be.

PATRICK JORDAN: You'll probably hear this quite often from the editors, but the main piece of advice that I would offer is to actually solve some of the puzzles published by the company or companies to which you'd like to contribute. You'll get a good feel for the kind of material they're looking for, and this knowledge, coupled with a copy of their style sheet, will reduce your chances of getting a rejection slip. Submit your first few puzzles to editors with reputations for being willing to take new constructors under their wings. (From my experience, these would include Stan Newman, John Samson, and Will Shortz.) If you do receive a rejection notice, don't be discouraged—if the puzzle is at all salvageable, these editors will usually include suggestions for improvement. Fix the puzzle (which may involve rebuilding the entire diagram, so be prepared for this!), and submit it again.

- Be tidy in your submissions.

- Keep a log of submissions and responses.

> *Well, back to the old drawing board.*
> *— Peter ARNO*

- Don't be discouraged by rejections.

RANDOLPH ROSS: Have fun with the puzzles and don't take criticism too seriously—just learn from it.

> *There is no substitute for hard work.*
> *— Thomas Edison*

WORKERS' COMPENSATION (?)

> *Excellence costs a great deal.*
> *— MAY Sarton*

If you're in the crossword construction game for the money, quit right now. Sure, there are some puzzles that will come easily, and for those you may actually make a decent wage—for the few hours it takes to create them. But others will take ten times as long as you think they should—and at the end, you're lucky to have made minimum wage (should you even manage to sell the puzzle). To top it off, when you do make a sale, it can be a year before you receive payment! And don't expect to get rich reselling your crosswords unless—like Merl Reagle and Henry Hook—you're enough of a brand name to retain rights. When you sell a puzzle, you typically sign away all rights, and you will rarely if ever be paid for reprints.

STAN NEWMAN: I remember reading about the history of television and how Jackie Gleason owned the rights to *The Honeymooners.* I remember reading how William Boyd bought back the TV rights for his Hopalong Cassidy movies right at the dawn of TV—and became a multimillionaire with his own show as a result. I knew all about rights—not to the degree I know now, but I understood what it was [*Newsday* was] giving me. I had no illusions of its value at the time—it wasn't very much. And even today, we're not talking about *Seinfeld* episodes here. Nevertheless, owning the rights to most of the crosswords I edit has made a big difference.

THE BASIC RULES OF CROSSWORD CONSTRUCTION
(by Will Shortz)

Here are the rules for beginning crossword contributors to the *New York Times.*

1. The pattern of black-and-white squares must be symmetrical. Generally this rule means that if you turn the grid upside-down, the pattern will look the same as it does right-side-up.

2. Do not use too many black squares. In the old days of puzzles, black squares were not allowed to occupy more than 16 percent of a grid. Nowadays there is no strict limit, to allow maximum flexibility for the placement of theme entries. Still, "cheater" black squares (ones that do not affect the number of words in the puzzle, but are added to make constructing easier) should be kept to a minimum, and large clumps of black squares anywhere in a grid are strongly discouraged.

3. Do not use unkeyed letters (letters that appear in only one word across or down). In fairness to solvers, every letter has to appear in both an Across and a Down word.

4. Do not use two-letter words. The minimum word length is three letters.

5. The grid must have all-over interlock. In other words, the black squares may not cut the grid up into separate pieces. A solver, theoretically, should be able to proceed from any section of the grid to any other without having to stop and start over.

6. Long theme entries must be symmetrically placed. If there is a major theme entry three rows down from the top of the grid, for instance, then there must be another theme entry in the same position three rows up from the bottom. Also, as a general rule, no nontheme entry should be longer than any theme entry.

7. Do not repeat words in the grid.

8. Do not make up words and phrases. Every answer must have a reference or else be in common use in everyday speech or writing.

These rules apply to almost all crosswords in all publications. The style sheet printed below lists some more special rules of the *New York Times. Note: Random House Puzzlemaker's Handbook* by Mel Rosen and Stan Kurzban (recently out of print, but widely available in libraries) contains detailed advice on creating and selling crosswords. This is the best starting point for new constructors.

The New York Times *Crossword Specifications*

GENERAL SPECIFICATIONS

The *New York Times* looks for intelligent, literate, entertaining, and well-crafted crosswords that appeal to the broad range of *Times* solvers.

Themes should be fresh, interesting, narrowly defined, and consistently applied throughout the puzzle. If the theme includes a particular kind of pun, for example, then all the puns should be of that kind. Themes and theme entries should be accessible to everyone (themeless daily puzzles using wide-open patterns are also welcome).

Constructors should emphasize lively words and names and fresh phrases. We especially encourage the use of phrases from everyday writing and speech, whether or not they are in the dictionary. For variety, try some of the lesser-used letters of the alphabet—J, Q, X, Z, K, W, etc. Brand names are acceptable if they're well known nationally and you use them in moderation.

The clues in an ideal puzzle provide a well-balanced test of vocabulary and knowledge, ranging from classical subjects like literature, art, classical music, mythology, history, geography, etc., to modern subjects like movies, TV, popular music, sports, and names in the news. Clues should be accurate, colorful, and imaginative. Puns and humor are welcome.

Do not use partial phrases longer than five letters (ONE TO A, A STITCH IN, etc.), uninteresting obscurity (a Bulgarian village, a water bug genus, etc.), uncommon abbreviations, or foreign words. Keep crosswordese to a minimum. Difficult words are fine—especially for the harder daily puzzles that get printed late in the week—if the words are interesting bits of knowledge or useful additions to the vocabulary. However, never let two obscure words cross.

Maximum word counts: 78 words for a 15 × 15 (72 for an unthemed); 140 for a 21 × 21; 168 for a 23 × 23. Maximums may be exceeded slightly, at the editor's discretion, if the theme warrants.

DIAGRAMLESS CROSSWORDS

Diagramlesses must be 17 × 17 in size. Follow the style as shown on the Sunday puzzle page. Puns & Anagrams and cryptics are done by assignment only.

Note: *Times* puzzles must never have been published anywhere before, either in print or electronically. The *Times* buys all rights, including first rights.

FORMAT

Use regular typing paper (8½" by 11"). Type the clues double-spaced on the left (no periods after the numbers), answer words in a corresponding column on the far right. Give a source for any hard-to-verify word or information. Down clues need not begin on a new page. Include a filled-in answer grid with numbers and a blank grid with numbers (for the editor's use). Put your name, address, and Social Security number on the two grid pages, and just your name on all other pages.

Send to:

Will Shortz, Crossword Editor
The New York Times
229 West Forty-third Street
New York, NY 10036

Please include a stamped return envelope—or an e-mail address—for reply.

PAYMENT

Compensation is as follows: $75 for a daily 15 × 15; $350 for a Sunday 21 × 21; $400 for a Sunday 23 × 23; $100 for a diagramless; $150 for a novelty puzzle.

There are very few human beings who receive the truth, complete and staggering, by instant illumination. Most of them acquire it fragment by fragment, on a small scale, by successive developments, cellularly, like a laborious mosaic.
—ANAÏS NIN

SCREEN GEMS

Depending on who you talk to, computers and the Internet have either (a) been the biggest boon to constructors since the dictionary, or (b) robbed the puzzle world of all innovation and creativity. The reality? Closer to the former—and, of course, it's all in how you use your tools . . .

MEL TAUB: A lot of constructors use computer models extensively. Don't know if this is good or bad—some good stuff, some evil comes out of it.

TRIP PAYNE: All of the filling programs in the world aren't going to help if you can't come up with an interesting theme or interesting clues, or if you can't decide on your own which is a better entry to use among two or three choices. I think software programs are helping a lot of constructors, but I also think they're giving rise to a lot of mediocre constructors. Those programs are a mixed blessing. I think some people are using them as a crutch. I think people should really at least start my way, with graph paper and pencil, just to get used to basic things, like in general consonants go next to vowels. Simple basics like that. No, you probably don't want a Q in that position. No, for your first puzzle you don't want a six-by-five corner of white squares. Stuff that you need to learn on your own, the hard way.

PATRICK JORDAN: The only downside I see is the continued prevalence of computer-generated puzzles in many newspapers. If a beginning solver is exposed only to these puzzles (which are usually themeless, crammed with esoterica, and completely lacking in wit and ingenuity), he or she may believe that all crosswords share these traits and, therefore, decide that the hobby is not worth pursuing.

BOB KLAHN: The one place where most constructors fall down is black-square placement. They seem to set up a certain arrangement of black squares, then immediately begin the fill. Then, if they run into trouble with the fill, they add "cheaters" (black squares that do not change the grid entry count) or they throw the problem section away and start just that section over. Rarely do they seem to recognize that the main problem is with the black-square structure itself.

I sometimes see discussions, for example, on the Internet Cruciverb-L constructors' forum, about using stock grids—about freezing the black-square placement before doing anything else. I think that's one of the worst things a constructor trying to achieve a top-notch fill can do. I might use a prestructured grid in a themeless construction—usually as a challenge to see if I can do it—but I would absolutely never do so in a themed puzzle.

Constructors should instead consider a variety of potential arrangements and try to articulate the plusses and minuses of each. To do that well requires a thorough knowledge of positional letter frequencies. My computer helps with that, of course, but you've got to have it in your head, too. Anyone with an Intel-based PC can go get Antony Lewis's Crossword Compiler and have it throw some words together, but the result is not likely to be that good. Certainly not nearly as good as it could be with a human in charge.

NANCY SALOMON: You'll find that most of the best-known constructors who use software use a program called Crossword Compiler. It completely eliminates all the drudge work from construction, and that's just for starters. It helps in every possible way.

KELLY CLARK: I recently purchased Antony Lewis's Crossword Compiler. I find it very helpful in grid construction, particularly black-square placement. You make a black square and it automatically places its symmetrical counterpart in the grid for you! I think that's terrific.

WILLIAM R. MACKAYE: Most of the people I know will use the automatic fill, then once it's filled, they'll start throwing things away. I have never tried very seriously to use any of that stuff—I just use the old bean.

JIM PAGE: Constructing on the computer makes it a lot easier. I go back to the days when it was all hand-done, which was a giant pain in the ass. I have some of those old puzzles, and some of the grids have holes in them from erasing the paper. Blood on them, too, from nearly blowing your brains out. But . . . the computer has made that far easier. At least you have a better look at the grid in terms of changes you might have to make.

DAVID J. KAHN: I use computer software to research clues and to prepare a submission, but not to fill in the grid, which I find the most fun in the process.

BILL ZAIS: Today's grids are *much* cleaner than in the past. A lot of this has to do with technology. I feel that within the next five to seven years, anyone will be able to push a button and get an elegant fill. Fills will still be important, but, like air, no one will pay for them. Thus I see themes and theme development becoming even more important than they are now. If fills become universally good, it's interesting to speculate on how this will affect the current oligopsonistic market.

MAURA JACOBSON: I use the software to get the diagrams, because it puts the black squares in. And then I work with it on the computer—it's easier to put in a letter and then take it away if need be.

RANDOLPH ROSS: I don't like computerized grid-filling—not because they don't produce good fill, but because they usually have compartmentalized interlocks: less appealing to the solver. I'm old-fashioned, and I enjoy the pleasure of filling in a grid myself, especially when I can use an entry that has never appeared before.

PETER GORDON: Computers are taking over the construction part. You no longer need a teacher, since the computer can do all the work of making the grid. But people who use them without having learned the craft don't know how to write clues that well, and coming up with good themes can't be done with a computer. So quality puzzle-writers will still be in demand, since good themes are the hard part.

GREG STAPLES: The Cruciverb Web site and Crossword Compiler have really lowered the learning curve, allowing many more people to give construction a try. The result is more constructors and better competition.

MARTIN ASHWOOD-SMITH: I've recently acquired Crossword Compiler. It helps in the editing and submission process.

ELIZABETH GORSKI: I use Crossword Compiler 4.0. That software allows me to create a library of words and clues.

DIANE EPPERSON: [I use] Crossword Compiler by Antony Lewis. Once the theme entries are in place and the grid [is] completed, I run AutoFill to see where the trouble spots, if any, are. If I can [use] AutoFill repeatedly with little reptition of entries, I feel I can make a good clean fill. If there are trouble spots, I rearrange entries (if possible) and blocks until satisfied. Thereafter, I use the Find Word feature to show what choices I have for each entry as I go.

DAVID MACLEOD: I use Crossword Compiler. It's a wonderful program, and I credit it (along with my mentors) with getting me as far as I've gotten.

CATHY MILLHAUSER: I previously used Mel Rosen's program, which freed me from hand-numbering and blocking of grids. It's awful to think how many years I did those tasks with a fine [felt-tip] pen and chunky marker! Now I am using Crossword Compiler. I find it very easy to use, except for the inability to export clues and answers in a columnar format.

JON DELFIN: [I use] Crossword Compiler (CCW 5) and Mel Rosen's CWP [The Crossword Puzzler] program (for Stan [Newman] the Luddite). I confess to having used CCW for grid fixes, and once let it make an entire 15 × 15 (around my theme answers). Much tweaking was required.

STAN NEWMAN: I am a late convert to the CCW package. This British gentleman, Antony Lewis, has done a remarkable job; invested untold hundreds of hours in a product that is useful to a very select few. I would like to think he's sold two million of these things, but I have a feeling he's sold closer to two thousand—maybe not even that many. I hadn't used it sooner—not because I wasn't interested in it, but because my editorial life is so hectic that the time investment required to learn new software, not to mention convert over procedures, that as long as my existing system was working, I resisted changing . . . but, now that I'm using CCW quite a bit, I congratulate Mr. Lewis on a triumph. This is an extraordinary piece of software. God bless him—we all owe him a big thank-you.

MANNY NOSOWSKY: Crossword Compiler—it helps as a word finder primarily, but the AutoFill feature can be quite helpful at times, especially in fat corners.

NELSON HARDY: When I first got started constructing, I didn't have a computer. For the first four or five years after I got a computer, the only piece of software I used as a crossword construction aid was a word-finding program called TEA (The Electronic Alveary), which was quite helpful. Since 1997, I've used Crossword Compiler. Its word-finder is similar to TEA's, only you can customize the word list. Also, Crossword Compiler prints out professional-looking grids (I used to draw them by hand) and has a clue library.

BARRY TUNICK: [My] clue database is on a simple word-processing system. I use CCW to make grids and to print out words to be clued, and to send grids to clients as bitmaps or EPS.

RICH NORRIS: I use CCW to make and edit puzzles. Among its features: displaying the grid on the screen; allowing various kinds of symmetry or no symmetry at all; any size grid; access to databases for fill words; helping to find words using a wildcard feature; built-in thesaurus, clue database.

FRED PISCOP: I use—as almost everyone in the business does now—Crossword Compiler for Windows. It's probably the best computer investment I've ever made. I don't use the AutoFill at all. Some people do, but I find it's faster, actually, to construct on my own. It would be much more time-consuming to keep my word lists clean enough [in the] AutoFill to give me a clean fill.

ARTHUR S. VERDESCA: Recently, I've begun using Antony Lewis's superb Crossword Compiler. I use it mainly to get the self-confidence incident to knowing that, at least in some way, the puzzle is doable. Then I get to work tweaking it by using words that I like.

BILL ZAIS: I use the Crossword Compiler Find Words feature to help with the fills, but I never use the AutoFill feature.

JOHN SAMSON: I use Crossdown and Crossword Compiler—both are excellent programs.

GAYLE DEAN: I use Bellotto's program Crossdown, which helps with the mechanical parts of the puzzle—controlling symmetry, entering the black squares in the grid, the editing, the printing, etc. I have several other programs that provide various other features, but Bellotto's program is my favorite.

MIKE SHENK: I don't use [software] to help construct, to fill a grid for me. Because of my background in publishing, I'm a Mac person, and there's very little out there. It's not just that I'm being a purist, it's that there isn't much for me to use.

TRIP PAYNE: I'm one of the holdouts. I have some of those programs, but I still do the old graph-paper-and-pencil thing. I'm used to it. There's just something about holding the pencil and having the grid in your hand that I just find very appealing. Everybody says, "Why do you want to fill in the black squares like that?" I say, "Well, big deal. It takes a couple of minutes." When it's ready to go, I use Mike Shenk's Gridsetter program and then throw it into Adobe Pagemaker so it looks professional when it's done.

PATRICK JORDAN: For the actual construction, I use a program called Cogix Crossword Wizard to keep track of the numbering and symmetry. It has a "Diagram Filling" feature, but I rarely use it. I prefer the challenge and fun of completing the diagram myself. Besides, the program's vocabulary includes no multiple-word entries and very few contemporary references.

WILLIAM R. MACKAYE: More and more, I'm getting most of my submissions by e-mail now. Mostly [done with Crossword] Compiler. The Sabins are going to start submitting in Crossdown, which you can read with Compiler. I also have the Crossdown software—the author of it sent me a copy of it.

TYLER HINMAN: I use Crossword Compiler 5, but it only aids me in saving me time, paper, and eraser, providing me with a list of words for a given slot (I choose what is interesting and fits best), and printing it out professionally without having to deal with complicated stuff in Microsoft Word.

TOM SCHIER: [I use] Crossword Compiler 5 and Crossdown 5. They provide grid setup and aid in word selection. They also simplify the submission process, since most editors now use these programs, and submission by e-mail beats snail mail.

MIKE SHENK: Right now, most of my correspondence, and even a lot of the submitting, is done all on-line. Like typical e-mail, it's much quicker than a whole letter explaining what you didn't like.

A CONVERSATION WITH ANTONY LEWIS, AUTHOR OF CROSSWORD COMPILER

I'm currently just finishing off my Ph.D. (I'm in astrophysics at the Cavendish Laboratory in Cambridge, U.K.) doing work on gravitation and cosmology. I did four years of undergraduate study here as well, and I'm now in the third year of my Ph.D.

I have sold puzzles to magazines in the past and done the odd cryptic for the student rag. And most of Crossword Compiler's sample puzzles, of course.

I started [programming] Easter 1993, just before my A-levels. At that point I didn't know anything about object-oriented programming and had only written some Qbasic programs, so I planned to teach myself programming as I

ANTONY LEWIS

went along. I bought a copy of Borland Pascal, quite a good investment as it turned out—though £110 seemed like a small fortune at the time. I spent more than half of all the holidays during my undergraduate years working on the program, and have done some more work in my free time whilst I've been doing my Ph.D. I've been using Borland Delphi since version CC4.

Way back in 1993 . . . Version 1 for DOS. Didn't sell very many! The first Windows version was the following autumn.

[I did] lots of work [on Crossword Compiler's dictionaries]. Took some freely available sources, added loads of words from other sources, made modifications as people suggested them, etc.

For the first few versions I only used a couple of testers (Mel Rosen being one). A couple of good testers is much better than hundreds of useless ones! For version 5, I made the test version freely available to current users so rather more people tried it out. I do all the programming myself. Lots of people have made suggestions that I've implemented.

[No definite future plans] at the moment—enough work finishing and writing up my Ph.D.! There are some enhancements to the solving applet that I'm planning on at some point, and a feature to automatically fill in clues from a database using some kind of moderately intelligent or random algorithm.

A CONVERSATION WITH SAM BELLOTTO, JR., AUTHOR OF CROSSDOWN

With Crossdown for Windows you can solve and construct professional crosswords on your Windows computer. New features include scrollable clue list, sound card support with speaking messages, dictionary "hot-link" support, and extensive on-line help. Crossword puzzle numbering is done for you by the computer, eliminating time-wasting mistakes. Crossdown's Autoclue feature guides you effortlessly through the cluing process so that no clues are overlooked or omitted.

Printing capabilities continue to be the best in the industry, with the ability to output puzzles in a variety of formats. You can also output puzzles for [desktop publishing] use as Encapsulated PostScript, Windows Metafile, or bitmap files, and as ASCII text. Software includes more than one hundred puzzles constructed by the top names in the field. You can also print manuscripts in either standard (clues on left) or Dell (clues on right) format.

Users also get free (within reason) crossword construction tutoring and marketing assistance. The latest version has been enhanced and improved to take full advantage of the Windows 98/2000 environment.

Obviously, there is no application available for crossword constructors (or solvers) to maintain a clue database. That is why I developed Cluebank. On the other hand, lots of other companies make dictionaries, thesauri, and specialized word lists. I did not wish to get into the dictionary business (folly to compete with Webster or Random House), so I simply gave Crossdown the ability to easily access third-party references.

TIMING IS EVERYTHING

MARTIN ASHWOOD-SMITH: If I'm creating a themeless, let's say a stacked fifteens themeless, I first spend several days and sometimes weeks playing with fifteen-letter phrases. When I find some fifteens that look promising, I then see if I can create a grid utilizing these stacks. Usually my first few attempts do not work, but if I'm patient, I'll end up with a first-draft grid. Then, I'll usually try to make as many different draft grids as possible and select the one with the cleanest fill.

GAYLE DEAN: It depends on the market. Some puzzles seem to appear before me in an hour without much effort. Others can take days or even weeks. On average, I can create a 15×15 puzzle in two to four hours. Of course, that doesn't count the time spent thinking about a theme, often the most difficult part of construction. I probably create two hundred puzzles a year when I'm working full-time.

TYLER HINMAN: My constructing time varies. Sometimes I'll strive for a low word count or a pangrammatic fill, and this takes longer. Sometimes, though, if I need to get a puzzle done, I'll do a low word count, which makes the fill easier and doesn't take me long at all.

RICH SILVESTRI: Once I come up with a theme (which can take forever), I can slap a 15×15 together in about two hours. A 21×21 takes five or six hours, on the average.

MARTIN ASHWOOD-SMITH: For a standard Monday- [or] Tuesday-level 15×15 that I construct for CrosSynergy (not including the time taken to dream up the theme), [it takes me] probably about an hour for the grid, if everything goes well . . . if not, possibly two or three hours. About another hour for the clues. So . . . probably on average about two to three hours total. The themeless (Friday to Saturday) puzzles I construct for the *New York Times* often feature stacked fifteens. Some of these puzzles take over two weeks to construct.

NELSON HARDY: A themed 21×21 with a word count of 140 (which is the maximum allowed by *New York Times* and *GAMES* magazine, among others) takes two or three days. A themed 15×15 with a maximum word count of 78 takes three to six hours. A themeless 15×15 with a maximum word count of 72 takes five to eight hours. I currently make about four hundred puzzles per year, but that number is deceiving; nearly half of these are themeless 13×13s that can be constructed in two hours or less.

RANDOLPH ROSS: I try to do one a week. From start to finish, once I have an idea for a theme, it takes about six hours on and off for a 21×21, less for a 15×15. Wide-open themeless puzzles, which I enjoy making, take longer than that. I really pain over them for hours.

BARRY TUNICK: Sylvia and I do a 21×21 in from ten to sixteen hours, depending on inspiration and luck. This includes preparation for our typesetter and coordinating responses from our two fact checker/proofers. We can do a 15×15 for other clients in four to six hours. (But factor in the time we spend doing research, checking other puzzles, making deals—some of which fall through—and trying to get paid, and the average time almost doubles.)

BERNICE GORDON: Every day that I can, I create a 15×15 and store it for future use. A Sunday size will take two or three days.

NORMAN WIZER: I can do a 15×15 in a couple of hours. Once I get the main words in and the grid set up, then the rest of it flows very easily. A 21×21 takes a long time. When you think you're about finished, [it turns out] you have an undone corner that drives you nuts.

SYLVIA BURSZTYN: Just coming up with a theme can take all day. Developing a theme can take hours. Filling a grid can take from four to eighteen hours. Then, proofing and editing [Barry's] clues can take a day. There's computer time for inputting stuff for our computer guy. Then, proofing our computer guy's output takes time. All told, and allowing for procrastination, interruptions, and for a cat settling in to nap on the desk, one *Los Angeles Times* crossword probably takes three days.

SAM BELLOTTO, JR.: Anywhere from a couple of hours for a 15 × 15 up to several days for a 21 × 21. Not only do I contribute regularly to all the traditional markets, but I have several vertical-market clients for whom I do a regular crossword feature. I must make four or five puzzles a week. I'm always up to my ears in grids.

My specialty is themed crosswords. I'm normally able, in addition to the typical long theme words, to pack quite a number of shorter secondary themed words into a grid. Some of my puzzles contain up to 50 percent themed entries. I guess this is why I'm in great demand.

WILLIAM CANINE: Even my dailies are themed, so I probably take a little longer than usual. Anyway, what's the hurry? I take my time and nearly always find changes to be made before I consider a puzzle done. Over twenty-five years, I've published more than 250 big puzzles and more than five hundred dailies. And that is only thirty a year average.

JON DELFIN: Anywhere from an hour (the wind was at my back) to several days. Years have gone by between constructions.

MEL TAUB: Two or three hours for a small crossword or acrostic. Longer for Puns & Anagrams and larger puzzles. I'm only semi-active nowadays, producing up to a dozen or so a year.

MARK DIEHL: Rough estimate: daily-size, themed, three hours; daily-size, unthemed, four hours; Sunday-size, eight hours. It all depends on the difficulty and word count. I usually create over several short sittings.

PETER GORDON: The hard part is coming up with a good theme. Once I have the theme, it takes usually an evening to make the grid, and then an hour or so to write the clues. I didn't write much in the mid-1990s, but lately I've been doing more. About one crossword a month sounds right.

MAURA JACOBSON: How long does it take? Oh, I'm slow: about four days, at least.

CHRIS JOHNSON: Generally, I spend between three and six hours on a puzzle.

NANCY JOLINE: So much of creating a puzzle is the thinking that may go on while I'm driving the car, or running the vacuum, or even in the middle of the night. As for output, a couple of puzzles a month is average for me.

PATRICK JORDAN: A 15×15 puzzle can take me from thirty to ninety minutes to construct, then another ninety minutes to write the clues. A 21×21 may require up to four hours to build, with an additional two or three hours for cluing. The cluing takes me nearly as long as the constructing because I try to avoid clichéd clues whenever possible. My yearly output is about seventy puzzles. I construct at least one per week, and usually two.

DAVID J. KAHN: A 15×15 typically will take me five to ten hours, including clue-writing. A 21×21 may take a few days. I write only thirty to forty puzzles a year, because the themes I want to explore don't come to mind that often. My *New York Times* submissions typically appear on Thursdays and Saturdays, and my Saturday puzzles almost always have a theme. I make my living as an actuary and employee benefits consultant, so writing puzzles in volume doesn't interest me.

SHAWN KENNEDY: It takes me anywhere from two to five or more hours to create a 15×15 crossword puzzle with well-polished clues. As far as other word games, it takes me about ten minutes to create a cryptogram, and sometimes even less to make a variety puzzle. Last year alone, excluding crosswords, I created about seven hundred variety puzzles.

DAVID MACLEOD: Some come quickly (a few hours), but I have some that are still unfinished after two years.

CATHY MILLHAUSER: I try for about fifty puzzles a year, of varying sizes. A really difficult theme such as my 21×21 "Eland" puzzle (no vowels used except E) can take weeks. But a 15×15 could take a couple of days if everything falls into place. I pretty much limit myself to punning themes. I've done a few cryptics, wide-open nonthematic, and straight factual puzzles, but I usually go for the punning or other wordplay puzzles.

MANNY NOSOWSKY: It takes two to one hundred hours to complete a 15×15 puzzle, and ten to one hundred hours for a 21×21 puzzle. I make about three to four puzzles a month.

TOM SCHIER: About three hours for a daily[-size], 15 × 15 grid and clues. About ten hours for a solid, themed 21 × 21 Sunday crossword. I construct about a hundred crosswords per year.

RICH NORRIS: It's going to be less now that I'm editing, but for the last two years I produced and sold about 160 and 190 puzzles, respectively. I can do a simple 15 × 15 with seventy-six to seventy-eight words in under an hour (grid only). The clues take another thirty minutes to an hour, depending on who I'm writing them for. My themeless *New York Times* puzzles, which can't have more than seventy-two words, might take anywhere from three to six hours to do, depending on how difficult the letter combinations turn out to be. Sunday puzzles, which are 21 × 21, take the longest: sometimes up to two full days (fifteen hours).

GREG STAPLES: A 15 × 15 can take as little as an hour or two—but usually it takes three to four hours. The 21 × 21s take about four or five times as long. I try to make four or five puzzles a month, but don't always get that many.

BILL ZAIS: It can vary from one day to two weeks, depending on the complexity of the theme.

ARTHUR S. VERDESCA: My fastest time in constructing a 15 × 15 has been forty or forty-five minutes. Some, of course, take much longer. As for 21 × 21s, I've been able to do one in five hours or so. I now turn out twenty to twenty-five puzzles a year. At my top speed, it was seventy-five or eighty per year.

STOCK EXCHANGE

STOCK GRIDS: YES OR NO?

BOB KLAHN: I would never—repeat, never—use a stock grid in a themed construction. That almost guarantees that the constructor will miss the best possibilities, and that he or she will be forced to use inferior vocabulary.

NANCY SALOMON: For themed puzzles, I can't recommend to beginners strongly enough that they master the art of designing their own grids. Stock grids very seldom provide the ideal fit for one's theme entries. In the end, constructors will spend *far less* time if they design their own grids than they will seeking out the right stock grid for their themes. Another problem with using stock grids for themed puzzles is that beginners often limit themselves to certain common configurations. They end up trying to force a theme into three fifteen-letter entries or four ten-letter entries. It's not often that the best potential set of theme entries lend themselves to one of these standard configurations. Designing one's own grids gives the constructor much more flexibility.

RICH SILVESTRI: Yes [I use stock grids]. Of course, I may modify a grid to fit a puzzle.

KELLY CLARK: I'm certainly not above pilfering another grid and altering it a bit to suit my needs.

RICH NORRIS: I do have a kind of unwritten formula in my head for placing theme entries, but from that point on, where the black squares go is determined by the letter combinations already in place. I find stock grids too confining. And sometimes too predictable.

RANDOLPH ROSS: My grids evolve with each puzzle, depending on the theme entries and letter placement.

TYLER HINMAN: I feel I must tailor each grid uniquely for each puzzle.

GAYLE DEAN: I have never used a stock grid. I create each one individually.

BILL ZAIS: I like to put a lot of theme [entries] in my puzzles, so I need to design the grids myself—but that's part of the fun!

NANCY JOLINE: Each new themed puzzle requires its own grid. I have reused grids for themeless, daily-size puzzles, though.

CATHY MILLHAUSER: I find that each theme idea needs its own grid. But when I was first starting out, I did use some stock grids that I found in a how-to book.

NELSON HARDY: I use stock grids for the themeless easy crosswords I make for Dell; there are only so many grids that lend themselves to this sort of puzzle anyway. All other crosswords have custom-made grids. I can't imagine trying to shoehorn a series of theme entries into a stock grid.

ELIZABETH GORSKI: I've made my own library of grids.

DIANE EPPERSON: I rarely use a stock grid, as each puzzle has its unique requirements and problems.

PETER GORDON: I sometimes flip through old puzzles of mine to look for a grid with the same lengths if I have unusual lengths (for example, if I have a thirteen- and two eleven-letter answers), but usually it's a straightforward theme with a fifteen and two of another length. Then I'll just wing it.

TOM SCHIER: I start with a copy of previously published grids and then adjust the design to fit my theme-word requirements.

MEL TAUB: I keep a few interesting grids around for possible future use or adaptation.

SYLVIA BURSZTYN: I have grids numbered from one to forty-eight, but use perhaps only half of them regularly.

BARRY TUNICK: For the *Los Angeles Times*, [we use a library of] about twenty-five [stock grids].

JON DELFIN: Black-square layout is my big construction block. I almost always use published grids.

PATRICK JORDAN: Will Shortz has told me that just about every constructor has a weakness in some area, and mine happens to be grid-plotting. I keep a large stack of books and magazines from every one of my regular buyers. When I've come up with my theme entries and decided to whom I'm going to submit the puzzle, I go to the stack and dig out recent releases from that publisher, and then [I] look through them for a grid that will accommodate my theme entries (either as-is, or with a bit of tweaking). This has the added advantage of ensuring that my puzzle won't be rejected simply because of the grid layout, since the grid has already been accepted and printed by that publisher.

CLUE ME IN

STAN NEWMAN: I'm, as you might imagine, fairly selective about where I send my puzzles these days. Not counting the ones I do gratis in-house for various promotional purposes, the places my puzzles appear now, most notably, are *Sport* magazine, for about twelve years now. I'm a reasonably interested baseball fan—my knowledge of other sports is somewhat limited, but because of the puzzles I need to make for *Sport*, I follow much more what's going on in the major sports. *People* magazine—I've been doing puzzles for them for nearly ten years, I believe. I'm one of three people now that make puzzles for *People* magazine weekly [the others are Stephanie Spadaccini and Fran and Lou Sabin]. Making a puzzle for *People*, I need to be aware with every word I enter into the diagram: Is there an entertainment-related or celebrity-related clue for it? My clue "The last word of *The Wizard of Oz*" was originally in *People*, where the word HOME came up. I don't want to say it's a cop-out to keep using fill-in-the-blanks for words, but given song titles and movie titles and TV series, for most words in the English language, you could probably find one of those and do a fill-in-the-blank. In fact, I hope it would distinguish my *People* puzzles [from] certain other people's . . . how I seldom fall back on [fill-in-the-blanks]. For HOME, I wasn't satisfied with [the clue] "The Green, Green Grass of _____." I let my mind wander, and fortunately, when my mind wanders, it often ends up somewhere like *The Wizard of Oz*. It's just one of the fortunate things about being a puzzle editor and having lived with so many clues and allowing my creativity to develop. I edited a puzzle just a few days ago with the answer ELEPHANT'S TRUNK. And again the "clue fairy" touched me on the shoulder, and I came up with the clue "circus squirter." That's a clue, I can immodestly say, that's evocative and funny, because you can picture a circus elephant squirting people. This mind-wandering process is how I come up with my best clues.

MERL REAGLE: I sort of feel that once I use a real clever one, I can't use it again—either ever, or in ages, or for a market that's different. Certainly not in the [*San Francisco*] *Examiner,* where I normally appear.

Some constructors think it's great . . . that the best kind of puzzle is one where all the clues are brand-new, even for the same old words. My experience has been that solvers find that stupendously difficult. If I want to make a really, really hard puzzle—yeah, do brand-new clues for even the commonest words. They don't have to be hard, but just brand-new clues. I've found that some degree of familiar clues have to be in there—you have to have a real mix of the familiar, the new, and the tricky.

It's got to be a real balance. I mean, how many ways are there to clue JAI, for example? Or ALAI? I mean, if I clue either word as "Game piece"? Well, that's pretty clever, but it's still a very hard clue for what is normally a gimme answer. I would have to make sure that what crosses it isn't quite so hard.

Sometimes these things just sort of hit you, and sometimes they don't, like cluing FANG as "The awful tooth." People out there in Puzzleland have to know that this is the sort of thing we think about quite a lot: How to clue the same old word with some clever little clue. WAND—which is almost always clued as "Baton" or "Magic stick" or something—is also part of a vacuum cleaner. Any brand-new, easy-to-get clue for something, I always think those are neat, too. You know, cluing TICKET as "Leadfoot's comeuppance." It's not a pun, it's not a twist, it's just really colorful and yet really terse. I like those a lot also. This is something that puzzle constructors think of: How do you clue the same old words in interesting but not impossible ways? You can't do it every other week, but it spices up everything. It's the mix—the balance and the mix.

STAN NEWMAN: I am blessed with a good memory and can recall odd facts very well. Being creative is not something I ever went to school for. As a mathematician by training, I was probably very ill-prepared for the life of words I find myself in now.

MAURA JACOBSON: I do something that is probably a time-waster and that probably most people do not do, and that is I keep a file of the clues I've used in [my] last twelve puzzles. That's one of the reasons I'm slow in constructing, because it takes a good couple of hours once I get to doing the clues. And, of course, for the common words, I try not to repeat anything I've used in [my] past twelve puzzles.

SYLVIA BURSZTYN: Barry keeps track of the clues he writes. I tend to remember the edits and suggestions I've made—or so I think. When we go over the clues together, he puts clue suggestions that are good but won't be used right now in what we call the bank.

BARRY TUNICK: I have to [keep track of clues used], because our puzzles reach the same solvers week after week, and I don't want to give them the same clues. I cross a clue out of my database printout as I use it, and every year I update the printout.

CHRIS JOHNSON: All my puzzles are stored on the computer. When I finish a puzzle, a program adds the words in it to an index that can be used to look up previous uses of any word.

GAYLE DEAN: I have a list of clues that I've collected over the years. It resides in a handy little program called Cluebank, which is one of Sam Bellotto's creations.

SAM BELLOTTO, JR.: Shameless plug: One of my products is Crossdown Cluebank, a computer database of puzzle definitions. It can hold up to two billion individual entries. Each entry can hold an unlimited number of definitions. It works integrally with Crossdown, my crossword construction software.

NANCY JOLINE: I just try not to overuse a particular clue. It's amazing how many ways you can clue something if you put your mind to it.

PATRICK JORDAN: The only time I really pay attention to this is when I'm sending a package of several puzzles to a single publisher. When this happens, I do make certain that I haven't repeated a clue for any word that happens to appear in more than one grid in the package.

TOM SCHIER: I have a computer database of clues that I have used as well as others. I developed it myself and update it daily from all crosswords that I access.

GREG STAPLES: Crossword Compiler has a built-in feature. I also save clues from high-quality puzzles (*New York Times*, etc.).

CATHY MILLHAUSER: I try not to repeat clues for submissions to a particular publication, and am beginning to experiment with the Crossword Compiler clue database.

NELSON HARDY: I used to keep a notebook full of frequently used words and a variety of clues for each word. Now I use the Crossword Compiler computer program, which automatically keeps a list of every clue I've ever used.

MERL REAGLE: I'm pretty good at cluing, but I would be better at it, I think, if I had the kinds of databases that all of my friends have. Bob Klahn, for example, has access to every clue from a certain year onward, so that if he needs to pick and choose, or to get ideas for new clues, he can just go to this massive database of his and just pick them out. This goes back . . . I don't know how many years. It might go back to the 1980s. Every *New York Times* puzzle, every *Washington Post* puzzle.

BOB KLAHN: Back in late 1991, when I decided to construct puzzles in earnest, I decided that my first step should be to write a little program to allow me to solve crosswords on-screen. My fast-typing fingers could keep my extremely astigmatic eyes from having to focus back and forth between grid and clues, because the clue for the current entry would always be right there in front of me, in one never-changing place. That's how I got started. I'd key in a puzzle first and solve it second. I never set out to build a fourteen-thousand-puzzle compendium of published puzzles, but that's roughly how many I have now. I've solved every one of them over the last nine years, and they're all in my computer. My "puzzlebase" is a by-product of my solving. I don't key in that many puzzles any more, as so many are on-line, but I try to stick to top-quality puzzles only. My "cluebase" is just a programmed extract from my puzzlebase. So for any entry, I can quickly tell you how many times it's appeared, in what markets, by what constructors, and, of course, how it's been clued. Counting the numerous duplicates, I have roughly 1.3 million clues so far.

I produce reports from my cluebase fairly often, for Cruciverb-L (if I have the time and I think the entry is decent; I refuse to help constructors salvage lousy entries), in response to private e-mail, and . . . for Will Shortz! Will gets inquiries from time to time about the content of past *New York Times* puzzles; he comes to me for the particulars. It may surprise you to hear that, while I may incorporate one in the future, I have no database per se. Everything is custom-programmed by yours truly, using flat files only, with no algorithm more complex than a binary search. My cluebase—which was never a goal of mine to develop—comes in quite handy now. When I'm creating a puzzle, and I've created the grid, I write my own clues first, then I check a number of them against my cluebase. If I find a similar clue therein, I'll usually try to create a new one instead. And I can always tell when a given clue is associated with a particular constructor, and avoid using it. On the other hand, if I see that a particularly witty clue has been used by a number of different constructors, then I'll feel free to use it myself. An added plus: Having so many clues so readily available together—so many jumping-off points all in one place—makes it easier to create new clues.

TYLER HINMAN: If it's a good clue and I want to remember it, I'll usually just put it in the back of my mind, and this memory will be jogged once I see the word again. I keep no documentation of my clues.

BILL ZAIS: One of these days I'll probably give in and get a clue database (a good one has already been offered to me), but right now I prefer doing them all from scratch because my cluing abilities need a lot of work.

MEL TAUB: I used to have a great memory so didn't need to write them down. Memory ain't what it used to be, but I still don't write 'em down.

EDITORS' SAY

MIKE SHENK: The main thing I look for is the theme. A theme that just doesn't seem very lively is reason to be rejected. If the theme is great and the puzzle construction is pretty good but has some problems with it, I'd be more likely to accept the puzzle and try to fix the things I don't like than to reject it for that. The theme is the most important part. Most of what I'm getting right now for the [*Wall Street*] *Journal* is from really good constructors who know what they're doing. I get very few first-time constructors, so there's very little that needs to be fixed.

FRANCIS HEANEY: One sure way to be a successful constructor is to try hard to emulate the quality of published puzzles. Certainly as an editor, I was surprised to discover that there really is a certain gap between submitted puzzles and published puzzles. Even from established constructors, a lot of puzzles by them often need work in terms of overused words or obscurities.

STAN NEWMAN: Knowing that a straightforward theme crossword need not have any obscure words, I set as a maximum 2 percent for unusual words. So for a seventy-eight-word crossword, that's two, if you round off. I believe my style sheet says something like, "Ideally, your puzzle should have no obscure words, and if you have more than two, it will not be accepted." As we've already established, that's something I feel very strongly about. It is not my job to teach puzzle solvers about Bulgarian fruit flies and seventeenth-century sopranos and thirteen-mile-long rivers in Angola and towns in Utah with 250 people. It is my job to entertain first, and inform and educate (about things worth knowing) second.

WILLIAM R. MACKAYE: What I like to some extent is turning the rules around. I don't have identical rules with other people. There are some things I won't accept that other people do accept, and vice versa. I will not permit a clue of the form "and kin," "and namesakes," and that sort of thing. In my view, if you're going to have a given name with an S on the end of it, you've got to have two people whose name that is. Good luck if you can find another [EARTHA]! Somebody did give me an EARTH AS quote, however. I will take partials of more than five letters.

JOHN SAMSON: Eugene Maleska had a strict rule forbidding all brand names from the answer grid and clues. I continued this policy for a few years until I realized the world around me was changing, becoming more and more commercial. Stadiums, golf tournaments, and various other events were being named after their sponsors. So I've modified my position on brand names within the squares and as clues. While I still prefer dictionary words to commercial ones, a clue like "Mercury and Saturn" is kind of a nice clue for CARS.

PETER GORDON: Too often I get rehashes of old stuff or puzzles that are just impossible to solve.

RICH NORRIS: Inconsistency in themes is a big pet peeve with me. "Same old same old" is another. Themes involving colors, trees, animals, etc., are so overdone—yet they keep on rolling in.

Obscure words in grids—particularly when they cross each other in the grid—are another. This is not to say that I'm some kind of authority on language, but in most cases, I figure if I've never heard or seen a word, probably most solvers won't know it either.

Crosswordese is a whole subject unto itself. Based on the numerous dialogues I've had with constructors and editors, one person's crosswordese is another's acceptable entry. What's obscure to one person is familiar to another. However, there does appear to be a body of "crosswordy" entries that most people agree is to be avoided. I won't allow those, though frequently I find I can tweak the grid to remove them.

JOHN SAMSON: I have no problem with crosswordese, and really, when you stop and think about it for a moment, just what is crosswordese? Is the ANOA crosswordese? Is the EMU crosswordese? The ERNE? The GNU? The NENE? (Please, not the NENE!) Who defines what is crosswordese and what isn't? Every solver I've talked with . . . [isn't] concerned about crosswordese. Constructors seem to care more about "crosswordy" words than solvers. What solvers object to is a puzzle containing dull, dry themes and clues. They complain when they've just spent an hour and a half solving a crossword and are left with an empty feeling inside. They could care less if the ANOA is in there or not.

I rejected a puzzle recently because one of the grid answers was TWO THUMBS OFF, clued thusly: *"The Texas Chainsaw Massacre* review?" My feeling is there's already too much violence in the world—we don't need any more in crosswords. While this constructor was reflecting the sad reality of a violent world, I felt compelled to reject it. If it bothered me, then it would bother others. Crosswordese doesn't bother me; lack of taste does.

JON DELFIN: [Some of my pet peeves are] misspellings in grids, and clue and answer disagreement. Some constructors have recurring flubs. One in the current rotation thinks there's an opera called *Der Fledermaus*. One I haven't heard from in a while thought Max von Sydow played *Pelle the Conqueror* (Max played Pelle's grandfather). Amazing how often PELLE can show up in a grid.

PETER GORDON: [My pet peeves include] inconsistent themes and too many bad filler words like partials, foreign words that are unknown, and obscure sports figures. Crosswordese is acceptable only if absolutely necessary and if crossed by easy words. The pros can write easy puzzles. Easy puzzles are much harder to write than hard ones, since you're limited to answers that aren't obscure. And the pros have better themes.

RICH NORRIS: The nontheme content of the grid—the pros are very good at filling in even the smallest corners with fresh, interesting words and phrases while avoiding obscurities. Creative, lively clues. And, perhaps most important to an editor, clues that match the difficulty level of the theme. The *Los Angeles Times* puzzles I edit are graduated in difficulty through the week: Monday the easiest, Saturday the hardest. The easy, straightforward themes appear early in the week and require easy, straightforward clues. All too often, I'll get a well-made puzzle with an easy theme and hard clues, necessitating a lot of time spent in clue editing. The pros seem to avoid this pitfall, which makes my job that much easier.

STAN NEWMAN: Differences in editorial styles are mostly generational. Having had an interest in trivia and facts long before I got involved in crosswords, I have some insight into this that predates my interest in crosswords. People love trivia, but people love trivia that relates to subjects they know something about. In fact, just by that definition, most people do like trivia, like testing themselves, like testing other people, like showing off what they know, like digging out from the back of their memory facts that they're surprised to have remembered. Anyone can create a trivia question in any category that no one will be able to answer. Anybody can show off their trivia knowledge, answering questions they happen to know.

5.

LEVEL BEST

IN CONCLUSION

And finally, I leave with you

Some favorites, both old and new;

Remember, puzzles keep evolving,

So stay in touch—and keep on solving!

Across

1. Be adequate
11. Request at the bar
15. Unyielding
16. Court actions
17. Summit participants
18. A state is named for them
19. Home of Commodore Perry's fleet
20. Pet's treat, perhaps
21. Kind of artist
23. Bambi's aunt
24. Golden, maybe
26. Aquarium residents
30. Like worshipers at a shrine
31. Befitting paradise
32. Indian Mr.
33. Sixties activists
34. Slap down
36. Ibiza, e.g.
39. Two Unsers
42. Lobbying grp.
44. _____ Zee, New York bridge
48. Place for a summary
51. Brosnan TV role
52. Akin
54. Jim Hawkins's creator
55. Spanish road
56. Word to Fido
58. 54-across, for one
59. Suffix with dactyl
60. Popular present for Pop
63. Back _____
64. Dry one
65. Uncle in *The Lion King*
66. Minstrels, e.g.

Down

1. South Seas city
2. Arrayed
3. Gorge
4. Never-Never-Lander
5. Con _____
6. Till
7. Newsmaker of 1998
8. Responses to the risible
9. Benz add-on
10. They're inactive
11. Sky sighting
12. Dos to Dos
13. Good place to dive
14. Maintains
22. *Sprechen* _____ *Deutsch?*
25. Lois of TV's *Lois & Clark*
27. TV series roles, often
28. Distress
29. They pay for others
35. St. _____
37. Bodybuilder's pride
38. Go _____
39. Common sources of relief
40. Wildly foolish
41. Athlete's need
43. Gather
45. Like some sheets
46. Finished
47. Empty-_____
49. Bakery item
50. Sweetie
53. Seville seven
57. Sci-fi film from 1982
58. Sardine's kin
61. Charge
62. Penn, e.g.

Across

1. *Intermezzo* actress
9. Teeming
15. Prepare the way for
16. Inventor Otis
17. Leveled off
18. Fingers
19. Teammate of "Stan the Man"
20. Hardly a traveler
22. Breaks
24. Polish money
25. Jazz org.
26. Fair-hiring abbr.
28. Observe
29. Stretched
30. Eden and others: abbr.
33. Henner's *Taxi* role
35. Feel
36. Appeal, e.g.
38. Villain
40. Leaves off
41. Kind of bar or roll
43. Country road feature
44. Secluded
45. Try hard (for)
46. Jacket part
48. Scrap
49. Make a mess of
51. Pick-me-up
55. Like some generators
58. Wrap tightly
59. Ruined
60. Not close at all
62. TV's Daniel Boone
63. It's found in preserves
64. Talks to the Lord?
65. Courses on carts

Down

1. *Street Scene* playwright Rice
2. Australian Governor-General since '96
3. Largest of the Cyclades
4. "_____ Fidelis"
5. Chum
6. Heroic verse
7. Maker of the Bearcat
8. Came to
9. Deodorize, in a way
10. Grayish
11. Dating
12. Vowel rhyme
13. Diamonds, e.g.
14. Femme fatales
21. "Appalachia Waltz" cellist
23. Berlin products
27. _____ de vie
29. It's served in spots
30. Introductions
31. Short notes
32. March 17th, for one
34. Good name
35. Arab's comment?
37. AAA offering
39. Bambi's aunt
42. Exclusive bunch
45. 1851 advice
47. Ready to go
49. Crams (with "up")
50. *Thin Ice* star
52. Floor
53. Start of a Bennett title
54. Conveys
56. Apple or pear
57. Reeves and Shannon
61. Sixties firebrands

by Rich Norris

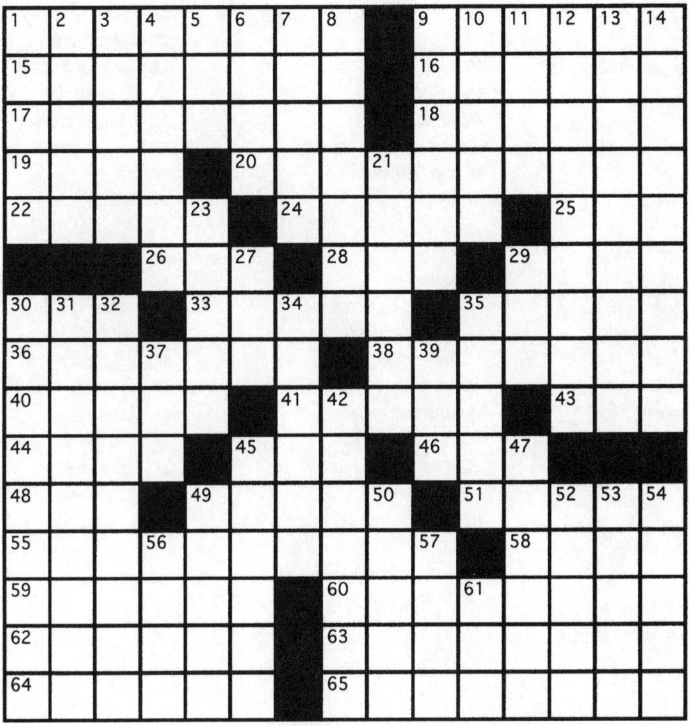

Across

1. Bill in a scope?
6. Lie adjacent
10. Evil face covering?
14. Give the slip
15. Steno reminder
16. Verdi heroine
17. "Here's the story of the Liberty Bell," Tom _____.
20. Likely to pat?
21. _____ wishes!
22. Engraves
23. Tutorial
25. Mason's Della
27. "Daily Planet" employee
29. Person in a shack
30. Where a deb sleeps?
33. Rite site?
36. Misophobiac's fear
38. Fiesta
39. "Get me off this mule," Tom _____.
42. Tennis great Lendl
43. "Runaround Sue" singer
44. Wight and Skye
45. Sn
46. Get long in the tooth
47. Ayn Rand hero
49. Take giant steps
52. Participated in a Haymarket Square event
56. "Way" between Rome and Capua
58. Branch part
60. Wallace film "Ben _____"
61. "Where did you get that meat?" Tom _____.
64. Role in scholarship?
65. Dehydrate
66. Utrillo's stand
67. Southern Togo denizens
68. E-mail command
69. Grinding grit

Down

1. Flower part
2. Take the honey and run
3. Indoctrinated groups
4. Kind of duck
5. Coast
6. Scrambled Spam?
7. Paragons of redness
8. *The Beach of Falesa* girl
9. Put up with
10. Lucy's Vivian
11. Get behind it
12. *Nuns on the Run* star
13. Produces eggs
18. *Little Big Man* filmmaker
19. Newsbreak in *Time*?
24. Struck down
26. Crowd
28. Moved with a circular air current
31. Palindromic fashion magazine
32. Malraux novel _____ of Wrath
33. Way in for the UMW
34. Vile novelist Primo?
35. Become known
37. _____ Jima
38. Zest
40. Tenseness
41. Delicate silver ornamentation
46. Syr Darya's outflow
48. Sutherland solo
50. Fundy's are high
51. Actor Hawke
53. "_____ Boots are Made . . ."
54. Swiss mathematician Leonhard
55. Blandly
56. Skillful
57. Frigate's front
59. Microsoft application
62. Astrologer to Elizabeth I
63. He sang with the "Pharaohs"

Double Croakers

by Gayle Dean

Across

1. Watches
8. User's waiting period
15. Sturdy-looking
16. Common fruitcake ingredients
17. Like a boys' choir
18. Land of Isaias Afwerki
19. Crosscurrents
20. Have a litter
22. Gun
23. US code and cipher group
24. Patent pending?
26. Brazilian soccer champion
27. Start of something?
28. Cincinnati baseballer once
31. What those with alopecia miss most
32. Lean against
34. Gulf state: abbr.
35. Chihuahua cheers
36. Pretty quick
39. Actress Swenson
42. Fluid lines
43. Shawm player
47. Rialto shiner
48. Where to find Mount Koussi
50. Cut a course?
51. Short fellow?
52. Rebuttal (page)
53. Skilled one
54. Not quite right
55. Most respectful (of)
58. Gertrud by another name
59. Not in the store yet
61. Money down
64. Distribute
65. Wide expanse
66. Commuters' bibles
67. Suspended progress for a while

Down

1. Merger with AOL
2. Fur-lined cloak
3. "None for me"
4. End of an O'Neill title
5. Secessionist org.
6. Unagi at the sushi bar
7. Cooked, in a way
8. Bide-_____
9. Jung man
10. Sound at the pedicurist's
11. Surg. subspecialty
12. Phantasmagoric
13. Heavy marble
14. Shortcuts, e.g.
21. When fans hit the fridge
24. Heavy metal
25. Menace in the paper
26. Popular family-page download
29. Seasonal employee?
30. As much as you want
33. Pitcher Luis
37. Reproduction needs
38. *Story of _____ Boy* (Aldritch)
39. Punctually
40. Is unrequired to
41. Blimp attachment
44. Stalemate
45. Made a raid
46. Like they came on the ark
49. A chimp's world
55. Pagoda sight
56. _____ *Zürcher Zeitung* (leading Zürich newspaper)
57. Special skills
58. Cell dweller, maybe
60. Member of 5-Down
62. Pollution police
63. In accordance with

Time's Up

by Manny Nosowsky

Across

1. Tabula _____
5. Train tracks
10. Trevi tosser's thought
14. Troop truant
15. Turn topsy-turvy
16. Topical treatment
17. Trey's trefoil
18. Torment
19. Toe the _____
20. Torquemada's territory
22. Trickery
24. Taxis
26. Truckee town
27. Tumbler
30. Tailors
33. Toast
34. Taunt
36. Tatter
38. Tokyo, to Takeshita
39. Tax tribulation
41. Temerity
42. Telepathy
43. Tyrant's title
44. Together, to Toscanini
45. Turn tail
49. Trustfulness
51. Tall-tale teller
52. Tucker
53. Terrifying
55. Tintinnabulated
59. Thailand
60. Thirst tamers
64. Twisted together
65. Too
66. Tie
67. *Tosca* tune
68. Transactor
69. Typesetter's text
70. Talk tempestuously

Down

1. Tear
2. Tannery tools
3. _____ tureen
4. Tuna type
5. Turnip
6. Thug
7. "This _____ test!"
8. The, to Therese
9. Tipsy
10. Thrash
11. Tennis troublemaker
12. TV threesome
13. Tee tail?
21. Trap
23. Tempest _____ teapot
25. Thicker through the tummy
26. Twinkling
27. Tylenol target
28. Took
29. Turnpike turnoffs
31. Traffic
32. Tours toast
35. Tabloids take them
37. Transport
40. Tramps
41. Tattled
46. Tumult
47. Televise
48. Tends to the tab
50. Temper
53. Tiller's tower
54. Tec's task
56. Traditional tales
57. Turpitude
58. Transaction
59. Tearful
61. _____ tear
62. Tunnel (though)
63. Took tiffin

T Party*

by S. E. Booker

*Stan Newman's favorite puzzle.

Across

1. Pilgrim's title
6. Blue
10. Current choice
14. From the top
15. One-named New Age singer
16. *Moonstruck* Oscar winner
17. The addled executioner _____
19. Miler's target
20. Born abroad
21. Obi-Wan player
22. Light-headed benefactors?
24. The Vegas oddsmaker _____
26. It sometimes needs boosting
29. Where It. is
30. Book after Joel
31. Seasick sailor's support
34. Blender brand
39. Diamond accessory
40. Raw fish dish
42. Irene of *Fame* fame
43. One of the Barrymores
45. Lock opener?
46. Passionate party
47. It comes before long?
49. Block houses
51. The clumsy album collector _____
57. Run
58. Smidgen
59. Jazz fan
62. Brain wave
63. The hayseed artist _____
66. Flat rate?
67. *The Grapes of Wrath* extra
68. "Not to worry"
69. Athlete's anathema
70. Kind of ring or swing
71. Elite divers

Down

1. Infamous Jessica
2. Fluish feeling
3. Miss Marple of mystery
4. Dublin dance
5. Behind bars
6. The 10 in *10*
7. Cooling
8. _____ Accord (1998 peace agreement)
9. Popular seaside resort
10. Play part
11. 1989 French Open champ
12. Profundity
13. Crown-polisher
18. Typo A ailments
23. Retro 'do
24. Clobber
25. Indian territory
26. Jerry Herman musical
27. Bypass
28. *Goodbye Columbus* author
32. Boring tool
33. Syr. neighbor
35. Nag
36. South Seas staple
37. As a result
38. Tanners catch them
41. Knuckleheads
44. Lustful look
48. Willy-nilly
50. On the house
51. '30s nightclub employee
52. Drive for big spenders
53. Hot spots?
54. "Endymion" poet
55. MacDonald's refrain
56. Intimidated
59. Chihuahua home
60. One who's off base
61. Condescending clucks
64. *Citizen Kane* studio
65. AAA recommendation

Workers

by Nancy Salomon

Across

1. Prepare greens
5. Producer of 1-Down
10. Empty remarks
14. Showy lily
19. Sore
20. Graff of *Mr. Belvedere*
21. It needs reeds
22. Like busy insects
23. Frequent caller's complaint?
27. It's west of Lake Pskov
28. Denomination
29. Michigan river
30. Small parcels
31. Las _____ (Cuban province)
32. Alice's boss
33. Came up
36. Miriam's brother
37. Expedited
39. Euro tax
42. Executive's affliction?
46. Canadian singer Vannelli
47. Rocky hills
48. Safe, on board
49. UFO crew
50. Wiped out
51. Lofty lyric
52. Balloonist's problem?
56. Verb form
57. It can heat or cool
60. Lair
61. It's legal
62. G, F, or C
63. Abzug
64. Cultivated
65. Falling star
68. Arc
69. Jaguars
73. Tracts
74. Landlady's woe?
76. Center of famous palindrome
77. Most worthless part
78. He wed Rita in 1949
79. Exude water
80. CAT, e.g.
81. Superior
82. Malady in 31-Across?
87. Sra. in Brooklyn
88. Toronto team
90. Units of loudness
91. Without equal
92. Pine kin
93. Little piggy
94. Clammy
96. Sluggishness
100. Admit a stock for trading
101. Type of number
105. Sticker shock?
109. Sheep-like
110. Held back
111. Saw
112. Olla
113. Very poor
114. Lip
115. Brings down the house
116. Warty amphibian

Down

1. Player insert
2. Baron in *Der Rosenkavalier*
3. Attempt
4. Summary
5. Permitted
6. Small, sporty cars
7. Actor Arthur
8. Med. specialty
9. Spare
10. Big beakers of the tropics
11. Drives the getaway car
12. _____ Gatos, California
13. Court designs
14. Sponged
15. "The cruelest month"
16. Celebrity
17. Buddhist monk
18. All over
24. Printer roller
25. Good place for salami
26. Reputation
31. Circus attraction
33. He's usually in a cast
34. Harper role
35. Like a trireme
36. "Lend _____ " (Channing hit)
37. Assail
38. "Hey there"
39. Food stuff
40. Fragrant seed
41. Facial cleanser
43. Main
44. Removed
45. Hotel Harry's wife
46. Jackson of *A Touch of Class*
50. Soak tea leaves
53. Unit of heat
54. Bisect
55. Straight edge
58. Glacial epoch
59. At _____ for words
61. _____ l'oeil
63. River markers
64. Attack
65. Word for Merman
66. Misplay
67. High schoolers
68. Kabalevsky's opera _____ *Breugnon*
69. Property claims
70. Right-hand page
71. Receive the waters of
72. Gist
74. Suggestive
75. Bird call
80. Most smooth and lustrous
83. Casual wear
84. Settle down for the night
85. Carousing
86. South African money
88. Small bus with a regular route
89. Operatic high spot
92. Palm leaf
93. Imposes a fine on
94. Clever plan
95. First sign of spring
96. User's image
97. Church's main part
98. One of HOMES
99. Refuges
102. Western defense org.
103. "Or to take arms against _____ of troubles" (*Hamlet*)
104. Lascivious
106. Verily's leader
107. Vitamin amts.
108. Nickname of great Boston outfielder

What's Up, Doc?

by Arthur S. Verdesca

Across

1. Experiences
4. With 19-Across, a certain pageant winner
8. Terminal info
11. Fischer finish
15. UTEP grid foe
18. Greenwich CT time
19. See 4-Across
20. *Laugh-In* first name
21. *Big Daddy* first name
22. Golfer Se Ri _____
23. "As state names go, it's the commonest first word"
25. "It's the part of the neighbor you never completely see on *Home Improvement*"
28. Winter runners?
29. Place for PIN money?
31. Prayer
32. Planet, e.g.
33. "This 1982 film starred Paul Newman"
36. Cookie-crumble candidate
38. Theater co.
39. Before, once
40. Chris Farley persona, often
41. Laziness
42. *Bosque* bear
45. Author Octavio
47. Very slow rate
49. "He's on first"
51. "Just Wilson's known for doin' it on PBS . . . I guar-awn-tee"
54. Asian nation
55. Eur. nation
56. Long time
57. Facilitators
60. The jig _____
64. *Jaws* town
66. "Will Rogers said that everything is funny as long as it is 'this' to somebody else"
70. *SNL* last name
71. German industrial region
72. Farm critters
73. Realms
74. "It's pretty much all that a great white shark has on its mind"
77. Lutelike instrument
78. Dutch portraitist Peter
79. Sound effect?
80. Super-sensitive subject?
82. _____ 's *Gold*, 1997
84. Lizard's tail?
85. "He's otherwise known as Bruce the rock star"
89. "It means 'batting' "
93. Financier Khashoggi
95. Yang's opposite
96. Seek answers
97. _____ zero
98. David Spade film, 1994
99. Ex-tree
101. Secret org.
103. Diamond decision
104. "A teacher needs to see it if you're tardy"
110. Prop for Norman
111. _____ leap tall buildings . . .
112. Sit in a dump all day
113. Ball-hiking cue
115. "It's the purpose of hooks and thumbtacks" (with 118-Across)
118. See 115-Across
120. That WNBA star
121. Big book
122. Chemical ending
123. Shower powder
124. *Exodus* hero
125. 2000 et al.
126. Gen. Lee, briefly
127. Dream sleep
128. Free, in a way
129. The present time?

Down

1. Chopped
2. Put on
3. Hide, in a way
4. Errors
5. Charged particle
6. Effort
7. _____ light (caught on)
8. Wallis's guy
9. Nevada resort
10. I shot _____ . . .
11. French plateau, the _____ Central
12. Committee type
13. Contaminate
14. Printing units
15. Piaf's nickname
16. Duncan's murderer
17. Small guitar, familiarly
24. Rend
26. Like waves
27. Silly people
30. Pfizer rival
34. Actor Kevin
35. Nabisco's _____ -Thin Pretzels
37. "So that's it!"
41. Plea at sea
42. Possess
43. Put into a scabbard
44. Healthy breakfast
46. Place with feeding times
48. Perform without _____
49. Contorts
50. OR site
52. Old, to a teen
53. Walk _____
54. Three-mile units
58. Pallid
59. "Get away!"
60. Three men's place
61. Mazatlán's place
62. Strip
63. Some ratings
65. _____ the season
67. Clog cause, often
68. "Rule, Britannia!" composer
69. Yale, Old _____
70. Rice athlete
71. Arose in bed
75. Jacob's twin
76. Clinic attire
77. Egyptian tour stop
81. Filthy place
83. Ulu user: abbr.
84. NYC to Atlantic City
86. Head light?
87. FDR book, _____ *Way*
88. Attach securely
89. Pugilists' org.
90. Actress Locklear
91. Listening
92. Rental sign
93. Behaved
94. Not as clean

Screamingly Obvious *Jeopardy!*

by Merl Reagle

98. Small movable platform

100. Cavern

102. Burmese Peace Nobelist, _____ San Suu Kyi

104. Leaping mackerel

105. Megaton monster

106. Auxerre's department

107. Farmer Frome

108. *Oh Dad, Poor Dad . . .* ending

109. Accustom, variantly

114. *The Longest Day*, e.g.

115. Motive

116. Orch. section

117. Lapidary concern

119. Lucas's FX company

Across

1. Least quiet quiet
12. Overstuffed prayer book
21. Charge from Rent-A-Streaker
22. In this spot, approximately
23. Singers of "Don't Cry for Us, Argentina"
24. Essays written in Rodents 101
25. Moving man of the year
27. Protests held by pep squads
28. "Quick . . . what's the 15th letter?" response
29. "The bearer will be repaid one chit"
30. Former litigant's remembrance
32. Composer Khachaturian
33. Deep-voiced opera singer heard on an album
35. Either of two anagrams for CAPES
38. Years spent as a U.S. soldier
39. One indication that Tarzan has taken his clan to the beach
41. Apr. and Aug., e.g.
42. Jackie K.'s future husband
43. The timber source notwithstanding
45. Whose competition is Kal-Kan?
47. Bring Senator Jake back to life
49. *Cogito* _____ ("I think, therefore I am the Greatest")
51. Some verses by Gershwin
52. The celebrity voters on *To Tell the Beast*
54. What this is
58. An "Unrestrained Acne" spell, perhaps
59. Taro-inspired tune
60. A question of distance
61. They're prescribed in cases of chocolate beverage deficiency
66. San _____, California
67. Take woods from Woods
69. *Portnoy's Complaint* author
70. Chemical ending
71. Group from western Virginia
73. Verdi opera
75. It only allows people to eat wheat, oats, barley, corn, rice, and rye

77. "What's your favorite woodwind, Ollie?" "Why, the _____"
79. Speaker of Quechua
80. Excoriates
81. Resemble Mr. Clean, perhaps
83. Journalist Nellie
84. Why you should never rely on garden pests to be perfectly accurate
86. Messages sent via the university computah?
89. Head of the rockpile
91. Make it to Anchorage
92. God's response when the committee presented plans for the Manx cat
93. How singer Janis responded to applause
94. What a fledgling appliance company aspires to be
95. Promotional gimmick designed by the Idaho Tourist Board

Down

1. Find _____ (think Mr. Iacocca poorly bred)
2. Possible cause of the two holes in a draft animal's neck
3. What "north" meant to those south of Rome's old port
4. Ellipsis parts
5. Answer when Isaac asked, "Which of my sons are you?"
6. Devilfish . . . or so they'd *like* you to think
7. Put you and me in a tricky position
8. Where you can buy all things wise and wonderful?
9. Remark from a jaded alien-watcher
10. Spoofed actor Hawthorne
11. "_____ Rebel" (1962 hit)
12. Distant
13. Ancient counting devices
14. End of a famous riddle's answer
15. Low-intensity sun god
16. _____ *Jury* (Spillane novel)

17. Music from Queen Latifah and Lil' Kim
18. All over half the place
19. Sports fan?
20. How Felix wanted Oscar to live
26. More well-to-do
31. A Baltimore bird-watcher might do it
34. Jaime Sommers or Steve Austin, in '70s TV
36. What a distant point on an orrery may do
37. Carpets made by Chia
40. Was indiscriminately imitative
44. Faster alternative to the Bunny Trail
46. "Once I borrowed ten trillion dollars . . .", et al.
48. If singer Cara married hockey player Bobby, she'd be . . .
50. Fix damaged classic paintings
53. What the minor deity Nicotinus was?
54. Tourist's terse assessment of the size of an English river
55. Movie where Gwyneth Paltrow inspires a musclebound Shakespeare to do his best work
56. "My wife is at home waiting" and "It's too crowded in here for me"
57. The money one's fellow emcee earns
62. Kind of like a particular hardwood
63. Attack the composer of "One O'Clock Jump"
64. Fan of a Sicilian volcano
65. Well-polished boys
68. C. S. Lewis's fight song
72. Miniature boor
74. Start of a memo between *Designing Women*'s producers
76. _____ -be (future jokes)
78. Exclude a follower of Attila
82. Olympic swimmer Janet
85. What a rolling enots doesn't gather?
87. Opera highlight
88. Crow's-nest location
90. Tarzan portrayer Ron

Something Different

by Trip Payne

Across

1. "_____ your name" (Mamas and Papas lyric)
6. Fell behind slightly
15. Euripides tragedy
16. Free
17. Forecast
19. Be bedridden
20. Journalist Stewart
21. Rosetta _____
22. 1960s espionage series
24. _____ Perignon
25. Quilting party
26. "Drying out" program
28. Umpire's call
30. Tease
34. Tease
36. Standard
38. "The Tell-Tale Heart" writer
39. Lead story in tomorrow's newspaper (!)
43. No Clue
45. Gold: prefix
46. _____ Lee cakes
48. Bobble the ball
49. Spanish aunts
51. Obi
53. Bravery
57. Small island
59. Daddies
61. Theda of 1917's *Cleopatra*
62. Employee motivator
65. Otherworldly
67. Treasure hunter's aid
68. Title for 39-Across next year
71. Exclusion from social events
72. Fab Four name
73. They may get tied up in knots
74. Begin, as a maze

Down

1. Disable
2. Cherry-colored
3. Newspaperman Ochs
4. Easel part
5. Actress Turner
6. Ropes, as dogies
7. Place to put your feet up
8. Underskirt
9. First of three-in-a-row
10. Lower in public estimation
11. Onetime bowling alley employee
12. Threesome
13. English prince's school
14. '60s TV talk-show host Joe
18. Superannuated
23. Sewing shop purchase
25. TV's Uncle Miltie
27. Short writings
29. Opponent
31. Likely
32. Actress Caldwell
33. End of the English alphabet
35. Trumpet
37. Ex-host Griffin
39. Black Halloween animal
40. French 101 word
41. Provider of support, for short
42. Much-debated political initis.
44. Sourpuss
47. Malign
50. *La Nausee* novelist
52. Sheiks' cliques
54. Bemoan
55. Popsicle color
56. Bird of prey
58. 10 on a scale of 1 to 10
60. Family girl
62. Famous _____
63. Something to make on one's birthday
64. Regarding
65. Quite a story
66. Dublin's land
69. _____ Victor
70. Hubbub

Election Day Puzzle, 1996*

by Jeremiah Farrell

*One of Will Shortz's favorite puzzles.

Across

1. Lord Byron poem
5. Loopy
9. "Uncle _____ " (Paul McCartney hit)
15. Boom causers
19. "Absolutely!"
20. Mighty mite
21. 1976 De Palma shocker
22. Tennis stroke
23. Flan
24. Royal pastime
25. Reservations
26. Recherche
27. Kind of planning
29. Legislators
31. Phoenix suburb
32. Kind of question
33. Plane's right
34. Paged
35. Kenneth Grahame character
38. "I cannot tell _____ "
39. Figures out at the beginning?
41. Abounding
44. Sliver
46. Second servings
48. Flynn portrayal
49. Record producer Brian
50. Program since 1965
52. " _____ may look on a king"
53. Summer of 1980 question
56. Madrid museum
57. "Yeah, sure"
61. To some degree
62. Magazine contents
65. Procrastinator
67. War story
68. It's depicted by parts of today's puzzle
71. Polynesian tongue
72. "Locksley Hall" poet
74. Hope and Crosby, often
75. Mickey's partner
76. Beat (out)
77. _____ 6
79. Lampoons
82. Slack-jawed
83. Most likely
85. _____ deus in nobis (there is God within us)
86. Remove

90. Part of a 1995 reunion
92. The _____ of the land
93. Ancient goddess of fertility
94. Today's soldier, e.g.
96. Bass _____
98. Tom Clancy hero Jack
100. Noisy gulps
101. Plesiosaurlike reptile, familiarly
103. The Taming of the Shrew setting
107. Author Ken
108. Salespeople push it
110. Wondrous
111. Bye
112. Thus
113. Magwitch of Great Expectations
115. 1979 disco hit
116. Kind of rack
117. Shop's replacement
118. Mooring site
119. Bed piece
120. Forward
121. Early English poet laureate
122. Major hit
123. Bang out, in a way

Down

1. Half a 1980s TV duo
2. Get a smile out of
3. Race do-overs
4. How to play "Loch Lomond"
5. Breach
6. From _____ z
7. Classroom reward
8. Slide sight
9. Familiarize
10. Artist Toulouse-_____
11. Form a queue
12. Perry's creator
13. Net supports
14. Parisian possessive
15. Brake sound
16. Movie for which Lee Grant won an Oscar
17. Sink
18. Went 80, say
28. More than enough
30. Traveler's guide
31. Leaves in the pot
34. Words in an anthology title
36. More than disdain

37. Japanese assembly
39. Tilting building?
40. Gentle _____ (Miss Manners salutation)
41. Newspaper's _____ desk
42. Had an inspiration
43. Foundation
45. Atlantic City resort, with "the"
47. Item in a lock
51. Downer
54. Classic film set in Wyoming
55. Delilah in Samson and Delilah
56. George Michael, for one
57. Mideasterner
58. Military decoration
59. Most like a ghost
60. Europe's Gulf of _____
63. Year in Louis XIV's reign
64. "O Sole _____ "
66. Foreign title
68. Get down, so to speak
69. Chant
70. "Over here!"
73. Brainpower
75. Fictional Walter
78. Baker's need
80. WWI grp.
81. Peter, once
83. George Cukor classic
84. Unversed?
86. Windows work area
87. Officially not working
88. Psych out
89. Southern stinger
91. Quarterback
93. Financial page figure
95. Kind of satellite
97. Perfume dispensers?
99. Classified ad abbr.
101. Very much
102. Pasta shape
104. Not very intelligently
105. Open, in a way
106. Talismanic stone
108. French Christian
109. Green light
110. Ingenue, perhaps
112. Honorary law degree
114. Uncle Tom's Cabin girl

Night Lights*

by Eric Albert

One of Will Shortz's favorite puzzles.

Across

2. Links org.
5. Hollers
10. Support
14. Speech fumbles
15. Charlotte cager
16. Mitch Miller's instrument
17. Bandleader Edmundo
18. Mr. Kosygin
19. "Lean _____ " (Bill Withers hit)
20. The Smothers Brothers, e.g.
21. Alice's restaurant
22. Make hand over fist
24. Open
26. Bottom-line amount
28. *Odyssey* enchantress
29. Antic
30. Chopin's "Butterfly" et al.
32. February 2 sighting
34. Brighton brew
35. Carved out
39. Cauldron
40. Like a certain period of burrowed time?
43. Singer Christie
44. Consent and Reason, e.g.
46. *Six Crises* monogram
47. 37-Down, e.g.
49. They're on the receiving end

52. Cross
53. Maid-for-TV?
56. *Steve Allen Show* regular
57. "Romancero gitano" poet
59. Handsome hunk
61. Cowboys and Indians, e.g.
63. Physicist Georg
64. Actress Diana
65. Casual coverup
67. Stock option
68. Clairvaux cleric
69. Elizabeth I, to poets
70. System start-up
71. Salt deposit?
72. Hornless, as cattle
73. *Citizen Kane* studio

Down

1. For the outlook, look out for his look out!
2. Lost in Lille
3. What 1-Down is
4. Hobnob
5. Shock treatments?
6. Pit
7. Blackmailer's words
8. Driver's aid
9. Be up and about

10. Fond of reading
11. Dogpatch denizen
12. "Cathy," e.g.
13. Nancy Drew's creator
23. Virtuoso
25. Postfix
27. Slipper
31. Adjudge
32. Toning-up spot
33. In fighting trim
36. George Gallup competitor
37. What 3-Down is
38. Ding-a-ling
41. Mutant cartoon superheroes
42. Site of 1905's Norway-Sweden split
45. "The Faerie Queene" poet
48. *Who Slew Auntie _____ ?* (1971 film)
50. Bard of boxing
51. Any soap opera
53. Set upon
54. Kind of brick
55. Kazantzakis character
58. "Are not!" response
60. What to do when you see red
62. D-Day river
66. Letters angels love

Groundhog Day Puzzle*

by Bob and Sharon Klahn

*One of Will Shortz's favorite puzzles.

Across

1. Riker's hoot
5. Groggy sound
10. Wad of gore
14. Maimed fountain in Thessaly
15. Tame coup
16. Soon for Tills
17. Freight for the stench
18. Do Nelly's land
19. Foil, as a spender
20. Kinks in a drab array
22. Knew Dooley
24. Site of fan's mall
25. To key, in ballet
26. Nip; in the hoe
29. Pick cheese
34. Lake mower
36. Booze and shoots have them
37. No lumber
38. "Moe is wee!"
39. Socko toss
41. Pinger that searches
42. Clone for Zox in Cal.
43. Rabbit in old home
44. Beagle rands
46. Sealer of the hick
49. Nap around the wreck

50. Poppy or carrot
51. Cart in the past
53. Home is near
56. He wears kites and a tape
60. Mend in the sail
61. Part of a gnat's frame
63. Rowing flock
64. Sensing Ford
65. Toast-of-the-mime
66. Thine mocs
67. Fix seat under
68. Lancer and Keogh, e.g.
69. Something seen eaten in groups

Down

1. It may see a bonnet
2. Mound in a history by Hammett
3. Russia's neater or pickle-less
4. Coated nape
5. Spate of studs?
6. Stayed for a shore
7. Rolls with peels
8. Row on gunners
9. Spear increases its feed
10. Farm-y bellows
11. Zoom or roan
12. Place for stocky hicks

13. Steak muffed
21. Way to be dairy?
23. Stitchers' pats
25. One who finds baits for Moes
26. Fake mitt
27. Rind of Cabot
28. Doe gown
30. Lighten with a toad
31. He's Sandy with a horde
32. Lack of the Shakers
33. Hell, or smearing
35. Boob to one's telly
40. Funny me
41. Rocking shout of 1815
43. Steer for a gable
45. Sand in the lea
47. Caught warty finks?
48. Barry or Hess
52. Stall phones
53. Laid mike
54. Gunning rate
55. Mailing on the sane
56. Batting oneself on the pack
57. Bash in Kahn
58. Fate as stacked
59. Spore involved with case
62. "Suo _____ day"

Done with Fiction*

by Sue Tilly and Jackie Westers

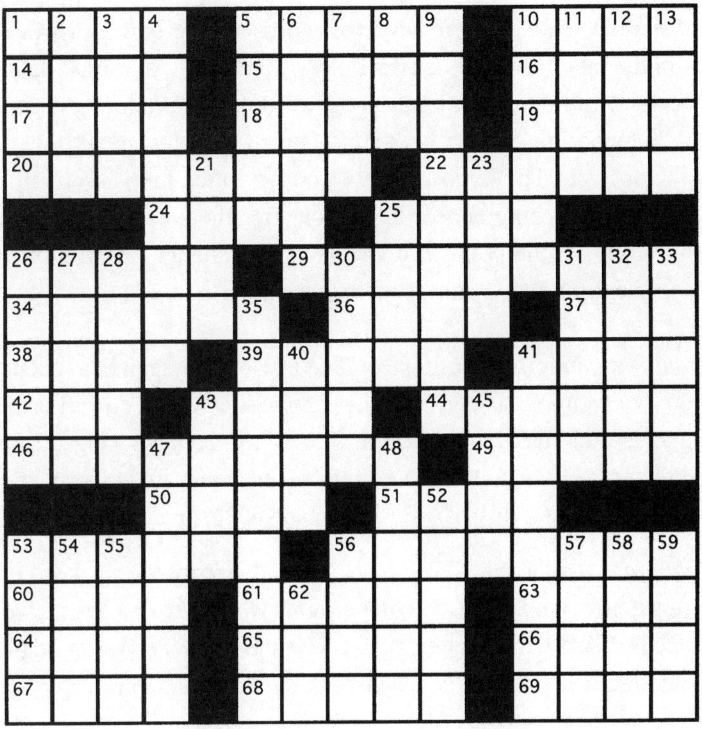

*From the 1999 American Crossword Puzzle Tournament.

HOW TO SOLVE CRYPTIC CROSSWORDS

(by Emily Cox and Henry Rathvon)

The difference between standard crosswords and cryptic crosswords is that the clues in the latter have two distinct parts. One part is a normal definition of the answer and the other is a hint using wordplay (common types are given below). A beginner might ask: Isn't a clue much easier to solve if it gives two hints to the answer? The hitch is that a good cryptic clue is worded misleadingly. The definition may appear before or after the wordplay, often with no punctuation to mark the point of division. The challenge and fun of a cryptic puzzle is to see through the clue-maker's deceptions.

1. *Double definitions.* The simplest kind of wordplay hint is a second definition. For example, HOOD can mean "gangster" or "a cover for the head." So a clue for HOOD might read: "Cover for the head gangster (4)." (The number in parentheses indicates how many letters are in the answer.) Here is another clue of this type for you to solve: "Trim a tree (6)."

2. *Anagrams.* A clue may show you what the letters of the answer would look like when scrambled, also giving a signal word such as *mixed, changed,* or *fractured.* An anagram clue for STEW could be "Wild West food (4)." Here is another clue of this type: "Noises in restless slumber (7)."

3. *Hidden answers.* Sometimes the answer will be hidden inside a longer word or phrase (as PLEAD is tucked inside "apPLE A Day"). Look for signals such as *caught in, buried in, part of,* and *housed by.* For example, CAT could be clued as: "Lover of birds imprisoned in Alcatraz (3)." Here's another example: "Karen always displays an engagement ring? (5)" (As in standard crosswords, a question mark at the end of a clue typically signals a punny definition.)

4. *Homophones.* The clue may tell you that the answer has the same sound as another word or words, giving a signal such as *we hear, so it's said,* or *orally.* A homophone clue for BEAR (which sounds like *bare*) could be: "Animal is naked, we hear (4)." See if you can solve this one: "Vocal gossip for a lodger (6)."

5. *Charades.* A clue may break the answer into two or more convenient parts and define them sequentially, as in the game of charades. FARM-ING (agriculture) breaks into *far* (remote) and *Ming* (Chinese dynasty), and could be clued as "Agriculture in remote Chinese dynasty (7)." Here is another charade: "A combo on leave (7)."

6. *Containers.* If the answer breaks into convenient parts not side by side but one within the other, the clue may say that one part *contains, holds, grips,* or even *swallows* the other. CALLOW (inexperienced, green) has *all* inside *cow*, yielding the clue "Bovine has eaten everything green (6)." A container for you to solve: "Mr. Crosby keeps it sharp (6)."

7. *Reversals.* The additional hint may tell you that the solution when seen backward makes another word or words. SMART (keen) is the word *trams* (railway cars) backward. Its clue could be "Keen—railway cars in reverse (5)." Here's another: "Strike friend's back (4)."

8. *Deletions.* If you take the "head" (first letter) from SENTRY, you'll get ENTRY. If you remove the "tail" (last letter) from BURRO, you'll get BURR. If you delete the "heart" (central letter) from FAUNS, you get FANS. Here's a clue using such a deletion: "Bird dog losing its head (5)."

9. *Complex clues.* Sometimes (especially with longer words) these different kinds of hints may used in combination. But however complicated the operations may seem, full instructions will always be available for obtaining the answer. Here is an example of a clue combining a charade and an anagram: "Pagans, strangely, hate barnyard birds (8)."

Answers to the sample clues: 1. SPRUCE (double def) 2. RUMBLES ("slumber" anag.) 3. ARENA (hid.) 4. ROOMER (homophone of "rumor") 5. A-BAND-ON 6. B(IT)ING 7. SLAP ("pal's" rev.) 8. (b)EAGLE 9. HEAT + HENS ("hate" anag.)

Across

1. Dromedary with no tail arrived (4)
3. Greek scientist chimed in "God of War" (10)
9. Only a bit of baloney (4)
10. Roundup producer in Arizona in summer (10)
11. Frayed cable repaired in an audacious way (11)
15. Wandering around hotel's front receptacle for butts (7)
16. Actual parking place for Dole again? (7)
17. Woman in a Greek play stirred treacle (7)
19. Greeting accepted by washed-up South American (7)

20. S & M allowed in newlywed's chamber of vice? (7,4)
23. The woman's B.A. names figures in folk medicine (10)
24. Money left for a waiter's bits of advice (4)
25. One small cell amid many odds and ends (10)
26. *Alien* showing in British school (4)

Down

1. Traitor in Celebes has a party (10)
2. Archie breaking Monday's rules? (10)
4. Dirty, wild, racy Hun (7)
5. Place for cigars I'd held in jokes (7)
6. Rude remark in gym festivity (11)

7. Almost 12—take a nap (4)
8. Sounded apologetic for woman's dress in India (4)
12. Feudal clergy leaving a will behind evergreens (5,6)
13. Kind of tale-teller upset legislator (10)
14. Construction worker in street with one mother and child (10)
18. CIA also badly disinclined to have company (7)
19. Fuzz brought in against 1990s president (7)
21. Fish food, pal (4)
22. Love god with aching back (4)

by Cox & Rathvon

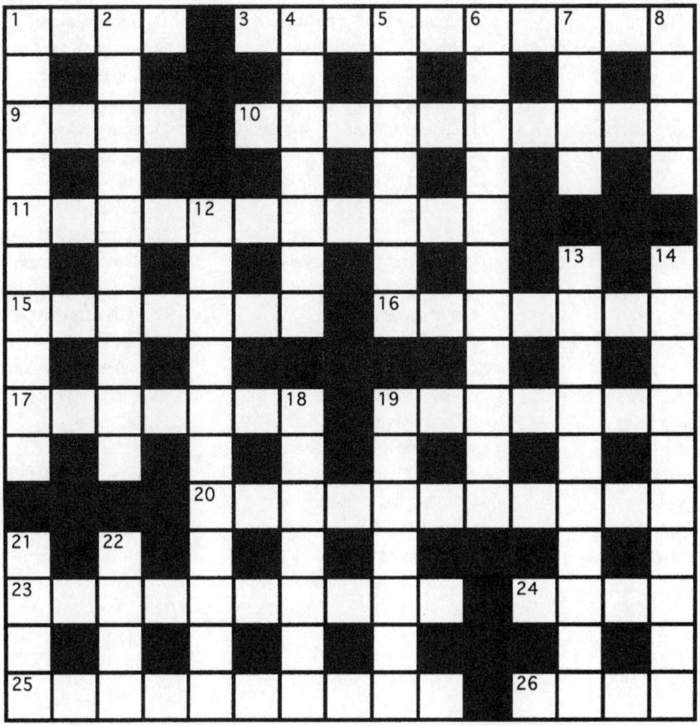

Across

1. Where one mowed a grass plot
7. Lines for Sadie
12. Where a man is at, down under
14. Rests? What else? Sp.
16. A c-clergyman? Correct!
17. Solitary one at the lady's school in Mass.
18. Picked Enoch's
19. She would, in short, take off
21. Peter's middle name
22. T'anger
23. It shuts out odor
24. Exult when you see quarrel
25. A little money in the bank
26. Figure of poetry? Why not?
28. 'Tain't lemon
29. The giving up of a meeting by the sound of it
31. Narrated Paul Revere's ride, etc.
33. 'ot weather phenomenon
34. Beginning of page
35. She's a moderate radical
39. Kid the musicians?
43. Letter in a game o' anagrams
44. Images conjured up by scion
46. Center of flood

47. Go off in high gear
48. See Myrna get sated
49. 'Tain't bull
50. Host follower
51. Heveryone
52. Dishes for small South American boys
54. Any girl may procrastinate
56. Who is a pretty girl?
58. Last under "E"
59. Acknowledged inmate gave up
60. Try S, A
61. Thwacks, as pets

Down

1. Device that slices ham nice
2. They accompany Ross, etc.
3. A Terpsichore or a Clio
4. How to challenge a Red
5. Anon. Biblical fellow
6. How to make rite write
7. Jacob's son as "The Woman"
8. But T and U were right behind
9. That is R, as used in comparison
10. It's time Red got a black mark
11. Pie, to me, is the ideal example
12. One sees it at battle
13. He would pose a moral

15. Like 500 sweet prunes
20. Hero of the fields
23. One can put this fellow on
24. See arm or leg go up
26. For Rita, a lid of sorts
27. Past tense of rite?
28. Sore points for strikers
30. S'border
32. Where they don't banish Hibernians
35. Esprit de corps from Rome-L.A.
36. Suppose I mean G.I.?
37. Feet?
38. Herb made 500 sick
39. He gets this from history
40. What Spaniards called a judge
41. What the old ones like in soup
42. Against the odds, we looked for water
45. Sees oil as a pain
48. Sounds like transport fellow
49. Wintry condition on Lee St.
51. Zeus gave _____ hard time
52. Yemen's capital is sultana's environs
53. What is left out of basics
55. He hangs around genius
57. Predecessor of rani

Puns & Anagrams

by Mel Taub

Chain Letters

by Coral Amende

Form words reading across and down, using only the letters provided. Don't repeat a word anywhere in the diagram, and don't use plurals, proper nouns, foreign words, prefixes or suffixes, abbreviations, or a different form of the same word (*give*, *gave*).

Point values for each letter are given. After you fill in all the squares, add up the columns vertically and enter the results in the scoring box. Total these, and then add 10 points for each letter you didn't use anywhere in the word squares to arrive at your grand total.

Letter Values

3 R	3 T	3 A
2 Y	2 O	2 N
1 C	1 E	1 D

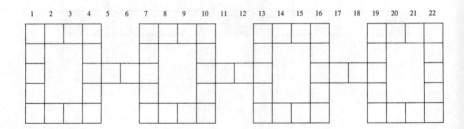

1 2 3 4 5 6 7 8 9 10 11 12 13 14 15 16 17 18 19 20 21 221 2 3 4 5 6 7 8 9 10 11 12 13 14 15 16 17 18 19 20 21 22

Score:

Column 1 _____   Column 12 _____

Column 2 _____   Column 13 _____

Column 3 _____   Column 14 _____

Column 4 _____   Column 15 _____

Column 5 _____   Column 16 _____

Column 6 _____   Column 17 _____

Column 7 _____   Column 18 _____

Column 8 _____   Column 19 _____

Column 9 _____   Column 20 _____

Column 10 _____   Column 21 _____

Column 11 _____   Column 22 _____

Total _____ + Total _____ + Letters unused _____ =

Grand total _____

Letter Gammon

by Coral Amende

Using the circled letter as a marker, land on any two different points. Select one of the two-letter groups from each point to form a five-letter word beginning with the marker letter. Use the letters in the order they appear, and cross off each two-letter group as it is used. Form fifteen five-letter words in this manner. When finished, arrange the last letters of each complete word to spell out the title of Howard Hughes's favorite flick, a Cold War suspenser with an all-male cast.

ZZ	RS	BU	DL	SI	NT
UG	LP	IC	LE	PT	OR
TA	SS	HA	CI	IS	LI
MA	GE	DA	SP	UD	ON
BI	IB	IO	DE	ER	BA

Your words:

_____ _____ _____

_____ _____ _____

_____ _____ _____

_____ _____ _____

_____ _____ _____

Last letters __ __ __ __ __ __ __ __ __ __ __ __ __ __ __

Film title _____

PUZZLE ANSWERS

(pages 260-61)

P	A	S	S	M	U	S	T	E	R		S	O	D	A
A	D	A	M	A	N	T	I	N	E		A	C	E	S
P	O	T	E	N	T	A	T	E	S		U	T	E	S
E	R	I	E		O	R	T		E	S	C	A	P	E
E	N	A			R	E	T	R	I	E	V	E	R	
T	E	T	R	A	S		R	E	V	E	R	E	N	T
E	D	E	N	I	C		S	R	I		S	D	S	
		S	L	A	M		I	S	L	A				
A	L	S		P	A	C		T	A	P	P	A	N	
N	U	T	S	H	E	L	L		S	T	E	E	L	E
A	N	A	L	O	G	O	U	S		R	L	S		
C	A	M	I	N	O		S	I	T		S	C	O	T
I	T	I	C		A	F	T	E	R	S	H	A	V	E
N	I	N	E		T	E	E	T	O	T	A	L	E	R
S	C	A	R		S	E	R	E	N	A	D	E	R	S

(pages 262-63)

E	D	N	A	B	E	S	T		A	S	W	A	R	M
L	E	A	D	U	P	T	O		E	L	I	S	H	A
M	A	X	E	D	O	U	T		R	A	T	S	O	N
E	N	O	S		S	T	A	Y	A	T	H	O	M	E
R	E	S	T	S		Z	L	O	T	Y		N	B	A
			E	O	E		E	Y	E		T	A	U	T
P	M	S		N	A	R	D	O		S	E	N	S	E
R	E	A	R	G	U	E		M	E	N	A	C	E	R
O	M	I	T	S		P	I	A	N	O		E	S	S
L	O	N	E		G	U	N		A	R	M			
O	R	T		B	O	T	C	H		T	O	N	I	C
G	A	S	P	O	W	E	R	E	D		B	A	L	E
U	N	D	O	N	E		O	N	E	S	I	D	E	D
E	D	A	M	E	S		W	I	L	D	L	I	F	E
S	A	Y	E	S	T		D	E	S	S	E	R	T	S

Double Croakers (pages 264–65)

```
P E C O S # A B U T # V E I L
E L U D E # M E M O # A I D A
T O L D A P P E A L I N G L Y
A P T # B E S T # E T C H E S
L E S S O N # S T R E E T #
# L A N E # H A M # B E D
A L T A R # D I R T # G A L A
D E R I D E D W O E F U L L Y
I V A N # D I O N # I S L E S
T I N # A G E # G A L T #
# S T R I D E # R I O T E D
A P P I A N # T W I G # H U R
B R I D L E D H O A R S E L Y
L O R E # S E A R # E A S E L
E W E S # S E N D # E M E R Y
```

Time's Up (pages 266–67)

```
* P I E C E S # A C C E S S *
W E L L S E T # W A L N U T S
A L L M A L E # E R I T R E A
R I P S # W H E L P # R E V
N S A # I D E A # P E L E
E S S # R E D L E G # H A I R
R E S T O N # F L A # O L E S
# I N N O * F L A T #
I N G A # I V S # O B O I S T
N E O N # S A H A R A # M O W
G E N T # O P E D # P R O
O D D # I N A W E # M A T A
O N O R D E R # D E P O S I T
D O L E O U T # O P E N S E A
* T A B L E S # M A R K E D *
```

T Party (pages 268-69)

```
R A S A . R A I L S . W I S H
A W O L . U P S E T . A L O E
C L U B . T E A S E . L I N E
E S P A N A . . W I L E S . .
. . C A B S . R E N O . . . .
A C R O B A T . A D A P T S .
C H A R . G O A D . . R A G
H O M E . A U D I T . G A L L
E S P . . T S A R . A D U E
. E S C A P E . N A I V E T E
. L I A R . T I R E . . .
. S C A R Y . . P E A L E D
S I A M . S O D A S . W O V E
A L S O . U N I T E . A R I A
D O E R . P A G E S . Y E L L
```

Workers (pages 270-71)

```
H A J J I . D O W N . A C D C
A G A I N . E N Y A . C H E R
H U N G J U R I E S . T A P E
N E E . A L E C . S A I N T S
. . P I C K E D A F I G H T
M O R A L E . E U R . . .
A M O S . R A I L . O S T E R
M I T T . S U S H I . C A R A
E T H E L . G R I D . O R G Y
. . E R E . I G L O O S
B R O K E A R E C O R D .
G O V E R N . I O T A . C A T
I D E A . D R E W S T R A W S
R E N T . O K I E . I T S O K
L O S S . M O O D . S E A L S
```

What's Up, Doc? (pages 272–73)

```
T O S S   L A B E L   T A L K   C A L L A
A C H Y   I L E N E   O B O E   A P I A N
P H O N I C F A T I G U E S Y N D R O M E
E S T O N I A   S E C T   S A G I N A W
      P K T S   T U N A S   M E L
A R O S E   A A R O N   S P E D   V A T
C H A I R M A N M E A S L E S   G I N O
T O R S   A L E E   E T S   S L A I N
O D E   S O A R T H R O A T   T E N S E
R A D I A T O R   H A U N T   T E N D E R
      C L E F   B E L L A   B R E D
M E T E O R   C U R V E   L E O P A R D S
A R E A S   R O O M E R T I S M   E R E
D R E G S   A L Y   W E E P   S C A N
A O N E   C A S T R O E N T E R I T I S
M R S   J A Y S   S O N E S   A L O N E
      F I R   S H O A T   D A N K
I N E R T I A   L I S T   O R D I N A L
C A R O N A R Y A R T E R Y D I S E A S E
O V I N E   K E P T   A D A G E   S T E W
N E E D Y   S A S S   R A Z E S   T O A D
```

ARTHUR S. VERDESCA: I wish I had saved Will Shortz's letter about [my "What's Up, Doc?"] puzzle. However, the essence of it was that, though he liked the construction, it was the illness theme that made him think his audience might be squeamish about it (or words close to that effect).

Screamingly Obvious *Jeopardy!* (pages 274–75)

1H	2A	3S		4M	5I	6S	7S		8E	9T	10A		11M	12A	13T	14E		15S	16M	17U
18E	S	T		19I	O	W	A		20D	A	N		21A	D	A	M		22P	A	K
23W	H	A	24T	S	N	E	W		25W	H	A	26T	S	H	I	S	27F	A	C	E
28N	O	S	E	S		29A	30T	M		31O	R	I	S	O	N		32O	R	B	
	33W	H	A	34T	S	T	H	E	35V	E	R	D	I	C	T		36O	R	E	37O
		38R	E	P		39E	R	E		40O	A	F			41S	L	O	T	H	
42O	43S	44O		45P	A	46Z		47C	R	A	48W	L		49W	50H	O	S	W	H	O
51W	H	A	52T	S	C	O	53O	K	I	N			54L	A	O	S				
55N	E	T	H		56E	O	N		57E	58A	59S	E	R	S		60I	61S	62U	63P	
	64A	M	I	65T	Y		66W	67H	68A	T	S	H	A	P	P	69E	N	I	N	G
70O	T	E	R	I		71S	A	A	R		72H	O	G	S		73L	A	N	D	S
74W	H	A	T	S	75E	A	T	I	N	G	76Y	O	U		77S	I	T	A	R	
78L	E	L	Y		79S	T	E	R	E	O		80E	81S	P		82U	L	E	E	83E
		84S	A	U	R			85W	86H	87O	S	T	H	E	88B	O	S	S		
89W	90H	91A	92T	S	U	P		93A	94D	N	A	N		95Y	I	N		96A	S	K
97B	E	L	O	W		98P	C	U		99L	O	G		100N	S	102A				
103C	A	L	L		104W	105H	A	T	S	106Y	O	U	R	107E	X	C	U	108S	109E	
	110T	E	E		111A	B	L	E	T	O		112R	O	T		113O	N	O	N	114E
115W	H	A	T	116S	H	O	L	D	I	N	117G	118T	H	I	119N	G	S	U	P	
120H	E	R		121T	O	M	E		122E	N	E		123T	A	L	C		124A	R	I
125Y	R	S		126R	O	B	T		127R	E	M		128O	N	M	E		129D	E	C

1 L	2 O	3 U	4 D	5 E	6 S	7 T	8 H	9 U	10 S	11 H	■	12 F	13 A	14 T	15 M	16 I	17 S	18 S	19 A	20 L
21 E	X	P	O	S	U	R	E	F	E	E	■	22 A	B	O	U	T	H	E	R	E
23 E	V	I	T	A	P	E	R	O	N	S	■	24 R	A	T	T	H	E	M	E	S
25 V	A	N	S	U	P	E	R	S	T	A	26 R	■	27 C	H	E	E	R	I	N	S
28 U	M	O	■	29 I	O	U	I	O	U	■	30 I	31 S	U	E	D	■	32 A	R	A	M
33 L	P	S	34 B	A	S	S	O	■	35 P	36 A	C	E	S	O	R	37 S	P	A	C	E
38 G	I	T	I	M	E	■	39 T	40 A	N	C	H	E	E	T	A	H	■	41 M	O	S
42 A	R	I	O	■	43 D	44 E	S	P	I	T	E	A	S	H	■	45 A	46 L	P	O	S
47 R	E	A	N	48 I	M	A	T	E	G	A	R	N	■	49 E	50 R	G	O	A	L	I
■	51 I	R	A	S	O	D	E	S	■	52 O	53 G	R	E	P	A	N	E	L
54 T	55 H	56 E	C	E	N	T	R	A	L	A	57 C	R	O	S	S	E	N	T	R	Y
58 H	E	X	O	N	T	E	E	N	■	59 P	O	I	D	I	T	T	Y
60 A	M	I	N	E	A	R	■	61 Y	62 O	O	H	O	O	D	O	S	A	63 G	64 E	65 S
66 M	A	T	E	O	■	67 R	68 O	B	A	G	O	L	F	E	R	■	69 R	O	T	H
70 E	N	E	■	71 R	72 O	A	N	O	K	E	S	E	T	■	73 E	74 R	N	A	N	I
75 S	I	X	76 G	R	A	I	N	D	I	E	T	■	77 O	78 B	O	E	S	T	A	N
79 I	N	C	A	■	80 F	L	A	Y	S	■	81 B	82 E	B	A	L	D	■	83 B	L	Y
84 S	L	U	G	85 S	E	R	R	■	86 H	87 A	R	V	A	R	D	E	88 M	A	I	L
89 B	O	S	S	S	T	O	N	90 E	■	91 R	E	A	C	H	A	L	A	S	K	A
92 I	V	E	T	O	T	A	I	L	■	93 I	A	N	C	U	R	T	S	I	E	D
94 G	E	S	O	M	E	D	A	Y	■	95 A	D	S	O	N	T	A	T	E	R	S

NANCY SCHUSTER: "Something Different" was a funny new idea and always entertaining. And [Trip is] truly brilliant puzzlewise.

Election Day Puzzle, 1996 (pages 278–79)

Left grid:

```
 I  C  A  L  L  ■  L  O  S  T  A  S  T  E  P
 M  E  D  E  A  ■  A  T  L  I  B  E  R  T  Y
 P  R  O  G  N  O  S  T  I  C  A  T  I  O  N
 A  I  L  ■  A  L  S  O  P  ■  S  T  O  N  E
 I  S  P  Y  ■  D  O  M  ■  B  E  E
 R  E  H  A  B  ■  S  A  F  E  ■  R  A  Z  Z
 ■  R  I  B  ■  N  O  R  M  ■  P  O  E
 B  O  B  D  O  L  E  ■  E  L  E  C  T  E  D
 A  U  R  ■  S  A  R  A  ■  E  R  R
 T  I  A  S  ■  S  A  S  H  ■  V  A  L  O  R
 ■  A  I  T  ■  P  A  S  ■  B  A  R  A
 A  W  A  R  D  ■  E  E  R  I  E  ■  M  A  P
 M  I  S  T  E  R  P  R  E  S  I  D  E  N  T
 O  S  T  R  A  C  I  S  M  ■  R  I  N  G  O
 S  H  O  E  L  A  C  E  S  ■  E  N  T  E  R
```

Right grid:

```
 I  C  A  L  L  ■  L  O  S  T  A  S  T  E  P
 M  E  D  E  A  ■  A  T  L  I  B  E  R  T  Y
 P  R  O  G  N  O  S  T  I  C  A  T  I  O  N
 A  I  L  ■  A  L  S  O  P  ■  S  T  O  N  E
 I  S  P  Y  ■  D  O  M  ■  B  E  E
 R  E  H  A  B  ■  S  A  F  E  ■  R  A  Z  Z
 ■  R  I  B  ■  N  O  R  M  ■  P  O  E
 C  L  I  N  T  O  N  ■  E  L  E  C  T  E  D
 A  U  R  ■  S  A  R  A  ■  E  R  R
 T  I  A  S  ■  S  A  S  H  ■  V  A  L  O  R
 ■  A  I  T  ■  P  A  S  ■  B  A  R  A
 A  W  A  R  D  ■  E  E  R  I  E  ■  M  A  P
 M  I  S  T  E  R  P  R  E  S  I  D  E  N  T
 O  S  T  R  A  C  I  S  M  ■  R  I  N  G  O
 S  H  O  E  L  A  C  E  S  ■  E  N  T  E  R
```

WILL SHORTZ: As I've often said, this is my favorite crossword of all time. It actually started back in fall 1980, when I was an associate editor at *GAMES*. Constructor Jeremiah Farrell sent me a crossword in which 1-Across could be either CARTER or REAGAN (clued as "Winner of the 1980 Presidential election," or something like that). Either answer fit with the clues for the crossing words. For some reason, Maleska, who was the editor at the *Times* then, had rejected this puzzle. I thought it was pretty amazing, and told Jerry so. Unfortunately, *GAMES* was a bimonthly magazine, and it was too late to get the puzzle into the November/December issue.

Sixteen years later, Jerry remembered my enthusiasm for the idea and constructed a new (and much improved) version of the puzzle involving CLINTON and BOB DOLE. When the puzzle appeared on Election Day, my phone at the *Times* started ringing at 9:00 and continued the whole day. Almost nobody seemed to realize that either answer fit the grid! The solvers who filled in CLINTON thought that I was being presumptuous at best, and maybe that I was inserting a political opinion into the puzzle. And the solvers who filled in BOB DOLE thought that I'd made a whopper of a mistake! Peter Jennings did a piece about the puzzle on *ABC News* that evening. He did explain both answers. And both answers appeared in the *Times* the next day, along with an explanation.

Night Lights (pages 280–81)

¹L	²A	³R	⁴A		⁵G	⁶A	⁷G	⁸A		⁹A	¹⁰L	¹¹B	¹²E	¹³R	¹⁴T		
¹⁹A	M	E	N		²⁰A	T	O	M		²¹C	A	R	R	I	E		
²³C	U	*	D		²⁴P	O	L	O		²⁵Q	U	A	L	M	S		
²⁷E	S	T	²⁸A	T	E		²⁹D	³⁰E	P	U	T	I	E	S			

WILL SHORTZ: An incredible construction. What a brilliant idea.

[Note the positions of the stars in the grid.]

Groundhog Day Puzzle (pages 282–83)

```
                    ¹P
 ²P ³G ⁴A  ⁵S ⁶H ⁷O ⁸U  T ⁹S  ¹⁰B ¹¹A ¹²C ¹³K
¹⁴E  R  S  ¹⁵H  O  R  N  E  T  ¹⁶O  B  O  E
¹⁷R  O  S  ¹⁸A  L  E  X  E  I  ¹⁹O  N  M  E
²⁰D  U  O  ²¹M  E  L  S  ²²R ²³A  K  E  I  N
²⁴U  N ²⁵C  A  P  ²⁶S  U ²⁷M  ²⁸C  I  R  C  E
   ²⁹D  I  D  O  ³⁰E  T  U ³¹D  E  S
³²S  H  A  D  O ³³W  ³⁴A  L  E  ³⁵H ³⁶E ³⁷E ³⁸N
³⁹P  O  T  ⁴⁰S ⁴¹I  X  W  E  E ⁴²K  ⁴³L  O  U
⁴⁴A  G  E ⁴⁵S  ⁴⁶R  M  N  ⁴⁷M ⁴⁸A  R  M  O  T
   ⁴⁹P ⁵⁰A  Y  E  E ⁵¹S  ⁵²R  O  O  D
⁵³H ⁵⁴A ⁵⁵Z  E  L  ⁵⁶N  Y  E  ⁵⁷L  O  R  C ⁵⁸A
⁵⁹A  D  O  N  I ⁶⁰S  ⁶¹P  R  O ⁶²S  ⁶³O  H  M
⁶⁴D  O  R  S  ⁶⁵T ⁶⁶S  H  I  R  T  ⁶⁷P  U  T
⁶⁸A  B  B  E  ⁶⁹O  R  I  A  N  A  ⁷⁰E  C  O
⁷¹T  E  A  R  ⁷²P  O  L  L  E  D  ⁷³R  K  O
```

BOB KLAHN: On New Year's Day, 1995, inside away from the freezing weather, I suddenly decided, "I'm going to make a Groundhog Day puzzle. I wonder if there's time to get it into the *Times* next month. I'd better make it now!" I thought, "Hmmm, Punxatawney Phil is just up in Pennsylvania; let's put him in." So I set up a 15 x 15 grid, stretched PUNXATAWNEY PHIL across the eighth row, put SHADOW, SIX WEEK, and MARMOT at right angles to Phil, threw GROUNDHOG and WOODCHUCK into opposite corners, laid out the critical black squares, and began the fill. Then it hit me: "Maybe I don't have the correct spelling! I had better look it up!" So I pulled my *Web Geo* off the shelf and discovered, to my horror, that it was PUNX-SUTAWNEY PHIL, sixteen letters long. "Oh no! Aargh!" But within the minute: "Oh, that's great! I can flip the grid and have the initial P sticking out the top!" And because it is formed like a head and neck, P is the perfect letter to be there, extending above the top of the grid, which has now magically become the surface of the ground. "Ah, this is tremendous!" A puzzle date of February 2 combined with a first clue of 2- rather than 1-Across was an added bonus. Then came the 1-Down clue, all at once: "For the outlook, look out for his look out!" Three separate meanings, and altogether a very smooth clue. Probably my best clue ever.

Done with Fiction (pages 284-85)

P¹	A²	T³	H⁴		M⁵	A⁶	R⁷	S⁸	H⁹		M¹⁰	A¹¹	R¹²	S¹³
O¹⁴	S	S	A		A¹⁵	W	O	K	E		A¹⁶	R	I	A
E¹⁷	T	A	T		I¹⁸	N	D	I	A		D¹⁹	E	N	T
M²⁰	A	R	T	I²¹	N	I	S		R²²	E²³	M	A	K	E
		E²⁴	D	E	N		E²⁵	T	R	E				
A²⁶	W²⁷	A²⁸	R	E		G²⁹	A³⁰	R	B	A	N	Z³¹	O³²	S³³
D³⁴	E	B	A	S³⁵	E		T³⁶	O	E	S		O³⁷	N	E
A³⁸	L	A	S		S³⁹	A⁴⁰	L	S	A		W⁴¹	R	E	N
P⁴²	S	T		T⁴³	O	G	A		T⁴⁴	I⁴⁵	A	R	A	S
T⁴⁶	H	E	R⁴⁷	A	P	I	S	T⁴⁸		S⁴⁹	T	O	L	E
		E⁵⁰	C	H	O		R⁵¹	O⁵²	L	E				
A⁵³	L⁵⁴	A⁵⁵	S	K	A		S⁵⁶	U	P	E	R	M⁵⁷	A⁵⁸	N⁵⁹
P⁶⁰	O	S	T		G⁶¹	A⁶²	M	M	A		L⁶³	A	V	A
E⁶⁴	P	E	E		U⁶⁵	S	U	A	L		O⁶⁶	R	E	S
D⁶⁷	E	A	D		S⁶⁸	I	G	N	S		O⁶⁹	K	R	A

Cryptic Crossword (pages 288–89)

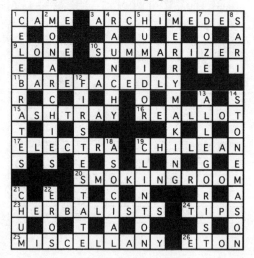

Across
1. CAME(L)
3. AR(CHIMED)ES
9. LONE (hidden)
10. SUMM(ARIZ)ER
11. BAREFACEDLY (anagram)
15. AS(H)TRAY
16. REAL + LOT
17. ELECTRA (anagram)
19. C(HI)LEAN
20. SM + OK + IN + GROOM

23. HER + BA + LISTS
24. TIPS (double definition)
25. M(I + S + CELL)ANY
26. ET + ON

Down
1. CELEB(RAT)ES
2. MON(ARCHIE)S
4. RAUNCHY (anagram)
5. HUM(ID)OR
6. MERRYMAKING (anagram)

7. DOZE(N)
8. SARI (homophone)
12. FIRS + TESTATE
13. ALLEGORIST (anagram)
14. ST + ONE + MA + SON
18. ASOCIAL (anagram)
19. C(LINT)ON
21. CHUM (double definition)
22. EROS (reversal)

Puns & Anagrams (pages 290–91)

MEL TAUB: My specialty is Puns & Anagrams crosswords, which used to appear every four weeks in the Sunday *Times* in Mrs. Farrar's day and also in the days of her successor, Will Weng. Under Maleska, they appeared every eight weeks, and currently, under Will Shortz, every eighteen weeks. In the 1950s, Puns & Anagrams crossword appeared every four weeks as the bottom puzzle in the *New York Times* Sunday magazine. These were freewheeling cryptic puzzles with an assortment of tricky clues. The strange clues baffled me until the process was explained by a genius friend who had learned how to solve them. I was smitten.

Soon after selling straight crosswords to the *Times*, I tried a Puns & Anagrams. Mrs. Farrar, to my surprise, ran it—after changing about 80 percent of the clues. Encouraged, I did another and another. With each successive submission, the degree of editing diminished. Before long I became the leading practitioner of the art, mainly by default. Most of the contributors doing them gave up, either on their own or with the prodding of Mrs. Farrar. One master of the art, J. F. Kelly (my role model), died. Saying I was now the only one around requiring minimal editing, Mrs. Farrar, in effect, gave me the job.

Chain Letters (pages 292–93)

1	2	3	4	5	6	7	8	9	10	11	12	13	14	15	16	17	18	19	20	21	22
T	A	R	N			R	O	A	R			T	A	T	A			C	A	R	T
A			A			O			A			A			C			R			A
R			T	O	R	T			T	A	R	T			O	N	T	O			R
O			T			O			T			T			R			O			R
T	R	A	Y			R	A	C	Y			Y	A	R	N			N	A	R	Y

SCORE:

Column 1	14	Column 12	3
Column 2	6	Column 13	14
Column 3	6	Column 14	6
Column 4	13	Column 15	6
Column 5	2	Column 16	11
Column 6	3	Column 17	2
Column 7	13	Column 18	3
Column 8	5	Column 19	10
Column 9	4	Column 20	6
Column 10	14	Column 21	6
Column 11	3	Column 22	14

Total 83 + Total 81 + Letters unused (E, D) 20 = Grand total 184

Letter Gammon (pages 294–95)

ALIBI	AORTA	ABUZZ
ASPIC	ADAPT	ASIDE
AISLE	ABACI	ADLIB
AMASS	AUDIO	AUGER
AGENT	ARSON	ALPHA

Last letters/film title: ICE STATION ZEBRA

APPENDICES

TOOLS OF THE TRADE

THE CROSSWORDER'S BOOKSHELF

I cannot live without books.
—Thomas Jefferson

JOE DIPIETRO: I pretty much survive with *Random House Webster's Unabridged Dictionary*, 2nd edition, *The Crossword Answer Book*, some foreign dictionaries, and *The Cambridge Factfinder*.

MARTIN ASHWOOD-SMITH: I have all of the major dictionaries with the exception of the [*Oxford English Dictionary*] 2nd edition. How do I get around not having the OED2? Well, I have the OED1 and the *New Shorter Oxford*. But this kind of huge reference is rarely needed in crossword construction (fortunately).

RICH NORRIS: Wow. Where do I start? Three or four dictionaries (two unabridged), several thesauruses, a few slang and idiom dictionaries, and a host of specialty encyclopedias and dictionaries on literature (American and English), sports, TV shows, Top-40 music, TV game shows, Broadway hits, movies, religion, and songs and songwriters. A *World Almanac*. A geographical dictionary. Two encyclopedias. A copy of *TV Guide*. *Consumer Reports'* annual "new cars" issue. A couple of quotation dictionaries. Oh, and I almost forgot: one of my most-used references, *The Random House Famous Name Finder*, by Coral Amende. (No, of course I didn't almost forget. I just saved it for last for dramatic effect.) Amende is so important because no other reference has a first-name index. I wish there were a first-name-indexed book for fictional characters—movies, TV, literature. That'd be a handy one to have.

TYLER HINMAN: I use a variety of dictionaries (the newest [*Oxford English Dictionary*], an old *Merriam-Webster's New Collegiate*, and an on-line program called WordWeb), and sometimes I go onto the Internet, specifically Yahoo!, if I wish to search for a good piece of trivia for a hard clue.

ELIZABETH GORSKI: I use [the *Random House Webster's Dictionary*] as a basic reference. I like to focus on contemporary language, so I try to use *Merriam-Webster's Third New International Dictionary* sparingly, only in a pinch.

KELLY CLARK: I've got a few good dictionaries. I wish I watched TV more, because there are, I gather, many television characters with beautiful, vowel-rich names.

BOB KLAHN: Did I mention Herbert M. Baus's *The Master Crossword Puzzle Dictionary*? It's out of print, but well worth finding. I use Baus quite a bit in theme and clue development; it's great for bringing two disparate ideas together because it helps me find vocabulary common to both ideas rather quickly and much more effectively than something as relatively rigid as a thesaurus ever could.

Other books I use quite a bit are Leonard Maltin's [yearly] *Movie & Video Guide*, Brooks and Marsh's TV books, Alex McNeil's *Total Television*, *Billboard*'s top-40 compilations, and the Jacobs' *Who Wrote That Song?* Nothing expensive. (If you want to be sure how a movie title is spelled or punctuated, head straight for Maltin. Period.) And the *Random House Thesaurus of Slang* often helps me liven up clues and develop themes. *Merriam Webster's Geographical Dictionary* helps a lot. And you already know I refer to a certain Amende publication quite a bit. I use Stetler's *Actors, Artists, Authors & Attempted Assassins* similarly, but unlike your compilation, it requires a double lookup. Boo, hiss.

Apart from various English dictionaries (*Random House Webster's Unabridged*, 2nd edition, stands head and shoulders above all the rest for puzzling purposes) and the Web, that's my complete "A list."

Quite a number of books I used to use have been supplanted by this or that URL. I use the IMDb heavily. And Napster (!) is great adjunct to *Billboard* for quickly identifying a given artist's titles, which titles are most popular, and who's recorded a given song; all of that information can be gleaned without ever downloading the music itself.

RICH SILVESTRI: Dictionaries (of course). I use mainly *Random House Unabridged* [2nd edition] and *Merriam Webster's Collegiate Dictionary*, 10th edition. *Directory of Prime-Time TV, Billboard Book of Top 40 Hits*, the *New Rolling Stone Encyclopedia of Rock & Roll, Merriam-Webster's Encyclopedia of Literature, Halliwell's Filmgoer's Companion, Roget's Thesaurus, Bartlett's*, and (sucking up here) the *Random House Famous Name Finder*.

SYLVIA BURSZTYN: Too many books to list. I love my three *Rock On* volumes by Norm N. Nite; my *People's Chronology* by James Trager; *Benét's Reader's Encyclopedia*, basic and American; *Bartlett's* and other quote books; a dozen dictionaries and encyclopedias; [*The*] *Film Encyclopedia* edited by Ephraim Katz [and coworkers]; trivia books; books of slang and idiom and phrases; foreign language dictionaries and phrase books; the *Random House Word Menu*; the new *Random House Famous Name Finder* and other first-name books; the *World Almanac;* Merriam Webster's geographical and biographical [dictionaries], and other biographicals. That scratches the surface. What's missing? A "sportographical." A who's who, who's been, and what's what in sports. I do the best I can without one by using general biographicals and the almanac.

GAYLE DEAN: With the vast array of wonderful Internet resources now available, I have my allowed my hard-copy references to dwindle. On-line I use some of the anagram-finders and general search features to verify facts. I utilize several CD-ROM dictionaries (*Random House* [2nd edition] is my favorite), Microsoft's Cinemania, which has a huge number of movies with everything anyone could possibly want to know about them, MS Bookshelf and Thesaurus, *Bartlett's Familiar Quotations, Larousse Dictionary of Literary Characters, Merriam-Webster's Geographical Dictionary* and [*Merriam-Webster's*] *Biographical Dictionary*.

BERNICE GORDON: My library contains two hundred reference books, including dictionaries in seven languages; thesaurus, quotations, biographies, and your book *Random House Famous Name Finder* (could not live without it).

I frequently call the Philadelphia Public Library for the information that I need.

NELSON HARDY: A few of the books I use quite a bit are the *Random House Webster's Unabridged Dictionary* (2nd edition), *Roget's Thesaurus*, the *World Almanac*, the *Rand McNally World Atlas*, NTC's *American Idioms* dictionary, *Total Television* by Alex McNeil, *The Film Encyclopedia* [edited] by Ephraim Katz, *Leonard Maltin's Movie & Video Guide*, and *The Billboard Book of Top 40 Hits*.

SAM BELLOTTO, JR.: [I use] too many books to name. In addition to dictionaries, atlases, and almanacs, I have such notable tomes as *The Emmys, Shakespeare Concordia*, and *Rock On*. You get the idea.

WILLIAM CANINE: *Webster's Deluxe Unabridged*; *Random House Webster's College Dictionary*; *Merriam-Webster's Biographical Dictionary*; world almanacs; *The Reader's Encyclopedia* (*Benét's*); *The Film Encyclopedia* (Katz); *Complete Directory . . . Network and Cable TV Shows* (Brooks and Marsh); Maltin's *Movie & Video Guide, Crossword Puzzle Dictionary* (Pulliam and Grundman); *Chambers Backwords for Crosswords*; *American Popular Songs* (Ewen); *New Rolling Stone Record Guide*; *Bartlett's*; *Dictionary of Given Names*; many sources of sports, classical music, and natural history, my personal major interests.

JON DELFIN: Shelves and shelves full. Between books on hand, the Web, and a few choice phone numbers, I can find most anything.

MARK DIEHL: *World Almanac, Grolier's Encyclopedia* (CD), Infopedia (CD), *Legends in Their Own Time*, Random House dictionary, *Merriam-Webster's Collegiate Dictionary*, 10th edition, *Merriam-Webster's Third New International Dictionary Unabridged*.

DIANE EPPERSON: Essentials: *Chambers Biographical Dictionary*; *Benét's Reader's Encyclopedia*; *Bartlett's Familiar Quotations*; *Merriam-Webster's Geographical Dictionary*; *Merriam-Webster's Collegiate Dictionary*, 10th edition; *Roget's International Thesaurus* (old-fashioned kind, grouped in categories); *VideoHound's Movie Retriever*; *World Almanac* (current year); Amende's *Random House Famous Name Finder*; Rodale's *Synonym Finder*;

Bibles (three versions); *Brewer's Dictionary of Phrase and Fable*; several mythology titles, including Hamilton's *Mythology*; Language phrase books (German, French, Spanish, Italian); Latin dictionary; atlases; Compton's reference CD (encyclopedia, thesaurus, dictionary, geographical dictionary, almanac, etc.). Other: miscellaneous dictionaries (music, biology, medicine, Bible, biography, technology); miscellaneous encyclopedias (history, science, natural history); crossword puzzle dictionaries; extensive collection of books on birds, geology, biology, botany; many other oddball references, like state names, flags, mottos, etc.; *A Glossary of Medieval Weapons*.

PETER GORDON: The usual. Lots of dictionaries (Random House's unabridged, Merriam-Webster's second and third *New International* dictionaries. *Random House Webster's College Dictionary*, American Heritage, Chamber's, *New World, Merriam-Webster's Collegiate*), almanacs, movie and TV books, and lots of other books—enough to fill more than one bookshelf.

MAURA JACOBSON: Okay, reference library: everything. Almanacs, film, TV, quotations, *Reader's Encyclopedia*, trivia. I'm just looking at what's on my desk here. Roget. One book that's marvelous for me is *The Crossword Answer Book*, from Random House, compiled by Stanley Newman [and Daniel Stark]. It has all the four-, five-, six-, and seven-letter words with the missing letters.

CHRIS JOHNSON: Several regular dictionaries: Compact *Oxford English Dictionary*; *Funk & Wagnalls Standard College*; *Chambers Twentieth-Century*; *Merriam-Webster's Collegiate*, 10th edition; *Collins Concise*; *New Lexicon Webster's Encyclopedic*; *Penguin Concise*. Specialized dictionaries: *Oxford Etymological*; Penguin dictionaries of science, music, geography; *Partridge's Dictionary of Slang and Unconventional English*; *Dictionary of Archaic Words; Harper Dictionary of Music; Harper Dictionary of Foreign Terms*; *Merriam-Webster's Pocket Dictionary of Proper Names*; Adrian Room's *Dictionary of Confusable Words*; Adrian Room's *Dictionary of Cryptic Crossword Clues*. Dictionaries of quotations: *Bartlett's Familiar Quotations*; *Oxford Dictionary of Quotations*; *Merriam-Webster's Dictionary of Quotations*. Various [thesauruses]. *The Canadian Encyclopedia* (1st edition); *The Cambridge Factfinder*; *The Timelines of History*; *Who's Who of*

Nicknames; *The Reader's Encyclopedia*; various foreign dictionaries; *The British Crossword Puzzle Dictionary*; *Capricorn Rhyming Dictionary*; *The Trivia Encyclopedia*; etc.

NANCY JOLINE: A book I use a lot is *Random House Famous Name Finder*. Also, *World Almanac, The New York Times Almanac, Reader's Encyclopedia, Bartlett's Quotations,* and the *World Book Encyclopedia*. The *Random House Webster's Unabridged Dictionary*, 2nd edition, is my word bible.

PATRICK JORDAN: I have four dictionaries of different thicknesses, two CD-ROM encyclopedias, three thesauruses (thesauri?), a mythology book, two almanacs (which I replace annually), two movie guides (also replaced annually), a TV show directory, a pop music anthology, a geographical dictionary, a world literature guide, *Random House Word Menu*, Coral Amende's *Random House Famous Name Finder*, and *The Crossword Answer Book* by Stanley Newman and Daniel Stark. I honestly can't think of any reference work not in existence that would be more useful in puzzle construction than what's available now.

DAVID J. KAHN: My main reference books are *Random House Webster's College Dictionary,* the *World Almanac,* a very good thesaurus, movie and TV books, etc. I also use the Internet occasionally for research.

SHAWN KENNEDY: I have dictionaries, foreign language dictionaries, geographical dictionaries, almanacs, writers' guides, style manuals, and quotation collections.

DAVID MACLEOD: *Random House Webster's Unabridged Dictionary* on CD-ROM, the *New York Public Library Desk Reference, Leonard Maltin's Movie and Video Guide,* my mind.

CATHY MILLHAUSER: I have an esoteric library that includes everything from a book of dog and cat names to one that has five thousand slogans. But more and more I am relying on Internet searches for my clues.

MANNY NOSOWSKY: I've used less and less of what's in my reference library as I've learned more about what's available on-line and on CD-ROM.

NANCY SALOMON: *Random House Webster's Unabridged* on-line version;

Merriam-Webster's Collegiate; *Merriam-Webster's New International Unabridged*; *Crossword Answer Book* (compiled by Stan Newman and Daniel Stark). This one is excellent for filling grids. *Random House Famous Name Finder*—thank you very much. Martin and Porter's *Video Movie Guide*: unlike other guides, this one has an index that makes it by far the most useful of the movie guides. Brooks and Marsh's *The Complete Directory to Prime-Time Network and Cable TV Shows*. *The Billboard Book of Top 40 Hits*; the *World Almanac*; Spanish–English dictionary; French–English dictionary; *Bartlett's Familiar Quotations*. *Master Crossword Puzzle Dictionary* (Baus): well and away the best of the lot. *The American Heritage Dictionary of Idioms*; *Barnes and Noble New American Encyclopedia*.

TOM SCHIER: Dictionaries, almanacs and encyclopedias, CD-ROMs of all types, on all subjects. If I'm missing reference information I go on-line for research.

GREG STAPLES: Lots of general dictionaries. I use Microsoft's Encarta a lot because it can be accessed from Crossword Compiler and contains a decent thesaurus. *Random House Webster's* version 2 is also used. [*Random House Famous Name Finder*] is never out of reach! Stan Newman and Dan Stark's *Crossword Answer Book* gets used. *Random House Word Menu* is useful for theme building.

MEL TAUB: I have an extensive reference library including a stack of dictionaries, foreign and domestic, plus numerous books of quotations, plus dictionaries and encyclopedias and compendia on ballet, music, opera, theater, movies, television, mythology, the Bible, slang, etc., etc. I also have an old set of *Encyclopedia Britannica*, a gift from my son who got the set for five dollars from a fellow college student who didn't want to cart them home after graduation.

BARRY TUNICK [*from Tunick's Sodamail Web site*]: I have two thousand reference works. . . . I have so many partly because I love books and love to collect them. Most of these references ("refs," for short) I picked up at used-book stores, lawn sales, and thrift shops. They're specialized books, dictionaries, and encyclopedias about gardening, ballet, geography, coins—you get the idea. I bought them because they were cheap and, well, you never know when they might come in handy. The problem with buying used refs is that they're often out of date, sometimes by decades. In some fields this is crucial—geography, politics, science—but in other cases it isn't. Ballet terms and mythology don't change a lot over the years. Anyway, as time went on and I could afford to spend more, I started to buy the latest editions. To tell the truth, for puzzle construction I usually look at maybe 1 percent of the refs in my library, but I hate to part with the rest. I mean, you never know when. . . . (Don't let my wife know about this; she can't understand why I need all fifty-five *World Almanacs* from 1945 to the present.) What reference materials are missing from the crossworder's canon? Up-to-date compilations of song titles, singing groups, and other pop culture stuff. *Random House Famous Name Finder*'s a big help.

ARTHUR S. VERDESCA: I am a book person (with a personal library of over eleven thousand volumes). So, since I love to buy books in general, I would guess that I have an extremely extensive reference library. It's almost "You name it, I have it."

LEONARD WILLIAMS: *New York Times Crossword Puzzle Dictionary*, *New York Times Crossword Answer Book*, *Random House Word Menu*, *Famous Name Finder*, *Roget's Thesaurus*, *Random House Webster's* dictionaries, *New York Public Library Desk Reference*, *Reader's Encyclopedia*.

BILL ZAIS: The typical dictionaries, gazetteers, [thesauruses], and almanacs. I do not own an unabridged dictionary. Two of my most helpful references are *The Crossword Answer Book* (Newman and Stark) and the *Random House Famous Name Finder* by one Coral Amende! (You're right . . . I have no shame!)

MERL REAGLE: I wrote down a list of things that are on my bookshelves. I have *Merriam-Webster's Third New International Dictionary*, which everybody has. I also have the latest *New World Dictionary*, which I think is the best dictionary in the country. It's only a college-size, but I think it's great. The *Random House Unabridged*, which is the most up-to-date unabridged. I've got the *Cyclopedia of Literary Characters*. The old *Reader's Encyclopedia*, not the new one—because it has more junk in it. The *Concordance to Shakespeare* and a Bible concordance—having a Bible concordance and a Shakespeare concordance is good, although you can get that stuff on-line now.

The one book I do have that I have never been able to find since I originally got it was the *Hammond World Atlas* of the sixties or seventies. I don't know why they don't do this now. It's an atlas; has all the countries of the world in the front, and every country has its own city list, and it goes on for a page or two, maybe even three, so that they can put all the cities on that same page. It's listed in the back also, under a grand index. It goes through all the countries, then it has all the U.S. states with all the cities of the states on the same page as the state. You would think that this would be an obvious thing to do, and yet nobody does this anymore. Either it's all world stuff, and it's got the states in the back, or it's world stuff with no states, and it's got just a smidge of cities on it—not everything. But mainly it's all in the back under one gigantic index. So you don't have any idea how big the cities are. I'm just amazed that nobody has done that since.

Merriam-Webster's Geographical Dictionary—everybody should have that. I do have volumes one and two of *Brands and Their Companies* by Wood. Page after page of things like Ty-D-Bol and Rol Eze Paints, with short explanations after each one. Stanley Newman saw it at one of those library sales, called me up and asked me if I wanted it. The reason I have such a good Shakespeare concordance is because when Stanley was visiting Jordan Lasher, he saw that Jordan had a couple of them just lying around and he asked me if I needed one. So now I have one of Jordan Lasher's Shakespeare concordances, thanks to Stanley Newman. Of course, now, though, the Internet has almost replaced a lot of these books—not completely, but in a lot of ways.

I've got the *VideoHound's Golden Movie Retriever*, and the *All-Music Guide to Rock, Total Television*—everybody should have that anyway. *The Film Encyclopedia* is a must—Ephraim Katz's book. *The Movie Guide*— looks the same, only it's red. It doesn't have as wide a movie selection as the *VideoHound* does, or even Leonard Maltin. But it does have lots and lots of stuff in it, including the names of all the characters in all the movies. You can get that on-line [now]. Until IMDb came along, it was hard to find that kind of stuff spelled correctly. The usual foreign language stuff, and a Bible, *Roget's International Thesaurus*—I like that one the best, but only the 1977 edition. I have the *Facts On File Encyclopedia of the 20th Century*, which comes in handy. *Oxford Dictionary of Music*. One of my favorite ones is the *American Thesaurus of Slang*. It's from the forties or something. Man, is it great. It's almost like if you're going to write a 1940s film, you can just pack it with this kind of stuff. I did a puzzle for Will Weng once . . . "In Other Words." It was army slang. I gave you the real food, and the answer was what it was called in the army. "Pancakes" were RUBBER PATCHES, "canned milk" was ARMORED COW, "beans" were AMMUNITION—I was glad that he actually used that one—"salt and pepper" was SAND AND DIRT, coffee was "BATTERY ACID". And, of course, I have a well-thumbed *Famous Name Finder* by someone named Coral Amende.

NANCY SCHUSTER: You know the *Master Crossword Dictionary*? The biggie? I proofread some of that. That's why people who use it as an authority—I always say to myself, "Wait a minute—I was one of those people. Don't trust it that much." I remember our instructions—we couldn't possibly go look everything up. You had to say, "How close is this?"

I revised the *Random House Crossword Dictionary*, which is a book nobody knows exists. It was the most awful book you ever saw. It required about six or nine months' editing, and they gave me two. It's the funniest crossword dictionary. It had every kind of dinosaur—doesn't matter if it's twenty-eight letters long, thirty-one letters long. I said to the Random House editor, "You know, these entries are completely useless. Nobody's ever going to look for this in a crossword!" It read like the Athens telephone book. It had more gods and goddesses and minor characters than you can believe, and they were all about thirty-one or twenty-two letters long. Completely useless information. Basically, I cut and slashed and added TV stuff, and that was all there was time to do. It was a huge job. At that point I did use the Master's for comparison, to see what the hell had been totally left out. The man who had done the first edition was a dictionary editor, so he didn't really have a concept of what was needed. I'd love to have another thorough go at that book one day.

There are some people who read too much: the bibliobibuli. I know some who are constantly drunk on books, as other men are drunk on whiskey or religion. They wander through this most diverting and stimulating of worlds in a haze, seeing nothing and hearing nothing.
—H. L. Mencken

SUGGESTED READING

Many of the books mentioned by constructors can be found in the list below (note: op = out of print).

Actors, Artists, Authors & Attempted Assassins: The Almanac of Famous and Infamous People, Susan Stetler, op.

All Music Guide to Rock: The Experts' Guide to the Best Rock Recordings in Rock, Pop, Soul, R&B, and Rap, Michael Erlewine (Editor), Chris Woodstra (Editor), Stephen Thomas Erlewine, Vladimir Bogdanov (Editor) (Miller Freeman Books, 1997).

American Heritage Dictionary of Idioms, The, Christine Ammer (Houghton Mifflin, 1997).

American Popular Songs, David Ewen, op.

Bartlett's Familiar Quotations: A Collection of Passages, Phrases, and Proverbs Traced to Their Sources in Ancient and Modern Literature, John Bartlett, Justin Kaplan (Editor) (Little, Brown & Company, 1992).

Benét's Reader's Encyclopedia, William Rose Benét (Editor), Bruce Murphy (Editor) (HarperCollins, 1996).

Billboard Book of Top 40 Hits, The, Joel Whitburn (Watson-Guptill Publications, 2000).

Brewer's Dictionary of Phrase & Fable, 16th ed., Ebenezer Cobham Brewer, Adrian Room, Terry Pratchett (HarperCollins, 2000).

British Crossword Puzzle Dictionary, The, op.

Cambridge Factfinder, The, David Crystal (Editor) (Cambridge University Press, 2000).

Capricorn Rhyming Dictionary: Aid to Rhyme, Bessie Redfield (Editor) (Perigee, 1986).

Chambers 20th Century Dictionary, Kirkpatrick, E. M., op.

Chambers Backwords for Crosswords, op.

Chambers Biographical Dictionary (6th edition), Melanie Parry (Editor) (Larousse, 1997).

Compact Oxford English Dictionary, The, Edmund S. Weiner (Editor) (Oxford University Press, 1991).

Complete Concordance or Verbal Index to Words, Phrases and Passages in the Dramatic Works of Shakespeare: With a Supplement Concordance to the Poem, A, John Bartlett (Editor) (St. Martin's Press, 1969).

Complete Directory to Prime Time Network and Cable TV Shows, The, Tim Brooks, Earle Marsh (Ballantine Books, 1999).

Concise Dictionary of Slang and Unconventional English: From a Dictionary of Slang and Unconventional English by Eric Partridge, Paul Beale (Editor), op.

Concise Oxford Dictionary of Current English, The, Judy Pearsall (Editor) (Oxford University Press, 1999).

Concise Oxford Dictionary of English Etymology, The, T. F. Hoad (Editor) (Oxford University Press, 1993).

Crossword Answer Book, The, Stanley Newman, Daniel Stark (Times Books, 1996).

Cyclopedia of Literary Characters, Frank Northen Magill (Editor), A. J. Sobczak (Editor) (Salem Press, 1998).

Dictionary of Archaic and Provincial Words, Obsolete Phrases, Proverbs, and Ancient Customs, from the Fourteenth Century, James O. Halliwell-Phillipps (AMS Press, 1990).

Dictionary of Confusable Words, Adrian Room (Fitzroy Dearborn Publishers, 2000).

Dictionary of Cryptic Crossword Clues, Adrian Room, op.

Dictionary of Given Names, F. H. Loughead, op.

Emmys: The Ultimate, Unofficial Guide to the Battle of TV's Best Shows and Greatest Stars, The, Thomas O'Neil, Peter Bart (Perigee, 2000).

Essential American Idioms: Makes Idioms, Clichés, and Phrases Easy to Understand and to Use, Richard A. Spears (NTC Publishing Group, 1999).

Facts on File Encyclopedia of the 20th Century, The, John Drexel (Editor), op.

Film Encyclopedia, The, Ephraim Katz, Fred Klein, Ronald Dean Nolen (Editor) (HarperPerennial Library, 1998).

Halliwell's Filmgoer's Companion: Everything You'd Ever Want to Know about Everyone in the Movies, John Walker, Leslie L. Halliwell (HarperCollins, 1997).

Harper Dictionary of Foreign Terms, Eugene Ehrlich, op.

HarperCollins Dictionary of Music, The, Christine Ammer (HarperPerennial, 1995).

Larousse Dictionary of Literary Characters, Rosemary Goring (Editor) (Larousse, 1996).

Leonard Maltin's Movie & Video Guide, Leonard Maltin (Editor), et al. (Signet, 2001).

Master Crossword Puzzle Dictionary: The Unabridged Word Bank, The, Herbert M. Baus, op.

Merriam-Webster Dictionary of Quotations, The (Merriam-Webster Mass Market, 1992).

Merriam-Webster's Encyclopedia of Literature (Merriam-Webster, 1995).

Merriam-Webster Pocket Dictionary of Proper Names, Geoffrey Payton, op.

Merriam-Webster's Geographical Dictionary (Merriam-Webster, 1997).

Mythology, Edith Hamilton (Back Bay Books, 1998).

New Rolling Stone Encyclopedia of Rock & Roll, The, Patricia Romanowski (Editor), Holly George-Warren (Editor), Jon Pareles (Editor) (Fireside, 1995).

New Rolling Stone Record Guide, The, Dave Marsh, John Swenson, op.

New Shorter Oxford English Dictionary, The, Lesley Brown (Editor) (Oxford University Press, 1993).

New York Public Library Desk Reference, The, Paul LeClerc (Preface), Paul Fargis (Editor) (IDG Books Worldwide, 1998).

New York Times Crossword Puzzle Dictionary, The, Tom Pulliam, Clare Grundman (Times Books, 1997).

Oxford Dictionary of Quotations, The, Elizabeth Knowles (Introduction and Editor) (Oxford University Press, 1999).

Oxford English Dictionary on CD-ROM (Windows), John A. Simpson (Editor), Edmund Weiner (Editor) (Oxford University Press, 1999).

People's Chronology: A Year-by-Year Record of Human Events from Prehistory to the Present, The, James Trager, op.

Rand McNally Quick Reference World Atlas (Rand McNally & Co., 1998).

Random House Crossword Dictionary, The (Ivy Books, 1995).

Random House Famous Name Finder, Coral Amende (Random House Reference, 1999).

Random House Thesaurus of Slang: 150,000 Uncensored Contemporary Slang Terms, Common Idioms, and Colloquialisms Arranged for Quick and Easy Reference, The, Esther Lewin (Random House Trade, 1989).

Random House Webster's College Dictionary (Random House, 2000).

Random House Webster's Unabridged Dictionary; Random House Webster's Unabridged Dictionary on CD-ROM (Random House Reference, 1999).

Random House Word Menu, Stephen D. Glazier (Ballantine Books, 1997).

Rock On: The Illustrated Encyclopedia of Rock 'n' Roll, Norm N. Nite, op.

Roget's International Thesaurus, Robert L. Chapman (Editor) (HarperCollins, 1992).

Synonym Finder, J. I. Rodale, Nancy Laroche, Faye C. Allen (Editor) (Warner Books, 1986).

Thesaurus of Slang, The, Esther Lewin, Albert E. Lewin (Checkmark Books, 1997).

Total Television: The Comprehensive Guide to Programming from 1948 to the Present, Alex McNeil (Penguin USA, 1996).

VideoHound's Golden Movie Retriever, Martin Connors (Editor), Jim Craddock (Editor) (Visible Ink Press, 2000).

Webster's Third New International Dictionary, Philip Babcock Gove (Editor) (Merriam-Webster, 1993).

Who Wrote That Song?, Dick Jacobs, Harriet Jacobs, op.

'NET WORTH

A miniguide to crossword resources found on the World Wide Web.

Note: These Web sites were current at the time of publication.

ACRONYMS

Acronym Finder www.acronymfinder.com/

World Wide Web Acronym and Abbreviation Server
www.ucc.ie/info/net/acronyms/index.html

ANAGRAMS

AnagramFun.com www.anagramfun.com/cgi-bin/anagrams.cgi

Andy's Anagram Solver www.ssynth.co.uk/~gay/anagram.html

Brendan's On-Line Anagram Generator www.mbhs.edu/~bconnell/anagrams.html

Internet Anagram Server www.wordsmith.org/anagram/index.html

Jumble ull.chemistry.uakron.edu/cbower/jumble.html

Mag's Word Finder www.w3tg.com/wordfinder/

Martin's Java Applet Anagram Generator
freespace.virgin.net/martin.mamo/anagram.html

The Anagram Engine www.easypeasy.com/anagrams/

The Anagram Genius Server www.anagramgenius.com/server.html

Wordplay Anagram Program pokey.itsc.uah.edu/~criswell/wordplay.html

BIOGRAPHY

28,000 Celebrity Birthdays from A to Z members.tripod.com/davytany/index010.htm

DT's Today in All Kinds of History (births and deaths)
www.geocities.com/Athens/Pantheon/1027

Lives, the Biography Resource amillionlives.com/

CONSTRUCTORS' SITES

Australian Crosswords by David Stickley ar.com.au/~stickley/index.html

Bob Klahn—The Crossword Beast www.magpage.com/~bobklahn/

A CONVERSATION WITH KEVIN MCCANN, ORIGINATOR OF WWW.CRUCIVERB.COM

What made you decide to do the Web site (were you a solver yourself?)?
I had just started constructing puzzles (I had been a long-time solver), and I had a few I wanted to share with anyone willing to try them. This was back in late 1994 or early 1995. The Web was a new phenomenon then, and there were very few crossword sites. Frank Longo stumbled upon my puzzles and gave constructive criticism. It was quite helpful. After having a few e-mail conversations with Frank, it occurred to me that a forum for crossword constructors would be a good thing. I tried a few Web-based forum tools, but none of them really worked well. There weren't a lot of sophisticated products at the time. I decided that a mailing list would be better, and so I set up the Cruciverb-L list in late 1995.

How did you find the constructors featured on the site?
I didn't, really. They just stumbled onto the Web site, which had instructions on how to join the mailing list. Also, I guess there was a bit of word of mouth via e-mail, too. There are about four hundred members of the Cruciverb-L mailing list, but only a small percentage of those people have created their own profile on the www.cruciverb.com Web site. Any registered member of the Web site can create and update his or her own profile at any time.

Who maintains the site?
That would be me. I do get some material from others, though. For example, Jon Delfin put together a list of corrections to [*The Random House Famous Name Finder*] and made that available. Patrick Jordan sends in the "Puzzle Calendar" once a month, and I put that up on the site. About a year ago, I contacted several editors and asked them to supply their style sheets and guidelines and contact info. They kindly made that available.

Is it income-producing for you (via advertisements or . . .)?
There aren't any ads, but there is some revenue generation through links to Amazon products. For every product sold (when someone clicks on a link on my site and follows through with a purchase), I get a small percentage. However, this goes toward the monthly Internet service provider fees. Unfortunately, the fees are higher than the Amazon revenue, so I do take a monthly loss. If I was a businessman, I could probably turn this into a money-making operation. But I'm not, so it's a labor of love more than anything.

Crosswords and Other Words by Barry Tunick sodamail/coravue.net/cgi-bin/gt/cw.shtml

Fred Piscop—MacNamara's Band Inc. Crossword Puzzles www.macnamarasband.com/

Merl Reagle's Sunday Crosswords www.sundaycrosswords.com/

Personalized Crossword Puzzles—Schier Delight www.schierdelightcrossword.com/

Peter Biddlecombe—Peter's Cryptic Crossword Corner www.biddlecombe.demon.co.uk/puzzles.html

Puzzles by Will Johnston world.std.com/~wij/puzzles/

Ray Hamel's Home Page www.primate.wisc.edu/people/hamel/

Timothy Parker's Universal Crosswords and Word Games www.arcenter.com/

Triple Stacks by Martin Ashwood-Smith www.gate.net/~minarcik/tripstak.html

CONTESTS AND TOURNAMENTS

American Crossword Puzzle Tournament www.crosswordtournament.com/

Board Games, Card Games & Puzzles—MSO Worldwide www.msoworld.com/

Boxerjam www.boxerjam.com/

Links from Yahoo! dir.yahoo.com/recreation/games/puzzles/puzzle_contests/

The Contest Center www.contestcen.com/

The Riddler www.riddler.com/

The World Puzzle Championship www.puzzles-usa.org/

CROSSWORD FORUMS

Puzzler www.puzzler.co.uk/common/forum.htm

Cruciverb-L www.cruciverb.com

The New York Times **on the Web** www.nytimes.com/

CROSSWORDS, GENERAL

Crosswords refdesk.com www.refdesk.com/crosswrd.html

Cruciverb-L www.cruciverb.com

John Gosnell's Barely Bad Web Site members.aol.com/xwdbarelybad/xwd.htm#timestracker

Links—Searchnerd Open Directory

www.searchnerd.com/scrbox/pod/pod.cgi/Games/Puzzles/Crosswords/

DICTIONARIES

Christian Classics Ethereal Library www.ccel.org/

Dictionary.com www.dictionary.com/

English Dictionary (With Multilingual Search) www.allwords.com/default.asp

Funk and Wagnalls www.funkandwagnalls.com/

Getty Thesaurus of Geographic Names shiva.pub.getty.edu/tgn_browser/

Legal Terms (law dictionary) www.lawyers.com/lawyers-com/content/glossary/glossary.html

Merriam-Webster On-Line (Dictionary, Thesaurus, Word of the Day, Word Games, Word for the Wise) www.m-w.com/dictionary.htm

On-Line Medical Dictionary www.graylab.ac.uk/omd/index.html

OneLook Dictionaries www.onelook.com/

WordNet www.cogsci.princeton.edu/cgi-bin/webwn/

Words of Art www.arts.ouc.bc.ca/fina/glossary/gloshome.html

YourDictionary.com www.yourdictionary.com/

FOREIGN LANGUAGES

Foreign Words and Phrases www.infoplease.com/ipa/A0001619.html

Latin Dictionary and Grammar Aid www.nd.edu/~archives/latgramm.htm

Text Foreign-Word List
ftp://ukanaix.cc.ukans.edu/pub/history/Europe/Medieval/aids/latwords.aid

LYRICS

Songfile songfile.snap.com/index_2.html

MERCHANDISE

eBay On-Line Auction Site www.ebay.com

It's Cubular! (Unusual Gifts for the Crossword Puzzle Enthusiast)
www.itscubular.com/

The National Puzzle Museum www.puzzlebuffs.com/cgi-bin/nph-tame/puzzlebuff/ museum.tam

WILL SHORTZ (ON HIS COLLECTION OF CROSSWORD COLLECTIBLES): I'll tell you, one of the most exciting things [I got from eBay] was a crossword bracelet from the craze in 1925. It's a bracelet with eight little enamel pieces with tiny crossword grids on them surrounded by silver, with a silver clasp. Beautiful. The seller really had no idea what it was. Well, I have an ad for this very bracelet from a 1925 book, so I knew exactly what I was getting, and I was the only person who bid on it. Fifty bucks. I actually bid *much* higher than that. I was the only person who bid on it, so I got it for the minimum amount. I get lots of bargains, but that's because most people don't care about puzzle stuff. I have all these treasures that no one but me cares about!

ON-LINE PUZZLES

2000 Boston Globe Sunday Crosswords www.fleetingimage.com/wij/xyzzy/00-bg.html

2000 Wall Street Journal Friday Crosswords www.fleetingimage.com/wij/xyzzy/00-wsj.html

3DCrossword.com www.3dcrossword.com/

Aboard Puzzle Depot Trivia, Puzzles and Games for Education or Recreation! www.puzzledepot.com/index.shtml

Acrostic www.phred.org/~michael/acrostic.htm

Archimedes' Laboratory www.geocities.com/TimesSquare/Labyrinth/2305/

Aristotle Games—Crosswords www.aristotle.net/games/crossword/

Atlantic Unbound (*The Atlantic Monthly*) www.theatlantic.com/

At the Crossroads—Daily Amusements www.atthecrossroads.com/asp/home.asp

BestCrosswords.com (Free On-Line Crossword Puzzles Daily) www.bestcrosswords.com/

Bible Crossword Fun www.gospelcom.net/gci/xword/

Billboard **On-Line Music Crossword** www.billboard.com/crossword/

Boxerjam www.boxerjam.com/

Brain Food (Tough Puzzles) www.rinkworks.com/brainfood/

British Crossword Puzzles, Word Searches and Word Games from the ClueMaster www.cluemaster.com/

Canada—CANOE Daily Crossword Puzzle www.canoe.ca/Crossword/home.html

Canada.com Crosswords www.networdcross.com/cgi-bin/dailypage/canada

Castle Networking Inc.—Internet Services www.castle.on.ca/crosswords/

CBC Interactive—Fun Crossword cbc.ca/interactive/fun/crossword/

Clue Me In On-Line Word Games Puzzles www.cashgames.com/

CNN (Word Games) www.cnn.com/books/crossword/index.html

CrossCraze Crossword Game by ORT Software www.ortsoftware.com/cc.html

crosswords.about.com (games and crosswords) crosswords.about.com/games/crosswords/

Crossword Puzzles, Trivia Questions, Word Searches, Other Puzzles of All Types www.dailypuzzler.com/

CrosSynergy Syndicate www.litsoft.com/across/Gallery/csynergy.htm#what

Discovery On-Line—Crossword Puzzles www.discovery.com/games/crossword/crossword.html

Excite Classic Games by pogo.com pogo01.excite.com/ten/game/word/crossword.jsp?tins=957159130019&game=xword &site=exci

FunkandWagnalls.com www.funkandwagnalls.com:/puzzle/getpage.asp?site/local& page=lobby.asp

Guardian Unlimited Crossword Crossword www.guardianunlimited.co.uk/crossword/

HoadWorks Puzzles www.hoadworks.com/

iVillage—Crossword Center www.ivillage.com/crossword/

Literate Software Systems—Crossword Puzzle Gallery www.litsoft.com/across/gallery.htm

London Sunday Times crosswords www.sunday-times.co.uk/news/pages/resources/puzzles1.n.html?999

Los Angeles Times—Hunter www.latimes.com/cgi-bin/login?Tag=/&URI=/extras/crossword/

Martin Ashwood-Smith's Triple Stacks www.gate.net/~minarcik/tripstak.html

Merriam-Webster's Word Puzzles www.m-w.com/game/

My AOL.COM Daily Crossword
my.aol.com/entertainment/crossword/crossword.tmpl

Newsday Crossword www.networdcross.com/cgi-bin/dailypage/newsday

NPR's Weekend Edition Sunday Puzzle www.npr.org/programs/wesun/puzzle/

NYT Crossword Talk Forum Links www.fleetingimage.com/wij/xyzzy/nyt-links.html

The Official Site of Major League Baseball (Fun and Games)
www.majorleaguebaseball.com/u/baseball/mlbcom/xword/

**One Across (Search for Crossword Puzzle Answers, Solve Crossword Puzzles
Online, Find Anagrams, Cryptogram Help)** www.oneacross.com/

Online Crosswords www.clearlight.com/~vivi/xw/index.html

Puzzability www.puzzability.com/

Puzzle Connection www.puzzleconnection.com/

puzzled.com www.puzzled.com/

Puzzler—UK puzzle site www.puzzler.co.uk/

Puzzles and Word Games www.startdl.com/index.html

Puzzles@Random! www.randomhouse.com/special/puzzles/

Puzzles by Will Johnston world.std.com/~wij/puzzles/

Puzzles—Chicago Tribune puzzles.webpoint.com/puzz/0,1097,chitrib,00.html

Salon Magazine Crossword www.salon.com/june97/games/xword970630.html

Shareware Games by Xdyne Inc. www.xdyne.com/cgi-bin/2.0/sharware.cgi

Software for Crossword Games www.cygcyb.com/catalog/software.html#CrossWise

Student.Com Fun & Games Crosswords www.student.com/feature/xwords

Style Daily Crossword www.washingtonpost.com/wp-srv/style/crosswords/daily/front.htm

Tampa Bay On-Line crossword page www.tampabayonline.net/features/puzzle.htm

Telegraph www.telegraph.co.uk/

The '80s Server Crossword Puzzle games.80s.com/Crossword/

The Crypto Drop Box www.und.nodak.edu/org/crypto/crypto/

The Game Report Online www.gamereport.com/index.shtml

The Herald—U.K. crossword www.theherald.co.uk/crossword/crossword.html

The Mind Breakers (Only the Best Puzzles and Riddles) mindbreakers.e-fun.nu/

The *New York Times* on the Web www.nytimes.com/

The rec.puzzles Archive einstein.et.tudelft.nl/~arlet/puzzles/

The Riddler (Free Games and Crosswords)
www.riddler.com/freegames/crossword/doc/crossword.html

Tidbits (The Sunday Puzzle on the Internet)
www.tidbitspuzzles.com/tidbits/tidframe.htm

TIME.com Crossword Puzzle www.time.com/time/crossword/puzzle01.html

TV Guide On-Line (Crossword Puzzle) www.tvguide.com/games/crossword/

USA Today Crossword www.usatoday.com/life/puzzles/puzzle.htm

Washington Post.com Style (crosswords) www.washingtonpost.com/wp-srv/style/crosswords/front.htm

Weekly Word Search Puzzle (Word Search Construction Kit)
www.puzzleconnection.com/weekwsk.htm

Word Prospector Start Page www.logophilia.com/WordPlay/WordProspector.html

Wordscramble at MindFun.com www.mindfun.com/wordscramble.htm

Yahoo! Games
login.yahoo.com/config/login?.src=ga&.done=http://games.yahoo.com/games/login
%3fgame=Crossword

PEEVES

Common Errors in English www.wsu.edu/~brians/errors/errors.html

Frequently Misused Words
www.amherst.edu/~writing/wb_html/misused_words.html

Notorious Confusables
webster.commnet.edu/HP/pages/darling/grammar/notorious.htm#xx

The Curmudgeon's Stylebook www.theslot.com/part4.html#start

Words That Should Be Banned for Life www.sevenquestions.com/banned.htm

National Puzzlers' League www.puzzlers.org/

The Australian Crossword Club (ACC) ar.com.au/~stickley/acc.html

World Puzzle Federation www.worldpuzzle.org/

REFERENCE MATERIALS

All About Cryptic Crosswords www.geocities.com/TimesSquare/Labyrinth/2519/

American Slanguages (American Slang—by City) www.slanguages.com

AMG All Music Guide allmusic.com/cg/x.dll

Crossword Puzzle Guide www.infoplease.com/ipa/A0001806.html

Crossword Star: Crossworders' Dictionary and Gazetteer www.crosswordstar.com

Bartlett's Familiar Quotations (1901) www.bartleby.com/99/

Digital Librarian www.servtech.com/public/mvail/home.html

Encyclopedia.com www.encyclopedia.com/

Facts, Information, Research www.refdesk.com/facts.html

Las Vegas SUN Crossword Cravings (A Passion for Puzzles Plus a Love of
    Language Equals a Lifelong Hobby)
    www.lasvegassun.com/sunbin/stories/do/1999/jun/01/508869204.html

Musical Cast Album Database www.eur.com/musicals/

Quoteland.com (Quotations on Every Topic, by Every Author, and in Every
    Fashion Possible) www.quoteland.com/

Research-It!—Your One-Stop Reference Desk www.itools.com/research-it/
    researchit.html

RhymeZone www.rhymezone.com/

Solving Cryptic Crosswords www.puzzlers.org/guide/cryptics-solving.html

The Collected Works of Shakespeare www.gh.cs.usyd.edu.au/~matty/Shakespeare/

The Internet Movie Database (IMDb) us.imdb.com/

The Internet Theatre Database www.theatredb.com/

The New Yorker's Guide to Solving Cryptic Crosswords
    www.primate.wisc.edu/people/hamel/newyorker.html

The World's First Crossword—The History thinks.com/crosswords/first1.htm

Tribune Media Services Spotlight www.tms.tribune.com/spotlight/9712.html

Val's Home Page—Cryptic Crosswords
www.home.gil.com.au/~vburton/cryptics/cryptics.htm

SOFTWARE

Across Lite Download www.litsoft.com/cgi-bin/serve/software/accept

Cross Sums Puzzles by X-Sums 98! members.aol.com/XSums98/

Crossword Builder (English Version) dezcom.mephi.ru/crossword/english/index.html

Crossword Compiler (Puzzlemaker Software) www.x-word.com/

Crossword Construction Kit (Windows Crossword Creator)
www.crosswordkit.com/

Crossword Express (The Complete Crossword System)
www.adam.com.au/johnstev/

Crossword Maestro for Windows www.genius2000.com/cm.html

CrosswordPlus home.clara.net/lnd/

Crossword Puzzle Maker Software by Variety Games Inc. www.varietygames.com/

Crossword Puzzles and Crossword Software by Crossdown
www.netacc.net/~crossdwn/

Crossword Puzzles from Word Pie www.wordpie.com/

Crosswords and WordSearch Puzzles cogix.com/cw/indexthinking.html

Crossword Weaver www.custompuzzles.com/prod02.htm

Crossword Wizard cogix.com/cw/CW20.htm

Cruciverbalist (Mac Construction Software)
members.aol.com/westpolesf/cruciv.html

E-Crostic Software www.teleport.com/~howorth/e-crostic/index.html

Franklin Electronic Publishers www.franklin.com/estore/fun/

Homeware (Crossword Puzzle Software with a Full Crossword Puzzle Dictionary)
www.homeware.com/

Literate Software Systems www.litsoft.com/

Oakley Data Services www.smartcode.com/cwk_scr.htm

Proverb: The Probabilistic Cruciverbalist www.cs.duke.edu/~keim/proverb/

Puzzle Assistant by Epsoft Computer Services www.powerup.com.au/~epps/puzzle/

Puzzle Express (Crosswords and More) www.puzzlexpress.com/

SoftSpot Software (Specializing in Great Word Games) www.softspotsoftware.com/

The Anagram Genius Server www.anagramgenius.com/server.html

WORDFIND www.auntannie.com/castoaks/wordfind.htm

Wordplay Anagram Program pokey.itsc.uah.edu/~criswell/wordplay.html

Wordsheets (Create Crossword, Word Search, and Word Scramble Worksheets) www.qualint.com/wordsheets.html

Word Wizard III from Coda Software www.laplace.demon.co.uk/codasoft/

THESAURUSES

ARTFL Project ROGET'S Thesaurus Search Form humanities.uchicago.edu/forms_unrest/ROGET.html

Merriam-Webster On-Line (Dictionary, Thesaurus, Word of the Day, Word Games, Word for the Wise) www.m-w.com/thesaurus.htm

Roget's Thesaurus web.cs.city.ac.uk/text/roget/thesaurus.html

Thesaurus.com www.thesaurus.com/

WORD COMPLETION

10C Dictionary Search www.fleetingimage.com/wij/xyzzy/10c.html

Amo's On-Line Crossword Puzzle Dictionary (English) www.amo.qc.ca/ODico/

Chris F. A. Johnson's Word Finder www.interlog.com/~cfaj/xword/wordfinder.cgi

Crossword Helper raru.adelaide.edu.au/craig/wow.html

Crossword Search www.logophilia.com/WordPlay/xword-companion.html

Crossword Solver from AllWords.com www.allwords.com/solver.asp

Crossword Solver www.ojohaven.com/fun/crossword.html

Crosswords Un-Crossed www.eecg.toronto.edu/~bryn/HTML/Crosswords.html

Jumble ull.chemistry.uakron.edu/cbower/jumble.html

National Puzzlers' League Dictionary Search
www.puzzlers.org/secure/wordlists/grepdict.html

Official *Scrabble Players Dictionary* Search
www.logophilia.com/WordPlay/dictionary-search.html

One Across (Search for Crossword Puzzle Answers, Solve Crossword Puzzles On-Line, Find Anagrams, Cryptogram Help) www.oneacross.com/

The Anagram Engine (Free Online Anagram Generator)
www.easypeasy.com/anagrams/

Wordsmyth www.wordsmyth.net/

WORDS AND WORDPLAY

A Collection of Word Oddities and Trivia members.aol.com/gulfhigh2/words.html

A Language Museum (English)
www.stir.ac.uk/departments/humansciences/celt/Museum/

Antagonyms www-personal.umich.edu/~cellis/antagonym.html

Dave Wilton's Etymology Page www.wilton.net/etyma1.htm

Cliché-Finder www.westegg.com/cliche/

Origin of Phrases members.aol.com/MorelandC/Phrases.htm

Palindromes www.rdg.ac.uk/~sssbownj/jnwobsss~/ku.ca.gdr.www//:ptth/

Phrases, Sayings and Clichés (With Their Meanings and Origins)
www.shu.ac.uk/web-admin/phrases/

Richard Lederer's Verbivore pw1.netcom.com/~rlederer/index.htm

Synonyms vancouver-webpages.com/synonyms.html

The Vocabula Review www.vocabula.com/vocabulareview.htm

Verbatim—The Language Quarterly www.verbatimmag.com/

Word for Word plateaupress.com.au/wfw/wfwindex.htm

Word Play www.wolinskyweb.com/word.htm

Words, Words, and More Words www.suite101.com/welcome.cfm/words/

Word Ways: The Journal of Recreational Linguistics www.wordways.com

World Wide Words www.clever.net/quinion/words/

ELECTRIC AVENUES

The modernization of the crossword construction biz has included our ever-increasing reliance on the Internet for quick answers. There are now multiple sites on just about every imaginable topic—and surfing the Web beats having to house huge stacks of reference works (although most constructors would have a hard time pruning their libraries, if pressed).

The Internet is an elite organization; most of the population of the world has never even made a phone call.
—NOAM Chomsky

SAM BELLOTTO, JR.: The Internet is the greatest thing that has happened to crossword constructing since felt-tipped pens. I use AltaVista quite a bit.

RANDOLPH ROSS: The Internet and CD-ROMs have filled in a lot of blanks. The Dogpile search tool is excellent.

RICH NORRIS: Anything I can't find in my references I try to look up on the Web. If I'm still not sure, I'll ask the Cruciverb-L group. Some of those people are amazing at finding sites I can never seem to unearth.

ELIZABETH GORSKI: I use the IMDb movie site to research film facts. I like to use google.com as a search engine. I use allmusic.com to research musical facts.

MARTIN ASHWOOD-SMITH: I find [search site] AltaVista very useful, especially if I need to check the usage (or nonusage) of a phrase.

MERL REAGLE: The *Random House Unabridged*, which is the most up-to-date contemporary thing [is] now on-line [and] searchable, even in the definitions. I use that all the time—that's the best source I've got. You just log on to Fleeting Image—that's the location—[and] all you've got to do, if you want to search for the word EEL, you just put in EEL, and it gives you not just the definition of EEL, but everyplace EEL appears throughout the dictionary in definitions. You can do that with the ones you buy on CDs, but I've always wanted one for free. I'm so computer-illiterate. Whenever I clue, I have [my browser] open to that page all the time. ONION: now you don't have to clue it as just "Hamburger option." You can actually go through and find all the dishes, and things that contain onions in them—chopped up or mixed in. There it is.

NELSON HARDY: I use the Internet often to check out hunches, but I never use information obtained from a Web site without confirmation from established print sources. Any moron can put up a Web site and load it with misspellings and erroneous information.

MARK DIEHL: Favorites: www.imdb.com [Internet Movie Database], www.allmusic.com, www.megacrawler.com for general searches.

DIANE EPPERSON: [I use the Internet for] specialized dictionaries: slang, 1950s tunes, etc.; databases—especially current entertainers (movies, singers, etc.) and sports figures; searchable literary collections: Shakespeare, Poe, etc.

PETER GORDON: If I need a particular word in a grid, I can usually find it in something I have, but if it's very new, I might use AltaVista or the Internet Movie Database to find it.

JOHN SAMSON: Although I own several sets of encyclopedias, dictionaries, CDs, etc., I have come to the conclusion that the Internet is my favorite reference source. It is the largest library on the planet and is constantly updated. When I first started constructing puzzles (before the Internet), I had Nagurski (the legendary Bear fullback) in a crossword and wanted to know if his first name was Bronco or Bronko. I ended up calling the NFL Hall of Fame in Canton, Ohio. Alex Webster answered the phone and wasn't sure himself, so he went to check the nameplate on a statue of Mr. Nagurski that was standing outside the Hall of Fame. "Yep, definitely Bronko with a K," said Alex (a great fullback himself for many years with the New York Giants.) Now, a simple click of the mouse achieves the same results. The Internet is also a great source of crossword themes. I'm presently constructing a puzzle on different roller coasters in the world—I would never have attempted this theme without the Internet to help me.

JIM PAGE: I use the Internet essentially for editing—meaning if I can't find a rock band with Snoopy Doopy Loopy Goopy in it, [and] I have to find out how the hell you spell Snoopy Doopy, I go to the Internet to find out exactly how you spell the artist or the song. It's just stuff that I could go to the library to look up, but it would take me twelve days. I will often just go to the Internet and do key word [searches]. Does Dove still make soap? Is Bic spelled B-I-C? Not just for editing, but sometimes for my own creative process.

MAURA JACOBSON: The Internet for research—I'm very unsuccessful at this. There's a way to do it, which I do not know. I'm computer-ignorant, and every time I try using the Internet, it takes me an hour just to get where I want to go, and often they don't have [what I'm looking for].

NANCY JOLINE: I began last year using the Internet for research, and wonder how I lived without it. I've looked up such things as s'mores and Smurfs, and found out all about them. IMDb (Internet Movie Database) is a treasure trove. I'd like to find its equivalent for TV programs and actors.

PATRICK JORDAN: I am very careful about this, because you simply can't trust anything you read on the Web unless the site is maintained by a highly reputable entity. I consult only two of them with any regularity: the AllMovie Guide and the official *Bartlett's Familiar Quotations* site.

DAVID MACLEOD: The Internet is my main reference source. The sites are too numerous to mention, but common ones are Internet Movie Database, AllMusic Guide, various dictionary and encyclopedia sites, *Bartlett's Quotations.*

CATHY MILLHAUSER: Most of the sites [I use] have come from the American Crossword Tournament links or from Cruciverb-L.

MANNY NOSOWSKY: *Encyclopedia Britannica,* a movie [data]base, and the AltaVista search engine. Also several on-line dictionaries.

NANCY SALOMON: I use the Google search engine. I also have a long list of research sites, but except for the IMDb movie and TV site, I don't use them that often.

TOM SCHIER: AltaVista, all sites. I'm not particular.

NANCY SCHUSTER: I first start with my own reference books, but then I use the Web search engines. For current info there's no other way. I had used AltaVista a lot, but I've lately switched to Google; it's so fast. IMDb is wonderful too.

GREG STAPLES: Various search engines—mainly dogpile.com, Internet Movie Database, AllMusic Guide, and others occasionally.

BARRY TUNICK: When my CD-ROM *Random House* dictionary is down, I'll go to the Merriam-Webster site for letter-fill help (??W??L?). I am a regular participant at the Cruciverb-L site.

ARTHUR S. VERDESCA: I use the Internet very, very sparingly for research. And when I do, I use Dogpile.

LEONARD WILLIAMS: Information Please and FAST Search, primarily.

BILL ZAIS: I find the Internet useful for finding phrases (which may become theme entries) that are fairly new to the language. I use AltaVista, onelook.com, dictionary.com, infoplease.com, and Metacrawler.

STAN NEWMAN: I was a very early user of the Internet because of Random House–related issues. I think I was probably one of the first half dozen people in the company to have Internet access. That came because of a games Web site that Random House invested in—at my behest, by the way. Random House encourages me to be on the cutting edge of technology . . . trying new things and thinking in a visionary way and making things happen that will benefit the puzzle world long-term and, of course, benefit Random House as well. The Internet was just one example.

The Internet is the greatest entertainment and educational tool ever developed. It's like a television with ten million channels, and it's a way to reach anybody in the world, get information from anywhere. The drawback is, of course, someone in the puzzle world needs to know what's accurate and what isn't. Fortunately, there are authoritative Web sites—if you need to know the correct spelling of Pepe Le Pew's name, you shouldn't get it out of a trivia question some guy wrote for high school homework. Chances are, you can find a Warner Bros. Web site that you could probably believe. With most corporations and most institutions now having Web sites, there is a huge amount of information available and accessible in just a few seconds, and that's a remarkable thing.

The fact that I'm on-line—the puzzle is on-line at the Philadelphia Inquirer—
*is sort of against my will in a way. I'd rather the puzzle not be on-line. I don't
want people to get it for free. But the* Inquirer *resets it—they reset all the
clues, so all the mistakes that can creep in, do. Sheesh!*
—Merl Reagle

GLOSSARY

Incomprehensible jargon is the hallmark of a profession.
—Kingman Brewster

15, 15×, 15 × 15 A puzzle whose grid size is fifteen squares by fifteen squares. Constructors and some solvers refer to the size of all standard crossword grids in this manner (e.g., 17× or 21 × 21). "15" can also refer to the size of a word or phrase included in the grid. See also *daily-size*.

acrostic A poem or series of lines in which the first letters (or other specified letters) of each line spell out a word, phrase, motto, or name.

Acrostic Puzzle See *Double-Crostic*.

Afrit's law The notable cryptic setter famously said, "A clue may not mean what it seems to say, but it must say exactly what it does mean."

American-style How non-cryptic crossword puzzles are described—the term is used for those puzzles that follow American crossword conventions (no unchecked letters, etc.).

anagram A word or phrase that forms a new word or phrase when its letters are rearranged (ANGEL/ANGLE). Also, a game played wherein players attempt to make new words by rearranging and sometimes adding letters.

answer, answer word A crossword grid entry, whether part of the theme or not.

bar diagram A cryptic-crossword grid in which thick black lines separate answers in the grid. No black squares are used in this style diagram.

beheadment A word's initial letter is dropped to form a new word (PAGE/AGE).

Boxquote One of Eugene T. Maleska's quotation-themed crosswords, in which the citation was entered going clockwise in a box shape within the grid.

British-style Cryptic (crosswords); this term is usually used by Americans.

charade An enigma or cryptic crossword clue in which the solver builds the correct answer (syllable by syllable) by answering questions that define each piece of the puzzle.

cheater A black square added to a crossword grid to make construction easier (see page 206).

checked A grid square that is part of both an across and a down entry (in most cryptic diagrams, "unchecked" squares are allowed—but never is an American-style crossword grid called "checked").

clue Sometimes incorrectly used as a synonym for *definition* (or *dictionary definition*), *clue* is a little broader in meaning: wordplay and new-wave conventions are used in clues; dictionary-style meanings are used for definitions.

compile A synonym for *construct* (crosswords) in the parlance of British cryptic creators ("setters").

conundrum A riddle that consists of a pun or puns, or is answered by a pun.

corner A section of a crossword diagram that is at one of the grid's four corners; typically, two remaining borders (making a box) are partially established by "fingers" (see page 347).

Crazy Crossword Humorous puzzle, focusing on trickery and wordplay; invented by Ted Shane.

crosswordese Words that are convenient for crossword constructors to use because of their letter patterns but that are unlikely to be found outside of crosswords because of their obscurity.

cruciverbalist Crossword constructor or habitual solver.

In general, puzzlemakers enjoy being called cruciverbalists about as much as fishermen enjoy being called piscatorialists.
—Merl Reagle

curtailment The opposite of beheadment: the final letter of a word is removed to form a new word (or series of words).

daily-size A puzzle whose grid is fifteen squares by fifteen squares (15 × 15).

definition See *clue*.

diagram Crossword grid.

diagramless A crossword that is unraveled from the ground up: the solver is faced with a blank grid (or at least the dimensions thereof) and must figure out both the diagram's pattern and the starting point of the entries. The diagramless was born during an editing session in the 1920s, when Margaret Farrar, Prosper Buranelli, and F. Gregory Hartswick discovered that one of their puzzles was missing a diagram. Hartswick, using the clues, was able to create the grid on the fly, and a new puzzle was born.

dictionary definition See *clue*.

double acrostic Similar to an acrostic, but the first *and* last letters of each line form words or phrases.

Double-Crostic In a Double-Crostic (also known as an Acrostic Puzzle), the answer is most often a quotation, and solvers must figure out answers to clues and write the answers into blanks and into correspondingly numbered white squares in a grid (often, the first letters of the clues spell out the author and/or source of the quotation). When the grid is complete, the quotation is revealed. According to Will Shortz, "Double-Crostic is the classic name for the puzzle. Acrostic Puzzle is what the *New York Times* calls this feature. Dell calls it an Anacrostic. *GAMES* calls it a Double Cross. Other puzzle magazines call it a Duo-Crostic, Twin-Crostic, etc. The traditional and original name, though, is Double-Crostic." The puzzle was invented by former English teacher Elizabeth Kingsley, who, after making a visit to Wellesley, decried the students' lack of knowledge of classical literature and created the Double-Crostic as a fun way to remedy this. The puzzles' solutions are always excerpts from literary works. The *Saturday Review of Literature* published her first puzzle on March 31, 1934. Kingsley's successors included Doris Nash Wortman and Thomas Middleton. She retired from puzzlemaking in 1952.

ARTHUR S. VERDESCA: My correspondence with Elizabeth Kingsley was in the 1940s, but, unfortunately, I didn't save it. It started when I had found an error. She graciously acknowledged that it was an error, as printed; however, she assured me that the editor (of the *Saturday Review of Literature*—which, at that time of my life, I was reading from cover to cover) had been responsible for the change. The other two or three times were fan letters about specific constructions. There is a specific memory about Miss Kingsley that you may enjoy: Her responses would come on a penny (in those long-bygone days!) postcard. Her very neatly penned, always readable, words were incredibly tiny. She could get a letter's worth of information on a little card.

The Double-Crostic is to the crossword puzzle what chess is to checkers.
It utilizes the basic form but contains an extra dimension that enables
the squares to emerge in a striking quotation.
—Norman Cousins

Double-Crostics have saved my sanity in the grim loneliness of hotel rooms
when I lecture my way around the country.
—Ogden NASH

entry The answer to a clue as written in a grid—usually a word or phrase, but sometimes a quotation, a string of letters, etc.

fill Answer words, usually unrelated to a puzzle's theme, that make up the bulk of a crossword grid.

fill-in-the-blank (also known as a missing-word definition) Definition that is a title, phrase, or snippet missing one or more words (e.g., "Once _____ blue moon" = IN A). These definitions can usually be answered only one way.

finger Two or more black squares perpendicular to the edge of a grid.

gimme Clue or definition that can be answered easily.

grid Crossword diagram, into which theme entries and fill are placed.

homograph, homonym, homophone Words that are pronounced or spelled the same (or both), but that differ in meaning. *Homophones* sound alike but may be spelled differently (bore/boar) or not (bore = dull person/bore = drill a hole). Homographs are words that are spelled the same but have different meanings and may have different pronunciations. The word *homonym* is used as a synonym for either of the other two words.

ladder A stair-step arrangement of black squares placed diagonally within a grid (see page 205).

light A white square in a crossword diagram.

missing-word definition See *fill-in-the-blank*.

palindrome A word, phrase, sentence, etc., that reads the same backward and forward (kayak; level).

pangram A sentence or verse containing every letter. A pangrammatic puzzle contains all letters of the alphabet in the grid.

partial (partial phrase) A two-word (or more) fragment of a commonly used cliché, lyric, title, or other citation or phrase. Partials are usually defined with fill-in-the-blanks.

portmanteau word A new word created from two others, e.g., smoke/fog = smog.

Puns & Anagrams (P&A) A themeless, 15 × 15 crossword puzzle that combines an American-style grid with cryptic-like clues. The first was composed by

Alfred Morehead (a *New York Times* bridge columnist), who'd come up with the concept, and Jack Luzzatto; it was published in the *Times* on the first day crosswords appeared in its pages. Today's preeminent P&A puzzler is Mel Taub.

rebus A puzzle whose solution is found by forming words and phrases from individual syllables or fragments, each of which is represented by a picture.

repeated-word theme A crossword theme using one word in most or all theme (long) entries (e.g., BLUE BAYOU, BLUE HAWAII, BLUE SKY).

repeater (1) A letter repeated in a word or phrase. (2) A word too often seen in crosswords (ARIA, ELI).

set; setter Construct (a cryptic crossword); cryptic constructor. Both terms are mostly used in the U.K.

solution Answers to a puzzle.

spoonerism Transposition of two words' initial syllables (room and board = boom and roared). The word derives from the name of a clergyman, W. A. Spooner (1844–1930), who was notorious for making such transpositions.

style sheet Specification sheets that detail editors' requirements and preferences for puzzle submissions.

Sunday-size 21×21.

symmetry American-style crossword diagrams typically feature diagonal symmetry, meaning the grid looks the same if turned upside down (if there's a black square in the uppermost left corner, there will also be a black square in the lowermost right corner); an imaginary line bisects the grid from the upper left to the lower right, and the black and white squares are identical on each side of the line. Left-right symmetry is the same concept, but with the imaginary line drawn vertically through the middle square of the diagram (square 11 in a 21×21 grid; square 8 in a 15×15 grid).

theme A crossword's longest (usually) diagram entries, that are related to each other in some manner.

Tom Swifty Apt adverbs: "It's a bomb," he said explosively.

unchecked An unchecked letter; a letter in a crossword diagram that is part of only one answer word. Almost exclusively seen in British puzzles.

variety cryptic A cryptic crossword with a gimmick above and beyond normal clue trickery; can involve answers, clues, and/or diagram.

word count The number of answers (answer entries) in a crossword puzzle.

word square An arrangement of words of equal length stacked in a square. The words read the same vertically and horizontally or, in the case of double word squares, differ going across and down (see page 5 for examples).

QUICK QUIZZES

The statistics on which these quizzes are based were compiled by Bob Klahn, who has created his own database of many years' worth of crosswords and clues (per Bob, "10,000 strong at the time [of this writing], all of which are from top-quality markets.") Note: proper nouns and names are included.

"Most Common" Quiz

How many of the ten most common crossword answer words in each category can you guess?

- Abbreviations and acronyms
- Animals
- Foreign words
- Place names
- People's names
- Phrases or multiple-word entries

- Three-letter words
- Four-letter words

Most Common Letters

What are the most common letters (hint: there are 11 total) used in the top 20 crossword answer words?

Top Fives Quiz

How many of the following most common crossword answer words can you guess?

Food and drink items (hint: they're all things you might find in your refrigerator)

All-consonant (excluding Y) words

QUIZ ANSWERS

"Most Common" Quiz (page 351)

ABBREVIATIONS AND ACRONYMS

ENE (487)
ETA (483)
IRA (447)
ESE (445)
EST (373)
ens (359)
SSE (342)
et al. (306)
Ste. (294)
AMA (287)

ANIMALS

ant (427)
eel (411)
ape (396)
ass (368)
roe (311)
ants (300)
asp (292)
ewe (274)
emu (254)
rat (253)

FOREIGN WORDS

ole (549)
tsar (337)
ete (316)
et al. (306)
oro (292)
etre (255)
este (249)
lei (246)
etre (241)
obi (222)

PLACE NAMES

Erie (579)
Asia (349)
Eton (322)
Erin (308)
Iran (301)
Etna (299)
Rio (288)
Oslo (268)
USA (260)
Eire (255)

PEOPLE'S NAMES

Eli (565)
Ali (525)
Ira (447)
Ari (416)
Enos (350)
Anne (343)
Alan (330)
Omar (325)
Ann (325)
Lee (323)

PHRASES

a la (488)
et al. (306)
I see (297)
I do (291)
on a (268)
a-one (259)
at a (251)
in a (247)
in re (245)
a lot (235)

THREE-LETTER WORDS

era (741)
ale (604)
ere (596)
ore (581)
ate (571)
one (569)
Eli (565)
ole (549)
are (539)
Ali (525)

FOUR-LETTER WORDS

area (661)
Erie (579)
aria (531)
Eden (492)
ante (480)

aloe (475)	else (417)	oral (391)
star (424)	idea (413)	E (20)

Most Common Letters (page 352)

E (20)	I (4)
A (14)	T, O (3)
R (7)	D (2)
L, N (5)	P, S (1)

Top Fives Quiz (page 352)

FOOD AND DRINK	ALL CONSONANTS
ale (604)	TNT (284)
tea (378)	SST (263)
oleo (356)	SSTs (220)
ade (353)	SSS (216)
ice (345)	nth (202)

KLAHN'S COMPLETE LIST

#	Word	#	Word	#	Word	#	Word	#	Word	#	Word	#	Word	#	Word
	ERA	372	EAT	317	IRON	286	LES	258	EVER	245	ALES	224	OTT	208	ALSO
	AREA	368	ASS	317	ELAN	285	IAN	257	EER	244	STEP	224	OMIT	207	OREL
	ALE	363	EROS	316	ETE	285	ELATE	257	ADA	244	OLD	224	OMEN	207	MAE
	ERE	359	ENS	316	ERAS	284	TNT	257	ABET	244	EELS	224	IRIS	207	BAR
	ORE	359	ARENA	314	ABE	284	ETTE	256	UNIT	243	ILL	223	ANNA	206	ABEL
	ERIE	358	ALAS	311	ROE	284	EAST	255	OREO	242	HER	223	ALIEN	205	TEEN
	ATE	357	ONES	311	ONCE	282	EDIT	255	ETRE	241	OPERA	222	OBI	205	SETS
	ONE	356	OLEO	310	RAE	281	EPEE	255	EIRE	240	RENO	222	NEST	205	SERA
	ELI	355	EASE	309	AGO	279	LIE	254	ITS	239	SRO	222	AURA	205	RYE
	OLE	353	ADE	308	ERIN	277	USE	254	INTO	239	ELLE	221	LIAR	205	RENT
	ARE	352	TEE	308	EDS	277	AVA	254	EMU	238	UTAH	221	IRS	205	REEL
	ARIA	350	ENOS	307	ERIC	276	AFAR	254	EDNA	237	OER	221	IGOR	205	NESS
	ALI	349	ASIA	307	ASA	275	ASTA	254	ARM	237	DEE	221	GAS	205	IOTA
	END	347	SHE	307	ANTI	274	RARE	254	ARID	236	ORA	220	SSTS	205	ERSE
	EDEN	345	ICE	307	ALEE	274	EWE	254	AMOS	236	NRA	220	REESE	205	EARL
	ALA	345	ACRE	307	ALEC	274	ARA	254	ALTO	235	RNA	220	OPEN	204	NILE
	ENE	343	ODOR	306	ETAL	273	URN	253	USER	235	OTTO	219	SNAP	204	NEA
	ETA	343	ANNE	306	AIR	272	ORR	253	RAT	235	ALOT	219	AMES	204	BEE
	ANTE	342	TEN	305	ERLE	272	IRENE	253	AXE	234	AERO	219	AIL	204	AJAR
	SPA	342	SSE	304	RED	272	IDLE	252	ETC	233	TOE	218	IRATE	203	SENT
	ALOE	342	ENDS	303	ACT	271	EVA	252	ELM	233	STU	218	INANE	203	RAP
	IRE	341	ELL	302	IDA	270	RAN	252	AGEE	233	ANY	217	TAN	203	RAM
	ERR	339	RES	301	RENE	270	ESP	251	NNE	232	OVAL	217	NEO	203	NEON
	EAR	339	ASEA	301	IRAN	268	OSLO	251	EYE	232	ASSET	217	EPA	203	AIDA
	ACE	339	AMEN	300	OBOE	268	ONA	251	ATA	231	OVER	217	EATS	202	SPAR
	ESS	337	TSAR	300	ANTS	268	INN	251	APT	231	ADORE	217	AROMA	202	OVEN
	NEE	337	TREE	299	ETNA	268	ARC	251	AND	230	STET	216	STEM	202	NTH
	ASH	336	AHA	297	ISEE	267	TSE	250	OPAL	230	ODES	216	SSS	202	ERODE
	IRA	334	TAR	294	STY	267	OTIS	250	NEED	230	ECO	216	ION	202	EPIC
	ESE	334	OAR	294	STE	267	LEO	250	DEN	230	ASTI	216	ETTA	202	EDIE
	ODE	334	ALL	294	ENID	267	ITEM	250	ALONE	229	ONTO	215	NEAT	202	EBB
	ADO	333	ECHO	293	ELLA	266	TRA	249	ORES	229	ITE	215	ERATO	202	EARN
	SEE	332	YES	292	ORO	266	NED	249	OAT	229	ILE	215	EGG	201	TIS
	ANT	332	SET	292	ASP	263	TRI	249	ESTE	229	ELK	215	AWE	201	MAR
	STAR	330	ALAN	291	IDOL	263	SST	249	ENTER	229	ADEN	214	SCAR	201	KNEE
	ELSE	329	ISLE	291	IDO	263	ADD	248	SAL	228	LEN	214	EVEN	201	HAL
	ARI	329	ACHE	291	ELS	263	ABLE	248	ELSA	228	ESAU	213	REO	201	ELF
	IDEA	325	OMAR	291	ATOM	262	TIE	248	ALIT	228	AVE	213	NIL	200	SARA
	ERASE	325	ARES	290	SIR	262	ORATE	247	TED	227	UTE	213	ASAP	200	ROD
	EEL	325	ANN	290	ELIA	261	URGE	247	INA	227	OGLE	213	AGRA	200	NEAR
	AGE	324	ANON	290	ARLO	261	LEA	247	APSE	227	LET	211	TRE	199	SEC
	EVE	323	STIR	290	AMI	260	USA	247	ANEW	227	EDAM	211	OLIO	199	BRA
	APE	323	LEE	290	ADS	260	RTE	246	SOS	227	ASI	211	EGAD	199	ASPS
	ORAL	322	ETON	289	ONO	260	OIL	246	RAH	227	ARTS	210	SLY	199	ALAMO
	EGO	322	EERIE	289	NERO	259	REST	246	PER	226	ERN	210	ACES	198	STA

KLAHN'S COMPLETE LIST (CONTINUED)

389	ART	321	NOR	289	EON	259	EVIL	246	LEI	225	AVER	209	TESS	198	ITO
379	SEA	321	ASHE	289	EDGE	259	EMIT	246	ATOP	225	ATONE	209	ALS	197	REDO
378	TEA	321	ADAM	288	RIO	259	ARTE	245	SAT	224	STOP	208	SRI	197	EKE
376	NET	320	ANA	288	ARAB	259	AONE	245	INRE	224	STAN	208	PRO	197	ALT
373	EST	319	ALAI	287	AMA	258	OGRE	245	ERRS	224	SAD	208	ESSE	197	AGES

CONSTRUCTOR/EDITOR
BIOGRAPHIES

MARTIN ASHWOOD-SMITH While Martin Ashwood-Smith was attending the University of Victoria, he attempted constructing both cryptic and standard-style crosswords for the student newspaper. They'd accept just about anything . . . so it was a good training ground! His first pro puzzle was accepted in 1990 by then–*New York Times* crossword editor Eugene T. Maleska and was published on June 5, 1991. Ashwood-Smith's puzzles have been featured in the *New York Times*, *GAMES* magazine, Dell

Photo by M.J. Ashwood-Smith

Champion publications, Simon & Schuster books, and *Attache* (the in-flight magazine of US Air). He is a founding member of CrosSynergy, a group of constructors that contribute crosswords to the Internet editions of several major newspapers including the *Washington Post*, *Houston Chronicle*, and *San Diego Tribune*.

Photo courtesy of Sam Belloto, Jr.

SAM BELLOTTO, JR. Sam Bellotto, Jr., has been selling puzzles since 1979 when he made his first sale to the Sunday *New York Times*. A very auspicious start! In his 1984 book *Across and Down*, Eugene T. Maleska called Sam "one of the most promising newcomers and a person to watch." Since, Bellotto's work has appeared in all of the major markets. He was recently named one of the top ten constructors in the field by Simon &

Schuster, and is a four-time winner of the coveted Margaret Award for crossword puzzle excellence. In addition to his puzzle success, Bellotto is a published writer, a huge science-fiction enthusiast, and a computer programmer/consultant. He is also the developer of Crossdown software, including Crossdown for Windows, Enigmacross for Windows and Quiptics cryptograms for Windows.

SYLVIA BURSZTYN Sylvia Bursztyn has, with Barry Tunick, written the *Los Angeles Times* Sunday Puzzler since 1980. Nearly thirty volumes of their crossword collections have been published, the most recent twenty by Random House. Their *Crossword Crosstalk* (Capra Press) appeared in 1988. Bursztyn and Tunick, together and separately, have custom-written crosswords and other puzzles for a variety of magazines, businesses, and individuals. Bursztyn, who lives in Los Angeles, takes pride in reviews that call the *Times* puzzles "intelligent, witty, punny, breezy, laid-back" and in herself at having been pronounced by a solver to be "a minor celebrity."

KELLY CLARK A hospital lay minister of the Eucharist, Kelly Clark also owns and operates a small advertising and design firm. She began creating crossword puzzles in 1997 when she realized she simply couldn't solve them. Her work has appeared in the *New York Times*, *GAMES* magazine, the *Los Angeles Times* Syndicate, and other publications. Clark's ambition is to one day complete a late-in-the-week puzzle without resorting to cheating.

EMILY COX AND HENRY RATHVON Emily Cox and Henry Rathvon live in Hershey, Pennsylvania, in the hills overlooking the town's chocolate factory. They write puzzles for the *Boston Globe*, *Atlantic Monthly*, and *New York Times,* among other publications. Cox is an avid rock climber and fossil collector. Rathvon has written three full-act plays in iambic pentameter (cast, director, and performance venue still unmaterialized).

GAYLE DEAN Gayle Dean has been constructing crossword puzzles full-time for all the major markets since 1985. She is known for her clever puns, such as "Bo Peep's Antiques" (SHEEPENDALE FURNITURE) and "Let the Sturgeon Beware" (CAVIAR EMPTOR). Dean's puzzles can be regularly found in Dell puzzle magazines, Simon & Schuster books, Book-Of-The-Month Club books, the *New York Times*, *Washington Post Magazine*, Universal Web sites, and  many others. Dean is currently working on two new crossword puzzle books with her friend and fellow punster Richard Lederer (Merriam-Webster, 2001).

JON DELFIN Jon Delfin constructs, edits, and test-solves crosswords and other puzzles for the *New York Times, Newsday*, and Random House books. He was seen on *Nightline* winning his fifth American Crossword Puzzle Tournament. The rest of the time, he plays the piano, accompanying and coaching singers and performing in cabaret acts and theater.

Photo courtesy of Mark Diehl

MARK DIEHL Mark Diehl concocts crosswords for the *New York Times*, Random House publications, *Los Angeles Times*, and other venues for the sheer joy and challenge of filling wide-open spaces. He pursues the same goal, as a dentist, with the Department of Veterans Affairs.

JOE DIPIETRO Joe DiPietro has been constructing since 1995. He specializes in theme-less, low-word-count puzzles, most of which appear in the *New York Times*. On January 19, 2001, he broke the record for fewest black squares (twenty) in a 15 × 15 puzzle. DiPietro twice has been selected to construct puzzles for the American Crossword Puzzle Tournament. He currently resides with his wife and child in Park Slope, Brooklyn, and owns a tavern in Manhattan.

DIANE EPPERSON When she's not constructing crossword puzzles, Diane Epperson writes a weekly on-line newsletter for subscribers in California's Imperial Valley. Her puzzles have appeared in the *New York Times, Los Angeles Times, GAMES* magazine, Simon & Schuster, Crosswords Club, and at a couple of on-line sites. A confirmed desert rat, she lives in the remote desert village of Ocotillo with hubby, Dave, and rottweiler, Worf.

BERNICE GORDON Bernice Gordon is one of the very old timers in the crossword puzzle field, having started over fifty years ago with Margaret Farrar, and has been published by every *New York Times* editor since. Her work has appeared in Simon & Schuster, Running Press, the Crosswords Club, and Dell magazines, as well as syndicated newspapers. Recently she won the Margaret Award for a puzzle in Simon & Schuster's Series 217. There is also a prize of $1000 given annu-

ally in her name by Masterpuzzles for outstanding work appearing on computers.

Photo by Chris Stavropoulos

PETER GORDON Peter Gordon is a puzzle-book editor and crossword puzzle writer who lives on Long Island with his wife, Chrissy (to whom he proposed marriage in a crossword); their daughter, Phoebe, and the family goldfish, Spike. Gordon and three U.S. teammates won the 1999 World Puzzle Championship in Budapest, Hungary, and he and five other contestants lost on the NBC game show *Twenty One* to the biggest winner in the history of network television, who earned $1.765 million. He has a collection of more than five thousand postcards that all say "Greetings from . . ." on them. Gordon is a widely published crossword constructor who is also the crossword editor for Sterling Publications.

ELIZABETH GORSKI Elizabeth Gorski has been published by Simon & Schuster, the *New York Times*, the *Wall Street Journal*, *GAMES* magazine, *Newsday*, Book-Of-The-Month Club, *Crosswords Club*, Crossword America, *Los Angeles Times* Syndicate, Running Press, Universal Puzzles, and others.

RAY HAMEL Ray Hamel leads the battle for truth, justice, and the pursuit of trivia in Madison, Wisconsin. His crosswords have appeared in such publications as *GAMES*, the *New York Times,* the *Los Angeles Times*, *Dell Champion Crosswords*, and the *Chicago Sun-Times*. He is a co-founder of the CrosSynergy group, which supplies crosswords to Web sites. He is also the author of *The New York Times Trivia Quiz Book* and provides two new trivia quizzes each week for the *New York Times* Web site.

FRANCES HANSEN Back in 1964, desperate editors of leading magazines and newspapers began filling the empty spaces of their publications with the puzzles of Frances Hansen. Despite angry protests from infuriated solvers, they persisted in this practice, sometimes even printing the puzzles upside-down in their efforts to make the puzzles interesting. Deaf to pleas for mercy, Hansen continued her evil course and is today, even as we speak, concocting another monstrosity.

Legal action may be taken. Hansen's puzzles have been published in all the major markets, and she had a second career for a while writing original verses for leading magazines.

NELSON HARDY Nelson Hardy is a professional pumpkin-carver who was drawn to the field of puzzle construction by the potential for enormous wealth. His puzzles have appeared in the *New York Times*, the *Washington Post*, the *Los Angeles Times*, *GAMES* magazine, most of Dell's puzzle magazines, and elsewhere. He lives in Rhode Island with his wife, Susan, and daughters, Melanie and Bailey.

FRANCIS HEANEY Francis Heaney has been writing puzzles professionally since 1993 and spent several years as *GAMES* magazine's editor at large, overlapping with his three-year tenure as editor of the National Puzzlers' League's monthly newsletter, *The Enigma*. He is currently a contributing editor to *Modern Humorist*, an on-line humor magazine.

TYLER HINMAN Tyler Hinman is a sixteen-year-old crossword constructor whose work has appeared in the *New York Times* and *TalkTeens*, a monthly publication aimed at teenagers. (He hopes to have work printed in a few other publications in the following months.) He is currently an American expatriate living in the county of Berkshire in England, but he plans to return to the United States for college.

KAREN HODGE Karen Hodge is a retired French teacher who has been constructing cross-word puzzles for about twenty years. She sings with a Sweet Adelines chorus, does square and round dancing, and plays duplicate bridge on a regular basis. She's been published in the *New York Times*, *GAMES* magazine, Dell Champion puzzle magazines, and Stan Newman–edited publications (such as *Masterpiece Crosswords* and *Newsday*). When the *Four-Star Puzzler* was around, she was a regular contributor there, as well as to *CROSSW RD*. For the past thirteen years, she has helmed a library crossword tournament in Westbrook, Connecticut.

MAURA JACOBSON Maura Jacobson has been the crossword puzzle constructor for *New York Magazine* for twenty years. During that time she has authored over twenty crossword books. She lives in the suburbs and works at home.

CHRIS JOHNSON Chris Johnson's puzzles have been published in the University of Toronto Alumni Magazine (*The Graduate*), *GAMES* magazine, *Four-Star Puzzler*, *Financial Post* (Moneywise) magazine, *Good Times*, and *TVOntario*.

NANCY JOLINE Nancy Joline is a native New Yorker, a graduate of Barnard College, and has worked as an editor/writer/journalist. She tried puzzle-constructing on a whim, but soon became hooked; she especially enjoys the mental stimulation and the new circle of friends it has brought. Her puzzles appear in the *New York Times*, the Simon & Schuster puzzle books, and numerous other places. When not puzzling, she enjoys travel, tennis, and most of all, "playing games with my four wonderful grandchildren."

PATRICK JORDAN Patrick Jordan, of Ponca City, Oklahoma, has kissed the Blarney Stone, attended a Mexican bullfight, interviewed Glen Campbell, and won a Disney World vacation through a contest on the back of a frozen-pizza box. He's been published in all three *GAMES* magazines, the *New York Times*, Creators Syndicate, the Simon & Schuster crossword book series, and CrosSynergy. His blood type matches his outlook on life—B positive.

Photo courtesy of the Ponca City News

Photo by Linda Kahn

DAVID J. KAHN David J. Kahn is a consulting actuary in New York City, where he lives. His puzzles appear regularly in the *New York Times, Los Angeles Times*, the *Wall Street Journal*, and Random House's "Editors' Choice" volumes. He's also written puzzles for the annual American Crossword Puzzle Tournament in Stamford, Connecticut. In July 1997, former President Clinton, who's an accomplished solver of crosswords, talked about one of David's puzzles, "Technophobe's Delight," during a White House news conference on technology and the Internet.

SHAWN KENNEDY Shawn Kennedy began publishing his puzzles at the age of thirteen. He authors *Gambit!*, a daily puzzle column sent to over one thousand subscribers each weekday. He has also written regular features for *GAMES* and *GAMES World of Puzzles* magazines, *TalkTeens*, Tribune Media Services, a game show distributed by FOX cable network, and over 150 regional and national newspapers. He is currently hard at work on his upcoming puzzle book.

Photo by Scott Hewitt

BOB KLAHN From his first construction at age eight, a 4 × 4 with four black squares in the center and "Animal" cluing the obvious answer BEAR, to first place in several national grid-construction contests in the early 1970s, to his syndicated work today, Bob Klahn has always loved puzzles. Language plus mathematical structure: Latin studies in Tennessee, French at Phillips Academy (Andover), and German at

Princeton; first place in statewide math competitions in Tennessee; a summer as a Siemens mathematician in West Berlin; a math major until he discovered computers. Today the Crossword Beast is a database administrator with Computer Sciences Corporation and lives with his wife, Sharon, and other critters of varying composition in Wilmington, Delaware.

WILLIAM R. MACKAYE William R. MacKaye is the editor of the *Washington Post* crossword puzzle.

DAVID MACLEOD David Macleod is a silviculture forester and inventor in the sticks of British Columbia. He constructs crossword puzzles because he loves seeing his name in print in big-city newspapers (forestry doesn't allow such opportunities). He has been published in the *New York Times*, *Los Angeles Times*, *Chicago Tribune*, and *Boston Globe*.

Photo by S. MacLeod

CATHY MILLHAUSER Cathy Millhauser is from Cincinnati (née Allis) where she grew up with a twin brother. After graduating from Indiana University, she had a twelve-year career as an occupational therapist working at various New York City–area hospitals. She met her future husband, a writer, when friends invited them over to play anagrams. She became hooked on the game and started solving and constructing crosswords shortly thereafter. Puzzlemaking has

Photo by Steven Millhauser

been her day job ever since her children, Anna and Jonathan (not Graham!) started school. When she's not playing with words, her family, or her cat (Kiki), she enjoys riding her old Schwinn and singing in a choral group. Millhauser is one of the *New York Times*'s most-published constructors.

STANLEY NEWMAN Stanley Newman is publishing director of Random House Puzzles and Games. Formerly a Wall Street executive, his prowess in crossword-solving won him the first U.S. Open Crossword Championship in 1982; he entered the puzzle business as a hobby the next year. After being involuntarily retired from Wall Street in the aftermath of the 1987 crash, Newman plunged into crosswords full-time, as a puzzle creator, editor, publisher, syndicator, and mail-order bookseller—becoming the first to achieve concurrent success in five different arenas of puzzledom. Newman is the author or editor of more than sixty of his own books, mostly for Random House. He has been crossword editor for the Long Island, New York, newspaper *Newsday* since 1988. As puzzle creator, his work appears regularly in *People* and *Business Week* magazines, And as puzzle solver, he holds the world's record, set in 1996 under *Guinness Book* conditions, for the fastest completion of a *New York Times* crossword: two minutes, fourteen seconds.

RICH NORRIS Rich Norris is co-editor of the Tribune Media Services, Inc. syndicated daily crossword appearing in the *Los Angeles Times* and a founding member of CrosSynergy, an on-line crossword puzzle syndicate. Norris is a prolific constructor as well, producing puzzles regularly for the *New York Times*, *Uptown Puzzle Club*, and Simon & Schuster puzzle books, among others. When not working on puzzles, he can usually be found playing golf, which he loves, he  says, because "it's yet another kind of puzzle." He lives with his wife and son in a suburb of New York City.

MANNY NOSOWSKY Beginning his crossword puzzle career upon retiring from his urology practice, Manny Nosowsky's work has graced the pages of the *New York Times* and other prestigious publications since 1991. A standard-setter with his wide-open themeless puzzles, Nosowsky is equally appreciated for his clever themes and entertaining wordplay. When he's not constructing puzzles, this native San Franciscan enjoys his tropical fish collection and bragging about his granddaughter, Sophie Rose.

JIM PAGE Jim Page edits for Simon & Schuster, including copyediting its John Samson crossword puzzle books. Jim's first puzzle was published in the *New York Times* in the seventies when Will Weng was the editor. Jim has constructed crosswords for the *Washington Post*, the *New York Post*, *Los Angeles Times*, *Crossword Club*, the *Wall Street Journal*, *Newsday*, and *USA Today*.

TRIP PAYNE Trip Payne is a world-renowned freelance puzzlemaker living in Atlanta. He has had over three thousand brilliant puzzles published in everything from the *New York*

Times to *TV Guide*, not to mention four universally admired puzzle books of his own. As Norman Payne, he was the first American contestant to win $32,000 on *Who Wants to Be a Millionaire*. When he's not reading the thousands of fan letters he receives daily, he enjoys tennis, Scrabble, and writing miniature autobiographical paragraphs about himself.

FRED PISCOP Fred Piscop is creator of the time.com crossword, and has been regularly published in the *New York Times*, Simon & Schuster, *GAMES*, the *Crosswords Club*, Creators Syndicate, and many other markets. Piscop also constructs custom crosswords of all descriptions and operates a crossword Web site at macnamarasband.com. In his spare time, Piscop enjoys riding his tandem bicycle with his wife, Laraine, playing keyboards with the Wes Houston Band, sampling excellent microbrews, and collecting spelling errors in comic strips.

Photo by Patricia Colombraro

MERL REAGLE Merl Reagle was born in Audubon, N.J., on January 5, 1950, made his first crossword at age six, and sold his first crossword to the *New York Times* at age sixteen. He was featured prominently on *Nightline with Ted Koppel* in July 1999 as one of the best crossword creators in America, and made the crossword commemorating the U.S. Postal Service's first crossword stamp in February 1998. Reagle wrote a widely acclaimed article about the crossword biz for the *Philadelphia Inquirer* in 1998, which was picked up that same year by *Reader's Digest*. He was commissioned by *Life* magazine to make its special puzzle celebrating the crossword's 75th birthday in 1988 (this is the only crossword *Life* has ever run). Reagle has been featured on CNN, the *Today* show, on National Public Radio and in *People* magazine, the *New Yorker*, and countless other newspapers and magazines. He makes the crossword every Sunday for the *Philadelphia Inquirer*, the *Seattle Times*, the *San Francisco Chronicle* (formerly the *San Francisco Examiner*), the *Cleveland Plain Dealer*, the *New York Observer*, and many other daily and weekly newspapers. He is the author of seven books of crosswords, worked as a writer on TV game shows in the 1980s, and plays a mean game of badminton.

RANDOLPH ROSS Randolph Ross, when not creating crosswords, is a high school principal, wherein he requires his students to solve his puzzles in order to graduate. To date, he has been the most featured constructor in the *Wall Street Journal* and frequently appears in the *New York Times*, *Washington Post*, and *Newsday*.

ERICA ROTHSTEIN After a some-might-think-too lengthy (twenty-five years, eight months, and fifteen days . . . but who's counting?) career as a puzzle editor, which culminated in vice president and editor in chief of the Dell puzzle magazines at Bantam Doubleday Dell, Erica Rothstein found new life as an ESL teacher and graduate student at Fordham University. Having received a master's degree in adult education, Rothstein now toils in relative obscurity at the Paul McGhee division of New York University's School of Continuing and Professional Studies, where she advises returning adult students who want to get an undergraduate degree, and supervises the Center for New Student Advisement, which she developed. As in the puzzle biz, the money's not so hot, but the good feelings are terrific.

NANCY SALOMON Nancy Salomon took up crossword construction in 1992 because of a disability that left her unable to hold a real job. Stan Newman got her started, and she hasn't looked back since. She, in turn, has helped a lot of novices get started. She leads a happy hermit's life in Rochester, New York.

JOHN M. SAMSON John M. Samson is the editor of Simon & Schuster's long-running crossword series and is responsible for six books annually. He also is the crossword constructor for A&E's *Biography* magazine and United Airlines' in-flight magazine, *Hemispheres*.

TOM SCHIER Tom Schier is a retired corporate executive who specializes in the design of sports, personalized, and corporate crosswords. He has challenged solvers for over thirty years with his creations. He was born in New York and now resides in Dallas, Texas, where he manages Schier Delight Crosswords. He contends that you will never find a "cross word" in his crosswords. Schier's puzzles have appeared in the *New York Times*, Simon & Schuster books, Dell crossword magazines, [Random House] Editor's Choice books, Universal Crosswords on-line, *CROSSW RD*, the *Crosswords Club*, *USA Today*, the *Washington Post Magazine*, *Newsday*, *Los Angeles Times*, *GAMES*, At the Crossroads on-line, and numerous other publications.

NANCY SCHUSTER Nancy Schuster began her crossword construction career in the 1960s; with a little help from Will Weng, she then turned to freelance editing for Dell magazines. Schuster also remained an active solver: at the first Stamford (ACPT) tournament in 1978, she took top prize, then placed in the top ten for five more years before being tapped as a judge for the event by Will Shortz. She retired from nine-to-five work in 1997 (as editor in chief of Dell Champion Puzzles) and now stays active test-solving, fact-checking, and proofreading for the *New York Times* puzzles. Other postretirement editorial work has included four volumes of *Crosswords for Dummies* and the *Random House Crossword Dictionary*, along with proofreading for Random House/Times Books and Boxerjam.

MIKE SHENK Mike Shenk is a former editor of *GAMES* and the current editor of the *Wall Street Journal's* crossword.

WILL SHORTZ has been the *New York Times's* crossword editor since 1993 and is Puzzlemaster for National Public Radio's *Weekend Edition Sunday* (since 1987). He was *GAMES* magazine's editor from 1978 to 1993. He is founder and director of the annual American Crossword Puzzle Tournament (since 1978), founder of the World Puzzle Championship (1992), and co-founder and chairman of the World Puzzle Federation, as well as being convention program director and historian for the National Puzzlers' League. He wrote the riddles featured in the movie *Batman Forever* (1995) and is the author or editor of more than forty books, including *The Puzzlemaster Presents, Will Shortz's Tournament Crosswords*, and *Will Shortz's Best Brain Busters*. He is the owner of more than twenty thousand puzzle books and magazines dating back to 1545; it is the world's largest library on the subject. He was named one of the "100 Best People in the World" by *Esquire* magazine in 1997. He lives in Pleasantville, New York.

Photo by Marilyn Huret

RICH SILVESTRI Richard Silvestri was born in Brooklyn (you got a problem with that?) and lives in Valley Stream, New York. When he is not explaining the mysteries of mathematics to students at Nassau Community College, he continues his quest to find the perfect beer.

GREG STAPLES Greg Staples is a relatively new constructor (he began in 1999), as well as being a sixth-grade teacher in suburban Milwaukee. His students help him with theme entries, and they have been rewarded with two class parties for their contributions, which include an entry he used in a Sunday puzzle soon to be published by the *New York Times*. Staples's puzzles have also been seen in the *Los Angeles Times*, GAMES magazine, and the *Uptown Puzzle Club*.

MEL TAUB Mel Taub is the composer of Puns & Anagrams puzzles for the *New York Times*.

BARRY TUNICK Barry Tunick has created crosswords and other word puzzles professionally for over twenty years. With Sylvia Bursztyn, he has constructed the last 1,100 *Los Angeles Times* Sunday Puzzlers. Author of the daily on-line column "Crosswords and Other Words" (at sodamail.com), Tunick is also the answer to the trivia question, "Who was the fourth and last creator of the *Saturday Review* Double-Crostic?" He lives with his wife, Trudi, in Culver City.

ARTHUR S. VERDESCA Arthur Verdesca is a man who loves his hobbies. They have included classical music (he had a radio program for eleven years), detective fiction (he has over six thousand titles in his collection), and solving and creating crossword puzzles. In his spare time he specializes in internal medicine. His puzzles have been published in the *New York Times*, the *Washington Post*, the *Los Angeles Times*, the Tribune Syndicate, Dell publications, the *Crosswords Club*, the Simon & Schuster crossword series, and the Running Press series.

LEONARD WILLIAMS More often than not, Leonard Williams teaches political science at Manchester College in North Manchester, Indiana. He has found that constructing crosswords can be almost as time-consuming as caring for a household of two children and two cats, but then it's much less maddening than trying to make sense of American politics. His work has been published by the *Los Angeles Times* Syndicate, Universal Crossword syndicate, *GAMES World of Crosswords*, Simon & Schuster, and the Crossroads Media Group.

NORMAN WIZER Norman Wizer is a Philadelphian, a University of Pennsylvania graduate, and a CPA by profession. From childhood he had a fondness for all games, including crossword puzzles. He decided to create his own crossword in 1981, which was published by the *New York Times*. He has constructed puzzles for Will Weng, Gene Maleska, John Samson, Will Shortz, Mel Rosen, Mike Shenk, and other great editors. He also does personalized puzzles for his friends.

BILL ZAIS Bill Zais was born and raised in Burlington, Vermont, and graduated from the University of Vermont (BS and MBA). He has worked in corporate finance and as an independent floor trader at the Mid-America Commodity Exchange in Chicago. His puzzles have been published in the *New York Times*, the *Los Angeles Times*, the *Washington Post*, the *Wall Street Journal*, *GAMES* magazine, and the *Crosswords Club*.